Let Us Reason Together

ESSAYS IN HONOR OF THE LIFE'S WORK OF
Robert L. Millet

Edited by J. Spencer Fluhman and Brent L. Top

Published by the Religious Studies Center and the Neal A. Maxwell Institute for Religious Scholarship at Brigham Young University, Provo, Utah, in cooperation with Deseret Book Company, Salt Lake City, Utah.

Visit us at rsc.byu.edu.

© 2016 by Brigham Young University. All rights reserved.

Printed in the United States of America by Sheridan Books, Inc.

DESERET BOOK is a registered trademark of Deseret Book Company.

Visit us at DeseretBook.com.

Any uses of this material beyond those allowed by the exemptions in US copyright law, such as section 107, "Fair Use," and section 108, "Library Copying," require the written permission of the publisher, Religious Studies Center, 185 HGB, Brigham Young University, Provo, Utah 84602. The views expressed herein are the responsibility of the authors and do not necessarily represent the position of Brigham Young University or the Religious Studies Center.

ISBN: 978-0-8425-2968-6
Retail US: $29.99

Cover design and interior layout by Madison Swapp

Library of Congress Cataloging-in-Publication Data

Let us reason together: essays in honor of the life's work of Robert L. Millet / edited by J. Spencer Fluhman and Brent L. Top.
    pages cm
  Includes bibliographical references and index.
    Collection of essays honoring Robert L. Millet's remarkable career as an administrator, teacher, and writer at Brigham Young University. These pieces range across topics, disciplines, and even religious traditions.
   ISBN 978-0-8425-2968-6 (alk. paper)
1. Church of Jesus Christ of Latter-day Saints--Doctrines. 2. Mormon Church--Doctrines. 3. Millet, Robert L.. I Fluhman, J. Spencer, editor. II. Top, Brent L., editor.
   BX8635.3.L48 2015
   230'9332--dc23
                         2015026821

Contents

INTRODUCTION
J. Spencer Fluhman   vii

Part I: Doctrine

1. "The First Principles of Man Are Self-Existent with God":
   The Immortality of the Soul in Mormon Theology
   Brent L. Top   3

2. To Know God Is Life Eternal
   Camille Fronk Olson   23

3. Instruments or Agents? Balancing Submissiveness
   and Anxious Engagement in Heavenly Father's Plan
   Lloyd D. Newell   37

4. Filling the Immensity of Space:
   The Titles and Functions of God's Revelatory Power
   Larry E. Dahl   51

5. Blessings Promised to the Faithful
   Richard O. Cowan   65

6. From Calvary to Cumorah:
   What Mormon History Means to Me
   Richard E. Bennett   81

Part II: Scripture

7. SYMBOLISM IN THE PARABLE OF THE WILLING
   AND UNWILLING TWO SONS IN MATTHEW 21
   John W. Welch 97

8. THE DIVINE PRINCIPLE OF FRIENDSHIP:
   SOME PROPHETIC AND SECULAR PERSPECTIVES
   Andrew C. Skinner 117

9. "THE WORK OF TRANSLATING":
   THE BOOK OF ABRAHAM'S TRANSLATION CHRONOLOGY
   Kerry Muhlestein and Megan Hansen 139

10. WAS NOAH'S FLOOD THE BAPTISM OF THE EARTH?
    Paul Y. Hoskisson and Stephen O. Smoot 163

11. THE "SPIRIT" THAT RETURNS TO GOD IN ECCLESIASTES 12:7
    Dana M. Pike 189

12. UNVEILING REVELATION AND A
    LANDMARK COMMENTARY SERIES
    Craig L. Blomberg 205

Part III: Christianity

13. MORMONS AND EVANGELICALS IN DIALOGUE:
    FINDING THE RIGHT QUESTIONS
    Richard J. Mouw 231

14. MORMONISM AND THE HERESIES
    Brian D. Birch 249

15. Atoning Grace on Progression's Highway: Explorations into Latter-day Saint Theological Anthropology
   Cory B. Willson   269

16. Embers and Bonfires: The Richard L. Evans Professorship and Interfaith Work at BYU
   J. B. Haws   291

17. Sin, Guilt, and Grace: Martin Luther and the Doctrines of the Restoration
   Daniel K Judd   311

18. Salvation by Grace, Rewards of Degree by Works: The Soteriology of Doctrine and Covenants 76
   Shon D. Hopkin   329

19. What Is Christianity?
   Dennis L. Okholm   357

   Curriculum Vitae   371
   Acknowledgments   395
   Contributors   397
   Index   401

Robert L. Millet

Introduction

J. Spencer Fluhman

A single volume cannot accurately measure the influence of a beloved colleague, but this one nevertheless stands as modest evidence of Robert L. Millet's prodigious impact over a career that spanned nearly four decades. His retirement in 2014 provided an opportunity to gather some of us who count him as a mentor, colleague, and friend. We offer the collection of essays that follows as a monument to his remarkable career as an administrator, teacher, and writer. That these pieces range across topics, disciplines, and even religious traditions seems especially appropriate given Millet's own broad reach. His students number in the thousands, his readers number perhaps ten times that, and his friends in academia, the Church Educational System (CES) of The Church of Jesus Christ of Latter-day Saints, and around the globe in many faiths would be difficult to number indeed. Both in terms of his staggering literary production and in his broad collection of colleagues, it is not an overstatement to place Bob, as he's affectionately known to us, among the most influential Latter-day Saint voices of the past quarter century.[1]

Millet's path as an educator and a writer was somewhat circuitous, but several aspects of his Southern upbringing predicted a life of influence. Born December 30, 1947, to Lou and Bobbi Millet, Bob's early years in

INTRODUCTION

Louisiana exposed him to good cooking and religious variety. His father was raised a Latter-day Saint and his mother a Methodist. Early on, the family drifted in and out of Church attendance at their local Latter-day Saint ward. That periodic activity notwithstanding, Bob grew into a spiritually sensitive youngster with a passion for religious learning. "I was one of those birds that was sort of drawn to church. I loved the Church," he recalls. Bob had a voracious appetite for Bible stories and Church manuals. His interest in religious topics was piqued in school, too. As one of the few Latter-day Saints in a veritable sea of Baptists and Roman Catholics, he gained both an appreciation for friends of other faiths and sensitivity to the fact that he stood somewhat apart. The interfaith nature of his young adulthood exposed him to the broad outlines of traditional Christianity and to a Latter-day Saint minority struggling to define itself over and against that majority. In one telling reminiscence, Bob remembers asking a family member about grace, only to be told, "That's what the Baptists believe." In some ways, his subsequent career seems to be an outgrowth of that early search for Latter-day Saint meaning in a broader Christian world.

After a stint at Louisiana State, Bob transferred to Brigham Young University. Though initially unsure what to study, he knew he loved people and wanted to help those who were struggling. Psychology seemed a good fit and, after realizing a bachelor's degree would not secure a career, he stayed at BYU for a master's degree in the same field. He started a doctoral program, too, but he impressed a supervisor in what was then called LDS Social Services and was hired at a Social Services office in Idaho, where he worked from 1973 to 1975. He was not long into that position when it became clear that his interests lay primarily with the *preventative* side of Church social work—and with teaching in particular.

Fortuitously, Millet had crossed paths as an undergraduate with a future mentor who would dramatically shape his academic future. Bob had innocently wandered into the old Joseph Smith Building one night as a homesick undergraduate, only to find himself at the feet of a lecturer named Robert J. Matthews. Matthews would win wide acclaim for pathbreaking work on the Joseph Smith Translation (JST) of the Bible, but Millet had no idea who Matthews was when he sat down in the auditorium. Matthews was among the first Latter-day Saints to gain access to the Reorganized

Church of Jesus Christ of Latter-day Saints' (now "Community of Christ") JST manuscripts and helped disarm longstanding Latter-day Saint mistrust of Joseph Smith's "Inspired Version," as it was known in RLDS circles. Bob was electrified by what he heard. The two eventually struck up an acquaintance and periodic correspondence after Millet embarked on his own careful study of the JST. Matthews, clearly impressed with his young protégé, kept an eye on Millet's progress and advised him about Church education once his zeal for social work fizzled.

Millet taught seminary for a couple of years in the mid-1970s and then accepted a transfer to direct the Church's Institute of Religion adjacent to Florida State University. The assignment not only took him back to his Southern roots, it exposed him to the joys and strains of both the institute classroom and the expansive world of secular religious studies. He learned quickly that an institute director recruits as much as teaches. And driven by the chance to enhance his academic training and by possible employment at BYU, he enrolled in a doctoral program at Florida State. As an institute director, a full-time student, a young bishop in his local Latter-day Saint ward, and a committed husband and father, Millet remembers the stint in Tallahassee as both dizzyingly busy and blissful. "I don't know how we lived through it," he said, looking back. "It was a blur."

At Florida State, he worked under Leo Sandon, a scholar of American religious history. The training at FSU stoked his fascination with the nation's Christian diversity, but it also fueled his theological streak. Bob had appreciated popular evangelical preachers on the radio as a young man, but his time at FSU brought enhanced exposure to Christianity's great thinkers. He relished the academic experience he gained with Christianity, but, with his advisor's encouragement, Millet centered his own research on the Latter-day Saints. Even so, he was exhausted after his coursework and qualifying exams and felt uninspired with the prospect of completing the doctoral dissertation. With his FSU coursework done, he had also accepted a new role in CES as a "Teaching Support Consultant" for the Southern States Area. Bob and Shauna moved to Athens, Georgia, and Bob traveled across a sizable portion of the South training other CES teachers. But when his area director moved to the College of Religious Instruction at BYU (later called Religious Education) and asked if Bob would be interested in coming to Provo,

INTRODUCTION

Bob—with Robert Matthews' ongoing encouragement—quickened his research and writing pace to become a viable candidate. Sandon had known something of Mormonism and urged Bob to study the concept of "Zion" in Latter-day Saint history. Partaking as it did of both doctrinal and historical development, it suited Bob's interests, and he crafted a dissertation that he describes as "not very well written" but nevertheless generative of some of his later academic fascination with Joseph Smith and the Restoration.

With Millet's completion of the PhD at Florida State and move to BYU in 1983, his passion for teaching and writing found greater resources and opportunities. Initially, he taught courses in the Bible and the Joseph Smith Translation. His leadership potential was not lost on his administrative superiors, however, and he quickly became a fixture in the leadership of both BYU's Department of Ancient Scripture and in Religious Education, an academic unit roughly equivalent to a college in the university's administrative structure. After a stint as chair of the Department of Ancient Scripture from 1988 to 1991, Millet was selected to replace Robert Matthews, his beloved mentor and friend, as dean of Religious Education in 1991, a position he held until 2000.[2]

As dean for nearly a decade, Millet led Religious Education into somewhat new territory. Long the center of religious instruction on campus, Religious Education had swung between periods of pedagogical and devotional emphasis that tilted the quasi-college towards being an institute of religion and moments of academic orientation that tended towards the model of a typical academic department, complete with publishing requirements and full academic standards. He inherited that ongoing identity crisis as dean. Was Religious Education's mission to effectively convey the gospel to the rising generation or to produce original scholarship on religious topics—or some combination of the two? If a combination, what would serve as the preferred training for faculty—experience teaching Latter-day Saint young people the faith or formal scholarly training in biblical studies and history? Suspended somewhere between the two models, Millet nevertheless pushed towards enhanced academic rigor while simultaneously safeguarding the teaching excellence that had become Religious Education's hallmark. To support teaching in Religious Education and in CES generally, he reinstituted graduate training specifically calibrated for Church educators and established a periodical to explore pedagogy and to provide in-depth content for Latter-day Saint readers, the *Religious Educator*. To spur academic rigor, he concentrated on faculty hiring and generally elevated the scholarly profile of both departments—Ancient Scripture and Church History and Doctrine.[3]

He found two additional areas needing immediate attention. First, he realized that Religious Education's place within the university was fairly isolated. Sensing that relationships with the university administration had been somewhat strained in the past, he worked to integrate Religious Education within the university community and have its mission better articulated and understood. Second, he moved towards détente with faculty and administrators in the sciences. Relations between Religious Education and the sciences had been at times rocky, stretching back to the early twentieth century when broader cultural clashes over Darwinian evolution and scriptural accounts of creation had erupted in Provo. To aid a broader rapprochement, Millet dispatched an associate dean, Larry Dahl, to establish a dialogue with science faculty. The conversations were productive; relations improved and collaboration between the two campus entities spurred the development of a packet of official Church statements related to science for student use in religion classes. Millet counts the improved relationships between Religious Education and the broader BYU community among the most significant legacies from his dean years. Millet's gifts as a bridge builder made success in both cases possible, and his penchant for bringing people together and spanning ideological divides was to be further elaborated and tested in his religious outreach efforts.

That story developed over many years. His passion for interreligious dialogue no doubt developed organically from his own upbringing, but it also sprang from a memorable exchange with a member of the Quorum of the Twelve Apostles. The search process for Religious Education's dean brought Millet into close association with several members of the Quorum of the Twelve (although their expanding administrative duties would make such a thing unlikely now). Multiple informal interviews with members of the Twelve not only preceded his formal appointment, but several Apostles traveled to Provo to announce his appointment to the faculty. One of those preliminary interviews proved to be profoundly influential for Millet's work as dean and subsequent involvement in religious outreach.

During that brief interview, Elder Neal A. Maxwell asked Millet to keep him informed about how things progressed and, particularly, to call on him

INTRODUCTION

if he needed help during the overwhelming early months. During a particularly difficult early stretch, Millet contemplated accepting Elder Maxwell's invitation. He hesitated, but with the weight of his new responsibilities bearing down, he summoned the courage to call Elder Maxwell's secretary on a Monday afternoon, when the Twelve are often out of the office, hoping to secure a few minutes in the Apostle's schedule for a phone conversation. To his surprise, Elder Maxwell himself answered the phone. After Millet's brief explanation and request for advice, Elder Maxwell responded characteristically, "Oh absolutely! I can be there in about forty-five minutes. Would that work for you?" Embarrassed, Bob reassured him that he would come to Salt Lake City. Finding time a few days later to meet, Bob went to Elder Maxwell's office hoping for direction on the thorny issues he faced as a new dean. Bob recalls the memorable conclusion to their visit:

> We had a wonderful conversation. He gave some encouraging counsel. Then he came around and put his hands on my head and said, "By the power of the Holy Apostleship"—that got my attention. . . . He said a lot of things that I still can't remember. I remember how inspired I felt by his blessing. But then [came] words that he repeated three different times through the course of what he was saying. "Brother Robert, you've got to find ways to reach out to those of other faiths more." "Now Brother Bob, you need to build some bridges between us and those of other faiths." And then he said [it] again just before he closed. And it just weighed on me. I didn't know what to do with it.

Bob left the interview impressed and inspired but unsure how to proceed. Initially, he broadened his reading load. He had taken up the habit of listening to prominent evangelical preachers on his drive to and from work as department chair, but after that 1991 interview with Elder Maxwell, he began reading contemporary Christian theological and devotional works to better understand the conservative Protestant world. He also took associate deans and visited the campuses of other religiously affiliated universities—such as Notre Dame, Baylor, and Wheaton—and made some valuable connections as a result.[4]

Grateful for what they learned from those campus visits, Millet still wondered about how to build more meaningful bridges with people of other faiths. After his stint as dean, and in recognition of his experience and contributions to interreligious understanding, he was appointed to BYU's Richard L. Evans Chair of Religious Understanding from 2001 to 2005 (see the essay in this volume by J. B. Haws). That endowed professorship provided a new platform from which to pursue Elder Maxwell's mandate. An unlikely opportunity grew out of Bob's friendship with a local Baptist pastor, Greg Johnson. Johnson had been raised Mormon but ultimately became an evangelical Christian as a teenager. After attending evangelical institutions Westmont College (Santa Barbara, California) and Denver Seminary, Johnson felt the call to ministry and to Utah, in particular, where he hoped to improve relations between the Latter-day Saint and evangelical communities. Uninspired by evangelical "countercult" approaches to Mormonism, rooted as they were in sharp-edged polemics that left most Mormons insulted, he sought a more relational approach to interfaith work, one grounded in mutual understanding and respect. One of his Denver Seminary mentors, Craig L. Blomberg, had coauthored a landmark volume of interreligious dialogue with one of Millet's colleagues in Religious Education, Stephen E. Robinson. (Johnson had introduced the two.) Their 1997 *How Wide the Divide?* modeled a new kind of conversation, one that was both respectful and engaging, and helped clarify respective positions and thaw some of the longstanding iciness between the two scholarly communities.[5] Critics charged that they downplayed some of Mormonism's more distinctive elements, or that each had been too soft towards the other side, or that they had even attempted to find common ground, but Johnson was inspired and so was Millet. Their own friendship, which began in 1997, would pave the way for a dramatic new stage in Latter-day Saint/evangelical relations.[6]

Millet and Johnson's extensive personal conversations opened them both to new understandings of the other's faith and, to a certain extent, new understandings of their own. They eventually opted for a two-pronged approach to share what they had learned. First, they offered to evangelical and Mormon groups something of a public dialogue, where they would engage each other with the kinds of questions and answers that had characterized their private conversations, followed by audience Q&A. Over the years, some seventy audiences across the United States, Canada, and England experienced the Millet/Johnson dialogue. Secondly, the pair established a formal Latter-day

Saint/evangelical dialogue group, comprising scholars from both traditions. The group ultimately opted for semiannual meetings—alternating in the spring between Mormon and evangelical locales and coinciding in the fall with the annual meeting of the American Academy of Religion/Society for Biblical Literature. The dialogue group lasted for fifteen remarkable years.[7]

After some tentative first steps, the dialogue became a productive engine for goodwill, understanding, and insight. Millet and Richard Mouw, then president of Fuller Seminary in Pasadena, California, became the de facto leaders of their respective sides and early on determined to keep the group relatively small, private, and focused on doctrinal matters. Bonds of friendship and love between dialogue members eventually replaced palpable early tension. Questions that participants guessed would be major stumbling blocks (grace versus works, for instance) seemed less daunting after careful consideration. Other matters (such as ontology and anthropology) proved far less conducive to common ground. Neither side had any interest in "watering down" their own perspectives or in doctrinal compromise. Neither side featured a unified systematic theology either, though, so theological diversity became a prominent feature of their shared experience. In the end, members of the group spoke publicly to clarify the others' positions and to correct misperceptions. Group members also quoted from each other's work, visited each other's institutions and classrooms, and eventually collaborated on several publishing projects. Millet himself led the way, authoring several titles directly related to the dialogue. Two volumes put the dialogue's process on display for a broad audience, each with a different evangelical conversation partner: *Bridging the Divide: The Continuing Conversation between a Mormon and an Evangelical*, with Gregory Johnson, and *Claiming Christ: A Mormon-Evangelical Debate*, with Gerald R. McDermott. And, in a first of its kind, Millet also authored an examination of Latter-day Saint teachings about Jesus Christ for an evangelical audience in a prominent evangelical venue: *A Different Jesus? The Christ of the Latter-day Saints*.[8] In 2015, a collaborative volume from its participants summed up the dialogue, marked its conclusion, and hinted at possibilities for future discussion: *Talking Doctrine: Mormons and Evangelicals in Conversation*.[9]

The tone and content of Millet's interfaith outreach efforts were not universally understood or appreciated, however. Some among Bob's own BYU colleagues worried that emphasizing the Christ-centered aspects of Mormon theology or the Book of Mormon so prominently effectively downplayed the more unique elements of Mormon thought and practice. Others doubted the sincerity of the evangelical counterparts. Once the effort broadened to include evangelical student visits to the BYU campus, some worried that Latter-day Saint students might get caught unawares in "stealth" evangelism. And, while some Church leaders lauded the efforts for the goodwill and understanding they generated, others worried that scholars might be perceived as speaking for the Church or that unique Church teachings might somehow get short shrift in the conversations. His outreach efforts cost him more than one friendship in Religious Education, Millet reported with regret. Even so, he felt inspired to take some risks given that 1991 apostolic mandate and the observable good accomplished during each step of the outreach process.

In the end, it seems warranted to place Millet in company with a circle of Latter-day Saints (from leaders such as David O. McKay to academics like Truman Madsen) who have influenced the tenor of Religious Education's, BYU's, and the Church's approach to interreligious endeavors. Simply put, Millet had a hand in many of the notable recent headlines related to interfaith cooperation or understanding: the two visits of renowned evangelist Ravi Zacharias to speak at the Tabernacle on Temple Square (in 2004 and 2014); the meeting of the National Association of Evangelicals governing board in Salt Lake City in March 2011 and an address of Elder Jeffrey R. Holland of the Quorum of Twelve Apostles to that body;[10] the visits of national evangelical leaders to Church headquarters in Salt Lake City or BYU, including Ravi Zacharias, Assemblies of God USA general superintendent George O. Wood, Southern Baptist Theological Seminary president R. Albert Mohler Jr., and Southern Evangelical Seminary president Richard D. Land; and the creation in 2014 of an Office of Religious Outreach connected to the BYU Religious Studies Center, which provides funding, support, and coordination to interreligious activities in Religious Education and across campus. Millet's unique blend of courage, sensitivity, conviction, and openhearted curiosity fit him well for this extraordinary chapter in Latter-day Saint history. Future histories will simply have to account for his influence when considering the twenty-first-century Church's engagement with other faiths.

His interfaith work punctuated a career of astounding literary output. Author, coauthor, or editor of over 70 books and 180 articles and book chapters, he has become one of the more recognizable and popular voices in Mormon publishing. By and large, he has calibrated his work for a broad Latter-day Saint audience. He remains a voracious reader of contemporary scholarship across a wide range of topics, but his own work tends to translate that world of sophisticated ideas for nonacademics. That approach resulted from a conscious decision early on in his career. Some of his more academically minded colleagues pushed him to write for scholarly audiences because of his training at Florida State. But while he appreciates the more scholarly work of others, he decided to set his focus at a wide angle. "Somebody's got to talk to the Saints," he explained. His writing is at once devotional, apologetic, scholarly, and pastoral. His interests vary widely, but the three sections of this Festschrift reflect his leading concerns as a writer: doctrine, scripture, and comparative Christianity. While one senses some significant shifts in his style and tone over time—especially a growing awareness of his non-Mormon conversation partners and readers—some steady themes are perceptible in his work.

First and foremost, Millet's work is "Christocentric" in its approach to Mormon theology. That is, despite his respect for Joseph Smith and Church history, the person and mission of Jesus Christ is in the forefront for Millet (and especially so in his later work). For him, topics range out from that center, but the Center is never far afield. Seen in context, Millet's work seems both reflective of, and undoubtedly contributive to, a broad shift in Mormon culture during the last half of the twentieth century. The 1990s reformatting of the Church's official logo, with "Jesus Christ" in noticeably larger type, nicely encapsulates that shift. Millet's writing is certainly part of that larger story. If twentieth-century Latter-day Saints are more conversant in their tradition's redemptive themes, more articulate concerning the role of grace in salvation, and more aware of the commitments they share with traditional Christians—and there is strong evidence that each is true—Millet likely deserves some of the credit (or blame, depending on one's perspective).

Secondly, the Millet corpus is rooted in a literalistic appreciation of scripture, especially the Book of Mormon and New Testament. This fact no doubt correlates with his pronounced Christocentrism, but it's worth noting how consistently Millet returns to the authority of scripture, and with an informed yet commonsensical reading of it, as an organizing principle.[11] Again, context matters. Millet came of age as a young professor just as Church President Ezra Taft Benson called Latter-day Saints to task for longstanding neglect of the Book of Mormon. While President Benson emphasized what he regarded as the Book of Mormon's lessons for American destiny, the millennial crescendo he sensed in world history, and the sin of pride, Millet and some of his like-minded Religious Education colleagues answered the call by focusing on another of the Church President's themes: the book's potential for increased personal spirituality. As they mined its pages, they rediscovered themes from the Church's earliest revelations: a strong emphasis on grace, Christ's Atonement, and salvation through his "merits." What has sometimes been taken as a "Protestant turn" in Millet's writings is likely often more the result of a fresh reckoning with early Restoration scripture. That his writing in the 1990s fit him well for détente with evangelicals is clear enough, but perhaps only in retrospect. When he started dialoguing with evangelicals in the early 2000s in earnest, in other words, he came with "Amazing Grace" already on his mind. Again, in this Millet both reflected and propelled a broader turn in Mormon culture. He has worked to harmonize Christ-centeredness and the more radical possibilities in the Mormon theological inventory, but by this point, if he were forced to choose, no one could question where he stands.

Much to his credit, the authors gathered here may or may not agree with Millet on any given topic. Certainly, it reveals a great deal that he invited several Mormon historians and philosophers into the Latter-day Saint/evangelical dialogue who spent as much time contesting his points as did the evangelicals! He has long been confident that Mormonism can more than hold its own under intense scrutiny, and he's keen to set a big table for the discussion. Simply put, he has personally mentored a large number of Mormon educators and has won the trust and respect of a significant contingent of Protestant fellow travelers. We who count ourselves grateful recipients of his generous influence hope this volume's collective thinking, faith, and lively conversation form a worthy "thank you" to our cherished colleague and friend.

Notes

1. Biographical information and quoted material without a citation is taken from author's interview with Robert L. Millet, January 16, 2015 (transcript in author's possession), and from "Engaging Intellect and Feeding Faith: A Conversation with

INTRODUCTION

Robert L. Millet" (interview by Lloyd D. Newell), *Religious Educator* 15, no. 2 (2014): 132–45.

2. Donald Q. Cannon served briefly as "interim dean" between Matthews and Millet. Cannon thereafter served as one of Millet's associate deans.
3. See "Engaging Intellect," 138–39.
4. See "Engaging Intellect," 137.
5. Craig L. Blomberg and Stephen E. Robinson, *How Wide the Divide? A Mormon and an Evangelical in Conversation* (Downers Grove, IL: IVP Academic, 1997).
6. See Craig L. Blomberg, "The Years Ahead: My Dreams for the Mormon-Evangelical Dialogue," *Evangelical Interfaith Dialogue* 3, no. 2 (Fall 2012): 8–11.
7. For a brief history of the dialogue, see Derek J. Bowen, "Mormon-Evangelical Scholarly Dialogue: Context and History," *Evangelical Interfaith Dialogue* 3, no. 2 (Fall 2012): 19–21.
8. Robert L. Millet and Gregory C. V. Johnson, *Bridging the Divide: The Continuing Conversation Between a Mormon and an Evangelical* (Rhinebeck, NY: Monkfish Publishers, 2007); Robert L. Millet and Gerald R. McDermott, *Claiming Christ: A Mormon-Evangelical Debate* (Grand Rapids, MI: Brazos Press, 2007); Robert L. Millet, *A Different Jesus? The Christ of the Latter-day Saints* (Grand Rapids, MI: Eerdmans, 2005). See also Robert L. Millet, "The Mormon-Evangelical Dialogue: Reflections after 12 Years," *Evangelical Interfaith Dialogue* 3, no. 2 (Fall 2012): 4–7; Richard J. Mouw, *Talking With Mormons: An Invitation to Evangelicals* (Grand Rapids, MI: Eerdmans, 2012).
9. Richard J. Mouw and Robert L. Millet, eds., *Talking Doctrine: Mormons and Evangelicals in Conversation* (Downers Grove, IL: IVP Academic, 2015).
10. The address was published in the Church's official organ: Elder Jeffrey R. Holland, "Standing Together for the Cause of Christ," *Ensign*, August 2012, lds.org/ensign/2012/08/standing-together-for-the-cause-of-christ?lang=eng.
11. While I discern a preponderance of references to the Book of Mormon and New Testament in my admittedly incomplete survey of his writings, it should be noted that Millet has written on every book of Latter-day Saint scripture. Indeed, he reflects an important reality in modern Mormon practice: as formalized in the 1981 editions of the Latter-day Saint canon with their extensive cross-referencing system, Millet reads those scriptures *together*. That is, while some of his Religious Education colleagues specialized in a particular book of scripture with its respective linguistic, historical, or textual particularities, Millet represents a more holistic approach—almost theological and yet not formally or systematically so. See "Engaging Intellect," 134–35.

Part I
Doctrine

"The First Principles of Man are Self-Existent with God"
The Immortality of the Soul in Mormon Theology

Brent L. Top

"I am dwelling on the immutability of the spirit of man," Joseph Smith taught in April 1844. "Where did it come from?" he rhetorically asked his Nauvoo, Illinois, congregation.[1] The emphatic answer was as much a repudiation of traditional Christian teachings on the immortality of the human soul as it was a declaration of unique Mormon doctrine—what Smith believed to be lost doctrines taught in antiquity, tenets that had been restored to earth through divine revelation: "I must come to the resurrection of the dead, the soul, the mind of man, the immortal spirit. All men say God created it in the beginning. The very idea lessens man in my estimation; I do not believe the doctrine, I know better. Hear it all ye ends of the world, for God has told me so."[2]

Other than on a very superficial level, it is highly unlikely that Joseph Smith was familiar with the great philosophical issues of the ages regarding man's immortality. While he may have heard of Aristotle, Socrates, and Plato, there is no evidence that he studied Greek philosophy or the works of the world's great thinkers. In his 1832 history, Smith said, "As it required the exertions of all that were able to render any assistance for the support of the Family therefore we were deprived of the bennifit of an education suffice it to say I was mearly instructed in reading writing and the ground rules of Arithmatic which const[it]uted my whole literary acquirements."³ His mother described him as "much less inclined to the perusal of books than any of the rest of the children, but far more given to meditation."⁴ It is reasonable to assume that Smith knew little, if anything, regarding issues such as Neoplatonism, dualism, absolutism, or materialism. His theological views were not shaped by studying the writings of philosophers or early Christian theologians like Clement, Justin Martyr, Origen, Tertullian, or Thomas Aquinas, though he may have been introduced to them by perusing some of the Bible commentaries and theological reference books of his day, such as *Bucks Theological Dictionary*. Smith claimed that his views concerning the soul of man came not by reason but by revelation. Even so, his teachings and revelations, and the teachings of subsequent Mormon prophet-leaders—including those espoused by the Church today—intersect with and sometimes directly respond to the great questions and issues raised by philosophers and theologians.

This chapter will explore significant teachings within early Mormonism that helped shape current doctrine regarding immortality as it relates to three phases of existence—preexistence, life on earth, and life after death. This paper offers a short examination of some of the most important and foundational doctrines relating to what Mormons would call man's three "estates"⁵ and argues that while Church leaders have hardly elaborated on every possibility, they've formulated their most potent challenges to traditional Christianity by shrinking the distance between humans and Deity. While many Christian critics worry about Mormon ideas about God, it's the Latter-day Saint doctrine of human souls that seems most striking given traditional theologies.

Intelligence: Primal Spirit Element

In 1833, Smith received a revelation—now canonized as section 93 of the Doctrine and Covenants—stating that "man was also in the beginning with God. Intelligence, or the light of truth, was not created or made, neither indeed can be" (D&C 93:29). Having rejected the traditional Christian view of *ex nihilo* creation, Joseph Smith later taught: "The Spirit of Man is not a created being; it existed from Eternity and will exist to eternity. Anything created cannot be eternal, and earth, water, etc.—all these had their existence in an elementary state from Eternity."[6] As early as September 1830—five months after the Church was organized and when Smith was only twenty-four years old—a revelation declared that all things were created, or organized, spiritually prior to being temporally (or naturally) created (see D&C 29:31–32). While we do not know exactly how Smith understood the concept in 1830—whether he perceived "spiritual creation" to mean merely God's foreknowledge or whether it referred to a literal creation (or organization) of all things in a pre-creation-of-the-earth, spiritual state—it is clear that a decade later he advocated an *ex materia* creation of both the natural world in general and man in particular.[7]

While in Washington, DC, during the winter of 1839–40, Joseph Smith was invited to preach in local churches and discuss Mormon beliefs with residents of the nation's capital, who were curious to hear the "Mormon Prophet." Matthew L. Davis, the Washington correspondent for the *New York Enquirer*, was in attendance at a gathering on February 5, 1840, and reported that Smith declared: "I believe that the *soul* is eternal; and had no beginning; it can have no end" and that "the soul of man, the spirit, had existed from eternity in the bosom of Divinity." What was Smith referring to? Davis stated that the explanation given "was so brief that I could not perfectly comprehend him."[8] What is it about the soul that "existed from eternity"?

Four years later in Nauvoo, Illinois, in what came to be known as the King Follett discourse, Smith amplified his earlier teachings. This may have answered some of the questions about man's immortality that had arisen in the minds of Church members from Smith's earlier piecemeal revelations and doctrines, but additional questions and controversies emerged. In one of the accounts of this sermon, Smith reportedly said:

> We say that God himself is a self-existing God; who told you so? it is correct enough but how did it get into your heads? Who told you that man did not exist in like manner upon the same principles? The mind of man is as immortal as God himself. . . . Is it logic to say that a spirit is immortal, and yet have a beginning? Because if a spirit have a beginning it will have an end . . . intelligence exists upon a self-existent

principle, it is a spirit from age to age, and there is no creation about it.... The first principles of man are self-existent with God.[9]

It is interesting to note the various terms Joseph Smith used in this discourse in referring to the immortal spirit of man. Earlier, he used the phrase "elementary state." In the 1844 discourse, however, he seems to more precisely define what that "elementary state" means. Terms such as "soul," "mind of man," "spirit," "intelligent part," "intelligence," and "first principles of man" appear to be used almost interchangeably. This portion of the discourse has generated considerable discussion and debate from 1844 to the present. Although there have been many interpretations through the years, it remains somewhat unclear what Smith meant by these terms. There is no doubt, however, that he taught that a central primal element of man was not created but has existed eternally. But questions remain concerning the exact nature of that eternal element. What is "intelligence"? Did man, as an individual entity, always exist? If so, how?

Even among Joseph Smith's contemporaries who heard this sermon there was disagreement as to what the Prophet meant. Perhaps this is nowhere more apparent than in the subsequent statements of the Pratt brothers, Parley and his younger brother Orson. Both were close associates of Joseph Smith, ardent defenders of Mormonism, prolific writers, and unlettered theologians in their own right. Yet each came to a different interpretation regarding the immortal or primal nature of man. Parley wrote that man, as an individual entity, was "created" or brought forth from uncreated, eternal, primal spiritual matter. Speaking of these "organized" entities, Pratt declared in 1853:

> Organized intelligence. What are they made of? They are made of the element which we call spirit.... Let a given quantity of this element, thus endowed, or capacitated, be organized in the size and form of man ... what would we call this individual, organized portion of the spiritual element? We would call it a spiritual body, an individual intelligence, an agent endowed with life, with a degree of independence, or inherent will, with the powers of motion, of thought, and with the attributes of moral, intellectual, and sympathetic affections and emotions.[10]

Like Parley P. Pratt, Brigham Young interpreted Smith's teachings about immortal "intelligence" to mean that man was created out of spirit element but did not exist as an individual, premortal entity prior to a literal spiritual birth.[11]

At the other end of the spectrum, Orson Pratt, one of Mormonism's most colorful and creative thinkers, argued eloquently, but often controversially, that immortal intelligence is a highly individualized existence. He proposed that "each particle [or intelligence] eternally existed prior to this organization; each was enabled to perceive its own existence; each had the power of self-motion; each was an intelligent, living being of itself."[12]

For decades, Orson Pratt feuded with Brigham Young over their differing views on the eternal nature of man and God. In 1865, Brigham Young and his counselors in the First Presidency issued a statement that Orson Pratt's views on the eternal nature of God and man were not to be viewed as the official doctrine of the Church. They stated that the members of the Church, along with all the "Prophets and Apostles," would have to be "content with the knowledge that from eternity there had been organized (created) beings, in an organized form."[13]

It was Brigham Young's, not Orson Pratt's, view that mostly "carried the day" and was viewed as the Church's doctrine in the latter half of the nineteenth century. It was even further solidified by an 1884 sermon delivered by Charles W. Penrose, a prominent Church leader and writer who would later serve in the First Presidency. In that discourse, Penrose argued that God "is an organized Being" and that "God had a beginning." Commenting on the eternal nature of God (which Pratt had advocated), he taught that the Almighty is viewed as the "Eternal Father" and that he "never had a beginning" only "in the *elementary particles* of his organism," not as a personal being. Penrose applied this same principle to the eternal nature of man: "The individual, the organized person may have had a beginning (a creation), but that spirit of which and by which they [were] organized never had a beginning. . . . The *primal particles* never had a beginning. They have been organized in different shapes [as individual entities]; the organism [or individual spirit] had a beginning, but the elements or atoms of which it is composed never had. . . . The *elementary parts of matter as well as of spirit*, using ordinary terms, never had a beginning."[14]

This seemed to settle the issue—at least temporarily. The accepted doctrinal view that man, as an individual entity, came about from the organization of primal spirit element remained virtually unchallenged until the early twentieth century. B. H. Roberts, one of Mormonism's most articulate defenders and doctrinal expositors and senior president of the Church's third-highest governing body (First Council of the Seventy), in 1907 published in the *Improvement Era*, the Church's official periodical, an article entitled "The Immortality of Man." Also, from 1907 to 1912, Roberts authored the *Seventy's Course in Theology*—a five-year theological curriculum for leaders and missionaries of the Church holding the position of Seventy. In that curriculum, Roberts sought to systematically explicate the revealed doctrines of the Church and support them by means of scientific evidences and philosophical arguments. In those publications, Roberts amplified what Orson Pratt had articulated a half century earlier. Roberts's notion of "personal eternalism" represented a more complex and developed view of human immortality in Mormon thought. He claimed that man existed as a personal, individual, self-conscious entity prior to what Mormons had come to accept as a "spirit birth." He wrote:

> There is a complex thing we call man, an intelligent entity, uncreated, self-existent, indestructible, he—for that entity is a person; because as we shall see he is possessed with power that go with the person. . . .
>
> Under this concept, the eternal ego of man was, in some past age of the other world dim to us, clothed with a spiritual body. That was man's spiritual birth and his entrance into the spiritual world. . . . The term "an intelligence" is then applied to the eternal ego of man existing even before the spiritual creation. . . .
>
> The difference between "spirits" and "intelligences," as here used, is this: Spirits are uncreated intelligences inhabiting spiritual bodies; while "intelligences," pure and simple, are intelligent entities, but unembodied in either spirit bodies or bodies of flesh and bone. They are uncreated, self-existent entities.[15]

Although neither Roberts nor the leadership of the Church viewed his teachings as official doctrine for the Church, "personal eternalism"—the view that man was an individual, self-conscious, self-acting "intelligence" prior to being created as a spirit—became widely taught and accepted in Church circles in the latter half of the twentieth century. However, the Church has never officially endorsed either philosophical camp—"primal particles" or "personal eternalism." As Mormon philosopher Blake Ostler has stated, "The conflict between absolute and finite theologies has yet to be resolved in Mormon thought."[16]

"Ye Are the Offspring of God": Spirit Sons and Daughters of a Heavenly Father

Although Joseph Smith's use of the terms "soul," "spirit," and "intelligence" was somewhat ambiguous, as evidenced by the conflicting opinions expressed by Church leaders in the decades after his death, the Latter-day Saint doctrine of a preexistent "spirit birth" decreased that ambiguity. An official proclamation by the First Presidency and the Council of the Twelve Apostles issued in 1995 stated: "All human beings—male and female—are created in the image of God. Each is a beloved son or daughter of heavenly parents, and, as such, each has a divine nature and destiny."[17] Nearly a hundred years earlier, the First Presidency had issued a doctrinal declaration regarding the spiritual and physical origins of man. "All men and women are in the similitude of the universal Father and Mother, and are literally the sons and daughters of Deity," the presidency of the Church wrote in 1909.

> The doctrine of the pre-existence—revealed so plainly, particularly in the latter days, pours a wonderful flood of light upon the otherwise mysterious problem of man's origin. It shows that man, as a spirit, was begotten and born of heavenly parents, and reared to maturity in the eternal mansions of the Father, prior to coming to earth in a temporal body to undergo an experience in mortality. It teaches that all men existed in spirit before any man existed in the flesh, and all who have inhabited the earth since Adam have taken bodies and become souls in like manner. . . . Man is the child of God.[18]

Every President of the Church since Joseph Smith has clearly and consistently taught that all humans are, as the Apostle Paul explained to the

Athenian intellectuals, "offspring of God" (see Acts 17:28–29). Not only that, but to Mormons, the phrase in Hebrews describing God as "the father of spirits" (see Hebrews 12:9) is to be taken literally.[19] Although this doctrine is ubiquitous today in official Mormon publications and curricula—as well as in sermons spoken, lessons taught, and hymns sung by leaders and lay members all over the world—it was not always so. There is little evidence that Mormons of the 1830s knew much, if anything, about this doctrine. The Latter-day Saint doctrine of preexistence and man's spiritual nature, as previously demonstrated, unfolded gradually. Even so, there is a paucity of evidence that Joseph Smith taught that men were spiritually begotten sons and daughters of God as preexistent spirit entities. The doctrine does not appear directly in any of Smith's public discourses or official Church publications in his lifetime; nor is it found in any of the Mormon canonical works.[20] However, it was widely taught by some of Smith's closest contemporaries, who attributed their understanding of the doctrine to the Mormon Prophet. For example, within months of Smith's death, Orson Pratt along with poetess Eliza R. Snow, one of Smith's plural wives, published writings that directly spoke of man's spirit birth to heavenly parents. "What is man? The offspring of God," Pratt wrote in his 1845 *Prophetic Almanac*. "What is God? The father of man. Who is Jesus Christ? He is our Brother. . . . How many states of existence has man? He has three. What is the first? It is spiritual. What is the second? It is temporal. What is third? It is immortal and eternal. How did he begin to exist in the first? He was begotten and born of God."[21] Some have suggested that Pratt actually wrote this work and prepared it for publication prior to Smith's death in June 1844.[22]

Similarly, a poem penned by Eliza R. Snow entitled "My Father in Heaven" was published in the November 15, 1845, issue of the Nauvoo *Times and Seasons*. Many secondhand accounts claim that Snow learned of spirit birth from Smith himself.[23] Today Snow's poem is a much-beloved Latter-day Saint hymn entitled "O My Father":

> O my Father, thou that dwellest
> In the high and glorious place;
> When shall I regain thy presence,
> And again behold thy face?

> In thy holy habitation
> Did my spirit once reside?
> In my first primeval childhood
> Was I nurtured near thy side?
> For a wise and glorious purpose
> Thou hast plac'd me here on earth,
> And withheld the recollection
> Of my former friends and birth:
> Yet oft times a secret something
> Whispered you're a stranger here;
> And I felt that I had wandered
> From a more exalted sphere.
> I had learn'd to call thee father
> Through the spirit from on high;
> But until the key of knowledge
> Was restor'd, I knew not why.[24]

In 1847, Orson Pratt stated that Joseph Smith, before his death, "advanced some new and glorious ideas, that we [h]ad never reflected on it. It was in reg[a]rd to the offspring of the Cel[estial] Male & Female. It was a new thing to me."[25] It is reasonable to assume that Brigham Young was likewise introduced to the doctrine by Joseph Smith, as reflected in this 1852 statement by Young: "Our Father in Heaven begat all the spirits that ever were, or ever will be on this earth; and they were born spirits in the eternal world. Then the Lord by His power and wisdom organized the mortal tabernacles of man. We were made first spiritual, and afterwards temporal."[26]

The Mormon notion of spirit birth is an interesting blend of Platonic thought on immortality, traditional Christian views concerning soul creation, Origen's beliefs regarding preexistence, and the dualists' views on body and mind, matter, and consciousness. Yet there are also great differences between each of these and Mormon thought. Latter-day Saint scholar Charles Harrell has pointed out that some aspects of the spirit birth doctrine were not as radical a departure from traditional Christianity as is usually assumed. "It is important to realize," Harrell writes, "that during the early nineteenth century there was a common tendency to view God's fatherhood much the same way as taught in Mormonism, except for the procreative process implicit in LDS teachings." As examples, Harrell cites Methodism's view of "man's divine sonship eventuating in his moral perfection," Universalists' view of the fatherhood of God, and an 1824 article in the *Christian Magazine* stating that man's soul possesses a "spark of [God's] intelligence, and continues to be in a high and peculiar sense 'his offspring.'"[27] Clearly, however, the Mormon doctrine of the literal relationship of man to heavenly parents is the great divide. It is this unique LDS doctrine that gives meaning to Latter-day Saints' understanding of their natures before they were born on earth, as human beings on earth, and what they will be like after death.

THE HAND AND GLOVE: SPIRIT AND BODY

There is a commonly used object lesson in Mormon circles that teaches in a simplistic manner the dual nature of man. It is the hand and a glove. The hand represents the spirit of man and the glove represents the physical body. Just as the glove cannot serve its purpose without the hand within it, the body is dependent upon and is the outward "clothing" of the immortal spirit. Clearly, the physical nature of man has a powerful effect on his existence and the "outward man" (or body) is an essential element in man's existence, but the "inward man" (or spirit) is central to eternal identity. Together, as Mormon scripture declares, "the spirit and the body are the soul of man" (D&C 88:15).

Within months after the organization of the Church, Joseph Smith spoke of the spiritual and temporal (physical) natures of man and all creation (see D&C 29:31–32). In 1832, Smith said that God revealed to him that "that which is spiritual [is] in the likeness of that which is temporal; and that which is temporal in the likeness of that which is spiritual; *the spirit of man in the likeness of his person*, as also the spirit of the beast, and every other creature which God has created" (D&C 77:2; emphasis added). A decade later, Joseph Smith elaborated further on the nature of spirits:

> The spirit, by many, is thought to be immaterial, without substance. With this latter statement we should beg to differ, and state that spirit is a substance; that it is material, but that it is more pure, elastic and refined matter than the [physical] body; that it existed before

the body, can exist in the body; and will exist separate from the body, when the body will be mouldering in the dust; and will in the resurrection, be again united with it.[28]

Similarly, Orson Pratt taught that spirits "have form and likeness similar to the human tabernacle."[29] His brother Parley went a step further in his classic *Key to the Science of Theology*, first published in 1855. He taught that the spirit being was not only "in the likeness and after the pattern of the fleshly tabernacle" but "it possesses, in fact, all the organs and parts exactly corresponding to the outward tabernacle."[30] That isn't official Mormon doctrine, but it is rather fascinating.

The Mormon view of the spirit body being in "the likeness of his person" also shapes Mormon perceptions of what spirit beings—both premortal and postmortal—do. Joseph Smith taught in 1843 that "the same sociality which exists among us here will exist among us there" (D&C 130:2). Contextually, he was speaking of post-Resurrection "sociality," but this notion has been applied by other Latter-day Saint leaders and scholars to preexistent spirits and those who have already lived on earth. For example, Brigham Young taught that "spirits will be as familiar with spirits in the spirit world—will converse, behold, and exercise every variety of communication with one another as familiarly and naturally as while here in tabernacles."[31]

Death—A Temporary Separation of Spirit from Body

When Joseph Smith castigated the "learned men and doctors of divinity" for what he considered their mistaken views on the immortality of the soul, he may well have been referring not only to their prevailing views regarding preexistence but also to their views concerning the soul's condition upon death. In contrast to nineteenth-century Christian materialist (or mortalist) teachings that many early Mormons would have known from their Protestant backgrounds, Joseph Smith proclaimed that death is merely a temporary separation of the spirit body from the physical body. The Book of Mormon teaches "concerning the state of the soul between death and the resurrection . . . that the spirits of all men, as soon as they are departed from this mortal body, yea, the spirits of all men, whether they be good or evil, are taken home to that God who gave them life" (Alma 40:11). Rather than "soul sleep" at death or a final judgment where righteous are taken immediately to the heavenly reward and the unsaved are thrust down to eternal torment, as many Christians advocated, the Book of Mormon and early Mormon leaders taught that at death the immortal spirits go to an intermediate realm "until the time of their resurrection" (Alma 40:14). Brigham Young taught that God, the Heavenly Father, was "pleased to organize tabernacles here, and put spirits into them, and they then became intelligent beings. By and by, sooner or later, the body, this that is tangible to you, that you can feel, see, handle, etc., returns to its mother dust. Is the spirit dead? No. You believe the spirit still exists, when this body has crumbled to the earth again, and the spirit that God puts into the tabernacle goes into the world of the spirits."[32]

Conditions in that postmortal spirit world, Mormons believe, are much like those in the premortal realm. Spirits, like men and women on earth, are capable of acting, thinking, feeling, and learning. Joseph Smith taught in 1843: "The spirits in the eternal world are like the spirits in this world."[33] The postmortal spirit world is an intermediate "estate"—a preparatory and purifying state where all will be given the opportunity to learn of and accept or reject the principles of eternal salvation. By this they can, as the Apostle Peter taught in the New Testament, be "judged according to men in the flesh" (1 Peter 4:6). This doctrine related to the eternal fate of the unevangelized is a distinctive feature of Mormon theology and practice. It was a prominent teaching of Smith's in Nauvoo before his death in 1844 and became even more institutionalized in Mormonism with the inclusion of a 1918 vision by Church President Joseph F. Smith known as the "Vision of the Redemption of the Dead" in the Latter-day Saint canon (see D&C 138).

"Resurrection from the Dead Is the Redemption of the Soul"

The foundation of Christianity is the Resurrection of Jesus Christ and the promise of man's Resurrection from death that results therefrom. "For as in Adam all die," the Apostle Paul taught the Corinthians, "even so in Christ shall all be made alive" (1 Corinthians 15:22). This is the cornerstone of LDS theology, as well: it is the "fundamental principle of the Gospel," Joseph Smith declared, and all other doctrines of the faith are mere "appendages" to it.[34]

Mormon scripture teaches that "the spirit *and* the body are the soul of man" (D&C 88:15; emphasis added). Therefore, "the resurrection from the dead is the redemption of the soul" (D&C 88:16). The culminating relationship between body and spirit is found, as taught in Mormonism, in a literal resurrection. Death results in a temporary separation of body and spirit. Resurrection is an eternal and inseparable union of both. The Book of Mormon speaks of the Resurrection as a "restoration" where "the spirit and the body shall be reunited again in its perfect form; both limb and joint shall be restored to its proper frame."

> Now, this restoration shall come to all, both old and young, both bond and free, both male and female, both the wicked and the righteous; and even there shall not so much as a hair of their heads be lost; but every thing shall be restored to its perfect frame, as it is now, or in the body. . . .
>
> Now, behold, I have spoken unto you concerning the death of the mortal body, and also concerning the resurrection of the mortal body. I say unto you that this mortal body is raised to an immortal body, that is from death, even from the first death unto life, that they can die no more; their spirits uniting with their bodies, *never to be divided*; thus the whole becoming spiritual and immortal, that they can no more see corruption. (Alma 11:44–45; emphasis added)

That there is a universal Resurrection; that all souls will live eternally with tangible bodies of flesh and bone; that these souls will know glory and joy, or the lack thereof, commensurate with their obedience to the law they were willing to obey in time and eternity (see D&C 88:21–38)—these things are widely taught in the Mormon canon and in the sermons and writings of Mormon leaders. What is less discussed, however, is *how* that Resurrection—the redemption of the soul—actually takes place. From the early years after the Church was first organized until today, Church leaders and lay members have speculated about the process of resurrection, but there is virtually no normative teaching in official Church publications regarding this process of resurrection.[35] For example, Brigham Young stated that "in the resurrection everything that is necessary *will be brought from the elements* to clothe and beautify the resurrected Saints who will receive their reward."[35] In 1854, Orson Pratt compared the death of the human body and its ultimate resurrection to a kernel of wheat that becomes a new organism:

> When a kernel of wheat falls into the earth, it dies, or rather a portion of its substance is disorganized; and the germ unites itself with other materials, and forms a stalk which heads and blossoms, and numerous other kernels of wheat begin to make their appearance which grow and ripen; and it is at length found that sixty or a hundred other kernels of the same, shape, size, and quality, as the one sown, are produced. Now these kernels are not the same identical materials sown; . . . they are each composed of almost entire new substance that never was before organized as wheat. . . . So likewise man sows not the body that shall be, but sows one containing form, and magnitude, and, in some degree, the elements of the new. Without the sowing of the old wheat, and its dissolution in the earth, the new could not be expected; so also, without our bodies sown in corruption, there would be no foundation for incorruptible bodies. And as the new wheat is mostly composed of new particles never before organized as wheat; so, it is probable, that the new immortal body will contain much matter never before organized in human bodies.[37]

These views—particularly the phrase "brought from the elements"—reflect the Mormon doctrine that all matter is uncreated and eternal and, as such, can be reorganized but not destroyed. Part of that "reorganization" would necessitate a change of what Paul called "corruptible" bodies that are fallen, die, and decay to an incorruptible, divine body (see 1 Corinthians 15:47–54). Joseph Smith taught: "God Almighty Himself dwells in eternal fire, flesh and blood cannot go there for all corruption is devoured by the fire [of God]—our God is a consuming fire—when our flesh is quickened by the Spirit, there will be no blood in the tabernacles,—some dwell in higher glory than others; . . . all men who are [im]mortal, dwell in everlasting burnings; . . . all men are born to die & all men must rise, all must enter eternity."[38]

Conclusion

During his April 7, 1844, sermon in Nauvoo, Illinois, when he was "dwelling upon the immortality of man," Joseph Smith took off the wedding ring from his finger, held it up before the crowd, and stated, "I take my ring from my finger and liken it unto the mind of man, the immortal spirit, because it has no beginning. Suppose you cut it in two; but as the Lord lives there would be an end."[38] Within Mormonism, man, like God, is an eternal being. Although neither Joseph Smith nor his successors were able to answer every question regarding how both God and man are uncreated and immortal or elaborate on every related doctrine, Mormons believe in a "two-way" immortality—an eternal past and an eternal future. Like all Christians, Latter-day Saints believe that Jesus Christ makes the immortality of the soul possible, in that he makes resurrected, glorified immortality possible. Mormon doctrine, however, parts company with traditional Christianity in unabashedly proclaiming that man is not only eternal but also the literal "offspring of God"—begotten daughters and sons of Deity with infinite potential. To be sure, that potential can be fully realized only as the Atonement of Jesus Christ is applied, so that lost and fallen men and women are redeemed from sin and put into a right relationship with Deity. Despite differences in doctrinal details, Mormons gladly join with many other Christians in declaring that death does not end man's existence but merely is a gateway to resurrection and eternal reward—a gift of God, through the power of his Son. A familiar Mormon scriptural passage from the Pearl of Great Price perhaps says it best: "For behold, this is [God's] work and [his] glory—to bring to pass the immortality and eternal life of man" (Moses 1:39).[40]

These unique views on the immortality of the soul and man's relationship to God powerfully affect the minds and lives of Mormons today. They are central to Latter-day Saints' approach to and worship of God. In addition to this "heavenly perspective," the Mormon theology of the immortality of the soul gives an "earthly view"—an understanding that all people on earth are linked together as brothers and sisters, children of God. As B. H. Roberts declared:

> I point out this noble relationship of man to Deity, not to flatter the former, but because I believe it to be a fact. It is a theme that I love to contemplate, not because it debases Deity, but because it elevates man, and must inspire him with noble aspirations, and to the performance of virtuous deeds. If but once understood and realized by mankind, I believe the conception would be a strong incentive to the reformation of the world.[41]

Notes

1. Wilford Woodruff, diary, 137, Church History Library, Salt Lake City. This discourse was delivered by Joseph Smith to an audience of nearly twenty thousand people during a general conference of the Church in Nauvoo, Illinois, on Sunday, April 7, 1844. Several of those present mentioned the sermon in their diaries. Smith stated that it was a funeral sermon given in response to a request from the family of King Follett, a member of the Church who had tragically been killed in an accident in March of that year. The discourse was recorded by four men who had experience and training in taking notes, some of whom at various times served as scribes for Joseph Smith. It was first published in the August 15, 1844, edition of the Mormon periodical *Times and Seasons*. This chapter will quote from these various early sources of the sermon. In 1855 the notes and accounts prepared by the four diarists were merged to form the official version of the sermon, which was published in the Salt Lake City *Deseret News* on July 8, 1857. That version has been published several times in official Church publications since that time, most familiarly in Joseph Smith, *History of the Church of Jesus Christ of Latter-day Saints*, ed. B. H. Roberts, 2nd ed. rev. (Salt Lake City: The Church of Jesus Christ of Latter-day Saints, 1932–51), 6:310–11.
2. "Conference Minutes," *Times and Seasons*, August 15, 1844, 615.
3. Karen Lynn Davidson, David J. Whittaker, Mark Ashurst-McGee, and Richard L. Jensen, eds., *Histories, Volume 1: Joseph Smith Histories, 1832–1844*, vol. 1 of the Histories series of *The Joseph Smith Papers*, ed. Dean C. Jessee, Ronald K. Esplin, and Richard Lyman Bushman (Salt Lake City: Church Historian's

Press, 2012), 11, available online at http://josephsmithpapers.org/paperSummary/history-circa-summer-1832.
4. Lucy Mack Smith, *Biographical Sketches of Joseph Smith the Prophet, and His Progenitors for Many Generations* (Liverpool: S. W. Richards, 1853), 84.
5. The term "estate" is used in the scriptures to mean a condition or dwelling place (see Ecclesiastes 3:18; Ezekiel 16:55; Jude 1:6). Latter-day Saint scripture uses the term "first estate" to mean man's pre-earthly spirit existence. Although not found in scripture, the term "second estate" is used within Mormonism to refer to earth life. By extension, life after death—either in the postmortal spirit world or after the Resurrection—could be referred to as the "third estate" or "fourth estate," respectively. Parley P. Pratt used these specific terms in his chapter, "Origin of the Universe," in *Key to the Science of Theology: Designed as an Introduction to the First Principles of Spiritual Philosophy; Religion; Law and Government; as Delivered by the Ancients, and as Restored in this Age, for the Final Development of Universal Peace, Truth, and Knowledge* (Liverpool: F. D. Richards, 1855).
6. *The Words of Joseph Smith*, ed. Andrew F. Ehat and Lyndon W. Cook (Provo, UT: Religious Studies Center, 1980), 9.
7. See Blake Ostler, "The Idea of Pre-Existence in the Development of Mormon Thought," *Dialogue: A Journal of Mormon Thought* 15, no. 1 (Spring 1982): 59–78; see also Ostler, "Out of Nothing: A History of Creation *ex Nihilo* in Early Christian Thought" (review of Paul Copan and William Lane Craig, "Craftsman or Creator? An Examination of the Mormon Doctrine of Creation and a Defense of *Creatio ex nihilo*," in *The New Mormon Challenge: Responding to the Latest Defenses of a Fast-Growing Movement*, ed. Francis J. Beckwith, Carl Mosser, and Paul Owen), *FARMS Review* 17, no. 2 (2005): 253–320.
8. Manuscript History of the Church, bk. C-1, 152–53, Church History Library.
9. Conference Minutes," *Times and Seasons*, August 15, 1844, 615.
10. Parley P. Pratt, in *Journal of Discourses* (Liverpool: F. D. Richards, 1855–86), 1:7–8.
11. See *Discourses of Brigham Young*, sel. John A. Widtsoe (Salt Lake City: Bookcraft, 1998), 47–51.
12. Orson Pratt, "The Pre-existence of Man," *The Seer*, July 1853, 103.
13. The First Presidency, 1865, in James R. Clark, comp., *Messages of the First Presidency*, 6 vols. (Salt Lake City: Bookcraft, 1965), 2:233.
14. Charles W. Penrose, in *Journal of Discourses* (London: Latter-day Saints' Book Depot, 1853–86), 26:23, 27; emphasis added.

THE FIRST PRINCIPLES OF MAN

15. B. H. Roberts, *The Seventy's Course in Theology* (Independence, MO: Zion's Printing and Publishing, 1907–11), 4:13–14; see also Roberts, "Immortality of Man," *Improvement Era*, April 1907, 403–23; see also *The Seventy's Course in Theology*, vol. 4, lessons 1–23.
16. Ostler, "The Idea of Pre-Existence in the Development of Mormon Thought," 72.
17. The First Presidency and Council of the Twelve Apostles, "The Family: A Proclamation to the World," *Ensign*, November 1995, 102.
18. The First Presidency (Joseph F. Smith, John R. Winder, Anthon H. Lund), "The Origin of Man," *Improvement Era*, November 1909, 75–81; reprinted in James R. Clark, comp., *Messages of the First Presidency*, 4:203–6.
19. A representative example of how this is taught within Mormonism today can be found in the following statement written in 1985 by one of Mormonism's most prolific writers and a prominent theologian, Apostle Bruce R. McConkie: "[God] is more than the Father of the Firstborn; more than the Father of the Only Begotten in the flesh; more than the Father in the sense that he created the first mortal man. He is, in deed and in fact, the Father of the spirits of all men in the literal and full sense of the word. Each of us was begotten by him in the premortal life. We are his spirit children." *A New Witness for the Articles of Faith* (Salt Lake City: Deseret Book, 1985), 61.
20. Some Mormon scholars today suggest that the "spirit birth" Joseph Smith would have understood and taught others, if he did so, was not a literal birth, but rather an "adoption" whereby God "claimed these intelligences as his own," "organizing them into a celestial kindred." See Samuel M. Brown, "Believing Adoption," *BYU Studies* 52, no. 2 (2013): 50; see also Terryl L. Givens, *Wrestling the Angel* (New York: Oxford University Press, 2015), 147–75. Tracing the historical development of the belief that most Latter-day Saints today espouse of "spirit birth" to "heavenly parents," Givens wrote: "Even though the transformation or progression of spirit matter or intelligence into spirit through a process analogous to birth, has no verifiable basis in Smith's teachings, this interpretation is the logical implication of a heavenly pattern—limned by Smith in his King Follett Discourse and in section 132—whereby exalted men and women become the creators of eternal offspring, in imitation of their own Heavenly Parents. . . . Smith may have been heading in the direction of reconciling eternal existence with spirit birth or spirit 'organization.' He may, in other words, have been working toward a scheme in which primordial intelligence is transformed into spirit corporeality. . . . When the language of spirit birth is used in the modern church, it is without the clarification that such

begetting may be our best near-equivalent for God's fathering of the human spirit." Givens, *Wrestling the Angel*, 160–61.
21. Orson Pratt, *Prophetic Almanac for 1845* (New York: Prophet's Office, n.d.), 7–8.
22. See Charles R. Harrell, "The Development of the Doctrine of Preexistence, 1830–1844," *BYU Studies* 28, no. 2 (1988): 88.
23. See Jill Mulvay Derr, "The Significance of 'O My Father' in the Personal Journey of Eliza R. Snow," *BYU Studies* 36, no. 1 (1996–97): 85–126.
24. Eliza R. Snow, "O My Father," *Hymns* (Salt Lake City: The Church of Jesus Christ of Latter-day Saints, 1985), no. 292.
25. Orson Pratt, general Church minutes, November 21, 1847, Church Historian's Office, CR 100 318, box 1, folder 58, November 15, 1847–November 30, 1847.
26. Brigham Young, in *Journal of Discourses* (London: Latter-day Saints' Book Depot, 1854), 1:50.
27. Harrell, "Doctrine of Preexistence," 89–90.
28. Joseph Smith, editorial, *Times and Seasons*, April 1, 1842, 745.
29. Orson Pratt, in *Journal of Discourses* (London: Latter-day Saints' Book Depot, 1873), 15:242.
30. Parley P. Pratt, *Key to the Science of Theology* (Salt Lake City: Deseret Book, 1979), 79.
31. Brigham Young, in *Journal of Discourses* (London: Latter-day Saints' Book Depot, 1860), 7:239.
32. Brigham Young, in *Journal of Discourses* (London: Latter-day Saints' Book Depot, 1855), 2:138.
33. Joseph Smith, journal, May 21, 1843, 215, MS 155, box 1, folder 6, Church History Library.
34. Joseph Smith, *Elders' Journal*, July 1838, 42.
35. For a discussion of Joseph Smith's views regarding a literal resurrection and his criticisms of others' philosophies regarding such, see Samuel Morris Brown, *In Heaven as It Is on Earth: Joseph Smith and the Early Mormon Conquest of Death* (New York: Oxford University Press, 2012).
36. Brigham Young, in *Journal of Discourses* (London: Latter-day Saints' Book Depot, 1862), 9:192; emphasis added.
37. Orson Pratt, "Resurrection of the Saints," *The Seer*, June 1854, 277.
38. Thomas Bullock, minutes of a discourse, May 12, 1844, Joseph Smith Collection, Church History Library.
39. "Conference Minutes," *Times and Seasons*, August 15, 1844, 615.

40. Mormons accept the Pearl of Great Price as a canonical work like the Holy Bible, the Book of Mormon, and the Doctrine and Covenants. Although not officially accepted by the Church as canon until 1880, portions of the works contained in it were published in the Church's official newspapers, *Evening and Morning Star* (Independence, MO) and *Times and Seasons* (Nauvoo, IL) as early as 1832. To assist the proselyting work of Mormon missionaries and their teaching new converts to Mormonism in Great Britain in the mid-nineteenth century, Apostle Franklin D. Richards compiled those previously published works into a small book entitled *The Pearl of Great Price*, published in Liverpool in 1851. The Book of Moses is one of the works contained within the Pearl of Great Price. It is an extract from Joseph Smith's "inspired translation" of the Bible and contains several visions purportedly given to Moses that differ from or expand the Genesis account. Mormons view this work as a "restoration" of unique doctrinal and historical concepts.
41. B. H. Roberts, *The Gospel and Man's Relationship to Deity*, 10th ed. (Salt Lake City: Deseret Book, 1965), 282.

To Know God Is Life Eternal

Camille Fronk Olson

Through the mercy, merits, and grace of Christ, we are saved and exalted but also changed to become more like him in the process. In his great intercessory prayer, Jesus proclaimed, "And this is life eternal, that they might *know* thee the only true God, and Jesus Christ, whom thou hast sent" (John 17:3; emphasis added). From the moment Peter witnessed the resurrected Christ, he was a different man. Fearless in his desires to serve others and be a witness for the Redeemer, he came to know the Savior more deeply and meaningfully. Over time, Peter's demeanor, attitudes, and actions became strikingly reminiscent of him whom he followed. Peter became a type of Christ. A similar process was working in other early Christians such as James and John, Paul, Prisca and Aquila, and Stephen. Coming to know the Father and the Son transforms our characters and desires to mirror theirs.

This chapter will explore the connections between knowing God, becoming like Christ, and receiving eternal life. It will also consider the parable of the unprofitable servant and other teachings by the Savior and his servants that assist believers to discover how to know God and recognize their deepening knowledge. Context and meaning of terms within these stories clarify and facilitate deeper appreciation for the process of becoming like him.

Context

Nowhere else in scripture is the focus on gaining knowledge of God more pronounced than in the Apostle John's writings in the New Testament. John's record of the Savior's prayer to the Father is set at the conclusion of the Last Supper, immediately before Jesus and the Eleven departed for the Garden of Gethsemane and his agonizing pleas to the Father on our behalf. Acknowledging that knowing the Father and Son leads to eternal life, the Atoning One prayed, "that they all may be one; as thou, Father, art in me, and I in thee, that they may be one in us: . . . that the love wherewith thou hast loved me may be in them, and I in them" (John 17:21, 26). In his prayer, Jesus linked eternal life with knowing God, being one with God, and loving others with God's pure love.

Life Eternal

Because the Father and the Son have eternal life, it is eternal life to know them (see John 5:26). Eternal life is experiencing life as God knows it. It is living forever *with* the Father and the Son and living *like* the Father and Son. Eternal life is the supernal salvific gift from God, and, as a gift, it is by definition "free" (see 2 Nephi 2:4; D&C 14:7; 6:13).

Drawing on the full canon of holy writ, Robert L. Millet has defined the term thus:

> Eternal life is God's life. It is life in the highest heaven, a life in which we enjoy fellowship with God our Father, his Son, the Lord Jesus Christ, with members of our family, and with friends who have developed like passions for Christ and his gospel. Enjoying eternal life is therefore being *with* God. But it is even more, so very much more. It is a state of being—being *like* God, having acquired many of his attributes and characteristics, having enjoyed the cleansing power of the Savior's blood, and having been sanctified by the Spirit made pure and holy and completely comfortable to stand (or kneel) in the divine presence.[1]

In this sense, eternal life is every bit as much the highest *quality* of life as it is *quantity* of life. God's life is endless life because God's name is "Endless" (see D&C 19:10), as are his attributes and existence.

To "Know" (Greek, *ginosko*)

Simply knowing *about* God or his Son and acknowledging their existence, however, does not constitute *knowing* them. In the extreme, evil spirits recognize Jesus and even testify of his divinity, but possess no knowledge that could merit God's promises (see James 2:19; Mark 1:24). President Joseph F. Smith explained, "Lucifer, the son of the morning, knows Jesus Christ, the Son of God, much better than we, but . . . knowing, he yet rebels; knowing, he yet is disobedient; . . . hence, . . . there is no salvation in him."[2] Neither do mortals' direct interactions with the Lord guarantee that they will know God. For example, the children of Israel were fed and led by God for forty years, without coming to know and fully trust him (see Psalm 95:10; Hebrews 3:10). Likewise, some first-century Jews heard, watched, and conversed with Jesus over a period of years, but did not ever *know* him (see Joseph Smith Translation, Matthew 7:33; Matthew 7:21–23). When the Savior invites us to "know God," he indicates that sufficient truth and tutelage are available and that we are capable of succeeding. From scriptural examples and exhortations, we may conclude that God is not incomprehensible, as sometimes claimed, but profoundly knowable.

From the inception of Mormonism, beginning with meditating on James 1:5, asking God for wisdom, and receiving answers that superseded all expectation, Joseph Smith stressed the importance of truly knowing God. Joseph's "First Vision" corrected false assumptions about the personages, desires, and accessibility of the Father and the Son. For example, the Father and the Son are two distinct "Personages" whose glorious light banishes all darkness, who know us by our names, and who provide direct answers to our questions (see Joseph Smith—History 1:17–20). Through his subsequent experiences with obedience to God's commands, the Prophet learned firsthand the life-changing effect that knowing God had on him.[3]

The early leadership of The Church of Jesus Christ of Latter-day Saints frequently expounded on revealed scriptures in their meetings to ensure a correct idea of God's attributes in their desire to know God. According to *Lectures on Faith*, for "any rational and intelligent being" to have faith in God, he or she must have "a correct idea of [God's] character, perfections, and attributes."[4] The *Lectures* further state that without knowing God, a person "could not center his faith in him for life and salvation, for fear there should be a greater one than [God], who would thwart all his plans, and he, like the gods of the heathen, would be unable to fulfil his promises; but seeing he is God over all, from everlasting to everlasting, the creator and upholder of all things, no such fear can exist in the minds of those who put their trust in him, so that in this respect their faith can be without wavering."[5] Knowing God therefore produces complete trust in him and confidence concerning his commands.

Furthermore, we must know that God, as stated in *Lectures on Faith*, "is merciful, and gracious, slow to anger, abundant in goodness, and that he was so from everlasting, and will be to everlasting."[6] If he were not, "such is the weakness of human nature, and so great the frailties and imperfections of men, that unless they believed that these excellencies existed in the divine character, the faith necessary to salvation could not exist; for doubt would take the place of faith, and those who know their weakness and liability to sin, would be in constant doubt of salvation, if it were not the idea which they have of the excellency of the character of God. . . . An idea of these facts does away doubt, and makes faith exceedingly strong."[7]

Because of God's constant grace, justice, and mercy, we may know that willingly following his path will lead us to eternal life and becoming more like him.

The essence of the Greek verb *ginosko*, translated into English as "to know," suggests the most complete sense of understanding which "relates to the knowledge acquired through experience . . . achieved in all the acts in which a man [or woman] can attain knowledge, in seeing and hearing, in investigating and reflecting."[8] New Testament scholars have also concluded that the Christian view of "knowledge" is shaped and informed by the concept of *ginosko* in the Septuagint and other Greco-Jewish sources. As such, "an obedient and grateful acknowledgement of the deeds and demands of God is linked with knowledge of God and what he has done and demands. It is . . . a gift of grace."[9]

For example, the Savior taught, "If any man will *do* [God's] will, he shall *know* of the doctrine" (John 7:17; emphasis added), and "Not every one that saith unto me, Lord, Lord, shall enter into the kingdom of heaven;

but he that *doeth* the will of my Father which is in heaven" (Matthew 7:21; emphasis added). When Jesus observed that eternal life is inseparably connected with knowing him and the Father, he conceived a depth of understanding that requires a willing heart, an engaged mind, active ears, and authentically *living* that knowledge in everyday life.

Other New Testament linguists have noted that this expanse of knowledge is a never-ending process of grateful obedience: "The knowledge of God from the creation (Rom. 1:19f) does not rest on a logical conclusion involving cause and effect but instead requires a recognition in obedience of the Creator. . . . [It is] a process that is never concluded (Eph. 1:17)."[10]

When we consider the Savior's teachings, prophetic experience, and the meaning of *ginosko*, we must conclude that knowing God is a dynamic concept borne of gratitude and profound love. Its potential for growth is infinite as is the fruit that it bears: increased reverence for the gift and the Giver.

Knowing God through Willing Obedience and Service

John's writings underscore that the earliest Christians understood that keeping the commandments of the Father and following the example of the Son is requisite to gaining knowledge unto eternal life. John taught the litmus test for knowing God: "And hereby we do know that we know him, if we keep his commandments" (1 John 2:3). Again, to profess that we know him therefore means that we "walk, even as he walked" (1 John 2:6). The test includes, however, our motive for keeping God's commands; we obey him because we love him (see John 14:15; 1 John 2:5). Expressions of love are not limited to words; as John wrote, "My little children, let us not love in word, neither in tongue only; but in deed and in truth" (Joseph Smith Translation, 1 John 3:18 [in 1 John 3:18, footnote *a*]). As we more fully develop the mind of Christ, we discover that "blessings from above" include "commandments not a few" (D&C 59:4). Furthermore, scripture informs us that when we love God and our neighbors, God's "commandments are not grievous" (1 John 5:3) because they actually inspire us (see D&C 20:7). When we know God, we love and show reverence for his commandments not as mere stepping stones to something greater but as a foundation to life with God. Building upon "the rock of our Redeemer" is not episodic but an approach to living woven into our very natures (see Helaman 5:12).

Robert L. Millet observed, "I am convinced that if we will seriously call upon the Lord and ask him regularly to bless us to feel what we ought to feel and see what we ought to see, we will sense the divine hand upon our shoulder, nudging us onward and upward, all the days of our lives. We will then begin to balance the divine discontent (a constant inner enticement to repent and improve) with what Nephi called 'a perfect brightness of hope' (2 Nephi 31:20) and thereby find peace and lead happy and productive lives."[11]

The Apostle Paul calls this authentic manner of knowing having "the mind of Christ" (1 Corinthians 2:16). Through a lifetime of selfless love and sacrifice, we may receive the mind of Christ, not as a single event but through a sacred journey built on *doing* truth rather than merely professing faith (see John 3:21). It is not a fanatical attempt to force spiritual knowledge, but a process whereby we learn to "wait on him," rely on him, develop deeper trust in him, and cheerfully serve him. By consequence, we may experience "the rest of the Lord," even in mortality, which President Joseph F. Smith described as "entering into the knowledge and love of God, having faith in his purpose and in his plan, to such an extent that we know we are right, and that we are not hunting for something else."[12]

Similarly, Eliza R. Snow wrote of unexpected blessings that accompany obedience:

> When you are filled with the Spirit of God, and the Holy Ghost rests upon you . . . do you have any trials? I do not think you do. For that satisfies and fills up every longing of the human heart, and fills up every vacuum. When I am filled with that spirit my soul is satisfied; and I can say, in good earnest, that the trifling things of the day do not seem to stand in my way at all. But just let me lose my hold of that spirit and power of the Gospel, and partake of the spirit of the world, in the slightest degree, and trouble comes; there is something wrong. I am tried; and what will comfort me? You cannot impart comfort to me that will satisfy . . . Is it not our privilege to so live that we can have this constantly flowing into our souls?[13]

Nothing is impossible. Fear dissipates. We sense a growing confidence in our ability to obey because of our deepening knowledge, love, and trust in God. This is not self-confidence; it is God-confidence.

Near the end of his life and the annihilation of the Nephite people, the prophet Mormon wrote a letter to his son Moroni in which he recorded a sermon he had preached to "the peaceable followers of Christ," who had "obtained a sufficient hope by which [they could] enter into the rest of the Lord, from this time henceforth until [they would] rest with him in heaven" (Moroni 7:3). Even amid continual war and civil unrest, Mormon judged these hopeful few to have found rest "because of [their] peaceable walk with the children of men" (Moroni 7:4). Their knowledge of and love for the Father and Son had been nourished through years of good deeds for others motivated by gratitude and reverence toward their Creator and Redeemer.

The Parable of the Unprofitable Servant

Through his timeless teachings and parables, Jesus encouraged all who would listen to trust God and walk in faith—to learn truth by *doing* truth. For example, after giving the Twelve a better appreciation for the tremendous power inherent in having faith in him, Jesus responded to their request for an increase in faith by relating the parable of the unprofitable servant. This is one of the lesser-known and lesser-cited parables, perhaps because its connection to a plea for increased faith appears obscure or even disjointed. The Apostles asked Jesus to increase their faith, or perhaps their knowledge of the Father and Son. In essence, they were asking, "Teach us to really know you." In response, Christ told them this parable:

> But which of you, having a servant plowing or feeding cattle, will say unto him by and by, when he is come from the field, Go and sit down to meat?
>
> And will not rather say unto him, Make ready wherewith I may sup, and gird thyself, and serve me, till I have eaten and drunken; and afterward thou shalt eat and drink?
>
> Doth he thank that servant because he did the things that were commanded him? I [think] not.

> So likewise ye, when ye shall have done all those things which are commanded you, say, We are unprofitable servants: We have done that which was our duty to do. (Luke 17:7–10)

The Savior is clearly the Master in the parable. He tells us that we are the servant, or more accurately the "slave" (*doulos*), as the Greek renders it. Important doctrines are alluded to in the parable that teach us how faith is strengthened during challenging times. Slaves were essential to the social and economic structure of the Roman Empire and an accepted norm among the Jews for generations. Considering the empire as a whole, an estimated one in six people was enslaved.[14] In contrast to American history, in New Testament times, slaves were neither recognized by race, nor a lack of education, nor even by necessarily being at the bottom of the socioeconomic ladder. Rather, slavery was a product of the widespread patron-client dynamic.

From the time of Augustus Caesar's Pax Romana, slaves in the Roman Empire were less likely to be prisoners of war or victims of kidnappers. More frequently, they were born to slaves, or forced into slavery to pay their debts, or abandoned by their family; some volunteered to become slaves. Because a slave's individual social standing, honor, and economic opportunity were dependent on the status of his or her owner, chances for improved social standing and careers enticed some individuals to sell themselves into slavery for a time. In contrast to the free poor, slaves may have enjoyed material advantages.[15] Not only did slavery offer job security when employment opportunities were thin, but slaves were exempt from heavy taxes levied against noncitizens and could inherit an improved lifestyle when manumitted. Not infrequently, freed slaves were even granted citizenship in recognition of their life's service to the empire.[16] No laws, however, protected slaves from abuse by the hand of their owners. Without control of their living conditions in times of sickness or health, and without possessions, even of their own bodies, slaves would have likely experienced psychological distress. On the other hand, a gracious and benevolent owner created living conditions so inviting that manumitted slaves sometimes elected to remain a working member of the owner's household.[17]

Understanding the potential for first-century slaves to receive added freedom and opportunities in life after years of dedicated service may inform our appreciation for the Lord's likening us to slaves in the parable.

Certainly the Apostle Paul, a Roman citizen and freeman from birth, was not offended by such imagery because he also used it to describe his willingness to turn over his life to the Master; he rejoiced at his good fortune to have become a slave in the service of Christ (see 1 Corinthians 7:22; 9:19). A similar teaching is found in the Book of Mormon. Amaleki invited us to "come unto Christ, who is the Holy One of Israel, and partake of his salvation, and the power of his redemption. Yea, come unto him, and *offer your whole souls as an offering unto him,* and continue in fasting and praying, and endure to the end; and as the Lord liveth ye will be saved" (Omni 1:26; emphasis added). Optimum trust is implicit in a person's willingness to give her soul to another, to selflessly serve indefinitely.

In the parable, we are not only the Lord's slaves, but we acknowledge that we are his "unprofitable servants." Jesus asked his disciples whether the servant in the parable who has been working all day in the fields should expect to be richly rewarded and finally served by the Master in return. Anticipating that his listeners would see the fallacy of such an expectation, Jesus instead explained that the servant would hasten to prepare and serve dinner to the Master before preparing something to eat for himself. Likening his disciples to the servant, the Savior concluded, "Likewise ye, when ye shall have done all those things which are commanded you, say, We are unprofitable servants: We have done that which was our duty to do."

We don't much like being called unprofitable. In this great era of entitlement, when consulting companies are reportedly hired for the sole purpose of stroking egos of new employees, when workers expect bonuses for merely showing up to work, and when students anticipate "A" grades because they attended and completed the class, the Savior's parable is difficult to swallow. On those days when our confidence is shattered, or we feel responsible for all the world's problems, the lesson that Jesus teaches in this parable is not particularly welcomed. It can sound like the Lord is asking us to add even more work to our already impossible daily demands. Instead of reminding us of our "nothingness" without Christ, we prefer a scripture which reads, "Thou art fine just the way thou art, my daughter, and hast worked hard enough, kick back now and rest, for I will do thy work for thee." After all, just five chapters later, Luke records another of Christ's parables that does indeed reverse the roles: "The lord . . . shall gird himself, and make [his servants/slaves] to sit down to meat, and will come forth and serve them" (Luke 12:37). The fact that the Lord has served and does indeed serve us daily, however, does not indicate that we are no longer indebted to him.

Through the parable of the unprofitable servant, Jesus provided a vital lesson for knowing God and thereby better appreciating his service to us. As in the parable, King Benjamin called his people unprofitable servants, even when they were previously described as "a diligent people in keeping the commandments" (Mosiah 1:11). In his sermon, this beloved Nephite monarch testified that everything that we are we owe "to that God who has created [us], and has kept and preserved [us], and has caused that [we] should rejoice" (Mosiah 2:20). All that God asks of us in return is to follow him, and when we do, he immediately blesses us all the more, increasing our debt to him. King Benjamin concluded, "Therefore, of what have ye to boast?" (Mosiah 2:24). Aaron, a great Nephite missionary, taught King Lamoni's father that "since man had fallen he could not merit anything of himself; but the sufferings and death of Christ atone for their sins, through faith and repentance" (Alma 22:14). The closer we come to the Savior, the easier it is to admit that we are nothing without the grace and power of Jesus Christ.

Another insight to knowing God becomes evident when we resist focusing on how long we work in the Lord's service, or how hard we work, or even what we are specifically assigned to do. Instead of answering *what* and *how*, what if the Master is teaching us *why* we work and *why* we serve? What if his message is what we learn and become along the way when we trust God completely? Two scriptural examples, one from the New Testament and the other from the Book of Mormon, illustrate how our motives in serving others can transform our character.

The epistle of the Apostle Paul to Philemon in the New Testament tells of Onesimus, a slave whose name means "profitable" in Greek, who ran away from his master Philemon. In truth, Onesimus was not profitable when he deserted his duty in Colossae but ended up in another city where he met the imprisoned Paul. There Onesimus was converted to Jesus Christ and returned to Philemon with a letter from Paul requesting that Philemon forgive his repentant slave. In a delightful play on words, Paul becomes a type of Christ who justified Onesimus because the slave was penitent, albeit still a work in progress. The Apostle Paul wrote to Philemon, "In time past [Onesimus] was to thee unprofitable, but now [is] profitable to thee and to me" (Philemon 1:11). Through his faith in the healing power of Christ, Onesimus was declared profitable, worthy, or righteous. Through the grace of Jesus Christ, he was made worthy of God's blessing.

Ammon, a Nephite missionary to the wicked Lamanites, embraced the blessing of being about the Lord's work without expectation of praise along the way. Captured by the Lamanites and taken as a prisoner to their king, the young missionary was given an offer to marry the king's daughter. Instead, Ammon requested to be the king's servant. He volunteered to be a slave for Christ. After hearing the incredible report of Ammon's labors during his first day at work in the king's field—gathering scattered sheep and fighting off those who attempted to steal them—King Lamoni inquired as to the whereabouts of this faithful servant, only to learn that Ammon was already preparing the king's horses and chariots as he had been previously directed. Upon hearing this, King Lamoni exclaimed, "Surely there has not been any servant among all my servants that has been so faithful as this man; for even he doth remember all my commandments to execute them" (Alma 18:10). Through his selfless service, Ammon inspired Lamoni to trust him and thereby come to know God. In a similar way, Jesus may have been telling his Apostles that as indentured servants their faith would increase when they lost themselves in the work, found joy and satisfaction in helping others, and did not seek recognition.

In his analysis of the parable of the unprofitable servant, Elder John K. Carmack of the Seventy observed, "Perhaps the Savior was teaching us [in the parable] that if we are serious about desiring greater faith, nothing short of maintaining a constant eternal perspective will do. If we place *any* condition on our willingness to serve the Lord with all our hearts, we diminish our faith. If we have complete trust in him . . . we will continue with pure intent and total commitment the rest of our lives."[18]

In a day when we may hear more criticism and mocking than praise for our work, the Master reassures us in the parable that he knows our heart and that he has not left us to serve alone. An oft-repeated phrase in the Book of Mormon promises prosperity for those who keep the commandments of God, and being "cut off from the presence of the Lord" for those who do not (Alma 50:20; see also 2 Nephi 1:20; Alma 37:13). When considered as a pair of opposites, God's blessing of prosperity is his presence, not necessarily wealth or health or family. In coming to know God, we count it a pleasure to serve him every hour of every day, forever and ever, because such service invites us into his presence. In the parable of the unprofitable servant, the blessing is not having an overabundance of time, money, or ease. The blessing is being in the presence of God, a gift he freely offers through the companionship of the Holy Ghost to all who covenant with him.

Jesus Christ as Exemplar

Considered yet another way, the servant in the parable can also be seen as a type of Christ who patiently waits on his Father and glorifies him in the process. As the Great Exemplar, Jesus never asks us to do what he does not do himself. Earlier the same evening that he offered his intercessory prayer, Jesus washed the Apostles' feet in the upper room and explained to them, "For I have given you an example, that ye should do as I have done to you. Verily, verily, I say unto you, The servant is not greater than his lord; neither he that is sent greater than he that sent him" (John 13:15–16). Throughout the Gospel of John, Jesus Christ is shown as the one who continually serves, obeys, and imitates the Father. To know the one is to know the other (see John 14:7–10):

> The Son can do nothing of himself, but what he seeth the Father do: for what things soever he doeth, these also doeth the Son likewise.
>
> For the Father loveth the Son, and sheweth him all things that himself doeth. (John 5:19–20)
>
> I do nothing of myself; but as my Father hath taught me, I speak these things.
>
> And he that sent me is with me: the Father hath not left me alone; for I do always those things that please him. (John 8:28–29)
>
> Many good works have I shewed you from my Father. . . .
> If I do not the works of my Father, believe me not.

> But if I do . . . believe, that the Father is in me, and I in him. (John 10:32, 37–38)

> For I have not spoken of myself; but the Father which sent me, he gave me a commandment, what I should say, and what I should speak.
> And I know that his commandment is life everlasting: whatsoever I speak therefore, even as the Father said unto me, so I speak. (John 12:49–50)

Jesus became like his Father by turning his life over to him, doing all that was asked of him, and doing this service with love. Even after paying the ransom for each of us with his perfect blood, Jesus Christ continued to serve, just as in the parable. He taught the righteous spirits in the spirit world and prepared a way for those who had died without receiving sufficient knowledge of him (see D&C 138), returned to report to his Father (see John 20:17), and afterwards ministered to his disciples in the old and new worlds as the Resurrected Lord (see Acts 1:1–8; 3 Nephi 11–28). His service to the Father and humankind never ends.

Conclusion

By entering into the covenant of baptism, we demonstrate to the Father, to the Son, and to ourselves that we need a Redeemer. We desire to make their work our work. In short, we choose to become servants, or slaves to the Lord, to go where he calls us to go, to say what he directs us to say, and to become what he alone enables us to become. Following Christ's example is how we grow in faith, obedience, and knowledge of the Father and the Son. To know them is the supreme mode of being, whether in this life or the next. It is founded on personal motivation to follow their commands because we love them and know that we were and are perfectly loved by them.

Notes

1. Robert J. Millet, *Coming to Know Christ* (Salt Lake City: Deseret Book, 1985), 90–91.

2. James R. Clark, comp., *Messages of the First Presidency*, 6 vols. (Salt Lake City: Bookcraft, 1965), 5:9.
3. In a discourse to the general Church membership on April 7, 1844, Joseph Smith taught, "I want to go back to the begin & so get you into a more lofty splen than what the human being generally understands I want to ask this cong: every man wom: & child to ans^r· the quest^n· in their own heart what kind of a being is God I ag^n· rep^t· the quest^n· what kind of a being is God does any man or woman know have any of you seen, him heard him, communed with him, here is the quest^n· that will peradventure from <this time> henceforth occupy your attent^n·— the Apos: says this is Eternal life to know God & J. C [Jesus Christ] who he has sent— that is etern^l· life if any man enquire what kind of a being is God if he will search deligently his own heart that unless he knows God he has no eternal life—my first object is to find out the character of the true God." General Church minutes, 2 (in handwriting of Thomas Bullock, who recorded the sermon), Church History Library. I am indebted to Michael MacKay for his assistance in finding this account.
4. *Lectures on Faith* (Salt Lake City: Deseret Book, 1985), 2:4.
5. *Lectures on Faith*, 3:19.
6. *Lectures on Faith*, 3:14.
7. *Lectures on Faith*, 3:20.
8. Gerhard Kittel, ed., *Theological Dictionary of the New Testament*, 10 vols. (Grand Rapids, MI: Eerdmans, 1964), 1:690.
9. Kittel, *Theological Dictionary*, 1:707.
10. Horst Batz and Gerhard Schneider, eds., *Exegetical Dictionary of the New Testament*, 3 vols. (Grand Rapids, MI: Eerdmans, 1999), 1:249.
11. Millet, *Coming to Know Christ*, 49.
12. Joseph F. Smith, *Gospel Doctrine* (Salt Lake City: Deseret Book, 1986), 58.
13. Eliza R. Snow, *Woman's Exponent*, September 15, 1873, 62.
14. William A. Simmons, *Peoples of the New Testament World* (Peabody, MA: Hendrickson, 2008), 311.
15. Simmons, *Peoples*, 90–92.
16. Simmons, *Peoples*, 306–22.
17. Keith R. Bradley, *Slavery and Society at Rome* (Cambridge: Cambridge University Press, 1994), 92.
18. John K. Carmack, "Lord, Increase Our Faith," *Ensign*, March 2002, 56–57.

Instruments or Agents?
Balancing Submissiveness and Anxious Engagement in Heavenly Father's Plan

Lloyd D. Newell

When most people in the English-speaking world use the term *agency*, they might be thinking of a government institution, such as the Environmental Protection Agency, or a business, such as an advertising or insurance agency. But to Latter-day Saints, agency has another, much more spiritually significant meaning—one that seems to be almost exclusive to Mormonism and is not even found in most major dictionaries.[1]

The concept of agency as the God-given privilege to choose and act for oneself is so central to the restored gospel of Jesus Christ that President David O. McKay called it "man's greatest endowment in mortal life."[2] He further declared: "Next to the bestowal of life itself, the right to direct that life is God's greatest gift to man. . . . Freedom of choice is more to be treasured than any possession earth can give. It is inherent in the spirit of man. [It] is the impelling source of the soul's progress. It is the purpose of the Lord that man become like him. In order for man to achieve this it was necessary for the Creator first to make him free."[3]

Our knowledge of the gift and principle of agency enlarges our perspective and gladdens our hearts. As Jacob declared to the people of his day, "Cheer up your hearts, and remember that ye are free to act for yourselves—to choose the way of everlasting death or the way of eternal life" (2 Nephi 10:23).

And yet, despite its importance in the Father's plan for his children (or perhaps because of it), the truth about agency or freedom to choose is frequently misunderstood—in the world generally and even among believing Latter-day Saints. This paper explores one element of this misunderstanding: the interplay and seeming contradiction between the meekness, submissiveness, and trust required of disciples of Jesus Christ and the active, bold, assertiveness implied in the principle of agency. Could it be that God wants us to develop both?

Instruments in His Hands

The scriptures use a variety of metaphors to describe different aspects of our relationship with God. The Book of Mormon, for example, compares servants of the Lord to "instruments" in his hands. This term is applied most frequently to Alma the Younger and the sons of Mosiah, who accomplished remarkable things in the work of the Lord but were quick to downplay their own abilities and attribute all of their success to the Lord. For instance, Ammon declared: "I do not boast in my own strength, nor in my own wisdom. . . . Yea, I know that I am nothing; as to my strength I am weak; therefore I will not boast of myself, but I will boast of my God, . . . and we have been instruments in his hands of doing this great and marvelous work" (Alma 26:11–12, 15).[4]

This metaphor emphasizes man's dependence on God and compliance with his will. An instrument does not act for itself; it cannot make music or accomplish any work of its own volition. It passively and obediently carries out the will of the one controlling it. To cite Isaiah's related imagery: "Shall the axe boast itself against him that heweth therewith? or shall the saw magnify itself against him that shaketh it? as if the rod should shake itself against them that lift it up, or as if the staff should lift up itself, as if it were no wood" (Isaiah 10:15).

This concept of our relationship with God is consistent with several other scriptures:

> Cry unto God for all thy support. . . . Counsel with the Lord in all thy doings, and he will direct thee for good. (Alma 37:36–37)

> Trust in the Lord with all thine heart; and lean not unto thine own understanding. (Proverbs 3:5)

> For my thoughts are not your thoughts, neither are your ways my ways, saith the Lord.
> For as the heavens are higher than the earth, so are my ways higher than your ways, and my thoughts than your thoughts. (Isaiah 55:8–9)

> [Become] as a child, submissive, meek, humble, patient, full of love, willing to submit to all things which the Lord seeth fit to inflict upon him, even as a child doth submit to his father. (Mosiah 3:19)

In fact, the Savior himself has used similar language to describe his relationship with the Father. "I can of mine own self do nothing," he said. "I seek not mine own will, but the will of the Father which hath sent me" (John 5:30). "I do always those things that please him" (John 8:29). From a young age, and throughout his life, Christ was "about [his] Father's business" (Luke 2:49). And, most movingly, when he trembled because of pain and "would that [he] might not drink the bitter cup" (DC& 19:18), he humbly said, "Nevertheless not my will, but thine, be done" (Luke 22:42).

Agents unto Ourselves

And yet, interestingly, along with scriptures that encourage meek submission to God's will, we find passages like these:

> For behold, it is not meet that I should command in all things; for he that is compelled in all things, the same is a slothful and not a wise servant; wherefore he receiveth no reward.
> Verily I say, men should be anxiously engaged in a good cause, and do many things of their own free will, and bring to pass much righteousness;
> For the power is in them, wherein they are agents unto themselves. And inasmuch as men do good they shall in nowise lose their reward. (D&C 58:26–28)

> And the Messiah cometh in the fulness of time, that he may redeem the children of men from the fall. And because that they are redeemed

> from the fall they have become free forever, knowing good from evil;
> to act for themselves and not to be acted upon. (2 Nephi 2:26)

When the Lord refers to us as "agents" who act for ourselves and are not acted upon, he seems to be emphasizing our independence and capacity for personal growth. He seems to be encouraging boldness and assertiveness—qualities that feel quite contrary to the meek submissiveness characterized by an "instrument" that is wholly dependent upon God. An agent is one who is trusted to act and make decisions; an instrument, on the other hand, is expected to trust its master and carry out his decisions.

Apparent contradictions like this one can cause confusion in some about the true nature of agency. Some might ask, How are we to be anxiously engaged and do many things of our own free will and yet at the same time counsel with the Lord and be directed by him in everything we do? How can a person use volition and initiative and at the same time submit to and depend upon God? How is it possible to be both a submissive instrument and a proactive agent?

Paradoxes like these should not scare us because the gospel is full of them. Whenever two gospel truths seem to contradict each other, that is simply an indication that our mortal understanding is limited—which is also an indication of an opportunity for more understanding! As John W. Welch once observed, "Because we know that there must be an opposition in all things, LDS thought often harmonizes traditional paradoxes. The world has fought wars over whether we are saved by faith or by works. We peacefully say, 'Both.' People argue over whether we come to know by study or by faith. We confidently say, 'Both.'"[5] To the question of whether God wants us to humbly submit to his will or actively exercise our own will, we could also say, "Both!"

The adversary, of course, would like us to get this wrong and err on one side or the other. This is one of his more effective tactics—if he can't convince us to accept false doctrine, he might just persuade us to take a true doctrine to an extreme. The result is the same. So, for example, if we depend solely upon God to run our lives, we run the risk of decisional paralysis, apathy, or indolence. And if we rely too much on our own flesh and understanding, we run the risk of pride and self-absorption and serious errors of judgment. Both of these extremes on the agency pendulum can lead to deception, bitterness, resentment, and anger. Over the life course, ours is the responsibility to find the right balance in any given moment.

The key to solving this paradox is in overcoming two faulty human tendencies. One is the tendency to resist commandments because we feel that they limit our agency. The other is the tendency to resign too easily to what we perceive as a predetermined fate that we cannot control.

Is Obedience to Commandments a Surrender of Agency?

We live in a world where many people see commandments or rules as shackles that limit and restrict our freedom. Evidence of this attitude is ubiquitous—it's almost impossible to grow up as a practicing Latter-day Saint and not hear, at least once during the teenage years, something to the effect of, "What? Mormons can't [insert behavior that is contrary to Church standards]? Your Church gives you no freedom! I'm free to do whatever I like, but you aren't!" Perhaps it hits closest to home when we're a little older, raising teenagers of our own, and they react to family rules with an objection like, "Dad [or Mom]! You're taking away my agency!"

When Elder Dallin H. Oaks was president of BYU, he used to hear arguments from students about the honor code or dress and grooming standards. The complaints went like this: "It is wrong for BYU to take away my free agency by forcing me to keep certain rules in order to be admitted or permitted to continue as a student." "If that silly reasoning were valid," Elder Oaks said, "then the Lord, who gave us our agency, took it away when he gave the Ten Commandments. We are responsible to use our agency in a world of choices. It will not do to pretend that our agency has been taken away when we are not free to exercise it without unwelcome consequences."[6]

The fact is that no one can take away our agency. God gave it to us as part of the condition of mortality. As President Joseph Fielding Smith wrote, "This great gift of agency, that is the privilege given to man to make his own choice, has never been revoked, and it never will be. It is an eternal principle giving freedom of thought and action to every soul. . . . There could be no satisfactory existence without [it]."[7]

INSTRUMENTS OR AGENTS?

In reality, when God gives us a commandment, he is really giving us an opportunity to *exercise* our agency, by either obeying or disobeying, by either turning to or away from God. Those options are not available to us if we do not have commandments. Agency can be exercised only when alternative choices are both possible and enticing and opposition is present (see 2 Nephi 2:16; D&C 29:39).

Thankfully, we are not left to our own devices, unaided and wandering on our own. We have the Spirit to guide us, we have the scriptures and teachings of apostles and prophets, and we have examples of holy men and women who can instruct us as they exemplify righteous living. "God has sent mortal servants who can, by the Holy Ghost, help us recognize what He would have us do and what He forbids," President Henry B. Eyring taught. "God makes it attractive to choose the right by letting us feel the effects of our choices. If we choose the right, we will find happiness—in time. If we choose evil, there comes sorrow and regret—in time. Those effects are sure."[8]

Here's how Lehi explained it to his family: "If ye shall say there is no law [which is exactly what many people are saying today], ye shall also say there is no sin. [Does this sound like moral relativism?] If ye say there is no sin, ye shall also say there is no righteousness. [If *nothing* is wrong, then how can we claim credit for choosing the right? Nothing is right or wrong.] And if there be no righteousness there be no happiness. . . . [You can see how this is spinning out of control for the moral relativists.] And if these things are not, there is no God" (2 Nephi 2:13).

How so? Because all power operates by law. Elder D. Todd Christofferson explained it this way: "It is by the operation of laws that things happen. By using or obeying a law, one can bring about a particular result—and by disobedience, the opposite result. Without law there could be no God, for He would be powerless to cause anything to happen."[9]

Indeed, choice as well as opposition are necessary for us to grow and progress. We cannot be faithful and true unless we have been confronted with the opportunity to be faithful and true. Similarly, we cannot be moral, merciful, kindhearted, or forgiving without having conquered circumstances which could have produced an opposite reaction. There can be no righteousness unless there is wickedness; thus all attributes of godliness have their opposite. We develop the attributes of godliness as we freely choose righteousness.

This is where commandments come in. Far from limiting our choices, commandments make it clear what our choices are. As the Lord told the early Saints: "I give unto you a . . . commandment, that you may understand my will concerning you; or, in other words, I give unto you directions how you may act before me, that it may turn to you for your salvation" (D&C 82:8–9). This is how God views his commandments: as a revelation to us concerning his will. Without commandments, we are in the captivity of ignorance about God's will. This is what the commandments save us from.

And this is what gave Jesus Christ his power—the fact that he obeyed God's laws, perfectly, always. A doctor who understands and follows the laws of human biology has the power to heal a person from physical illness. An organist who understands the laws that govern how to manipulate the sounds that come out of the Salt Lake Tabernacle organ has the power to make beautiful music with that instrument. Someone like me who does not understand those laws has limited freedom to make anything other than irritating sounds with that organ. But I could learn those laws, and if I did, my freedom in that regard would be enhanced.

Similarly, a follower of Christ who understands the laws of God has the power to become like God. "That which is of God is light; and he that receiveth light, and continueth in God, receiveth more light; and that light groweth brighter and brighter until the perfect day" (D&C 50:24). That is ultimate freedom, and it is the essence of the Father's plan for our eternal growth and happiness.

Satan has the opposite goal. He wants us to receive less and less light and truth, keeping us in ignorance of God's laws, which will make our range of choices narrower and narrower until we are completely in his power—in darkness. As Alma explained, "They that will harden their hearts, to them is given the lesser portion of the word until they know nothing concerning his mysteries; and then they are taken captive by the devil, and led by his will down to destruction. Now this is what is meant by the chains of hell" (Alma 12:11). That is ultimate captivity. This is why the Savior said, "If ye continue in my word, then are ye my disciples indeed; and ye shall know the truth, and the truth shall make you free" (John 8:31–32). Again quoting Elder Christofferson:

INSTRUMENTS OR AGENTS?

> The beauty of the gospel of Jesus Christ is that it pours knowledge into our souls and shows things in their true light. With that enhanced perspective, we can discern more clearly the choices before us and their consequences. We can, therefore, make more intelligent use of our agency. . . . As our understanding of gospel doctrine and principles grows, our agency expands. First, we have more choices and can achieve more and receive greater blessings because we have more laws that we can obey. . . . Second, with added understanding we can make more intelligent choices because we see more clearly not only the alternatives but their potential outcomes.[10]

Similarly, when we choose to submit our will to the Father's by obeying his commandments and directions, we are not *surrendering* our agency but *expressing* it—in the highest, noblest way possible. As Elder Neal A. Maxwell taught, this kind of submission "is not resignation or a mindless caving in. Rather, it is a deliberate expanding outward. . . . [It] is not shoulder-shrugging acceptance, but, instead, shoulder-squaring to better bear the yoke."[11]

So when the Savior said, "Not my will, but thine, be done," he was not giving up, he was rising up! He was not abandoning his own will but aligning it—as he had done since premortality and throughout his life—to the will of his Father. This is what God wants from us as well: not to throw our own will away and passively accept his but to change our will until we actively, passionately, eagerly desire what he desires. It is appropriately described in the scriptures as a "wrestle"—not with God but with ourselves, to bring our will in line with his (see Enos 1:2; Alma 8:10; Genesis 32:24). We need the strength and power that comes from this wrestle. It is the only way we will be strong enough to cling to and defend his will in the face of intense opposition—it must become our will too.

It was this eternal truth that inspired C. S. Lewis to write these words: "A world of automata—of creatures that worked like machines—would hardly be worth creating. The happiness which God designs for his higher creatures is the happiness of being freely, voluntarily united to Him and to each other in an ecstasy of love and delight compared with which the most rapturous love between a man and a woman on this earth is mere milk and water. And for that they must be free."[12]

How Much Does God Micromanage Our Lives?

While sometimes we resist commandments because we mistakenly think our agency is being limited, at other times we seem to have the opposite problem—we too readily resign our agency because we mistakenly overestimate what is out of our control. This attitude manifests itself, for example, in a self-defeating attitude in which we seek to blame our circumstances or our genes or other people for our choices.

Often our favorite target for this blame is the adversary himself. And ironically, he probably gladly accepts that blame, because if we believe that the devil can cause us to sin, then it is an easy task to convince us that we are powerless to improve ourselves. This direct contradiction to God's declaration, "The power is in them" (D&C 58:28), is one way Satan attempts to "destroy the agency of man" (Moses 4:3).

We are here in mortality to volitionally choose righteousness, without coercion or force. The truth is that the devil cannot compel us to choose evil, just as God will force no one to heaven. The Prophet Joseph Smith observed: "Satan was generally blamed for the evils which we did, but if he was the cause of all our wickedness, men could not be condemned. The devil cannot compel mankind to do evil, all was voluntary. Those who resist the Spirit of God, are liable to be led into temptation, and then the association of heaven is withdrawn from those who refuse to be made partakers of such great glory—God would not exert any compulsory means, and the Devil could not; and such ideas as were entertained [on these subjects] by many, were absurd."[13] In all the commands and expectations of God, as well as in the enticements of the adversary, we are free to act for ourselves and freely choose.

Interestingly, however, just as we may give the devil too much blame for our sins, we may also place upon God too much of the responsibility for our salvation.[14] As such, Latter-day Saints do not believe in fate or in predestination. We are not locked in to a pre-programmed response or destiny. We make choices all along the way that can forever alter our course. The *Encyclopedia of Mormonism* explains the Latter-day Saint perspective:

> Fate, as usually interpreted, is the antithesis of self-determination and responsibility. Latter-day Saints reject on scriptural grounds all appeals to precausation whether as "fate," "the stars," "blind chance," or even the

predestination of man by God. Fate in these forms implies a precaused outcome of one's life. Instead, man is seen as having innate autonomies and capacities—the gift of agency—that the divine will guarantees all men: "I the Lord God make you free, therefore ye are free indeed: and the law also maketh you free" (D&C 98:8; cf. 2 Ne. 2:25–27; Alma 12:31; Moses 4:3). People are free to choose obedience or disobedience, good or evil, and most other aspects of their lives, and they are accountable for their choices. The belief that all is fated, stifles, discourages, and hinders the progress and growth possible for the children of God. . . . The gospel of Jesus Christ opens to all mankind the opportunity to rise above chance fate in this life and choose eternal life with God.[15]

The Apostle Paul taught that God "will render to every man according to his deeds" and that "there is no respect of persons with God" (Romans 2:6, 11). Likewise, we are to "look unto [God] in every thought" (D&C 6:36), because we cannot save ourselves or earn our salvation. But neither can God redeem anyone without that person's effort and collaboration. All are free to accept or reject God's help and powers of redemption.[16] For this reason, there is danger in saying "everything happens for a reason" or "it was all part of the plan" because that could imply that everything that happens is according to God's will. But that is not consistent with scripture, doctrine, or personal experience. All is not decided for us.

Our Father is a God of order. He created systems and structures and principles that govern the laws of nature. He does not have to command the sun to rise each morning or decide where and when it will rain every moment of each day. Certainly God can and often does intervene in world and personal events.[17] But often he chooses not to, leaving us to make choices and deal with the natural consequences of our actions, both good and bad. If he were to manipulate every detail of our lives, he would interfere with our moral agency and our eternal growth.

This does not mean, however, that God is distant or distracted or uncaring. In fact, it is truly amazing how much our Father interests himself in the small and simple moments of the lives of his children. "God's personal shaping influence is felt in the details of our lives—not only in the details of the galaxies and molecules but, much more importantly, in the details of our own lives," Elder Neal A. Maxwell testified. "Somehow God is providing these individual tutorials for us while at the same time he is overseeing cosmic funerals and births, for as one earth passes away so another is born (see Moses 1:38). It is marvelous that He would attend to us so personally in the midst of those cosmic duties. . . . Be assured that God is in the details and in the subtleties of the defining and preparatory moments of discipleship."[18]

Yes, those who are observant can see God's hand in our lives in very personal, customized ways. But he doesn't wave a giant magic wand or utter some magical word to accomplish his purposes. Rather, when he does intervene, he does so within the framework of our agency, and his purpose in doing so is to give us enhanced opportunities to exercise our agency. He intercedes to teach, reprove, inspire, warn, comfort, and encourage us—not to control us. He is not the Great Micromanager, controlling and determining each moment and every event of our lives. He is so dedicated to our personal growth and happiness that he leaves much of the decisions and work up to us. Righteousness must be freely chosen.[19] C. S. Lewis wrote:

> God created things which had free will. That means creatures which can go either wrong or right. Some people think they can imagine a creature which was free but had no possibility of going wrong; I cannot. If a thing is free to be good it is also free to be bad. And free will is what has made evil possible. Why, then, did God give them free will? Because free will, though it makes evil possible, is also the only thing that makes possible any love or goodness or joy worth having. . . . If God thinks this state of war in the universe a price worth paying for free will—that is, for making a live world in which creatures can do real good or harm and something of real importance can happen, instead of a toy world which only moves when He pulls the strings—then we may take it it is worth paying.[20]

This truth has important implications when we are faced with difficult decisions. Consider this true story of a couple who had been trying for years to decide whether or not to move from their current home. Every time they had made a decision, in a few weeks or months they began to have doubts and decide to do nothing. They had come close a few times but could never quite make a final decision to move. One time they had purchased a residential lot, hired an architect to draw up house plans, and

INSTRUMENTS OR AGENTS?

made plans to build. But again, in a few weeks and months they pulled back and decided to wait and think about it some more. They sincerely prayed and sought the Lord's counsel; they fasted and went to the temple regularly to seek guidance; they just couldn't seem to make a final decision and go forward. Why did it seem the Lord was not responding? If we are to counsel with God in everything, they thought, why couldn't they get a confirming witness of what they should do and then make a final decision? Were they not living righteously enough to be granted heavenly guidance? Or, could it be that God didn't really care whether or not they moved or built a new home?

Often, in a surge of obedience, we wish Heavenly Father would simply tell us what to do and we would gladly do it. But perhaps this desire is inspired not only by a willingness to obey but also by an unwillingness to choose for ourselves and accept responsibility for our choices. God, we discover, wants proactive, initiative-taking agents as much as he wants submissive, obedient instruments.

When it comes to missions, marriage, parenting, career choices, or a host of other decisions large and small all along life's pathway, we are to study it out and do our research, ponder and pray and seek the guidance and peace of the Lord, and go forward. Some choices are made quickly and easily, while others take much time and serious deliberation. Some good choices need to be made and remade many times during a lifetime. Sometimes we seem to get an answer that is clear and immediate, and other times no answer seems to come at all. It could be that no answer is *the* answer—perhaps he either lets us figure it out, or it doesn't matter all that much, or it's simply up to us.

President Ezra Taft Benson said:

> Usually the Lord gives us the overall objectives to be accomplished and some guidelines to follow, but he expects us to work out most of the details and methods. The methods and procedures are usually developed through study and prayer and by living so that we can obtain and follow the promptings of the Spirit. Less spiritually advanced people, such as those in the days of Moses, had to be commanded in many things. Today those spiritually alert look at the objectives, check the guidelines laid down by the Lord and his prophets, and

then prayerfully act—without having to be commanded "in all things." This attitude prepares [us] for godhood.[21]

And therein lies the answer to the paradox, "Does God want his children to be submissive instruments or proactive agents?" It should not surprise us that the answer is "both." He wants his children to become as he is, and that requires that we acquire the attributes of both a trusting instrument and a trusted agent. In other words, he wants us to eagerly and anxiously exercise our agency, of our own free will, to choose to meekly submit to and adapt to his will. He wants us to humbly and willingly learn from our experiences in the hands of the Master so that we may one day be masters ourselves.

Notes

1. Multiple definitions of *agency* are given in *Merriam-Webster's Collegiate Dictionary*, 11th ed. (2003); the *Oxford English Dictionary* (1971); and the *American Heritage Dictionary*, 4th ed. (2000), but none of them fully captures the idea of the right or privilege to make one's own choices or act for oneself. Interestingly, when the word *agency* is used in Latter-day Saint scriptures (primarily the Doctrine and Covenants and Pearl of Great Price), it is often translated into non-English languages as a word that means something closer to "free will" or "independence" than to the common English word *agency* (Spanish: *albedrío*, not *agencia*; German: *Selbständigkeit* or *Entscheidungsfreiheit*, not *Agentur*; French: *libre arbitre*, not *agence*).
2. David O. McKay, *Gospel Ideals* (Salt Lake City: Deseret News, 1953), 299.
3. McKay, *Gospel Ideals*, 299, 301.
4. See also Mosiah 27:36; Alma 2:30; 17:9, 11; 26:3; 35:14. Alma's father, Alma the Elder, also refers to himself as an instrument in God's hands in Mosiah 23:10.
5. John W. Welch, "Thy Mind, O Man, Must Stretch," Brigham Young University forum, May 17, 2011, 7, speeches.byu.edu.
6. Dallin H. Oaks, "Weightier Matters," Brigham Young University devotional, February 9, 1999, 2, speeches.byu.edu.
7. Joseph Fielding Smith, *Answers to Gospel Questions* (Salt Lake City: Deseret Book, 1958), 2:20.
8. Henry B. Eyring, "A Priceless Heritage of Hope," *Ensign*, May 2014, 24–25.

9. D. Todd Christofferson, "Moral Agency," Brigham Young University devotional, January 31, 2006, 2, speeches.byu.edu.
10. Christofferson, "Moral Agency," 2.
11. Neal A. Maxwell, "Swallowed Up in the Will of the Father," *Ensign*, November 1995, 23–24.
12. C. S. Lewis, *Mere Christianity* (New York: Simon & Schuster, 1996), 52.
13. Entry for Sunday, May 16, 1841, in "History, 1838–1856, volume C-1 [2 November 1838–31 July 1842]" (bracketed explanation added), third volume of "Manuscript History of the Church," Church History Library, josephsmithpapers.org/paperSummary/history-1838-1856-volume-c-1-2-november-1838-31-july-1842.
14. We need to be clear here: we are saved through the grace of Jesus Christ. The Book of Mormon teaches: "For we labor diligently to write, to persuade our children, and also our brethren, to believe in Christ, and to be reconciled to God; for we know that it is by grace we are saved after all we can do" (2 Nephi 25:23). The Book of Mormon adds "all that we could do [was to] repent of all our sins" (Alma 24:11). Lehi also taught, "There is no flesh that can dwell in the presence of God, save it be through the merits, and mercy, and grace of the Holy Messiah" (2 Nephi 2:8).
15. Gerald E. Jones, "Fate," in *Encyclopedia of Mormonism*, ed. Daniel H. Ludlow (New York: Macmillan, 1992), 2:502–3. See also *Gospel Principles* (Salt Lake City: The Church of Jesus Christ of Latter-day Saints, 1978), 18–21.
16. For an insightful explanation of how God and humanity are working together for the salvation of souls, see Robert L. Millet, "The Perils of Grace," *BYU Studies* 53, no. 2 (2014): 7–19.
17. A full and thorough discussion about the degree to which God actively intervenes in day-to-day events is beyond the scope of this paper. Suffice it to say here that much of the time he forbears out of respect for our agency.
18. Neal A. Maxwell, "Becoming a Disciple," *Ensign*, June 1996, 17, 19.
19. See Richard W. Cracroft, "We'll Sing and We'll Shout: A Mantic Celebration of the Holy Spirit," Brigham Young University devotional, June 29, 1993, speeches.byu.edu.
20. Lewis, *Mere Christianity*, 52–53.
21. Ezra Taft Benson, in Conference Report, April 1965, 121–25.

Filling the Immensity of Space
The Titles and Functions of God's Revelatory Power

Larry E. Dahl

Doctrine and Covenants 88:5–13 speaks of "the power of God," identified as the "light of truth," or "the light of Christ," which light "proceedeth forth from the presence of God to fill the immensity of space." There are five functions of this power included in these nine verses: (1) creation (verses 7–10), (2) the source of light (verse 11), (3) the source of life (verse 13), (4) the "law by which all things are governed" (verse 13), and (5) the power that "enlighteneth your eyes" and "quickeneth your understandings" (verse 11). The fifth function listed here, the revelatory role of the power of God, is the focus of this article.

There are many terms used in the scriptures, in Church literature, in prayers, in teaching, and in common communication to refer to this revelatory power and its numerous dimensions and levels of application. Some of these include the Spirit of God, the Spirit of the Lord, the Spirit of Christ, the Spirit of Truth, the Light of Christ, the gifts of the Spirit, the Holy Ghost, the Holy Spirit, the Comforter, the Holy Spirit of Promise, thy Spirit, his Spirit, the Spirit, the Spirit of the Living God, the more sure word of prophecy, and more.

Because these terms are often used indiscriminately and even interchangeably, it can lead to the confusion President Joseph Fielding Smith acknowledged:

> These terms are used synonymously: Spirit of God, Spirit of the Lord, Spirit of Truth, Holy Spirit, Comforter; all having reference to the Holy Ghost. The same terms largely are used in relation to the Spirit of Jesus Christ, also called the Light of Truth, Light of Christ, Spirit of God, and Spirit of the Lord, and yet they are separate and distinct things. We have a great deal of confusion because we have not kept that clearly in our minds.[1]

Perhaps, then, more important than trying to determine consistent, precise, and unique terms for the various functions of the revelatory power that comes from God, would be to have an understanding of the levels of that power available to mankind and to recognize that all spiritual gifts, of whatever level, are manifestations of the same power.

A framework for such an understanding was given by President Marion G. Romney, while serving as Second Counselor in the First Presidency. When he spoke in the priesthood session of the general conference of the Church in April 1977, he taught, "There are three phases of the light of Christ that I want to mention. The first one is the light which enlighteneth every man that cometh into the world; the second phase is the gift of the Holy Ghost; and the third is the more sure word of prophecy."[2]

The First Phase of the Light of Christ—Light to All

As noted, the first phase, variously termed "the Spirit of Christ" (Moroni 7:16), "the Spirit of Jesus Christ" (D&C 84:46), "the light of Christ" (Moroni 7:19; Alma 28:14; D&C 88:7), "the Spirit of truth" (D&C 93:26; John 1:9), or "true light" (D&C 93:2; John 1:9) inherent in the Savior's presence, is given to "every man that cometh into the world" (John 1:9; D&C 84:46; Moroni 7:16). Anyone who hearkens to that light will be enlightened "that he may know good from evil," persuaded "to believe in Christ," and invited "to do good" (Moroni 7:16).

Down through the ages, all those who have sought to do good have been recipients of this revelatory power of the Light of Christ, bringing progress to the world in every field of endeavor—philosophy, religion, music, art, poetry, science, education, government. For example, the Book of Mormon pays tribute to Columbus, not by name, but by mission. Led by the Spirit of God, he discovered America. In so doing, he paved the way for the establishment of a great Gentile nation on this land, a choice land that has a critical role in the work of God in the last days. That critical role includes the Restoration of the gospel, the establishment of Zion, and taking the gospel to the whole world in preparation for the Second Coming of the Lord.[3] In the Doctrine and Covenants, the Lord affirms that he "established the Constitution of this land [America], by the hands of wise men whom I have raised up unto this very purpose [that men might be free from bondage]" (D&C 101:80). President Joseph F. Smith adds to the list of those who were inspired to make significant contributions for "the advancement of the human race": Washington, Lincoln, Bacon, Franklin, Stephenson, Watts, Edison, Calvin, Luther, Melanchthon, "all the reformers," and the Revolutionary Fathers.[4] Truly, anyone who has contributed to the advancement of the human race has done so with the aid of the Light of Christ.

The Light of Christ not only helps people bless the world but also blesses individuals personally. The Lord has promised that anyone who hearkens consistently to the light and "continueth in God" (D&C 50:24) will personally be brought to the fulness of the gospel of Jesus Christ, the "everlasting covenant" (D&C 66:2), which was restored to the earth through the Prophet Joseph Smith: "Every one that hearkeneth to the voice of the Spirit cometh unto God, even the Father. And the Father teacheth him of the covenant which he has renewed and confirmed upon you" (D&C 84:47–48). That covenant, or fulness of the gospel, includes having a testimony of Jesus, having faith in him, repenting, being baptized, receiving the gift of the Holy Ghost, and enduring in righteousness.[5] But men are endowed with moral agency and are free to hearken to the light and be led to more and more light and truth, or to ignore or reject the light and be left in spiritual darkness to their own condemnation: "Behold, here is the agency of man, and here is the condemnation of man; because that which was from the beginning is plainly manifest unto them, and they receive not the light. And every man whose spirit receiveth not the light is under condemnation" (D&C 93:31–32; see also John 3:16–21).

The Book of Mormon prophet Alma described this increase or decrease in spiritual understanding, which depends on how people respond to the light given them:

> And therefore, he that will harden his heart, the same receiveth the lesser portion of the word; and he that will not harden his heart, to him is given the greater portion of the word, until it is given unto him to know the mysteries of God until he know them in full.
>
> And they that will harden their hearts, to them is given the lesser portion of the word until they know nothing concerning his mysteries; and then they are taken captive by the devil, and led by his will down to destruction. Now this is what is meant by the chains of hell. (Alma 12:10–11)

The Light of Christ is generously provided to all mankind, but there are some limits to its availability. The Lord has said, "For I the Lord cannot look upon sin with the least degree of allowance; nevertheless, he that repents and does the commandments of the Lord shall be forgiven; and he that repents not, from him shall be taken even the light which he has received; for my Spirit shall not always strive with man" (D&C 1:31–33). When men defiantly reject the light given them and rebel against the commandments of God, becoming degenerate and depraved and ripe in iniquity, even the Light of Christ will cease to strive with them. They are then left to their own destruction, whether by the wrath of God or by their own swords. Such was the case with the ancient Jaredites, Nephites, Lamanites, and the inhabitants of the land of Canaan whom the Israelites were commanded to destroy. And such will be the case for any individuals or nations who reject the light of heaven and become ripe in iniquity.[6]

Truly, with the Light of Christ given to all people who come into the world and with their God-given agency, "they are their own judges, whether to do good or do evil. Now, the decrees of God are unalterable; therefore, the way is prepared that whosoever will may walk therein and be saved" (Alma 41:7–8). Thus, hearkening to the universally available initial phase of the Light of Christ will lead men and women to greater revelatory power, even to the power and gifts of the Holy Ghost, President Romney's "second phase" of the Light of Christ.

The Second Phase of the Light of Christ—The Holy Ghost

It is important to understand what has been revealed concerning the personage, power, and gift of the Holy Ghost. "Much of the confusion existing in human conceptions concerning the nature of the Holy Ghost arises from the common failure to segregate His person and powers."[7] The Holy Ghost is the third member of the Godhead and is in perfect union with the Father and the Son in presiding over all the works of God in this world.[8] He is included with the Father and the Son, in whose names saving ordinances are performed, and will be with the Father and the Son at the final judgment bar, before which all mankind will be arraigned.[9] Unlike the Father and the Son, who are resurrected, glorified beings with bodies of flesh and bones, "the Holy Ghost has not a body of flesh and bones, but is a personage of Spirit" (D&C 130:22). His spirit body is in the form of a man, just as the Savior's spirit body was before his birth into this world.[10] As to the Holy Ghost's omnipresence, President Joseph F. Smith explained, "The Holy Ghost as a personage of Spirit can no more be omnipresent in person than can the Father and the Son, but by his intelligence, his knowledge, his power and influence, over and through the laws of nature, he is and can be omnipresent throughout all the works of God."[11] President Joseph Fielding Smith further commented on his father's teaching: "Thus when it becomes necessary to speak to us, he [the Holy Ghost] is able to do so by acting through the other Spirit, that is, through the Light of Christ [the power of God that fills the immensity of space]."[12]

Even though for the most part the Holy Ghost does his work through the Light of Christ, there may be special occasions when he personally attends, such as when Jesus was baptized (see Matthew 3:13–17);[13] when Abraham and later Moses were able to see God and speak with him face to face (see Abraham 2:12; 3:11; and Moses 1:1–2, 11, respectively); when the Holy Ghost appeared to Nephi (see 1 Nephi 11:11–12); when Isaiah, Nephi, and

Jacob were able to see the Lord (see 2 Nephi 11:2–3); when the brother of Jared saw and spoke with the Lord (see Ether 3:6–20); when Joseph Smith saw the Father and the Son during the First Vision (see Joseph Smith—History 1:17–19); or any number of like occasions that require mortal beings to be transfigured or "quickened by the Spirit of God" in order to see God (see D&C 67:11; 130:22).

The central mission of the Holy Ghost is to bear witness of the Father and the Son[14] and to administer the gifts of the Spirit to those who have received the gift of the Holy Ghost and who live worthy of the blessings promised. Listings of many of the gifts of the Spirit are found in the New Testament, the Book of Mormon, and the Doctrine and Covenants.[15] Not everyone has all the gifts, but "to every man is given a gift by the Spirit of God," and all are encouraged to "seek ye earnestly the best gifts" (D&C 46:11, 8). The Prophet Joseph Smith taught, "The greatest, the best, and the most useful gifts would be known nothing about by an observer."[16] Such gifts might include testimony and the quiet whisperings of guidance, assurance, peace, and happiness that come with the companionship of the Holy Ghost.

There is an important difference between receiving a *testimony* from the Holy Ghost and having the *gift of the Holy Ghost.* The Prophet Joseph Smith explained:

> There is a difference between the Holy Ghost, and the gift of the Holy Ghost. Cornelius received the Holy Ghost before he was baptized, which was the convincing power of God unto him of the truth of the Gospel; but he could not receive the gift of the Holy Ghost until after he was baptized. Had he not taken this sign or ordinance upon him, the Holy Ghost which convinced him of the truth of God, would have left him.[17]

Any honest seeker after truth who will "ask God, the Eternal Father, in the name of Christ, if these things [in this case the Book of Mormon] are not true; and if ye shall ask with a sincere heart, with real intent, having faith in Christ, he will manifest the truth of it unto you, by the power of the Holy Ghost. And by the power of the Holy Ghost ye may know the truth of all things" (Moroni 10:4–5). Having the *gift of the Holy Ghost,* however, requires faith, repentance, baptism, and receiving the gift through the laying on of hands by an authorized servant of the Lord.[18]

If everyone has the revelatory power of the Light of Christ, what advantage comes with having the gift of the Holy Ghost? First and foremost, only with the gift of the Holy Ghost, through the ordinances of the gospel, can one be sanctified and thus attain salvation in the celestial kingdom of God. Even those who are the honorable men of the earth and who have a testimony of Jesus but who are not valiant in that testimony sufficient to receive the ordinances of salvation, are limited to a terrestrial glory in the hereafter.[19] In addition, receiving the gift of the Holy Ghost maintains and enhances the testimony of the truth originally given by the Holy Ghost. Further, the gift of the Holy Ghost magnifies a person's understanding of the scriptures and truths of the gospel.[20] Still further, the gift of the Holy Ghost may also strengthen and amplify whatever spiritual gift one is given. One of the gifts of the Spirit is the gift of teaching (see Moroni 10:9–10). Cannot a person be an effective, even powerful teacher without having the gift of the Holy Ghost? Certainly, but it is highly probable that that person would be even a better teacher if he enjoyed the gift of the Holy Ghost. The same principle may hold true with other gifts of the Spirit—language, wisdom, differences of administration, perhaps even faith in Jesus Christ to be healed, and so forth. Honest, honorable people can develop many good attributes with the help of the Light of Christ but not to the extent that those same attributes can be enjoyed if one has the gift of the Holy Ghost. Still another significant advantage of having the gift of the Holy Ghost is the promise that "the Holy Ghost shall be thy constant companion" (D&C 121:46) rather than the possibility of somewhat intermittent episodes of testimony or inspiration. That promise does not mean that the Holy Ghost, in person, will be constantly present. It does mean, however, that the *power* of the Holy Ghost is always near and available, comforting, teaching, urging one to an ever-growing commitment and obedience. President Joseph F. Smith taught, "Therefore, the presentation or 'gift' of the Holy Ghost simply confers upon man the right to receive at any time, when he is worthy of it and desires it, the power and light of truth of the Holy Ghost, although he may often be left to his own spirit and judgment."[21] This constantly available power of the Holy Ghost to those who have received the gift of the Holy Ghost, and who keep their gospel covenants, will in fact "show unto you all things what ye should do" (2 Nephi 32:5). That includes, eventually, putting off the "natural man" and becoming a true Saint "through the atonement of Christ the Lord," by yielding to the enticings of the Holy Spirit, becoming "as a child, submissive, meek, humble, patient, full of love, willing to submit to all things which the Lord seeth fit to inflict upon him, even as a child doth submit to his father" (Mosiah 3:19). During the process of becoming sanctified and putting off the natural man, the Holy Ghost is very much involved in his role as the Holy Spirit of Promise. "All covenants, contracts, bonds, obligations, oaths, vows, performances, connections, associations, or expectations, that are not made and entered into and sealed by the Holy Spirit of Promise . . . are of no efficacy, virtue, or force in and after the resurrection from the dead; for all contracts that are not made unto this end have an end when men are dead" (D&C 132:7; see also D&C 76:50–54). Latter-day prophets and apostles have taught that when covenants are made and ordinances performed in worthiness, the Holy Ghost will seal or approve the action and the promised blessings. However, if there is subsequent disobedience, the Holy Ghost will withdraw his seal of approval, and the promised blessings will be withheld. To then have the seal and promised blessings restored requires genuine repentance and obedience.[22]

Once a person passes through "the gate" of repentance, baptism, and receipt of the Holy Ghost, Nephi testifies that all is not yet done. "Wherefore, ye must press forward with a steadfastness in Christ, having a perfect brightness of hope, and a love of God and of all men. Wherefore, if ye shall press forward, feasting upon the word of Christ, and endure to the end, behold, thus saith the Father: Ye shall have eternal life" (2 Nephi 31:20). The promise of eternal life leads to a discussion of President Romney's third phase of the Light of Christ, "the more sure word of prophecy."

The More Sure Word of Prophecy

"The more sure word of prophecy means a man's knowing that he is sealed up unto eternal life, by revelation and the spirit of prophecy, through the power of the Holy Priesthood" (D&C 131:5). It means one's calling and election has been made sure, and his exaltation is assured unless he becomes a son of perdition. President Joseph Fielding Smith taught:

> Those who press forward in righteousness, living by every word of revealed truth, have power to make their calling and election sure. They receive the more sure word of prophecy and know by revelation and the authority of the priesthood that they are sealed up unto eternal life. They are sealed up against all manner of sin and blasphemy except the blasphemy against the Holy Ghost and the shedding of innocent blood.[23]

Concerning blasphemy against the Holy Ghost, the Prophet Joseph Smith explained:

> If men have received the good word of God, and tasted of the powers of the world to come, if they should fall away, it is impossible to renew them again, seeing they have crucified Son of God afresh, and put Him to an open shame, . . . and the power of Elijah cannot seal against this sin, for this is a reserve made in the seals and power of the Priesthood.[24]

Additional information is given in the Doctrine and Covenants concerning what is required for a person to blaspheme against the Holy Ghost, thus becoming a son of perdition: "Thus saith the Lord concerning all those who know my power, and have been made partakers thereof, and suffered themselves through the power of the devil to be overcome, and to deny the truth and defy my power—they are they who are sons of perdition . . . concerning whom I have said there is no forgiveness in this world nor in the world to come—having denied the Holy Spirit after having received it, and having denied the Only Begotten Son of the Father, having crucified him unto themselves and put him to an open shame" (D&C 76:31–35), doing so "after the Father has revealed him" (D&C 76:43). Thankfully, as President Spencer W. Kimball taught, "The sin against the Holy Ghost requires such knowledge that it is manifestly impossible for the rank and file to commit such a sin."[25]

But what of those who have been sealed up to eternal life and then commit sins that do not constitute denying the Holy Ghost but which are sins nonetheless? The Lord has made it clear that he "cannot look upon sin with the least degree of allowance" (D&C 1:31). That is true—even, and perhaps, especially—for those who have achieved high levels of spiritual knowledge and experience. Certainly deep repentance will be required. Beyond that, there may be suffering, even the buffetings of Satan, until justice is served and mercy redeems them and they are ultimately granted the promised eternal life (see D&C 132:26). Hence the Lord's warning voice: "But there is a possibility that man may fall from grace and depart from the living God; therefore let the church take heed and pray always, lest they fall into temptation; yea, and even let those who are sanctified take heed also" (D&C 20:32–34).

How might a person come to know that he or she is sealed up unto eternal life and understand what must be done to merit such a blessing? One way of knowing is to have the Lord personally deliver the message. President Romney cites several scriptural examples of the Lord letting his servants know that they have received this blessing, including Enos, the Nephite disciples, Moroni, Paul, and Joseph Smith.[26] He also cites the experience of Heber C. Kimball, who was told, "Thy name is written in heaven, no more to be blotted out for ever."[27] The Prophet Joseph Smith added, "Isaiah, Ezekiel, John on the Isle of Patmos, . . . and all the Saints who held communion with the general assembly and Church of the Firstborn."[28] Undoubtedly, many of the ancient patriarchs and prophets such as Moses, Alma, Enoch, the whole city of Zion, and hosts of others were so blessed (see Alma 45:18–19; Moses 7:18–21).

Another way of knowing is "by revelation and the spirit of prophecy, through the power of the Holy Priesthood" (D&C 131:5). Using the priesthood in this way requires the keys of the sealing power, restored to the earth by Elijah on April 3, 1836, in the Kirtland Temple to Joseph Smith and Oliver Cowdery (see D&C 110:13–16; 2:1–3). The priesthood keys restored by Elijah seal husbands, wives, and children through generations and dispensations, as families, for time and all eternity. In addition, the Prophet Joseph Smith taught that "the power of Elijah is sufficient to make our calling and election sure."[29] All priesthood keys restored to the earth in this last dispensation, including the sealing power brought by Elijah, have been passed down from the Prophet Joseph Smith to every succeeding President of The Church of Jesus Christ of Latter-day Saints. Those keys and the exclusive right to exercise them are held only by the current President of the Church. He may delegate to others certain priesthood functions, including any that have to do with the more sure word of prophecy, but all that is done must be done by virtue of the sacred priesthood keys he holds, and under his direction. Thus, when the Lord revealed that Hyrum Smith was "to hold the sealing blessings of my church, even the Holy Spirit of promise, whereby ye are sealed up unto the day of redemption" (D&C 124:124), it follows that Hyrum would function under the direction of Joseph Smith, who was "to be a presiding elder over all my church, to be a translator, a revelator, a seer, and prophet" (D&C 124:125) and the only one holding all the keys of the priesthood, including the sealing power.[30] Whether the more sure word of prophecy comes from the Lord himself or through the "power of the Holy Priesthood" by those authorized to exercise that function of the sealing power, it comes as an invitation and not by application.

Although it is not appropriate to campaign to receive the more sure word of prophecy according to one's own timetable, the Prophet Joseph Smith said, "I would exhort you to go on and continue to call upon God until you make your calling and election sure for yourselves, by obtaining this more sure word of prophecy, and wait patiently for the promise until you obtain it."[31] While pressing forward and waiting patiently, where should one's focus be? It is interesting to note that not one of those who are named in the scriptures as receiving the more sure word of prophecy was seeking such a blessing at the time it was given. All of them were totally involved in the Lord's service and seeking to know how to serve better. Consider, for example, the experience of Alma, recorded in Mosiah 26 and that of Nephi, son of Helaman, recorded in Helaman 10. Perhaps serving the Lord and waiting patiently as these brethren did is the best way for anyone to prepare to receive the more sure word of prophecy. Those who immerse themselves in the service of the Lord with "all [their] heart, might, mind, and strength"(D&C 4:2) are in the process of making their calling and election sure, even though they may not receive the more sure word of prophecy during their mortal lives. They can in the meantime enjoy the quiet whisperings of the Spirit that their lives are in harmony with the will of heaven and have the utmost confidence that the Lord's promise of eternal life is sure.

Conclusion

God the Father, the Savior Jesus Christ, and the Holy Ghost have provided a revelatory power that proceeds forth from their presence to fill the immensity of space to bless all mankind. Although this power is referred to by different names and operates at varying levels, it is all the same "power of God" (see D&C 88:5–13). Thus what is usually referred to as the Light of Christ is a certain measure of this power given to every person born into the world, to enlighten them in all righteous endeavors, teach them right from wrong, and encourage them to believe in Christ. This Light of Christ will not cease to strive with humankind until they willfully reject the light and become degenerate and ripe in iniquity. Those who faithfully follow the Light of Christ will be led to the fulness of the gospel of Jesus Christ, which provides them with a higher manifestation of the revelatory power, even the power and gifts of the Holy Ghost, who uses the Light of Christ to perform his labors. And those who live in harmony with the guidance of the Holy Ghost in their strivings for salvation may receive the more sure word of prophecy, which means they will *know,* "by revelation and the spirit of prophecy, through the power of the Holy Priesthood" that they are sealed up unto eternal life (D&C 131:5). Those who are not so informed can make their calling and election sure by steadfast righteousness.

Even beyond the more sure word of prophecy, the Prophet Joseph Smith taught of the possibility of receiving not only the first Comforter, who is the Holy Ghost, but the second Comforter, who is the Lord Jesus Christ himself:

> There are two Comforters spoken of. One is, the Holy Ghost. . . . The other Comforter spoken of is a subject of great interest, and perhaps understood by few of this generation. After a person has faith in Christ, repents of his sins, and is baptized for the remission of his sins and receives the Holy Ghost, (by the laying on of hands), which is the first Comforter, then let him continue to humble himself before God, hungering and thirsting after righteousness, and living by every word of God, and the Lord will soon say unto him, Son, thou shalt be exalted &c. When the Lord has thoroughly proved him, and finds that the man is determined to serve Him at all hazards, then the man will

find his calling and election made sure, then it will be his privilege to receive the other Comforter. . . . Now what is this other Comforter? It is no more or less than the Lord Jesus Christ himself. . . . When any man obtains this last Comforter, he will have the personage of Jesus Christ to attend him, or appear unto him from time to time, and even he will manifest the Father unto him, and they will take up their abode with him, and the visions of the Heavens will be opened unto him, and the Lord will teach him face to face, and he may have a perfect knowledge of the mysteries of the Kingdom of God; and this is the state and place the ancient Saints arrived at when they had such glorious visions—Isaiah, Ezekiel, John on the Isle of Patmos, St. Paul in the three heavens, and all the Saints who held communion with the general assembly and Church of the First Born &c.[32]

The revelatory power of God will indeed lift humankind spiritually as high as they choose to go through obedience to the laws of heaven, which laws also govern in all the immensity of space.

Notes

1. Joseph Fielding Smith, *Doctrines of Salvation*, comp. Bruce R. McConkie (Salt Lake City: Bookcraft, 1954), 1:50.
2. Marion G. Romney, "The Light of Christ," *Ensign*, May 1977, 43.
3. See 1 Nephi 2:20; 13:12–19; Ether 2:9–12, 15; 13:1–12; D&C 57:1–3; 101:16–23; 1:1–7; 42:58.
4. Joseph F. Smith, *Gospel Doctrine* (Salt Lake City: Deseret Book, 1970), 31.
5. See 3 Nephi 11:32–40; 27:13–22; D&C 39:6; 76:50–53.
6. See Ether 2:9–12, 15; 9:20; 15:19; Mormon 5:16; Moroni 8:28; 9:4; 1 Nephi 17:32–38; Alma 10:19, 23; 37:28, 31; 45:16; Helaman 13:14; 2 Nephi 28:16; D&C 18:6; 29:9; 86:7.
7. James E. Talmage, *Articles of Faith* (Salt Lake City: The Church of Jesus Christ of Latter-day Saints, 1962), 160.
8. See Alma 11:44; 3 Nephi 11:27, 36; 2 Nephi 31:21; John 17:20–22.
9. See Matthew 27:19; 3 Nephi 11:25; D&C 20:73; Alma 11:44.
10. See 1 Nephi 11:11; Ether 3:4–16; see also Talmage, *Articles of Faith*, 159–60.
11. Smith, *Gospel Doctrine*, 61.

12. Smith, *Doctrines of Salvation*, 1:40.
13. See Joseph Smith's explanation that the Holy Ghost was not transformed into a dove but that the dove's lighting upon Jesus was a prearranged sign given to John that Jesus was the Son of God. Joseph Smith, Journal, December 1842–June 1844; book 1, in Andrew H. Hedges, Alex D. Smith, and Richard L. Anderson, eds., *Journals, Volume 2: December 1841–April 1843*, vol. 2 of the Journals series of *The Joseph Smith Papers*, ed. Dean C. Jessee, Ronald K. Esplin, and Richard Lyman Bushman (Salt Lake City: Church Historian's Press, 2011), 251.
14. See Moses 1:24; 5:9; 7:11; 2 Nephi 31:18; 3 Nephi 11:32, 36; 16:6; 28:11; D&C 20:26–27.
15. See 1 Corinthians 12:1–31; Moroni 10:8–23; D&C 46:8–33.
16. Joseph Smith, "The Gift of the Holy Ghost," *Millennial Star*, July 3, 1876, 427.
17. Joseph Smith, "Sabbath Scene in Nauvoo," *Millennial Star*, August 1842, 59.
18. See 2 Nephi 31:4–18; D&C 20:43; 33:15; 35:6; 39:23; 49:14; 55:1; 68:25; 76:52.
19. Compare D&C 76:71–80 with D&C 76:50–70; see also D&C 88:20–24.
20. See Joseph Smith—History 1:73–74; D&C 76:5–10, 114–18.
21. Smith, *Gospel Doctrine*, 60–61.
22. Smith, *Doctrines of Salvation*, 2:98–99; Bruce R. McConkie, *Mormon Doctrine* (Salt Lake City: Bookcraft, 1977), 361–62.
23. Smith, *Doctrines of Salvation*, 2:46–47.
24. Joseph Smith, "History of Joseph Smith," *Millennial Star*, February 9, 1861, 88.
25. Spencer W. Kimball, *The Miracle of Forgiveness* (Salt Lake City: Bookcraft, 1969), 123.
26. See Enos 1:5, 27; 3 Nephi 28:1–3; Ether 12:37; 2 Timothy 4:6–8; and D&C 132:49, respectively.
27. Orson F. Whitney, *Life of Heber C. Kimball* (Salt Lake City: Bookcraft, 1975), 24.
28. Joseph Smith, *History of the Church of Jesus Christ of Latter-day Saints*, ed. B. H. Roberts, 2nd ed. rev. (Salt Lake City: Deseret Book, 1978), 3:381.
29. Joseph Smith, quoted in Joseph Fielding Smith, "Elijah the Prophet and His Mission," *Utah Genealogical and Historical Magazine*, January 1921, 16.
30. See D&C 132:6–8; 21:1, 9.
31. Smith, *History of the Church*, 5:389.
32. Joseph Smith, "History of Joseph Smith," *Millennial Star*, May 5, 1855, 278–79.

Blessings Promised to the Faithful

Richard O. Cowan

Through his inspired prophets, our Heavenly Father has promised wonderful blessings to his children who keep his commandments. While most of these relate to our condition following mortality, other blessings relate more especially to our sojourn here on earth. Among these are the promises made to Abraham and those who would be descended from him.

Blessings for Abraham and His Descendants

The Lord repeatedly made wonderful promises to Abraham and his posterity. While Abram was still living in Haran, the Lord revealed to him, "I will make of thee a great nation, and I will bless thee, and make thy name great.... And I will bless them that bless thee, and curse him that curseth thee: and in thee shall all families of the earth be blessed" (Genesis 12:2–3). After Abram settled in Canaan, the Lord continued to unfold his future: "Look from the place where thou art northward, and southward, and eastward, and westward: for all the land which thou seest, to thee will I give it, and to thy seed for ever. And I will make thy seed as the dust of the earth:

so that if a man can number the dust of the earth, then shall thy seed also be numbered" (Genesis 13:14–16).

On another occasion, the Lord directed Abram, "Look now toward heaven, and tell the stars, if thou be able to number them: and he said unto him, So shall thy seed be" (Genesis 15:5). Finally, in Genesis 17, the Lord changed Abram's name to Abraham (verse 5) and promised him that he would be fruitful and become known as the "father of many nations" (verse 4) and that kings would be among his posterity (verse 6).

Eventually Sarah, though advanced in age, was blessed to bear a son, Isaac. Through him, the promises to Abraham concerning a great posterity would need to be fulfilled. Hence the Lord's command that Abraham sacrifice Isaac was a significant test. When Abraham passed this test, he was again assured that his posterity would become "as the stars of the heaven, and as the sand which is upon the sea shore" and that in his "seed shall all the nations of the earth be blessed" (Genesis 22:17, 18). Modern-day revelation gives us more insight into the Lord's covenant with Abraham:

> And I will make of thee a great nation, and I will bless thee above measure, and make thy name great among all nations, and thou shalt be a blessing unto thy seed after thee, that in their hands they shall bear this ministry and Priesthood unto all nations;
>
> And I will bless them through thy name; for as many as receive this Gospel shall be called after thy name, and shall be accounted thy seed, and shall rise up and bless thee, as their father . . .
>
> For I give unto thee a promise that . . . in thy seed after thee . . . shall all the families of the earth be blessed, even with the blessings of the Gospel, which are the blessings of salvation, even of life eternal. (Abraham 2:9–11)

These blessings were reconfirmed to Abraham's son Isaac, who by this time had married Rebekah: "Unto thee, and unto thy seed, I will give all these countries, and I will perform the oath which I sware unto Abraham thy father; and I will make thy seed to multiply as the stars of heaven, . . . and in thy seed shall all the nations of the earth be blessed" (Genesis 26:3–4). These blessings were renewed yet again to Isaac's son Jacob: "God Almighty bless thee, and make thee fruitful, and multiply thee, that thou mayest be a multitude of people; and give thee the blessing of Abraham, to thee, and to thy seed with thee" (Genesis 28:3–4). So closely identified were these three patriarchs in the memories of their descendants that the Lord sometimes simply identified himself as the God of Abraham, Isaac, and Jacob (see, for example, Exodus 3:15–16). Likewise, the promises made to these three great leaders are similarly referred to as the blessings of Abraham, Isaac, and Jacob.

Elder Bruce R. McConkie testified, "Elias [who appeared at Kirtland in 1836] gives the promise—received of old by Abraham, Isaac, and Jacob—that in modern men and in their seed all generations shall be blessed. And we are now offering the blessings of Abraham, Isaac, and Jacob to all who will receive them."[1] More specifically, he explained, "Every person married in the temple for time and for all eternity has sealed upon him, conditioned upon his faithfulness, all of the blessings of the ancient patriarchs, including the crowning promise and assurance of eternal increase, which means literally, a posterity as numerous as the dust particles of the earth."[2]

As descendants of Abraham, either literally or by adoption, we are heirs to this covenant (see, for example, Matthew 3:9 and 3 Nephi 21:6), but being a covenant people does not make us better than others. For us, receiving the blessings of Abraham, Isaac, and Jacob not only includes such promises as an innumerable posterity but also the responsibility to reach out to others in order to be instruments in the Lord's hands to bless all the world with the gospel of Jesus Christ. The prophet Brigham Young affirmed, "I expect to obtain the same as Abraham obtained by faith and prayer, also the same as Isaac and Jacob obtained; but there are few who live for the blessings of Abraham, Isaac and Jacob." President Young insisted that being heirs to a blessing will not "do us any good, unless we live for it."[3] Thus, even though we may be promised in our patriarchal blessing that we are heirs to these great blessings, we need to live to be worthy of them.

The Resurrection

One of the most marvelous blessings that comes to all unconditionally is the Resurrection, enabling us to live forever. Were it not for this assurance, the promise of an eternal increase could not be fulfilled. The Master left ample evidence that the Resurrection is not just figurative but actual. When he appeared to the eleven disciples who were meeting in a closed room, he directed them, "Behold my hands and my feet, that it is I myself: handle me, and see; for a spirit hath not flesh and bones, as ye see me have" (Luke 24:39). The Book of Mormon provides a powerful second witness. When the risen Savior visited the 2,500 who had gathered at the temple in the land Bountiful, he took enough time to let them have experiences that would enable them to bear testimony of his literal Resurrection: "And it came to pass that the multitude went forth, and thrust their hands into his side, and did feel the prints of the nails in his hands and in his feet; and this they did do, going forth *one by one* until they had all gone forth, and did see with their eyes and did feel with their hands, and did know of a surety and did bear record, that it was he, of whom it was written by the prophets, that should come" (3 Nephi 11:15; emphasis added). Even if each individual had only a few seconds with the Lord, the whole experience would still have required more than two hours.

Book of Mormon prophets explained what actually occurs in the Resurrection. They testified that "the spirit and the body shall be reunited again in its perfect form; both limb and joint shall be restored to its proper frame, even as we now are . . . and even there shall not so much as a hair of their heads be lost (Alma 11:43–44; compare Alma 40:23). Specifically, President Joseph Fielding Smith assured, "If there has been some deformity or physical impairment in this life, it will be removed."[4] Many of us have loved ones dealing with physical challenges who can therefore look forward eagerly to having an immortal tabernacle perfect in every detail. Elder Orson Pratt, undoubtedly tongue in cheek, worried that we might have abnormally long, uncut fingernails or hair when everything is restored. He therefore explained, "I do not believe that every particle that is ever incorporated in the systems of human creatures will be resurrected with them. . . . But a sufficient amount of the particles . . . will be used . . . to make perfect and complete tabernacles for celestial spirits."[5]

Even though every resurrected body will be physically perfect, not all will be prepared to enjoy the same level of glory. In his great chapter on the Resurrection, Paul taught, "There are also celestial bodies, and bodies terrestrial: but the glory of the celestial is one, and the glory of the terrestrial is another. There is one glory of the sun, and another glory of the moon, and another glory of the stars: for one star differeth from another star in glory. So also is the resurrection of the dead" (1 Corinthians 15:40–42).

A latter-day revelation clarifies that we will inherit a body suited for the kingdom whose law we have lived and thereby have qualified to receive. The Lord declared, "He who is not able to abide the law of a celestial kingdom cannot abide a celestial glory" (D&C 88:22). The Lord then added that those who have lived the celestial law will receive a body suited for that glory (see D&C 88:18–32).

What does it mean to live a celestial law? This is the law on which the gospel of Jesus Christ is based. In his Sermon on the Mount, the Lord contrasted lesser standards with those he was requiring. For instance, "Ye have heard that it was said by them of old time, Thou shalt not kill"—perhaps at least a terrestrial standard—"But I say unto you, That whosoever is angry with his brother without a cause shall be in danger of the judgment"— the higher celestial standard. Similarly, "Thou shalt not commit adultery"—the terrestrial standard—was supplanted by "whosoever looketh on a woman to lust after her hath committed adultery with her already in his heart"—the celestial requirement (see Matthew 5:21–22, 27–28). We can apply this same principle to judging other aspects of our gospel living. For example, *Am I a celestial or terrestrial home or visiting teacher?*

President Joseph Fielding Smith pointed out that the resurrected bodies suited for different degrees of glory "will differ as distinctly as do bodies here." He explained that the faithful "will gain celestial bodies with all the powers of exaltation and eternal increase. These bodies will shine like the sun as our Savior's does." Those who are exalted in the celestial kingdom will "have the 'continuation of the seeds forever.' They will live in the family relationship."[6]

The Apostle Paul also spoke of an order or sequence of resurrection. Not all will be resurrected at once, but all will arise, "every man in his own order" (1 Corinthians 15:23). Here again, modern revelation elaborates on Paul's statement (see, for example, D&C 88:96–102).

There are two major phases of the Resurrection (see John 5:28–29 and Acts 24:15): The "first resurrection," or "resurrection of the just," began with the Resurrection of Christ and will close with the end of the

Millennium. Those going to the celestial and terrestrial kingdoms will be resurrected during this phase. The "second resurrection," or "resurrection of the unjust," will follow the Millennium and will include those who are going to the telestial kingdom and those who have become sons of perdition during mortality.

The first resurrection, or resurrection of the just, may then be further subdivided into two parts. "Those being resurrected with celestial bodies, whose destiny is to inherit a celestial kingdom," Elder Bruce R. McConkie explained, "will come forth in the *morning* of the First Resurrection."[7] This includes not only those who were resurrected with Christ but those who will be resurrected and meet him in the clouds of heaven at the time of his Second Coming.

Terrestrial resurrections, which might be called the evening of the first resurrection, will begin only after Christ arrives to reign over the earth for a thousand years. The remaining dead will be judged at the beginning of the Millennium but will be found unworthy; as a result, they will spend the thousand years in the spirit prison (see D&C 43:18) and will be resurrected after the Millennium has ended (compare D&C 88:100–102 with D&C 76:84–85).

The Lord has revealed that only when the physical body and its eternal spirit are "inseparably connected" by the Resurrection can we "receive a fulness of joy" (D&C 93:33). President Joseph Fielding Smith taught, "No man in mortal life can receive the fulness of joy which the Lord has in store for him. Only after the resurrection from the dead, only when the spirit and the body are inseparably connected—when through the resurrection the spirit and the body are welded together inseparably—can that fulness come. That is the beauty of the resurrection," he insisted, "that is the objective of the resurrection from the dead."[8]

Visions of Eternity

The gospel of Jesus Christ promises more than the Resurrection, as wonderful as it is. The Lord told Moses, "This is my work and my glory—to bring to pass [1] the immortality and [2] eternal life of man" (Moses 1:39). Notice there are two distinct objectives. To Martha, who was grieving following the death of her brother Lazarus, the Savior similarly declared, "I am [1] the resurrection, and [2] the life: he that believeth in me, though he were dead, yet shall he live: and whosoever liveth and believeth in me shall never die" (John 11:25–26). In this declaration he again made two promises. First, through his Atonement all humankind will overcome the physical death. Second, as President Joseph Fielding Smith explained, "In giving to those who believed on him the power that they should never die, he had no reference to the mortal or physical dissolution, but to the second death, which is . . . the condemnation of those who are consigned to immortality outside of the kingdom of God."[9]

Robert L. Millet clarified the difference between how the gospel offers each of these two gifts. The Atonement of Jesus Christ gives us Resurrection unconditionally, as well as the opportunity to inherit eternal life. As he explained, "Immortality . . . is a free gift to all. Eternal life, on the other hand, is something for which one must qualify through faithful obedience to the statutes and commandments provided through the plan of salvation. Both of these conditions are made available through our Lord's suffering in Gethsemane and on Golgotha, as well as his rise to glorious immortality from the Arimathean's tomb."[10] There is a significant difference between these two gifts, pointed out Elder Marion G. Romney: "Immortality denotes *length* of life—deathless. Eternal life denotes *quality* of life—the quality of life God enjoys."[11]

Latter-day Saints often make the distinction between salvation and exaltation. We actually need both to achieve our maximum potential. Elder Russell M. Nelson explained:

> To be saved—or to gain salvation—means to be saved from physical and spiritual death. Because of the Resurrection of Jesus Christ, all people will be resurrected and saved from physical death. People may also be saved from individual spiritual death through the Atonement of Jesus Christ, by their faith in Him, by living in obedience to the laws and ordinances of His gospel, and by serving Him. To be exalted—or to gain exaltation—refers to the highest state of happiness and glory in the celestial realm. These blessings can come to us after we leave this frail and mortal existence. The time to prepare for our eventual salvation and exaltation is now.[12]

BLESSINGS PROMISED TO THE FAITHFUL

The Lord has promised that the faithful will "come forth in the first resurrection; and if it be after the first resurrection, in the next resurrection; and shall inherit thrones, kingdoms, principalities, and powers, dominions, all heights and depths, . . . and they shall pass by the angels, and the gods, which are set there, to their exaltation and glory in all things, as hath been sealed upon their heads, which glory shall be a fulness and a continuation of the seeds forever and ever. Then shall they be gods, because they have no end" (D&C 132:19–20). The same passage of scripture adds, "This is eternal lives" (D&C 132:24), and the plural "lives" suggests the multiplicity of the blessings promised. Some may be uncomfortable with the notion that we may become gods. However, just as any child has the potential to become like his or her parents, so do we, as the spirit sons or daughters of God (see Hebrews 12:9), have the capacity to become like him. In his Sermon on the Mount, Jesus commanded, "Be ye therefore perfect, even as your Father which is in heaven is perfect" (Matthew 5:48).

Of course, this perfection doesn't come all at once. "Just as Christ 'received not of the fulness' of the glory of the Father at the first, but 'continued from grace to grace'—grew line upon line, developed from one level of spiritual grace to a higher," Millet explained, "and just as Christ received in the resurrection the fulness of the Father, so may all men and women follow such a path and grow in spiritual graces until they inherit all that the Father has" (see D&C 93:12–20).[13]

The Lord has revealed relatively little concerning the telestial and terrestrial kingdoms, or even the lower two levels of the celestial kingdom. Perhaps they are included in his revelations merely to emphasize the lofty state to be inherited by those who are exalted in the highest level of the celestial kingdom—the condition our Father wants us to strive for. "Those who qualify for this kingdom of glory," Elder Dallin H. Oaks taught, "'shall dwell in the presence of God and his Christ forever and ever' (D&C 76:62). Those who have met the highest requirements for this kingdom, including faithfulness to covenants made in a temple of God and marriage for eternity, will be exalted to the godlike state referred to as the 'fulness' of the Father or eternal life."[14] Still, Elder Charles W. Penrose reminded us that Jesus Christ and Heavenly Father "will always be above us."[15]

The physical condition of that exalted state was described graphically by Orson Pratt: "[God the Father] will light up that world; they will have no need of the rays of the sun, as we now have, neither of the moon, nor stars, so far as light is concerned, for the Lord God will be their light and their glory from that time henceforth and forever."[16] But how can we attain this exalted state?

The Atonement and the Gospel of Jesus Christ

Jesus Christ, our Savior, has established the means by which we can access the marvelous blessings he offers to us, including the power to overcome both physical and spiritual death. Elder Marion G. Romney explained why Christ was uniquely qualified to overcome physical death. Like all of us, Christ was a spirit son of God, but our physical bodies "are begotten of mortal men and are, therefore, subject to death, being descendants and inheritors from Adam, while Christ's physical body was begotten of God, our Heavenly Father—an immortal being not subject to death."[17] Hence the Savior inherited from his mortal mother, as do we all, the capacity to die. But unlike us, he inherited from his immortal Father the power to live forever. Therefore, it is not accurate to say that the Savior was killed on the cross, because no person had the power to take his life from him. The Savior himself explained this as he likened himself to the Good Shepherd. Directly after the well-known reference to his "other sheep," he specifically testified, "No man taketh [my life] from me, but I lay it down of myself" (John 10:18).

The Savior also had power over the spiritual death—an estrangement from God caused by sin. The Apostle Paul testified that even though Christ was "tempted like as we are," he was "yet without sin" (Hebrews 4:15). Hence he is able to plead our cause with the Father, saying, "Behold the sufferings and death of him who did no sin" (D&C 45:4).

Jesus Christ was willing to accomplish the Atonement because of his great love for us. One of the most-beloved and oft-quoted biblical passages affirms, "For God so loved the world, that he gave his only begotten Son, that whosoever believeth in him should not perish, but have everlasting life" (John 3:16). A latter-day revelation clarifies that the Savior shared the

Father's love and therefore was a willing participant in the great atoning sacrifice. Jesus Christ emphasized that he also "so loved the world that he gave his own life, that as many as would believe might become the sons of God" (D&C 34:3).

The Lord's teaching about how the Atonement applies in our lives is called the gospel, which means "glad tidings" or "good news." Alma gratefully acknowledged, "He will take upon him the pains and the sicknesses of his people. And he will take upon him death, that he may loose the bands of death which bind his people; and he will take upon him their infirmities, that his bowels may be filled with mercy, according to the flesh, that he may know according to the flesh how to succor his people" (Alma 7:11–12).

Covenants are an important means for implementing the gospel in our own lives. They are solemn agreements in which God specifies blessings to be received and what we must do to receive them. The Lord equated "mine everlasting covenant" with the "fulness of my gospel" (D&C 66:2). This overarching covenant has several subcategories such as the covenant we make at baptism and the oath and covenant pertaining to the priesthood, as well as the covenants made in connection with eternal marriage in the temple. The phrase "new and everlasting covenant of marriage" (such as in D&C 131:2) is so often heard that many have erroneously concluded that eternal marriage is always what is meant by "the new and everlasting covenant." Elder Joseph Fielding Smith lamented, "I regret to say that there are some members of the Church who are misled and misinformed in regard to what the new and everlasting covenant really is." Actually, he insisted, "the new and everlasting covenant is the sum total of all gospel covenants and obligations."[18] He concluded, "Marriage properly performed, baptism, ordination to the priesthood, everything else—every contract, every obligation, every performance that pertains to the gospel of Jesus Christ, which is sealed by the Holy Spirit of promise according to his law here given, is a part of the new and everlasting covenant."[19]

The gospel is certainly "everlasting" because it was ordained from the beginning, and its beneficial effects are never-ending. It may be regarded as "new" for at least two reasons. The Savior established his new covenant based on love in contrast to the requirements under the law of Moses. Elder Marion D. Hanks pointed out, "Jesus referred repeatedly to the old law by which they had been governed—and then fitted those teachings into the higher and holier context of the law of love he had come to invoke among God's children."[20] A second reason the gospel may be called "new" is because it has been newly restored in these latter days. Stephen E. Robinson eloquently taught the power we can access through the Savior's Atonement and gospel: "In the new covenant of faith, perfect innocence is still required, but it is required of the team or partnership of Christ-and-me, rather than of me alone. Because Christ and I are one in the gospel covenant, God accepts our combined total worthiness, and together Christ and I are perfectly worthy."[21]

REQUIREMENTS FOR THESE BLESSINGS

Concerning what we must do to inherit these great blessings, Elder M. Russell Ballard testified, "Your Heavenly Father has promised in return that He will give marvelous blessings to those who honor their covenants, keep His commandments, and endure faithfully to the end. They will be sealed by the Holy Spirit of promise and will be 'given *all* things' (D&C 76:55; emphasis added; see also D&C 76:50–54, 70), including an inheritance in the celestial kingdom."[22]

Elder David A. Bednar explained what is meant by this sealing: "The Holy Spirit of Promise is the ratifying power of the Holy Ghost. When sealed by the Holy Spirit of Promise, an ordinance, vow, or covenant is binding on earth and in heaven. (See D&C 132:7.) Receiving this 'stamp of approval' from the Holy Ghost is the result of faithfulness, integrity, and steadfastness in honoring gospel covenants 'in [the] process of time' (Moses 7:21)."[23]

As noted above, the Resurrection comes to all unconditionally while eternal life is a conditional gift. The "conditions of this gift," Elder Russell M. Nelson emphasized, "have been established by the Lord, who said, 'If you keep my commandments and endure to the end you shall have eternal life, which gift is the greatest of all the gifts of God.' Those qualifying conditions include faith in the Lord, repentance, baptism, receiving the Holy Ghost, and remaining faithful to the ordinances and covenants of the temple."[24] Specifically, Elder Nelson noted that "no man in this Church can obtain the highest degree of celestial glory without a worthy woman who is sealed to him." Hence, as he concluded on another occasion, "While salvation is an individual matter, exaltation is a family matter. Only those who are married in the temple and whose marriage is sealed by the Holy Spirit of Promise will continue as spouses after death."[25]

Thus, even though the gospel incorporates the power of love, it is still based on law. The Prophet Joseph Smith declared, "There is a law, irrevocably decreed in heaven before the foundations of this world, upon which all blessings are predicated—and when we obtain any blessing from God, it is by obedience to that law upon which it is predicated" (D&C 130:20–21). Hence, the Lord acknowledged, "I . . . am bound when ye do what I say; but when ye do not what I say, ye have no promise" (D&C 82:10). What then may we think of as the law of the gospel? Elder William R. Bradford declared:

> I have never seen this law, but, like gravity, I have seen its effects and felt its powerful influence in my life. This is the law of the Son of God, even Jesus Christ. . . . He would have us know that "that which is governed by law is also preserved by law and perfected and sanctified by the same" (D&C 88:34). . . . The law of the gospel of Jesus Christ has decreed that every man must repent and be baptized by immersion, after the pattern of the Lawgiver, or he cannot be saved. . . . We could talk about the law of sacrifice and service to one another, moral cleanliness, tithes and offerings, honesty. Indeed, we could review all the many laws that together comprise the law of the gospel. But perhaps enough has been pointed out to draw focus on their exactness, the protection and salvation they provide us if we obey, and the serious consequences for noncompliance.[26]

Robert L. Millet and Joseph Fielding McConkie also stressed the importance of law in the gospel: "If God is no respecter of persons, then all will be called upon to accept or reject the gospel and work out their salvation in circumstances that the wisdom of heaven holds as equal. None of Adam's family were to be born in the Garden of Eden in a paradisiacal state."²⁷ Hence, these authors concluded, "It cannot be stated more plainly. It will be the seeds of obedience planted and nurtured in the soil of mortality that produce the delicious fruits upon which one feasts in the paradise of God."²⁸

The Lord has provided temples where we can gain a clear vision of the goal for which we are striving, and learn what we must do to attain it. The temple and its ordinances play a key role in giving us the knowledge and power we need to ultimately become exalted. "*Why is the temple especially suited to provide this knowledge?*" Truman G. Madsen asked. "Because the temple is dedicated to that purpose, because there we make covenants to be true to what we understand, not just learning out of curiosity but absorbing into our souls what we most need to understand."²⁹ Elder D. Todd Christofferson also testified, "Our covenant commitment to Him permits our Heavenly Father to let His divine influence, 'the power of godliness' (D&C 84:20), flow into our lives. . . . In all the ordinances, especially those of the temple, we are endowed with power from on high. This 'power of godliness' comes in the person and by the influence of the Holy Ghost. The gift of the Holy Ghost is part of the new and everlasting covenant."³⁰

In the temple, frequently described as the "Lord's University," we are taught in an effective way the laws we need to obey. "The ordinances of the endowment," explained Elder James E. Talmage, "embody certain obligations on the part of the individual, such as covenant and promise to observe the law of strict virtue and chastity, to be charitable, benevolent, tolerant and pure; to devote both talent and material means to the spread of truth and the uplifting of the race; to maintain devotion to the cause of truth; and to seek in every way to contribute to the great preparation that the earth may be made ready to receive her King,—the Lord Jesus Christ."³¹

Then, in the climaxing ordinance of sealing, a worthy couple is promised a series of almost incomprehensibly marvelous blessings (compare D&C 132:19–24). Thus, as Eldred G. Smith, former Patriarch to the Church, noted, "Temple marriage is not just another form of church wedding; it is a divine covenant with the Lord that if we are faithful to the end, we may become as God now is."³²

To some, this exalted goal may seem unattainable. Robert Millet, however, sought to keep us from becoming too discouraged: "There is no ceiling on the number of saved beings in eternity, no cap, no quota by which the Father of us all must and will be governed."[33] Millet continued, "I know you are not perfect and that you make mistakes. You are mortal. You are human. But I know also that you are trying to keep your covenants, not only with deeds but with your whole heart. You truly love God and want to please him. You qualify to hold a temple recommend. These are not things to be dismissed lightly. They place you in a remarkable minority in this world."[34]

Elder Bruce C. Hafen similarly acknowledged, "I sense that an increasing number of deeply committed Church members are weighed down beyond the breaking point with discouragement about their personal lives. When we habitually understate the meaning of the Atonement, we take more serious risks than simply leaving one another without comforting reassurances—for some may simply drop out of the race, worn out and beaten down with the harsh and untrue belief that they are just not celestial material."[35]

Rather, as we think of our quest to attain the blessings promised to the faithful and the enabling power of the Atonement, we can take to heart the injunction which the Prophet Joseph Smith gave to the beleaguered Saints in 1842, "Brethren, shall we not go on in so great a cause? Go forward and not backward. Courage, brethren; and on, on to the victory!" (D&C 128:22).

Notes

1. Bruce R. McConkie, "The Keys of the Kingdom," *Ensign*, May 1983, 22.
2. Bruce R. McConkie, *The Millennial Messiah* (Salt Lake City: Deseret Book, 1982), 264.
3. Brigham Young, in *Journal of Discourses* (London: Latter-day Saints' Book Depot, 1854–86), 11:117.
4. Joseph Fielding Smith, *Doctrines of Salvation*, comp. Bruce R. McConkie (Salt Lake City: Bookcraft, 1955), 2:292.
5. Orson Pratt, in *Journal of Discourses*, 16:355–56.
6. Smith, *Doctrines of Salvation*, 2:286–87.

7. Bruce R. McConkie, *Mormon Doctrine*, 2nd ed. (Salt Lake City: Bookcraft, 1966), 640.
8. Smith, *Doctrines of Salvation*, 2:284.
9. Smith, *Doctrines of Salvation*, 2:266.
10. Robert L. Millet and Joseph Fielding McConkie, *The Life Beyond* (Salt Lake City: Bookcraft, 1986), 133.
11. Marion G. Romney, "Easter Thoughts," *Ensign*, May 1975, 84–85; emphasis added.
12. Russell M. Nelson, "Salvation and Exaltation," *Ensign*, May 2008, 8.
13. Robert L. Millet, *Selected Writings of Robert L. Millet* (Salt Lake City: Deseret Book, 2000), 232.
14. Dallin H. Oaks, "Apostasy and Restoration," *Ensign*, May 1995, 86.
15. Charles W. Penrose, in *Journal of Discourses* (London: Latter-day Saints' Book Depot, 1854–86), 26:25.
16. Orson Pratt, in *Journal of Discourses*, 21:205.
17. Romney, "Easter Thoughts," 83.
18. Smith, *Doctrines of Salvation*, 1:156.
19. Smith, *Doctrines of Salvation*, 1:158.
20. Marion D. Hanks, "The Royal Law," *Ensign*, May 1992, 10.
21. Stephen E. Robinson, *Believing Christ: The Parable of the Bicycle and Other Good News* (Salt Lake City: Deseret Book, 1992), 43.
22. M. Russell Ballard, "Keeping Covenants," *Ensign*, May 1993, 6.
23. David A. Bednar, "Ye Must Be Born Again," *Ensign*, May 2007, 22.
24. Nelson, "Salvation," 9.
25. Nelson, "Salvation," 9; Russell M. Nelson, "Celestial Marriage," *Ensign*, November 2008, 92.
26. William R. Bradford, "The Safety of the Gospel Law," *Ensign*, November 1977, 64, 65.
27. Millet and McConkie, *The Life Beyond*, 57–58.
28. Millet and McConkie, *The Life Beyond*, 60.
29. Truman G. Madsen, *The Temple: Where Heaven Meets Earth* (Salt Lake City: Deseret Book, 2008), 30.
30. D. Todd Christofferson, "The Power of Covenants," *Ensign*, May 2009, 22.
31. James E. Talmage, *The House of the Lord: A Study of Holy Sanctuaries, Ancient and Modern* (Salt Lake City: Bookcraft, 1962), 100.
32. Eldred G. Smith, in Conference Report, October 1948, 93.
33. Robert L. Millet, *Within Reach* (Salt Lake City: Deseret Book, 1995), 18.

34. Millet, *Within Reach*, 4.
35. Bruce C. Hafen, *The Broken Heart: Applying the Atonement to Life's Experiences* (Salt Lake City: Deseret Book, 1989), 5–6.

From Calvary to Cumorah
What Mormon History Means to Me

Richard E. Bennett

Fifty years ago, when as a young boy I first visited Nauvoo and other Latter-day Saint historical sites, I wrote in my little diary such fleeting comments as "Went to Palmyra [New York] and slept on the Hill Cumorah" (July 23, 1956); "Arrived at Independence, Missouri, today. Saw the place where the Missouri Temple will be built" (July 1, 1956); and finally, "Saw the old Carthage Jail where the Prophet Joseph Smith was martyred. Also we saw other historic sites of the Mormons in Nauvoo."[1] Nauvoo was then a far cry from what it is today. There was no Nauvoo Restoration, Incorporated. There were no beautifully restored buildings, no Williamsburg-like effort to manicure and professionally preserve and restore the past, no missionary-oriented visitors' center, and certainly no temple restoration as we see today. Rather, Nauvoo slumbered on the banks of the Mississippi—dusty, unkempt, and not at all sure if it had a future. Thanks to the work of a few farsighted private Latter-day Saints, it became possible to resurrect the past. And, of course, families like mine kept coming in ever-increasing numbers to connect with the history of the Restoration.

Awakening to the city's possible future, the leadership of The Church of Jesus Christ of Latter-day Saints changed its policy and determined to invest in Nauvoo's future by professionally restoring this site. Said Elder Delbert L. Stapley of the Quorum of the Twelve in the early days of the Nauvoo restoration:

> Many thousands in the Church today have no real understanding of the personality, power, and mission of the Prophet Joseph Smith and other Church leaders. By developing our understanding and appreciation of Church history, we gain perspective and strengthened sense of purpose. It will aid us in making present-day choices and in obtaining present-day testimonies. . . . History carries the torch of light from the past into the present and illuminates the future. . . . This approach to Church history at Nauvoo demonstrates that Church pioneers were real people, living in the real world of America. History can enable us to ease the transition from one type of living to another and increase our effectiveness in the work of the Kingdom of God. . . . [It] would allow the student to vicariously relive the lives and experiences of these faithful pioneers and to point the way toward increased devotion and perspective. . . . To appreciate the fruits of Mormonism, one must understand its roots.[2]

Developing in parallel with Nauvoo's restoration was the intellectualization of Church history and the rise of what many term the "new Mormon history,"[3] which have changed the intellectual landscape of our past, invigorating the faith of some while sorely testing others.

A historic place like Nauvoo provides a pause from our busy lives and hectic schedules to ponder on the gospel of Jesus Christ and the meaning of history. Nauvoo is a tangible, physical expression of the spiritual reality of the Restoration, which in turn is the modern, downstream reiteration of the Resurrection of the Lord Jesus Christ. It has power as a sacred place because it reminds Church members of the importance of their heritage—it brings the past to the present. Behind the buildings and the structures, beyond the pioneers and their families, and before the temple and the Red Brick Store is the First Vision of the Prophet Joseph Smith, which is a revelation anew of our risen Lord and Savior, Jesus Christ. Fundamentally, if Nauvoo does not point to Christ, then it means very little.

Perhaps the best starting point to understand what sacred space can mean to all of us is to remember the imprint of the divine in our individual lives. From my experience, there are three essential elements to the sacred moments in my personal life: time, place, and people. I look back at the YMCA Hall on Elm Street in the hardscrabble, heavy-drinking mining town of Sudbury, Ontario, where I was baptized on May 23, 1954. Although the building has been razed and the swimming pool, changing rooms, and doorways no longer exist, the memory remains, and thankfully the record attests that on that day my life changed forever. It will ever remain a sacred time and space to me.

Similarly, the Sudbury Moose Hall on Pine Street—hardly a sacred place with its moose head, beer hall, and dancing floor—became a sacred spot for me. It was the place where Church meetings were held, where my testimony of the living gospel of Jesus Christ began to take root, and where I began to feel those "swelling motions," as Alma describes, and the power of conversion and testimony (Alma 32:28). Richard J. Mouw recalls something similar in the "gospel tent meetings" of his youth: "I can still smell the sawdust, and this aroma carries with it spiritual associations that have shaped my understanding of what it means to be a Christian human being. And I think it is important—not only for myself but for the evangelical movement in general—to keep smelling the sawdust."[4] I am sure that to all of us there are such sacred moments, hallowed places in each of our individual lives that still stir our devotions and recollections.

And as for people, I came to know the Savior most intimately through my study of the scriptures. I remember reading Jesse Lyman Hurlbut's *Story of the Bible for Young and Old* with its helpful illustrations.[5] I was given my first Bible when I was ten. I can still remember the smell of the leather, the cool crispness of the pages and the warm invitation to read from them. I recall the many stories of Jesus taught to me in Sunday School and Primary by loving teachers. In my very early life, the Holy Bible became the anchor of my faith, the authority of my life, my illuminated passageway to Christ, a companion with prayer to personal revelation. The Bible made Christ a present, living person in my life. Neither a collection of ethical statements nor a mere standard for a moral life, the Bible was a call to Christ and to the Restoration of the gospel.

When I was eighteen, one of my greatest religious experiences came in my own grove of trees while working for the railroad in the Canadian wilds. That spiritual experience, with the Book of Mormon in hand, remains forever engraved in my heart, not only as a witness of the book's truthfulness but also of my Heavenly Father's personal love and concern for me. To me, the Bible and the Book of Mormon are far more than mere publications: they are living water from a living Christ. As one scripture in the Book of Mormon says of these things, "They [the plates of brass] have *enlarged the memory of this people*, yea, and convinced many of the error of their ways, and brought them to the knowledge of their God unto the salvation of their souls" (Alma 37:8; emphasis added).

Memory connects us to the physical places where we have experienced the Lord's Spirit. Just as Paul could never disassociate his conversion from the road to Damascus, so we, as members of the Church who have been touched by the grace of Christ and by the enticing of the Holy Spirit, can never disconnect ourselves from our own history in these sacred places. We find meaning for our living in the history of our lives, those times and places that God has touched.

Similarly, there is a compelling sense of Christian history that should bind our collective experiences. From the New Testament's accounts, places such as Calvary, Gethsemane, the Tomb, Mars Hill, and the Isle of Patmos are of lasting importance. We remember them for what historically transpired there, but for those of us who have been converted, such locations mean more because of their connections to our own experience. Places such as these teach us the mighty truth that Christianity, as the great Protestant scholar J. Gresham Machen has so well stated, "is more than just a way of life but a historical fact." Faced with a growing opposition intent on socializing and secularizing the faith, Machen continued:

> The great weapon with which the disciples of Jesus set out to conquer the world was not a mere comprehension of eternal principles; it was an historical message, an account of something that had recently happened, it was the message, "He is risen."
>
> The world was not to be evangelized by the spread of a wonderful new philosophy but would "be redeemed through the proclamation of an event. . . . Christianity is based, then, upon an account of

something that happened. . . . Christianity is based on a real Person and a real series of historical events in that Person's life which, if He or they did not exist or happen means the end of Christianity.[6]

In more recent times, Adolf Koberle has likewise argued against what he calls the "nonhistorical trend of thought which, as our present age discloses all too clearly, constantly seeks to dominate not only philosophy but also theology. Today it is popular to say that faith is the historical event per se." He continued, "The proud spirit will always maintain that he can grasp the Absolute with equal immediacy at all points of history and that he is in no way dependent on any particular historical events for the appreciation of truth."[7] Koberle rejects such views with this argument: "If Jesus did not live, if He did not die on Golgotha, if the crucified one was not resurrected, then all existential appropriation of these things is left hanging in air. How is it possible, therefore, to disparage the 'facts of salvation,' to totally compress the objective occurrence into its subjective consummation in the life of the believer, when everything depends upon the fact that faith has firm ground beneath it because God has acted in Christ as the Saviour."[8]

Charles Colson has written in a similar vein: "What we need to understand about our faith is that it is not based on wise writings or philosophies or books written in so-called prophetic trances. It is not based on ideologies, which come and go. It is based on the facts of history, real events. . . . That's what Christianity is: history."[9] Again, I quote from Machen: "Give up history and you can retain some things. You can retain a belief in God. But philosophical theism has never been a powerful force in the world. You can retain a lofty ethical ideal. But be perfectly clear about one point—you can never retain a gospel. For gospel means 'good news,' tidings, information about something that has happened. In other words, it means history. A gospel independent of history is simply a contradiction in terms."[10]

Latter-day Saints share this view of Christianity's historicity—that Christ actually lived, died, and was resurrected, that the glad tidings of his Resurrection spawned a movement and a doctrine that continue to change lives. If there is a recurring theological position of the Book of Mormon, it is that Christ was born, that he lived and died in Jerusalem, that he was literally resurrected, and that his atoning sacrifice for sin happened in time and place. The Book of Mormon prophet Abinadi prophesied of Christ some 150 years before the Lord was born:

> And now if Christ had not come into the world, speaking of things to come as though they had already come, there could have been no redemption.
>
> And if Christ had not risen from the dead, or have broken the bands of death that the grave should have no victory, and that death should have no sting, there could have been no resurrection.
>
> But there is a resurrection, therefore the grave hath no victory, and the sting of death is swallowed up in Christ.
>
> He is the light and the life of the world; yea, a light that is endless, that can never be darkened; yea, and also a life which is endless, that there can be no more death. (Mosiah 16:6–9)

Elder LeGrand Richards, a former Latter-day Saint Apostle, in a 1955 Easter address, wrote of our understanding of the risen Christ's historicity:

> The resurrection which we celebrate today has lost all its significance if Jesus did not retain his body following the resurrection. Why should some assume that he is now but a personage of spirit, while he declared so emphatically to the apostles: "For a spirit hath not flesh and bones as ye see me have"? Why did he take up his body from the tomb at all if the work he had to do following his crucifixion could have been done better while in the spirit only? Why did he not leave his body lying in the tomb? Where in the scriptures is there justification for the belief that he has laid his body down again since he took it up from the tomb. . . . Is it possible that our Lord has died a second time, that he can be but a personage of spirit? If so, why do we celebrate Easter in commemoration of his resurrection?[11]

The Latter-day Saint view of biblical Christianity's historicity is similar to our views of the Restoration. Just as Machen argues that without Christianity's history there is no real Christianity, in similar fashion Latter-day Saints argue that without the factuality of our history, there is no Restoration. The First Vision—the appearance of the Father and Son to Joseph Smith in a very real grove of trees near Palmyra in upstate New York in the spring of 1820—actually happened or Mormonism is a fraud. "Every claim that we make concerning divine authority, every truth that we offer concerning the validity of the work, all finds its root in the First Vision of the boy prophet," taught President Gordon B. Hinckley. "That becomes the hinge pin on which this whole cause turns. If the First Vision was true, if it actually happened, then the Book of Mormon is true. Then we have the priesthood. Then we have the Church organization and all of the other keys and blessings of authority which we say we have. If the First Vision did not occur, then we are involved in a great sham. It is just that simple."[12]

Such tangibility in Latter-day Saint history includes a book of scripture written on actual gold plates, which were accompanied by a real object called the Urim and Thummim, the restoration of priesthood by heavenly messengers on the banks of the Susquehanna River in 1829, and the laying of heavenly hands on earthly bodies. Just as the irreligious mind recoils at having to see Christ as the center of history—that the accent of eternity should be placed upon this one point of history—so too many take offense at the Mormon emphasis on the literality of the Restoration.

Of course, the theology of Christian history, as Machen later said, was not merely that Christ died—a historical fact—but that he died *for our sins*. This becomes the theological expression of the historical reality—the spiritual meaning of a physical experience. Latter-day Saints agree with this theology but take it one vital step further. The Restoration of the fulness of the gospel is not merely a historical fact but a doctrinal necessity—that it happened for the *endowment of our eternal life*. The fulness of Christ, the fulness of the gospel, its complete set of teachings and ordinances, the supernal gift of the Holy Ghost made possible through the restoration of divine authority—these constitute the theological meaning of our history. These doctrinal truths make our historical facts invaluable and memorable, symbolic reminders of modern revelation and its centrality in our restored faith. This is why we seek to remember and keep sacred such places as Nauvoo. But to separate these places, the Sacred Grove or the Hill Cumorah, from the Christ of the Bible is to ensure that historical memory of them will inevitably fade. Ultimately, Nauvoo is sacred not just because of the pioneers, not merely because of Joseph Smith or his martyrdom, but because the Christ of the Restoration *is* the Christ of the Resurrection. For us, the

Resurrection and the Restoration are a continuum, running from Calvary to Cumorah, from the River Jordan to the Mississippi.

There are, however, other compelling reasons why we Latter-day Saints revere these sacred sites. One of these surely must be that they point to the importance of *the institution* and the establishment of an organization, a church, a very corporeal expression of the gospel message. The Restoration of the Church is of signal importance, for with it came authority and ordinances, levels of government and jurisdiction, hierarchies and bureaucracies—the very things that many who wish to spiritualize or individualize religion despise. Yet this has given weight and structure and permanence to the Restoration at a time when many others were downplaying the ecclesiastical structures of Christianity. Leonard I. Sweet spoke of such modern trends when he wrote of the anti-institutionalism of the late 1960s: "For the first time in American religion, the authority of the church was widely discredited. Many Christians abandoned an understanding of the church as an institution that sets standards for society in favor of an institution that meets the needs of society, a change in definition that had shuddering consequences for the formation of religious and personal identity."[13]

Likewise the restoration of such sites, and in particular the City of Joseph, or Nauvoo, points to the importance of *community* to the Latter-day Saints. Every careful observer of the Latter-day Saints will recognize that although salvation is essentially an individual affair, much is accomplished collectively. The Saints did not come west as individuals; rather, they came as a group or they did not come at all. As William Clayton penned in his famous hymn "Come, Come Ye Saints," it was always a sense of the collective—that "*We'll* find the place." Nauvoo represented a gathering of converts to Zion in great numbers, the building of a new city of believers. Nauvoo, then, represents a *community* of Saints who shared common beliefs and values. Even in temple worship, Latter-day Saints go through in companies, not by themselves. Though Mormonism preaches individual responsibility, it advocates interdependency on one another as well. Its emphasis on marriage, particularly eternal marriage and the family, points to family exaltation as much, if not more, than individual salvation. It is this community of believers, this family of support, which means so much to modern Mormon worshippers. And with it has come a strong sense of tradition, family history, or what might be termed an LDS "legacy." Some Latter-day Saints see more of this than anything else when visiting such places as Nauvoo. Many who have ancestors who lived and were persecuted there see in such a place the establishment of lasting family values and of compelling individual family stories.

This emphasis on heritage, on preserving our legacy, has kept The Church of Jesus Christ of Latter-day Saints from the loss of identity, from what Sweet called "culturalist Christianity," an age when promoting social causes has come to mean more than preserving historical consciousness. He writes:

> What a religious tradition does with its past has everything to do with the establishment of a distinctive identity. The preservation and transmission of the tradition is an ineluctable obligation of the church. But culturalist Christianity discarded the cultivation of religious belief and the preservation of the heritage for social engagements in changing national and international society. . . . In the 1960s . . . the goal was not to prepare a new generation for the church but to promote social and personal values among the young and to translate religious symbols into ethical and political imperatives among the adults. . . . Thus Protestantism raised a generation of kids who were robbed of their history and without inheritance. . . . A tradition cannot long survive without a living memory. By failing to generate among church members a sense of living out their past, much of Protestantism cuts the cords of community in the present and endangered its survival.[14]

A combination of collective and individual memory in Mormonism is reflected in the Nauvoo Temple. No more sacred space exists in Mormonism than its holy temples. Such are sacred not only as monuments to our history but as places for personal revelation, covenant making, sanctification, and personal holiness. Though the inscriptions on such buildings invariably say "Holiness to the Lord," they are invitations to personal holiness, consecration, and sacrifice that no ordinary Church history site can ever afford.

Not that the reconstruction of these temples came without debate among those in the highest councils of the Church. Even with the work of President Joseph F. Smith in the late nineteenth and early twentieth centuries to purchase historical properties, many modern Church leaders did not support such expenditures. Considered by some to be a peripheral part of the Church's mission, the preservation of such places as Nauvoo by the institution of the Church was slow in coming. Brigham Young tried desperately to sell the Nauvoo Temple to the Roman Catholic Church, and the temple lot in Independence, Missouri, and Ohio's Kirtland Temple were let go out of a desire to establish the Church in the West. Restoration of Church history sites would have to wait until the survival of the Church was assured. All would come in order. Thanks to the vision, tireless efforts, and financial sacrifices of such modern preservation pioneers as Wilford Wood and Dr. LeRoy Kimball, Nauvoo is the classic expression of the inspiration of the rank-and-file membership who insisted on remembering this place. The restoration of Nauvoo is a wonderful example of how fluid revelation in Mormonism can be, inspiration coming almost as much from the bottom up as from the top down.

There are, of course, problems and pitfalls for a Church that insists on preserving its history. I will mention but two. The first rests in the selectivity of what the institution chooses to remember and celebrate—i.e., while we emphasize some parts of our history, we also de-emphasize some other things that happened at a given site. In Nauvoo, there is little in the corporate memory and even less in the missionary tours that ever speaks to such practices as plural marriage. It is as if such a practice never happened or was part of the Prophet's teachings. Such selectivity of what to remember and honor and what to discard may lead to a sense of misunderstanding, if not suspicion, for some. For when some of these realities come out—as they invariably have done and will continue to do—some inevitably feel let down. In attempting to engage the many critical interpretations of the Prophet Joseph Smith in candid, professional, and even faith-supporting ways, several modern Latter-day Saint scholars have broached topics that the rank-and-file members know little about. What was best left unsaid by those wanting to project a modern image of our past has become for others an issue of honesty.

The point is, if we believe in literal history and the power of sacred place, excessive selectivity for corporate public image purposes may do a disservice in the long run. The reaction, for instance, to Richard L. Bushman's *Joseph Smith: Rough Stone Rolling* by several Latter-day Saint readers has often been one of suspicion: why has so little of this been told? Is it possible that the image makers in Church art, film, and literature are doing a disservice to the faith-building power of our own history? If the Restoration is, like the New Testament, history, then what history are we remembering? One of Bushman's contributions is to show how to take it, warts and all.

The second problem is somewhat the reverse: seeing what was never there. Some time ago, a colleague of mine approached me with a question. He had just read a chapter in one of my books dealing with the succession of Brigham Young to the presidency of the Church in the Kanesville (Iowa) Log Tabernacle in December 1847. "Why didn't you tell about the earthquake?" he wondered. "What earthquake?" I asked. "The one some later said happened on that day in that place. Surely it was a sign of God's benediction." I could only respond that there may have been a retrospective account somewhere that spoke of such things, but from my research into scores of contemporary letters, diaries, and sermons, the Spirit of the Lord was in abundance without any earthquake occurring. "But it's such a faith-building story," he argued. "It had to have happened!"

I have reflected on our conversation many times since. Why is it, I wonder, that many Latter-day Saints "go beyond the mark" in wanting to believe in that which never happened, in seeking more than truth, in relying on myth when fact and faith are sufficient? Elder Bruce R. McConkie spoke of this tendency when discussing the miracle of the 1978 revelation, which opened the Mormon priesthood to all worthy men regardless of color:

> Latter-day Saints have a complex: many of them desire to magnify and build upon what has occurred, and they think of miraculous things. And maybe some of them would like to believe that the Lord himself was there [at the temple], or that the Prophet Joseph Smith came to deliver the revelation, which was one of the possibilities. Well, these things did not happen. The stories that go around to the contrary are not factual or realistic or true, and you as teachers in the Church Educational System will be in a position to explain and to tell your students that this thing came by the power of the Holy Ghost, and that

all the Brethren involved, the thirteen who were present, are independent personal witnesses of the truth and divinity of what occurred.[15]

None of us appreciates being purposely deceived. Bearing false witness is both a crime and a sin. There is only hurt, sorrow, and diminishment in lying and deception. Satan himself is "the father of lies" (2 Nephi 9:9). Why is it, then, that we hate lies but often love supposedly faith-promoting myths? I believe that in doing so, we not only twist the truth but also damage our faith for the simple reason that faith must be based in truth. As the Apostle Paul said, "Faith is the substance of things hoped for, the evidence of things not seen" (Hebrews 11:1). The Book of Mormon prophet Alma added, "Faith is not to have a perfect knowledge of things; therefore if ye have faith ye hope for things which are not seen, which are true" (Alma 32:21). Truth, not embellished myth, is the bulwark of faith.

The dictionary defines *myth* as "a belief, opinion, or theory that is not based on fact or reality," an "invented story," or "made-up person or thing."[16] Mormon history, or rather Mormon popular memory, is strewn with such misconceptions of fact. Spurious accounts of the appearance of the Three Nephites are everywhere. There are even published accounts of oversized Nephite warriors who protected temple doors during the antipolygamy raids of the late nineteenth century. And, as a child, I remember reading the book *Fate of the Persecutors*, which assigned the most cruel sufferings and ignominious deaths to those responsible for Joseph Smith's martyrdom.[17] If they escaped justice, surely they deserved divine punishment! Never mind that Elder Dallin H. Oaks and Marvin S. Hill have debunked these accounts in their excellent history, *Carthage Conspiracy*.[18]

Yet these pitfalls and problems are a price we are willing to pay for remembering our history and traditions. Much better we have these problems than those of the more serious kind: the loss of the sense of our history and heritage altogether. We can afford and must encourage differing interpretations, but we cannot afford relegating the glad tidings of Cumorah to myth or the oblivion of forgetting.

In the end, one thing unites Latter-day Saints and believing Christians of all other faiths. And that is a mutual recognition of what Timothy George calls "a true bottomless pit," what Machen described as "the abyss between belief and unbelief."[19] As Christians, we all believe in our Lord and Savior, Jesus Christ; we all share an "unflinching allegiance to the Holy Scriptures"; we all share in a mutual desire to live lives of personal purity and holiness in opposition to the secularizing influences rampant in modern society, in protecting the sanctity of human life, in opposing the destruction of family values, and in spreading the good word of the gospel of Jesus Christ.

Notes

This presentation was made to a combined audience of Latter-day Saint and evangelical Protestant scholars at a special interfaith dialogue conference held in Nauvoo, May 17, 2006.

1. Personal diary of Richard E. Bennett, entries for July and August 1956.
2. Delbert L. Stapley, "The Importance of Church History," *Brigham Young University Speeches of the Year* [April 15, 1969] (Provo, UT: Brigham Young University Press, 1969), 2, 13–14.
3. The term "new Mormon history" suggests a Renaissance-like return to original manuscripts with emphasis on revised interpretation, on seeing things as they really were, and on professional historical study.
4. Richard J. Mouw, *The Smell of the Sawdust: What Evangelicals Can Learn from Their Fundamentalist Heritage* (Grand Rapids, MI: Zondervan Publishing House, 2000), 8.
5. Jesse Lyman Hurlbut, *Hurlbut's Story of the Bible for Young and Old* (Philadelphia: Universal Book and Bible House, 1952).
6. J. Gresham Machen, *Christianity and Liberalism* (Grand Rapids, MI: Eerdmans, 1923), 25, 28–29, 53.
7. Adolf Koberle, "Jesus Christ, the Center of History," in *Jesus of Nazareth: Saviour and Lord*, ed. Carl F. H. Henry (Grand Rapids, MI: Eerdmans, 1966), 64–65, 70.
8. Koberle, "Jesus Christ, the Center of History," 68.
9. Charles Colson, in *Evangelical Affirmations*, ed. Kenneth S. Kantzer and Carl F. H. Henry (Grand Rapids, MI: Academic Books, 1990), 48–49.
10. J. Gresham Machen, *What Is Christianity?* (Grand Rapids, MI: Eerdmans, 1951), 171.

11. LeGrand Richards, "Faith in Action," radio address delivered April 10, 1955 (Salt Lake City: The Church of Jesus Christ of Latter-day Saints, 1955).
12. *Teachings of Gordon B. Hinckley* (Salt Lake City: Deseret Book, 1997), 227.
13. Leonard I. Sweet, "The 1960s: The Crisis of Liberal Christianity," in *Evangelicalism and Modern America*, ed. George Marsden (Grand Rapids, MI: Eerdmans, 1984).
14. Sweet, "The 1960s," 42–43.
15. Bruce R. McConkie, "'All Are Alike unto God'" (CES religious educators symposium address, August 18, 1978), 4–5.
16. *The World Book Dictionary* (Chicago: World Book, 2000), "myth."
17. N. B. Lundwall, comp., *The Fate of the Persecutors of the Prophet Joseph Smith* (Salt Lake City: Bookcraft, 1952).
18. Dallin H. Oaks and Marvin S. Hill, *Carthage Conspiracy: The Trial of the Accused Assassins of Joseph Smith* (Urbana: University of Illinois Press, 1975).
19. Timothy George, "Evangelicals and Others," *First Things*, February 2006, 23.

Part II
Scripture

Symbolism in the Parable of the Willing and Unwilling Two Sons in Matthew 21

John W. Welch

Deeply valuable symbolism is thoroughly embedded in two of Jesus' parables, both of which begin, "A certain man had two sons." The more famous of these two is commonly called parable of the prodigal son, found in Luke 15. The less often mentioned can be called the parable of the willing and unwilling two sons, found in Matthew 21. Even people who have written much and taught profoundly about the parables of Jesus have rarely had much to say about this brief text, which is nevertheless freighted with significantly authoritative cargo. In explicating this lesser-known of the two-sons parables, I hope to honor and recognize Robert L. Millet for his consummate willingness to do the will of the Father and to go down this day to work in his vineyard, wherever the needs may be found.

Reading the Parables of Jesus

In approaching this or any other parable of Jesus, as Bob has elegantly and cogently written, one needs to be alert to the fact that every communication may contain several symbols that convey, intentionally or unintentionally, multiple levels of meaning: "Some of the messages are crystal clear, while others are intentionally veiled," depending on "the openness and spiritual receptivity of the listeners." Furthermore, "a parable can have many applications."[1] Each element in the parables of Jesus works as an analog, as one thing representing, or "re-presenting," something else. Indeed, all art (whether visual or verbal) can be seen as analog, for without analogy, one has artifacts or artifice but not art.

With numerous possible applications to choose from, readers must selectively decide how to interpret what they see in a parable.[2] But at the same time, some readings will always be stronger than others. A strong reading is grounded in close attention to details. The more one can see the interlacing and reinforcing textures of symbolism at work in a parable, a painting, or any other work of meaningful communication, the stronger the reading. Moreover, strong readings make use of all the elements, not just a few selected elements, in the text or work being interpreted. Furthermore, strong readings explain or ameliorate elements that otherwise appear as if they do not fit with the rest of the parable. In addition, strong readings must not stretch the symbolism in a text so far as to thin out its texture.

As I have discussed elsewhere in connection with the parable of the good Samaritan in Luke 10,[3] Jesus' parables have long been profitably read as comprising bundles of extended symbolic messages.[4] Thus, for example, second-century Christian readers and exegetes linked "the man going down" and his "falling among robbers" with Adam and the Fall in Genesis; the robbers were seen as symbolizing the minions of Satan; and the Samaritan was interpreted as a reference by Jesus Christ to himself as the one who rescues. Many things help make this early Christian understanding of the parable of the good Samaritan plausible, elegant, and instructive. Indeed, this two-level reading allows that Jesus marvelously answered both of the questions raised by his interlocutory lawyer—not only the more definitional question, "And who is my neighbor?" (Luke 10:29), but also the lawyer's more seminal initial inquiry, "Master, what shall I do to inherit eternal life?" (Luke 10:25).

To my mind, all of Jesus' parables are to be read at multiple levels. Indeed, Jesus was remembered as having purposefully intended his parables to be seen at least at two levels. One level was for ordinary listeners, who might be edified by the publicly accessible, straightforward narrative value of the story; the other was only for those with eyes to see and ears to hear

(Matthew 13:11, 16),[5] and to them Jesus may frequently have unfolded or discussed his deeper meanings in private conversations (as he did in Matthew 13:19–23, 36–43; 19:10–11). Indeed, Joseph Smith taught that the hidden meanings of all the parables were "plainly elucidated" by Jesus to his disciples.[6] These symbolical readings do not diminish or supplant ordinary, plain, practical readings of the parables. Indeed, multiple readings enrich and magnify these extraordinary texts.

Amplifying and extending these two levels of reading, Christian interpreters, especially in the Middle Ages, saw in all biblical texts four levels of meaning:

1. The literal, factual, historical, or cultural. This approach focuses on explaining what happened in the story, either actually or fictively. The domain of this objective approach is the "is," and it limits itself to a close reading of the text itself.

2. The moral or ethical. Often, the telling of a story or the projection of a symbol is intentionally laden with moral overtones. In response to favorable portrayals, readers or viewers should go and do likewise, whereas unfavorable conduct embedded in negative depictions is to be eschewed. The domain of this social approach is the "ought," and it adds to the discussion the implications of cultural mores and expectations.

3. The allegorical. Here, figures and scenarios are laid for purposes of comparison beside other figures, groups, or developments. Sometimes these paralleling referents are transparent and obvious; other times, and for various reasons, the allegorical counterparts are more obscure and esoterically coded. Although some have discounted the allegorical nature of the parables of Jesus,[7] the roots of the allegorical mode of interpretation reach deeply into the earliest Hebrew and Christian literature; it was commonly used at least from the times of Jesus (who often spoke of such things as the brazen serpent[8] or the sign of Jonah[9] as analogies of himself) and Philo (20 BC–AD 50),[10] as well as in the writings of Irenaeus (c. AD 140–c. 202), Clement of Alexandria (death c. AD 215), and onwards. Although some allegories can be drawn between events in heaven and events on earth, more often allegories are located between two characters or characteristics found in this world, such as the allegorical juxtaposition of a seed to faith or a fisherman to a missionary. The domain of this comparative

approach is typically the "horizontal," and it thrives on comparative and analogical reasoning.

4. The anagogical. When an allegory or parable leads the mind and the soul upward, projecting worldly events, human relations, and natural purposes onto a higher metaphysical or celestial level, the linkage is anagogical. Sometimes called mystical, spiritual, or doctrinal, the anagogical reading highlights heavenly things and especially draws connections between patterns in this life and truths pertaining to the life beyond this mortal realm. The domain of this elevating approach is the "vertical." It is open to impressions that transcend the strict or obvious meaning of the text. These subtle meanings or double entendres are invited by the elevated spiritual vantage point from which Jesus spoke.

These four modes of reading may be seen as basic elements of the world of traditional scriptural interpretation.[11] In these four, one might see a reflection of a four-square approach to the gospel: the physical, social, intellectual, and spiritual (see Luke 2:52). Indeed, it always helps to read the parables of Jesus not only historically and practically but also symbolically and sublimely.

In addition, one further tool was given to the Church by the Prophet Joseph Smith. Speaking about the parables of the lost sheep, the lost coin, and the prodigal son in Luke 15, on Sunday, January 23, 1843, Joseph taught: "I have a Key by which I understand the scriptures—I enquire what was the question which drew out the answer?"[12] As will be seen, these four modes of reading and especially Joseph's key unlock the meaning of the parable of the certain man who had two sons in Matthew 21:28–31.

The Setting of the Parable of the Willing and Unwilling Two Sons

With these general thoughts as guiding principles, consider first the setting of this short parable, which comes at a crucial moment in Matthew's Gospel narrative. Immediately after Jesus' triumphal entry into Jerusalem, he went straight to the temple, knocked over the tables of the overreaching merchants and money changers, miraculously healed the blind and the lame, and was heralded by children (21:12–16). At the end of that momentous day, after spending the night with friends in the nearby village of Bethany, he returned the next morning to the temple (21:17, 23). There he was accosted by the chief priests and the elders of the people, who challenged him, demanding to know, "By what authority doest thou these things?" and "Who gave thee this authority?" (21:23).

As he usually did, Jesus answered their affront with a question of his own: "The baptism of John [the Baptist], whence was it?" he asked. Was it "from heaven, or of men?" (21:25). When they were unwilling to respond, Jesus used this as an opportunity to address the fundamental issue of authority. Although he declined to say directly by what authority he did these things (see 21:27), he immediately[13] went on to answer their question indirectly by giving this trenchant parable about two sons—one of whom ultimately was willing and the other not.

This was Jesus' first teaching in the temple after his triumphal entry, and this short parable effectively took this crucial question of authority all the way back to fundamental principles, not only to the current unwillingness (or inability) of the chief priests to answer the question about the source of John's authority but also beyond that to things pertaining to the foundation of the world relevant to the source of Jesus' and all true authority. At a deep level, this parable calls to mind a particular dichotomy of enduring eternal character and consequence.

According to the King James Version, Jesus said: "But what think ye? A *certain* man had two sons; and he came to the first, and said, Son, go work to day in my vineyard. He answered and said, I will not: but afterward he repented, and went. And he came to the second, and said likewise. And he answered and said, I *go,* sir: and went not. Whether of them twain did the will of his father? They say unto him, The first" (Matthew 21:28–31).

Objective Elements in the Parable

Several significant factual or cultural points are embedded in this instructive story. At the literal, factual level, this is a story of a man. The first word in this parable is *anthrōpos* (21:28), a man. This also is the first word in the parables of the good Samaritan (Luke 10:30) and the prodigal son (Luke 15:11). From the words of this story, all one knows is that this man was a father of two sons, that he had a vineyard or orchard (*ampelōn*, the word may mean either), and that he needed someone to go down to work immediately in that vineyard.

The work was needed *sēmeron*, "today, this day." Perhaps it was harvest time or planting time; either way, the need was rather urgent.

The two sons are referred to as the father's *tekna*, his own immediate offspring (not slaves or servants); although referred to with this term of endearment, which is often used in speaking of young children, these sons[14] must be old enough and mature enough to do this work. For some unstated reason, the father was either unable to hire other workers or did not want to entrust this work to slaves or dayworkers. He needed one of his own sons to go down and do this work.

From these straightforward facts, the message speaks in everyday terms: In such a case, Galilean society would have expected sons to drop whatever they were planning to do that day and go and help their dear, perhaps somewhat elderly, father in his time of need. This story "expects that listeners should pronounce judgment upon the son who did not obey," for children in this world were "expected to honour [their] parents."[15] One son eventually does this; the other does not.

All this is well and good, but it is clear from the context that Jesus was not giving the chief priests and the venerable men of the city a cultural commentary about family relations. As he was being challenged there in the temple by the highest authorities in Jerusalem about his own authority, this was not the time for him to deliver a homely description of family behaviors.

Moral Principles in the Parable

At the broader ethical level, this parable gives helpful domestic guidance to all sons and daughters on how they ought to behave. In happy families everywhere, it is ethically good for children to decide, in the end, to go and do what their parents have reasonably asked them to do; and it is always a problem for children to promise that they will do something they have been asked to do but then, for whatever reason, leave their parents disappointed. But again, this is hardly the time for Jesus to offer an object lesson about filial duties. I disagree that "this is little more than an expanded proverb" employed as a "parable of judgment."¹⁶

In addition, at the moral level, the parable might also be understood as simply teaching the general point that "it is never too late to make a decision and to act upon it."¹⁷ And indeed, this parable may well have been originally used by Jesus in this context, or it was eventually placed in this setting in Matthew 21, for the purpose of suggesting that Jesus wanted to persuade the chief priests and the Pharisees that it was still not too late for them to change their opinions and behavior toward him. This view has been embraced by several commentators¹⁸ because at the end of verse 31 Jesus indicted his challengers, saying that the publicans and harlots would enter the kingdom of God before they would because the publicans and harlots believed John the Baptist but the chief priests and elders did not. And at the level of moral persuasion, this parable serves very well in this regard. But it seems to me that more must be involved here. If that was all that was intended by Jesus, a simpler story involving only one son who at first disregarded his father's wishes but then changed his mind might have been sufficient and more appropriate in showing that those sinners had ultimately done the right thing by repenting and following John. And without a further point of reference in connection with the dual story, the chief priests and elders would well have been left puzzling when they had not done what they had specifically said they would do? When had they said they would follow John but then did not do so?

Allegorical Readings of this Parable

Thinking allegorically, this parable offers other interpretive outcomes. The vineyard (*ampelōn*) is a favorite and common symbol for how God sees humankind: either representing the people of Israel (as in Isaiah's parable of the vineyard in Isaiah 5)¹⁹ or the whole world (as in Zenos's parable of that olive tree that stood in a large vineyard or orchard in Jacob 5). Because of this symbolic element, it is often suggested that this parable should be read nationally, as a statement about God's two ethnic sons, so to speak, the Israelites and the Gentiles: one of the sons (Israel) said (and covenanted) that he would do what God wanted but then did not, while the other (the Gentiles, or the publicans and the harlots) said he would not go, but reconsidered and did go. Consistent with this allegorical reading, it is clear that Jesus intended the chief priests and elders to see themselves and their own failure to do the will of the Father in this little parable, as Jesus concluded this part of his conversation with them by saying, "Verily I say unto you, that the publicans and the harlots go into the kingdom of God before you" (Matthew 21:31), and by extension this point of judgment would fall upon anyone else who had rejected John.

But, while this allegorical reading emphasizes the way in which this little parable silenced Jesus' critics, it does not really answer either of the two questions they had asked him about his authority, and so this collective or national allegorical reading—useful though it certainly is in Matthew's rhetorical agenda—still leaves us wanting more. In fact, logically, the comparative failure of the Jewish leaders to do the will of God has nothing to do with Jesus' authoritative empowerment to do or to say all the things he was teaching and doing. Indeed, when the chief priests and elders refused to answer Jesus' question about the origins of John the Baptist's admittedly lesser authority than Jesus' asserted Melchizedek authority (Psalm 110:1–4), Jesus at first said to them, "Neither tell I you *by what authority* I do these things" (21:27; emphasis added), thereby setting aside the first of the chief priests' two questions. But when he went on to tell the ensuing parable of the two sons, he answered in effect their second question: "*Who gave thee* this authority?" As mentioned above, Joseph Smith taught that readers should pay close attention to "the question which drew out the answer."[20] In this case, that question was the source of Jesus' authority, and ultimately that is the question the parable particularly answers.[21]

Reading the Parable Anagogically

With the foregoing in mind, I suggest that readers might most meaningfully look at this parable through a spiritual or anagogical lens. Here one finds a strong reading of this text, conceptually engaging all of its elements. Indeed, most potently, this parable takes the question of authority into divine realms. Anagogically involved here is no ordinary father, no ordinary vineyard, and no ordinary pair of sons. An attentive reader can see in Jesus' answer a number of elevated doctrinal points about the nature of authority received from God in general and about Jesus' authority in specific. Consider the following:

The two sons were asked by their father. In the end it becomes clear that this father is not just their father, but God the Father.[22] The King James Version chose to supplement the text by inserting the word *his* in italics, when Jesus asks, "Whether of them twain did the will of *his* father?" (21:31). Nevertheless, the Greek reads, "Which of the two did the will of *the* father (*epoiēsen to thelēma* tou *patros*)?" (emphasis added). While it is possible that the definite article here (*tou*) can simply be understood as taking "the place of an unemphatic possessive pronoun when there is no doubt as to the possessor,"[23] which would allow the KJV rendition "*his* father" as a legitimate translation, Jesus' wording here echoes the Greek wording found in Matthew 7:21 regarding the one who enters the kingdom of heaven, namely he "who does the will of the Father of mine who is in heaven" (*ho poiōn to thelēma tou patros mou tou en tois ouranois*). Thus the use of the definite article in the question, "which did the will of *the* father" at least invites an anagogical reflection, seeing the father and willing son in this parable as representing Jesus and his Father in Heaven.[24] The sons were thus called to serve by and with authority directly from the divine principal whom they would serve. Those with authority do not take that authority upon themselves but are "called of God, as was Aaron" (Hebrews 5:4).

These two sons were both offered their commission to "go" by way of commandment from the Father. This invitation came, not as a polite request, but as an imperative, literally, "go [*age*] down [*hyp-*]" (*hypage*, Matthew 21:28; the father said the same to the second son in 21:30). While the word *hypage* can have a number of meanings, including to "go away," "withdraw," "depart," "go forward," or simply to "go,"[25] its sense always depends on the context in which it is used. Here, if the setting is in the father's house, the sons are being asked to leave the comforts of home and go work in the fields; if the setting is in the father's mansion on a hill, or in heaven, then the sons will be going down from there. In any case, the prefix *hyp-* (from the preposition *hypo*, under) in composition conveys some sense of being "under, as well of rest as of motion," or, interestingly, "of the agency or influence under which a thing is done, to express subjection or subordination."[26] Moreover, in being asked to go, the two sons were told when and where they were to serve—today, and in the vineyard—so their authority was specific. Those with specific authority do not have the option of selecting another time or place. They can either respond with a yes or a no, but they cannot modify the father's request.

To carry out their assignment with authority they need to be in tune with the will of the one who has sent them. Those having divine authority may need to repent or change their attitude in order to accommodate themselves to do what God wants, not what they might want.

Beyond these important points about the nature of authority and legal agency, this parable draws its listeners back to the heavenly realms where Jesus and all the holy apostles and prophets—including John the Baptist—were called and foreordained to hold the priesthood of God. In so doing, this story calls to mind events in the Council in Heaven, where a Father indeed had two very different sons and where Jesus received his commission and authority from the Father. In fact, the Father's command to his first son, "go *down*" (*hypage*), which says more than just "go," as in the KJV, and thus invites the listener to understand this dialogue as having transpired somewhere above.

These heavenly, primeval overtones are a bit more evident in the Greek text of Matthew than in the Latin Vulgate or in the English of the King James Version or other translations. The most widely supported Greek texts literally read as follows: "A man had two sons, and going to the first he said, 'Go down this day to work in the vineyard.' He answered, 'Not as I will,' but then reconciling himself to the task he went. Going to the other, he [the Father] said the same. And he answering said, 'I, Lord!' And he did not go."[27] The differences between this rendition of the Greek and the usual English translations of this text—which is clearly much more than a fable—may be explicated as follows:

In the Greek, it is more evident that Jesus is casting himself as the first of these two sons. In most manuscripts, at the end of the story in verse 31, he is called "the first" (*ho prōtos*).[28] Just as he was the Firstborn, this son was the first son that the Father approached. In some other early manuscripts, he is called "the last" (*ho eschatos*), apparently because in the narrator's mind that son is the farthest back in the story. Being called "the first" and "the last" evokes Isaiah 44:6; 48:12; Revelation 1:17; and 22:13: "I am the first, and I am the last." Either way, this submissive, obedient son is the one who does the will of his Father. I will simply call him "the first."

Indeed, the first son initially answered the Father's request by saying, "*Ou thelō*," which the KJV translates as "I *will* not" (emphasis added). But *thelō* is not a future-tense verb. It does not mean "I *will* not, or *shall* not." *Ou thelō* is a present-tense verb, meaning "I don't want to," or "I don't wish to," or "I'd rather not," or, idiomatically, "Not (*ou*) [what or as] I will (*thelō*)." In Elizabethan English, "I will not" could mean "I do not will it," as does the Latin *nolo*, but this is not how modern readers hear this crucial word.[29] Doing the Father's will (*thelēma*—which is the noun cognate to the verb *thelō*) is a central theme in the Gospel of Matthew leading up to Christ's teaching in this parable and immediately beyond (see Matthew 6:10; 7:21; 12:50; 18:14; 26:42). In Gethsemane, as the Savior reconciled and submitted himself to the will of the Father, he said, "not my will [*mē to thelēma mou*] but thine, be done" (Luke 22:42).[30] These words in Matthew 21:29 take on an elevated meaning when the "first son" is taken as referring to Jesus himself.

The two sons were commanded by the Father to go down "this day" to do what the Father wanted to have done at the time when that work was needed below. Timing was important for the coming of Christ. Many things had been put in place for the Son of God to appear in the flesh at the promised and prophesied time, and people in Jerusalem were counting down the days and years for the fulfillment of the prophecy given in the book of Daniel, to say nothing of the prophecies given in the Book of Mormon. As mentioned above, to Jesus and his listeners, the vineyard was a potent symbol of the house of Israel (see Isaiah 5:1–7).

The first son "goes *away*" or "departs *from*" (*apēlthen*) the Father's presence. This verb is translated simply as "went" in the KJV in Matthew 21:29, 30. This word, along with the Father's command, "go *down*" (*hypage*),[31] may call to mind the condescension or incarnation of Jesus leaving his Father's presence. These words were used by Jesus himself in referring to his own going away or departure, as a euphemism for his impending death and descent into the spirit prison: "Then said the Jews, Will he kill himself? because he saith, Whither I go (*hypagō*), ye cannot come" (John 8:22); "It is expedient for you that I go away (*apelthō*)" (John 16:7). Indeed, speaking

WILLING AND UNWILLING TWO SONS

prophetically of his death in the longer and immediately following parable of the vineyard and the wicked tenants at the end of Matthew 21, Jesus clearly referred to himself as the son of a landowner in a faraway country who planted a vineyard and sent his servants, whom the tenants beat and killed; and when he sent his own son, they cast him out and killed him too (see Matthew 21:33–41). In hearing that parable, the chief priests and the Pharisees "perceived that [Jesus] spake of them" and their desire to kill him (21:45). With a little further reflection, they may also have perceived that Jesus had spoken of himself as the first son in the immediately preceding parable of the willing and unwilling two sons.

The onerous burden of the work asked by the Father seems to have given even the ultimately submissive first son ample reason for pause. Perhaps this son knew when he was asked to go down that there were or would be wicked tenants in the vineyard who had or would have already killed the two sets of servants sent by the landowner-father, and now in desperation the father needed a son to send. No wonder even that first son might need to think things over a bit. At this point in Matthew 21:29, the KJV reads, "but afterward he *repented*" (emphasis added), which might seem unbecoming of the Savior. But the idea that the first son repented of some sin (an idea which is implicit in *paenitentia*, the Latin word used at this point in the Vulgate) is actually not necessarily implied in the little parable. The Greek word used here is not the ordinary verb used to mean "repent" (*metanoeō*),[32] but rather *metamelomai*, which does not primarily mean "to repent." In the Septuagint and in Koine Greek, with rare exception, it always means to feel sad about something or to change one's mind;[33] in Classical Greek it means to regret, or to change one's purpose or line of conduct; or, as one might say, to reconcile oneself to the task of serving a difficult part in a larger plan. Viewed objectively or ethically, a son might need to change his mind and decide to obey his father's command. And seen allegorically, the Jewish leaders, unlike the first son, had not felt any need to adjust their preferences or change their minds (*oude metamelēthēte*), let alone repent, as even the publicans and harlots had done when they saw John the Baptist "in the way of righteousness" (21:32). But ultimately and anagogically, the willingness of the first son to submit to the Father's will is an understandable and appropriate reaction—just as the First Son contemplated shouldering his daunting assignment and aligned his own will with that of the Father.

At the same time, there was another son. Most manuscripts call him "the other" (*ho heteros*),[34] while some call him "the second (*ho deuteros*)."[35] This son stood in utter contrast to the first, as in the expression "on the one hand, or on the other hand." He is more than numerically second; he also stands in contradistinction, being the "other," being of another mind or having some other purpose. He was eager at first, but in the end he would not serve his father.

Significantly, when this other son answered, he did not actually say, "I go, Lord," as the KJV reads, following the Vulgate, which uses the words "*eō* [I go], *domine*." The word "go," however, is italicized in the KJV because it is actually not present in the strongest Greek manuscripts. Except in a few NT manuscripts,[36] the other son simply says *egō, kurie*, "I, Lord." In ordinary parlance, this might sound something like "Yes, sir." But in an anagogical mode, the pronoun *egō* adds connected significance. For this second son, it seems that it was all about ego. This is the first word he says. He seems caught up with the fact that *he* had been called. In this context, what does this word *egō* entail? "I *what?* Lord." "I *will gladly go?*" "*OK,* I *will [grudgingly] go?*" or "I *get to go!?*" "I *have been chosen!?*" "I will do it;" I *want the glory!* Lord."[37] All of these are possibilities. Moreover, the second and only other word (*kurie*) in his reply to his father a bit stiffly calls his own father "Lord," which may well convey an underlying sentiment that for that son this matter was not primarily about close personal love or filial devotion.[38] For whatever reason, that son did not go. He was called but not chosen.

If the first son is identifiable as Jesus, the second son in this parable can be understood as Lucifer, his brother. For Latter-day Saints, this calls to mind the familiar scene in the Council in Heaven in which Jesus was given his commission and authority from the Father.[39] While not exactly the same as in this parable, certain similarities are unmistakable. On that occasion the Father asked, "Whom shall I send?" (Abraham 3:27). In the texts we have, Lucifer then responded with a barrage of six first-person pronouns, "Here am *I*, send *me*" (Abraham 3:27; Moses 4:1; emphasis added), adding, "*I* will be thy son, . . . *I* will redeem all mankind . . . ; surely *I* will do it; wherefore give *me* thine honor" (Moses 4:1; emphasis added). Jesus, however, simply "answered like unto the Son of Man: Here am I, send me" (Abraham 3:27), adding, "Father, *thy* will be done" (Moses 4:2; emphasis added). These two responses typify the contrast between the course of self-interested unrighteousness and the way of submissive righteousness in answering a call from God. Because Lucifer sought to usurp God's own honor, glory, power, and authority, he was cast down (Moses 4:3) and, as in Jesus' parable to the Jewish leaders, Lucifer did not go. Whether he was not allowed to go or took himself out of the running, the outcome was the same. In either case, it is interesting to note that the Father was apparently open to sending either (or perhaps, in some way, both), if they would be willing to be his agents and to do his will within the scope of the authority and assignment given to them.

Whether or not the chief priests and elders had any knowledge from traditional sources about the heavenly council in which the eternal plan was established from the foundation of the world,[40] that primal event would have been well known to the Savior and perhaps to his disciples and others of his contemporaries. Indeed, the Apostle John knew and testified that the power and authority of Jesus came from the premortal world, where Jesus obtained his right to rule on this earth, not to do his own will, but to do the will of the Father. The authority of Jesus was traceable back to "the beginning" (John 1:1); his judgment was just because he sought "the will of the Father" who had sent him (John 5:30). Jesus taught openly, "For I came down from heaven, not to do mine own will, but the will of him that sent me" (John 6:38), and at the Last Supper, only a few days after his triumphal entry in to Jerusalem and his confrontation with the chief priests and elders in the temple, Jesus affirmed to his disciples, "I am in the Father, and the Father [is] in me. . . . the words that I speak unto you I speak not of myself: but [of] the Father" (John 14:10). "I have given unto them the words which thou gavest me" (John 17:8). So, it would not have been out of character or out of season if Jesus had taken his disciples aside as they returned to Bethany after that day in the temple, at the beginning of the Holy Week, to remind them of the source of his authority and explain this meaning of this parable of the willing and unwilling two sons. But, in any event, this parable clearly answered the question, "Who gave thee this authority?" (namely, God the Father); and it even hints at when and where that happened (namely, in the divine council, where two sons were involved).

In the end, whatever the chief priests and elders knew about the traditional teachings of God's heavenly council, or whether they could have surmised the implications of the dichotomous two-sons typology that permeates much of scripture,[41] they did not have ears to hear on this occasion. Unlike the meek and obedient Son of Man and too much like the second son in the parable, they refused to accept God's emissaries and do the will of the Father. Thinking too much of their own self-interests, they failed to learn this eternal lesson—that when people seek unrighteous dominion, the heavens withdraw, and "amen to the . . . authority of that man" (D&C 121:37). Having challenged Jesus' authority, the chief priests and elders found their own authority challenged. As always, true authority can only be maintained by virtue of humility, long-suffering, kindness, and love unfeigned, exercised for the glory and honor of the Father, as exemplified by his First and eternally willing Son.

Notes

1. Robert L. Millet and James C. Christensen, *Parables and Other Teaching Stories* (Salt Lake City: Shadow Mountain, 1999), 7. Concurring, Arland J. Hultgren, "Interpreting the Parables of Jesus: Giving Voice to Their Theological Significance," in *Hermeneutic der Gleichnisse Jesu: Methodische Neuansätze zum Verstehen urchristlicher Parabeltexte*, ed. Ruben Zimmermann (Tübingen: Mohr Siebeck, 2011), 639–40.
2. See, generally, Ruben Zimmermann and Gabi Kern, eds., *Hermeneutik der Gleichnisse Jesu* (Tübingen: Mohr Siebeck, 2008); Stefan Nordgaard Svendsen, *Allegory Transformed: The Appropriation of Philonic Hermeneutics in the Letter of the Hebrews* (Tübingen: Mohr Siebeck, 2009).
3. John W. Welch, "The Good Samaritan: A Type and Shadow of the Plan of Salvation," *BYU Studies* 38, no. 2 (1999): 50–115, and also "Parable of the Good Samaritan," *Ensign*, February 2007, 40–47, and *Liahona*, February 2007, 26–33.
4. Kurt Erlemann, "Allegorie, Allegorese, Allegorisierung," in Zimmerman and Kern, *Hermeneutik der Gleichnisse Jesu*, 482–93.

5. Jesus may have had several reasons for veiling his meanings, all of which could have been operating on the occasion of Matthew 21. Those reasons include avoiding controversy, protecting himself from accusation, protecting the sacredness of certain revelations, softening the impact of his teachings, and allowing his listeners to discover the meaning of his messages as they might be ready to internalize and accept their implications and applications.
6. Joseph Smith, "To the Elders of the Church of the Latter Day Saints," *Latter Day Saints' Messenger and Advocate*, December 1835, 225–30.
7. Notably C. H. Dodd, *The Parables of the Kingdom* (New York: Charles Scribner's Sons, 1961), 4–5.
8. As in John 3:14.
9. As in Matthew 12:39–41.
10. See, for example, the discussion of the role of allegory in Stoic literature as well as the use of allegory by Philo and his Alexandrian predecessors in Svendsen, *Allegory Transformed*, 9–52.
11. This type of thinking has a parallel in the four progressively better types of seeds in the parable of the sower, or the four types of learners who go to study Torah. See *Abot* 5:15, discussed in Brad H. Young, *The Parables: Jewish Tradition and Christian Interpretation* (Peabody, MA: Hendrickson, 1998), 265 (quick to learn, quick to forget; slow to learn, slow to forget; slow to learn, quick to forget; quick to learn, slow to forget).
12. Andrew F. Ehat and Lyndon W. Cook, eds., *The Words of Joseph Smith* (Provo, UT: Religious Studies Center, 1980), 161.
13. Commentators often assert that this parable has been taken out of its original context in some Galilean village setting and inserted here, where it does not really belong. However, this parable is introduced by the question, "But what think ye?" (*ti de hymin dokei*, "but how then would it seem to you?") which is a common introductory question used in various forms (such as *ti oun*, "what then?" or *ti de*, "but what about?") in the dialogues of Plato, where Socrates uses this expression to continue a line of questioning or to press forward with a discussion, as for example, *ti soi dokei*, "how does it seem to you?" in *Phaedo* 96e5, John Burnet, ed., *Platonis Opera* (Oxford: Oxford University Press, 1967).
14. The male gender of these children becomes clear in the male adjectives, "the first" and "the other."
15. See Peter Balla, *The Child-Parent Relationship in the New Testament and Its Environment* (Peabody, MA: Hendrickson, 2003), 126.

16. Charles H. Talbert, *Matthew* (Grand Rapids, MI: Baker, 2010), 251.
17. Young, *The Parables*, 137.
18. For example, Joachim Jeremias, *The Parables of Jesus*, 2nd ed. (New York: Charles Scribner's Sons, 1972), 80–81.
19. "The vineyard is here, as elsewhere (Isaiah 5:1–7; Matthew 21:33–43), a metaphor for Israel." Arland J. Hultgren, *The Parables of Jesus: A Commentary* (Grand Rapids, MI: Eerdmans, 2000), 221.
20. See note 6 above.
21. On the importance of the two questions in Matthew 21:23 and 25 for the interpretation of this parable, see Wesley G. Olmstead, *Matthew's Trilogy of Parables: The Nation, the Nations and the Reader in Matthew 21:28–22:14* (Cambridge: Cambridge University Press, 2003), 99, 108.
22. Hultgren, "Interpreting the Parables of Jesus," in *The Parables of Jesus: A Commentary*, 637: "It should go without saying that a father can represent God, and so it is."
23. Herbert Weir Smyth, *Greek Grammar* (Cambridge, MA: Harvard University Press, 1963), section 1121.
24. There is no grammatical doubt as to the referent of the possessive *tou*: it obviously refers to the father of the son, and if the willing son represents Jesus in this parable, then his father is, by extension, "the Father," his Father in Heaven.
25. Henry George Liddell, Robert Scott, and Henry Stuart Jones, *A Greek-English Lexicon* (Oxford: Clarendon, 1968), 1850.
26. Liddell, Scott, Jones, *Greek-English Lexicon*, 1875.
27. I first suggested this reading in "'Thy Mind, O Man, Must Stretch,'" *BYU Studies* 50, no. 3 (2011): 71.
28. Most manuscripts say that the father went first to the son who eventually goes and is referred to as "the first." This reading is most widely supported in the early New Testament manuscripts, and I follow it here. For discussions of the textual variants, see Olmstead, *Matthew's Trilogy of Parables*, 167–76, and the editorial comments reported by Bruce M. Metzger, *A Textual Commentary on the Greek New Testament* (London: United Bible Societies, 1971), 55–56; see also Hultgren, *Parables of Jesus*, 218–19. Metzger calls this reading "probably the original," 56.

    In a small minority of manuscripts, another version of this parable likewise has the father approach the ultimately willing son first, but in the end he is called not "the first" but "the last" or "the least" (*ho eschatos*). One possible explanation for this textual oddity is that the ultimately willing son is the furthest back in the story in the audience's mind. Or it may be that the willing son could be seen as both the first and the last, or as having reduced himself to the least in the kingdom of heaven. Or this reading may simply be "nonsensical." Metzger, *Textual Commentary*, 55.

    A few other manuscripts reverse the order of the appearance of the two sons, so that the father first asks the son who eventually does *not* go, even though he initially says yes, and in these texts the answer to Jesus' final question about which of the two did the father's will is accordingly either "the latter" (*ho hysteros*) or "the last" (*ho eschatos*). It might mean that the Jewish leaders, who were chronologically asked first, but did not do the will of the father, were seen as coming first in the parable, whereas the tax collectors and harlots were asked second, and then went, were transposed into second position. But this form of the parable is "inferior" to the first. Metzger, *Textual Commentary*, 56. Moreover, it is unclear which group was actually asked by John the Baptist first.

29. H.W. Fowler, *A Dictionary of Modern English Usage* (London: Oxford University Press, 1926), 729. The phrase "I shall not" would have been the correct translation of expression of future intent in the first person, whereas "I will not" expressed desire "as far as one has the power" (Fowler).

30. On the importance in this parable of doing the will of the father, see Olmstead, *Matthew's Trilogy of Parables*, 100–105, 108.

31. See discussion above accompanying notes 23–26.

32. Johannes P. Louw and Eugene A. Nida, eds., *Greek-English Lexicon of the New Testament Based on Semantic Domains*, 2nd ed. (New York: United Bible Societies, 1988), domain 41.52 (p. 510).

33. Louw and Nida, *Greek-English Lexicon of the New Testament*, domains 25.270 (p. 318); 31.59 (p. 373). In the Septuagint, God does not bring Israel through the land of Canaan so that they will not *change their minds* (*metamelēsēi*, Exodus 13:17; but here the KJV reads "repent"). Likewise, it is not that the Lord "repented that he had made Saul king over Israel" (1 Samuel 15:35), but rather that he felt *sorrowful or regretful* (*metemelēthē*). See also Psalm 106:45; Jeremiah 20:16; Ezekiel 14:22. In Zechariah 11:5, "repent" (*metemelonto*) parallels "sorrow" (*epaschon*). Regarding his oath and covenant of the Melchizedek priesthood in Psalm 110:4, the Lord promises that he "will never change his mind" (*ou metamelēthsetai*). Much less frequently, this word refers to repentance (Proverbs 5:11).

34. Including ℵ*C D K W X Δ Π.

35. Including ℵ²B C L Z Θ f¹.

36. In D, the second son says *egō kurie hypagō* ("I, Lord, I go down") and occasionally others, including Θ 0233 f¹³, will likewise supply the verb in "I go down," which seems to be implied but which then renders the pronoun *egō* superfluous, except for added emphasis—which is still consistent with my point.
37. Compare Moses 4:1, "and surely I will do it; where give me thine honor." It would not appear here that Satan approached God first, for the first son, the Father's "Beloved Son," who had been "Chosen from the beginning," said, "Father, thy will be done, and the glory be thine forever" (Moses 4:2).
38. Recalling to mind that not everyone who simply says, "Lord, Lord [*kurie, kurie*] shall enter into the kingdom of heaven" (Matthew 7:21).
39. See generally Jeffrey M. Bradshaw and Ronan James Head, "Mormonism's Satan and the Tree of Life," *Element: The Journal of the Society for Mormon Philosophy and Theology* 4, no. 2 (2008): 5–7 (Satan in the heavenly council), and 18–19 (the issue of proper authority).
40. They may have known of the pattern of authoritative callings and the heavenly council from several passages, including 1 Kings 22:19–23; Psalms 82:1; 110:3; Isaiah 9:5 LXX; Jeremiah 23:18; Daniel 7:9–14; Amos 3:7; 1 Enoch 12:3–4. See John W. Welch, "The Calling of a Prophet," in *The Book of Mormon: First Nephi, the Doctrinal Foundation*, ed. Monte S. Nyman and Charles D. Tate Jr. (Provo, UT: Religious Studies Center, 1988), 41, 46; Hugh W. Nibley, "Treasures in the Heavens: Some Early Christian Insights into the Organizing of Worlds," *Dialogue* 8, no. 3–4 (1973), 76–98, reprinted in The Collected Works of Hugh Nibley, 1:171–214 (see p. 174); see generally E. Theodore Mullen Jr., *The Divine Council in Canaanite and Early Hebrew Literature* (Chico, CA: Scholars, 1980). In Acts 2:23, Peter's text assumes that his audience on the day of Pentecost was familiar with the idea of God's primordial council (*boulēi*) and foreknowledge (*prognōsei*) that sent Jesus to his fate.
41. For example, Cain began as "a man from the Lord" (Genesis 4:1), but killed Abel (Genesis 4:10) and was cast out. Eber also had two sons, Peleg and Joktan, and in their days the earth was "divided" (Genesis 10:25). Abraham had two sons, Ishmael and Isaac (see Genesis 16 and 21), one the son of a slave born after the flesh, the other born of the freewoman by everlasting promise, which Paul saw as an allegory (see Galatians 4:22–26). Isaac had two sons, Jacob and Esau; the one wrestled with God and received an eternal blessing, and the other sold his birthright. Joseph had two contrasting sons, Manasseh and Ephraim (see Genesis 41:50). Moses has two sons (Exodus 18:3), one negatively named Gershom (from

ger, alien), the other favorably named Eliezer (from *Eli*, my God, and *ezer*, help). For Lehi, the dichotomy gave people the choice between liberty and eternal life through the great Mediator, or captivity and eternal death under the power of the devil (see 2 Nephi 2:27).

The Divine Principle of Friendship
Some Prophetic and Secular Perspectives

Andrew C. Skinner

Friendship is a vital relationship and a great blessing in our lives, but also a concept that many of us may not have contemplated theologically as a fundamental principle of the gospel of Jesus Christ. This essay seeks to explore, through Latter-day Saint lenses, friendship as a divinely established doctrine undergirded by such traits as honesty, loyalty, faithfulness, forgiveness, mercy, and tolerance.

Discussing friendship is tricky business. Some readers may feel it is not a topic worthy of discussion in a scholarly volume. Others will want to know why the essay does not treat such things as the scholarly literature on friendship. Still others will question why the essay does not delve into the negative aspects of friendship. But our present interest is to try to understand the mind of God on this subject through examination of scriptural and modern prophetic pronouncements. We seek to understand what the scriptures and prophets say about friendship and how those teachings might be applied in real life. After all, if scriptures have no application to real life they are of very limited value. But, as Paul declared, "all scripture is given by inspiration of God, and is profitable for doctrine, for reproof, for correction, for instruction in righteousness: that the man of God may be perfect, thoroughly furnished unto all good works" (2 Timothy 3:16–17).

This Festschrift seems an appropriate venue for discussion of our topic since Robert Millet has offered his friendship to many religious educators over the last four decades—a kind of friendship that can be characterized as radiating an active and constant interest in seeing others succeed, and, along the way, facilitating the doctrinal education of the Latter-day Saints. His goodwill and total absence of pettiness cause us to think more deeply about the divine concept of friendship.

Because all we do as Latter-day Saints is influenced by the Restoration of the gospel of Jesus Christ through the instrumentality of Joseph Smith, it seems logical to begin with the Prophet of the Restoration and examine his statements on friendship. Those statements tell us much about the principle as well as the man. We next look at the expressed views of Joseph Smith's successors, including a paradigm-shifting teaching by Elder Richard G. Scott of the Quorum of the Twelve about the principle of true friendship. We try to illuminate Latter-day Saint views of friendships against the backdrop of what many consider to be the greatest philosophical discussion of friendship in Western secular literature—Aristotle's discourse in his *Nicomachean Ethics*. We conclude with an examination of Jesus' teachings on friendship and offer personal observations about the far-reaching doctrinal implications of his statements.

Joseph Smith's View of Friendship

Significantly, the historical record indicates that Joseph Smith not only appreciated true and faithful friends, but revealed to us the place of friendship in the restored gospel of Jesus Christ. "Friendship," he said in July 1843, "is one of the grand fundamental principles of Mormonism [designed] to revolutionize and civilize the world, and cause wars and contentions to cease, and men to become friends and brothers."[1] For Joseph, friendship was not predicated upon utility but loyalty. So important to him were the qualities of faithfulness and unwavering loyalty in friends that he felt to express this strong statement: "I don't care what a man's character is, if he's my friend, a true friend, I will be a friend to him, and preach the

Gospel of salvation to him, and give him good counsel, helping him out of his difficulties."[2]

Loyalty and faithfulness in friendship formed something of a theme in the Prophet's thinking. Of family and friends who visited him when he was in hiding on August 11, 1842, he said: "How good and glorious it has seemed unto me, to find pure and holy friends, who are faithful, just and true, and whose hearts fail not; and whose knees are confirmed and do not falter, while they wait upon the Lord, in administering to my necessities, in the day when the wrath of mine enemies was poured out upon me. . . . How glorious were my feelings when I met that faithful and friendly band, on the night of the eleventh on Thursday, on the Island, at the mouth of the slough [swamp], between Zarahemla and Nauvoo. . . . There was brother Hyrum who next took me by the hand, a natural brother. Thought I to myself, brother Hyrum, what a faithful heart you have got."[3] Indeed, Hyrum shared much of the same adversity as his brother, or, more accurately, *with* his brother, even to the point of being shot to death alongside of him in Carthage, Illinois (see D&C 135:1). Here one immediately thinks of Proverbs 17:17, and it is quite possible Joseph himself knew these words, given his familiarity with the entire Bible: "A friend loves at all times, and a brother is born for adversity." Like Joseph, Hyrum certainly seems to have been born for adversity, and perhaps this helps explain their close friendship.

Clearly, Joseph Smith's views on friendship were shaped by his sufferings. On August 23, 1842, a time of ongoing tribulation, he spoke again of faithfulness in friendship: "I find my feelings . . . towards my friends revived, and while I contemplate the virtues and the good qualifications [qualities], and characteristics of the faithful few, which I am now recording in the Book of the Law of the Lord[,] of such as have stood by me in every hour of peril, for these fifteen long years past; say for instance; my aged and beloved brother[,] Joseph Knight, Sen., who was among the number of the first to administer to my necessities, while I was laboring, in the commencement of the bringing forth of the work of the Lord, and of laying the foundation of the Church of Jesus Christ of Latter Day Saints; for fifteen years has he been faithful and true . . . and it shall be said of him by the sons of Zion, while there is one of them remaining[,] that this man was a faithful man in Israel; therefore his name shall never be forgotten."[4]

Although there is no evidence that Joseph Smith's fundamental beliefs about friendship were informed by literary sources other than the Bible, it seems almost certain that he would have agreed with Shakespeare, who said through the character Cassius in his play *Julius Caesar*, "A friend should bear his friends' infirmities."[5] The ancient Greek biographer Plutarch also reflected a concept which seems to underlie Joseph's experience with friends, namely that "prosperity is no just scale; adversity is the only balance to weigh friends."[6] Consider as well the words of another Greek writer in relation to Joseph Smith's beliefs—the Athenian dramatist Menander (341–290 BC), who was one of the most popular writers of antiquity: "As gold is tried in the furnace, so friends are tried in adversity."[7] One might say Joseph Smith's views on friendship reflect the generally noble outlook of Western culture.

Not surprisingly, the qualities of friendship that Joseph regarded as paramount in others are those same qualities that others saw in him. His personal secretary, Benjamin F. Johnson, said of him, "As a friend he was faithful, long-suffering, noble and true."[8] And, it seems clear that Joseph thought of himself as Brother Johnson saw him: "There are many souls whom I have loved stronger than death. To them I have proved faithful—to them I am determined to prove faithful, until God calls me to resign up my breath."[9] In a letter to his wife Emma, written while he was in chains in Richmond, Missouri, Joseph wrote, "Oh my affectionate Emma, I want you to remember that I am a true and faithful friend to you."[10] Canonized scripture records that Joseph Smith considered himself "a never deviating friend" (D&C 128:25).

Thus, for Joseph Smith, true, faithful, constant friendship was an ideal, a standard to live by. For him a fundamental virtue of friendship was its power to unite the human family with its influence—an idea we shall return to later.

The Necessity of Friendship

Though few of Joseph Smith's more immediate apostolic successors spoke of the principle of friendship, per se, they did speak about humankind's relationships to each other in terms such as the importance of loving one's fellow man, having compassion for each other, and showing charity. President Brigham Young can be taken as a good representative of other Church leaders. He said, "Love each other—go on until we are perfect, loving our neighbor more than we love ourselves. . . . Let us have compassion upon each other, and let the strong tenderly nurse the weak into strength and let those who can see guide the blind until they can see the way for themselves. . . . Let us be just, merciful, faithful, and true. . . . Let all Latter-day Saints learn that the weaknesses of their brethren are not sins. . . . Let us be patient with one another."[11] Again the qualities of being just, faithful, and true come to the fore.

One of the most significant statements on friendship in the last seventy-five years came from President David O. McKay (1873–1970), ninth President of The Church of Jesus Christ of Latter-day Saints. During the April 1940 general conference, he said, "Next to a sense of kinship with God come the helpfulness, encouragement, and inspiration of friends. Friendship is a sacred possession. As air, water and sunshine [are] to flowers, trees, and verdure, so smiles, sympathy, and love of friends [are] to the daily life of man! 'To live, laugh, love one's friends, and be loved by them is to bask in the sunshine of life.'"[12]

Here we have it. President McKay, then a counselor in the First Presidency, publicly stated that next to a sense of kinship with Deity stands the kinship we feel with friends. Friendship is an important, even necessary, part of our mortal lives. In fact, true friendship is the second most important relationship mortals enjoy, according to President McKay. Friendship is a *sacred* possession! Few possessions in our lives are as precious as true, loyal, faithful friends.

Practically speaking, what does this mean? I believe the implications are stunning. Friendship can be one of the greatest blessings people enjoy in mortality, or like much of the world today, individuals can discount friendship and cut themselves off from a divinely established relationship that comes through association with other human beings. True and loyal friends can help one another get through tough and challenging times. Friendships can lift the burdens of loneliness that come to individuals as a natural result of mortality. True friends can and will build each other up when they have been torn down.

THE DIVINE PRINCIPLE OF FRIENDSHIP

Here I echo the musings of one of the founders of our Western intellectual tradition, the Greek philosopher Aristotle (384–323 BC), who devoted two entire books (sections) of his *Nicomachean Ethics* to a discussion of the concept and principles of friendship. He introduces the topic by declaring that friendship is "most indispensable for life. No one would choose to live without friends, even if he had all other goods."[13] He continues:

> In poverty and all other kinds of misfortune men believe that their only refuge consists in their friends. Friends help young men avoid error; to older people they give the care and help needed to supplement the failing powers of action which infirmity brings in its train; and to those in their prime they give the opportunity to perform noble actions. (This is what is meant when men quote Homer's verse:) "When two go together . . .": friends enhance our ability to think and to act. . . . When people are friends, they have no need of justice, but when they are just, they need friendship in addition. In fact, the just in the fullest sense is regarded as constituting an element of friendship. Friendship is noble as well as necessary: we praise those who love their friends and consider the possession of many friends a noble thing. And further, we believe of our friends that they are good men.[14]

From the standpoint of personally improving our lives, Aristotle seems to be telling us that friendships can help us break out of our shells of self-absorption and even selfishness by causing us to turn our energy to help others.

Philia and *Agape*

The Greek word Aristotle uses in discussing friendship is *philia*. "It designates the relationship between a person and any other person(s) or being which that person regards as peculiarly his own and to which he has a peculiar attachment."[15] However, the connotations of *philia* are much broader than "attachment," as one would expect, since the root meaning of *philia* is "love" (*phileō*, *philos*, and so forth),[16] and love in some form, it seems to me, must be at the heart of true friendship. However, *philia* does not denote the highest form of affection or friendship, especially from a Christian viewpoint. That is embodied in the term *agape*.

Principally, *philia* in the Greco-Roman mind constituted "the bond that holds the members of any association together, regardless of whether the association is the family, the state, a club, a business partnership,"[17] and so forth. But *agape* comprehends a selfless concern for the welfare of others that is not called forth by any quality of loveableness vested in the person loved. *Agape* in scriptural terms is the product of a desire to love in obedience to God's command, in contrast to *philia*. One either possesses *philia* or does not. This is reflected in the Greek proverb *Koina ta tōv philōn*,[18] "friends are what they have in common." Not so with *agape*. It may be worked for, prayed for, increased by a desire to be strengthened (see Moroni 7:48). Significantly, *agape* is "charity," as defined by Lidell and Scott's Greek lexicon.[19]

Contrast *agape*, or charity, with Aristotle's dissection of friendship as he asks, "What is the object worthy of affection?" He continues, "For it seems, we do not feel affection for everything, but only *for* the lovable, and that means what is good, pleasant, or useful." This is different from a relationship grounded in *agape*, or charity. For, says Aristotle, when we ask, "Which good, then, is it that men love?" it seems apparent that "each man loves what is good for him: in an unqualified sense it is the good which is worthy of affection, but for each individual it is what is good for him."[20]

Aristotle goes on to elucidate the "three causes of affection or friendship," namely, usefulness, pleasure, and goodness.[21] He concludes, "The perfect form of friendship is that between good men who are alike in excellence or virtue." But, notice here, again, the implications of Aristotle's analysis for an understanding of *philia* versus *agape*: "For these friends wish alike for one another's good because they are [both] good men."[22] In other words, *philia* is manifest in its ultimate form when two parties are both good and appreciate that the other individual is good. In contrast, *agape* is concerned with loving or having affection for those others who are not necessarily good, in the sense Aristotle uses the term. That is, the person being loved or receiving *agape* may not be concerned for the welfare of the one possessing *agape*, may not even appreciate the goodness of the one offering love, or may not possess any quality of lovableness.

In the Greco-Roman world, *philia* (Latin, *amicita*) was even used of patron-client relationships. Society was highly stratified, and *philia* was suitable to denote relationships between the rich and powerful and their social inferiors. This is undoubtedly why the Apostle Paul largely avoids such language in his letters to branches of the Church[23] and why he expends considerable effort in discussing *agape*, or charity. Notable is 1 Corinthians 13, where Paul uses the word *agape* throughout and which the King James Version translates as "charity."

Charity as Paradigm

Probably most Latter-day Saints would agree that Paul's equal in discussing the doctrine of charity is Mormon, who is quoted by his son Moroni (see Moroni 7:45–47). I have long believed that this passage in the Book of Mormon describes Christ-centered friendship as well as Christlike love. A short article by Elder Richard G. Scott, "The Comforting Circle of True Friendship," also links Mormon's discussion with the essence and fundamental nature of genuine friendship. After quoting Moroni 7:45–47, Elder Scott muses, "What a priceless message for any that would enjoy the comforting circle of true friendship."[24] He noted it was prayer and application of this familiar scripture that guided him to new depths of understanding and appreciation of the principle of friendship.

Indeed, the words of Mormon regarding charity take on new meaning as we contemplate friendship as a divine doctrine. Those words provide a kind of blueprint, a paradigm, to be followed by all who desire to *be* true and loyal friends, and enjoy the blessings of *having* true and loyal friends. Ultimately, only charity makes possible the attainment of Joseph Smith's ideal—true, loyal, faithful, constant friendship. In this light, it not only becomes easy but imperative to substitute the word "friendship" for the word "charity" in the following verses of Mormon's instruction:

> And charity [friendship] suffereth long, and is kind, and envieth not, and is not puffed up, seeketh not her own, is not easily provoked, thinketh no evil, and rejoiceth not in iniquity but rejoiceth in the truth, beareth all things, believeth all things, hopeth all things, endureth all things. . . .

> But charity [friendship] is the pure love of Christ, and it endureth forever; and whoso is found possessed of it at the last day, it shall be well with him. (Moroni 7:45, 47)

According to Mormon's paradigm, true and loyal friendship "*suffereth long and is kind*"—that is, friends bound together by charity are patient; they allow others to make mistakes or errors in judgment and to say or do thoughtless things at times without becoming critical, unkind, mean-spirited, or vengeful or adopting a "holier than thou" attitude.

Orthodox rabbi and professor Stanley Wagner often told a story attributed to the Talmud, the great repository of Jewish law and tradition, about Father Abraham, who is called the *friend* of God in both Jewish *and* Christian scripture (see 2 Chronicles 20:7; Isaiah 41:8; James 2:23). The patriarch is camped out in the wilderness and invites a traveler into his tent to enjoy some hospitality. During the course of their conversation, Abraham learns that the stranger is a fire worshipper and won't pray with the patriarch. Abraham immediately throws the man out of his tent. He goes to bed, satisfied, I suppose, that he has upheld Jehovah's honor. That night, Abraham has a dream in which the Lord comes to him and says, "Abraham, Abraham, I have borne with that ignorant man for all these many years. Could you not have suffered him one night?"[25] The message is clear: if Abraham was "the friend of God," he was supposed to act like his friend by exercising patience in the face of ignorance.

According to Mormon's paradigm, true and loyal friends know and remember that *all* human beings are subject to the foibles, follies, and weaknesses of mortality; all make mistakes, and thus friends can help each other out of their difficulties by exercising patience.

True and loyal friendship "*envieth not, and is not puffed up*." True and loyal friends do not gossip, backbite, think they are better than everyone else, or denigrate others to exalt themselves. True and loyal friends are *not* jealous of the success of others. Rather, they celebrate the achievements and happiness of their friends. They pay sincere compliments to their associates. They embrace cooperation.

I have spent my entire professional life associated with universities—a seedbed of fierce competition. And yet the irony is that the greatest scholars I have known are those who have been ever-present mentors—cheering on their colleagues—encouraging their work, congratulating them for their breakthroughs—and expressing genuine pleasure at the accomplishments of associates. These mentors offer real help. They remember their debt to others.

Are we not all mentors and protégés at different stages in our lives? A relatively recent publication on the life of Albert Einstein and his close circle of colleagues describes, among other things, how Einstein, arguably one of the greatest minds of the twentieth century, was glad to hear of the accomplishments of his friends. He encouraged them and even remained a loyal friend to those with whom he disagreed—sometimes vociferously. Yet Einstein and his associates did not deal with inconsequential questions or with concepts that could not instantly establish the reputation of their "first" discoverer. When it came to attempting to understand something as profound as the structure of the universe, there were no bigger issues than relativity on the one hand (Einstein's position) and the uncertainty principle on the other (others' positions). Yet if a discovery, proposal, or theory advanced the state of the discipline, Einstein was one of the first to congratulate the concept's proponent.[26] There does not seem to be pettiness or smallness of soul in truly big people.

True and loyal friendship *"seeketh not her own"*—meaning that real friends do not look out for their own welfare to the exclusion or detriment of others. They prize cooperation over competition. A heartwarming story may serve to illustrate the point. Several years ago during the Seattle Special Olympics, nine contestants lined up at the starting line for the 100-yard dash. All nine were either physically or mentally disabled or both. At the sound of the gun, they all started out with the same excitement and desire to win that any athlete would have in a race. However, this race turned out to be unlike any other. One of the runners, a boy who had an especially hard time, stumbled on the track, tumbled over, and began to cry. The other eight contestants heard the boy and without hesitating, stopped running, turned around, and went back to their fallen competitor. They helped the boy up, and then all nine competitors linked arms, finished the rest of the race, and walked across the finish line together. By cooperating, the result desired by each of these competitors was not diminished but greatly enhanced because they worked together. In this case, all nine were winners, and literally no one lost.[27]

True and loyal friends are "*not easily provoked, . . . [think] no evil, . . . [and bear] all things.*" Perhaps the single word that summarizes theologically this part of Mormon's message is "meekness." True and loyal friends are meek. Yes, they are humble, but meekness means something more. It denotes calmness in the face of provocation, poise under pressure, returning goodness for evil, helping others when those others lose control or have a meltdown (in modern parlance).

Scripture teaches that Jesus and the prophet Moses were the meekest of all men on earth (see Numbers 12:3; Matthew 11:29; 2 Corinthians 10:1; D&C 19:23). When one contemplates the provocation these two figures endured, their responses to external threats and violence are stunning. The Apostle Peter tells us that though Jesus was reviled against, he did not return revilement or hostility. When he suffered at the hands of wicked men, he did not threaten retribution (see 1 Peter 2:23). Can we imagine how different the universe would be for all of us—for eternity—if Jesus had actually called on twelve legions of angels to respond to the undeserved abuse and suffering heaped upon him, as Matthew 26:53 says he could have? Instead, he meekly submitted to the Father's will. True and loyal friends seek to cultivate the godly attribute of meekness.

Elder Neal A. Maxwell (1926–2004) of the Quorum of the Twelve Apostles offered profound insight on the attribute of meekness, as it relates to the concept of true and loyal friendship. He said:

> Meekness . . . is more than self-restraint, it is the presentation of self in a posture of kindness and gentleness, reflecting certitude, strength, serenity, and healthy self-esteem and self-control. . . . Meekness does not mean tentativeness. But thoughtfulness. Meekness makes room for others. [The Apostle Paul said:] "Let nothing be done through strife or vainglory; but in lowliness of mind let each esteem other[s] better than themselves" (Philip. 2:3). . . . Meekness cultivates in us a generosity in viewing the mistakes and imperfections of others. [As Moroni said:] "Condemn me not because of mine imperfection . . . but rather give thanks unto God that he hath made manifest unto you our imperfections, that ye may learn to be more wise than we have been" (Morm. 9:31).[28]

Elder Maxwell went on to provide an example of meekness from the life of President Brigham Young, who viewed with charity and generosity a situation in which he received a scolding, undeserved, from someone he so much loved and admired—someone he regarded as one of his truest and closest friends. He "took it" without protest, said Elder Maxwell, "because he was meek. Yet, surely, none of us . . . would think of Brigham Young as lacking in boldness or firmness!" Some clever pundit has said, if you think meekness is weakness, try being meek for a week!

True and loyal friendship recognizes that charity, "*the pure love of Christ . . . endureth forever.*" True and loyal friends seek to cultivate charity; they pray for it, as they are commanded to do in Mormon's urging (Moroni 7:48). *Agape* is the foundation of the most profound kind of friendship—meaningful and everlasting. Friendships that are based on—and imbued with—charity are eternal.

Aristotle recognized that friendships based on usefulness or pleasure are fleeting, for "such friendships are easily dissolved when the partners do not remain unchanged: the affection ceases as soon as one partner is no longer pleasant or useful to the other. . . . Accordingly, with the disappearance of the motive for being friends, the friendship, too, is dissolved."[29] By extension, we add that relationships based on anything other than *agape* stand in danger of dissolving.

True, loyal, and lasting friendship "*rejoiceth not in inquity, but rejoiceth in the truth, . . . believeth all [good] things, hopeth all things.*" True friendship grounded in charity (*agape*) demands that human beings forgive one another and hope for better days. It seems to me that those possessing charity will naturally understand and appreciate the Lord's declaration that he "will forgive whom [he] will forgive," but the rest of us are "required to forgive all men" (D&C 64:10). Thus true friendship disdains grudges—even when we believe that hurtful wrongs have been perpetrated. True and loyal friendship means that we will forgive. We will let go of the impulse to remember the hurt. True friendship demands that we extend mercy to others.

One of the most impressive illustrations of such magnanimous behavior comes from the life of Job, who is described foremost as a righteous, wealthy man. After multiple tragedies strike (loss of family, loss of wealth, debilitating illness, and so on), Job's friends come forth to "help" him out of his misery. They pronounce their diagnoses: there is a cause for every effect; therefore, wickedness must be behind Job's suffering. After all, "who ever perished, being innocent? or where were the righteous cut off?" (Job 4:7). Those who are cut down are they who have forgotten God. God doesn't cast away the innocent, but he will not uphold evildoers (see Job 8:5, 8, 11, 20).

Perhaps the lessons of Job's friends seem so powerful because they have such significant application to our own circumstances: when we sit in judgment of others under the guise of friendship, especially when we do not know all the facts, we make their burdens greater.

Job's friends made quite an impression on the Lord. When he was consoling the Prophet Joseph Smith during a time of extreme tribulation, he used the example of Job's friends as the ultimate measure of the Prophet's circumstances: "Thy friends do stand by thee. . . . Thou art not yet as Job; thy friends do not contend against thee, neither charge thee with transgression, as they did Job" (D&C 121:9–10).

In the end, Job's friends are chastised by the Lord (Job 42:7). But the greatest lesson of all comes from Job himself. He did not hold a grudge, he dealt with his friends charitably, he extended mercy, and he prayed for them, the very ones who had compounded his misery. By so doing, he was given release from the physical, spiritual, and emotional torment and bondage brought on by his suffering: "And the Lord turned the captivity of Job, when he prayed for his friends: also the Lord gave Job twice as much as he had before" (Job 42:10).

Friendships give us the privilege of being able to feel what God feels when he helps one of us overcome a problem, or answers one of our prayers, or extends mercy to any one of his children. As Elder Jeffrey R. Holland reminded us in the April 2012 general conference, "Surely the thing God enjoys most about being God is the thrill of being merciful, especially to those who don't expect it and often feel they don't deserve it."[30] In other words, friendships in mortality allow us the thrill of knowing the joy of both *extending* mercy *to* others, extending acts of love and compassion, and *receiving* mercy *from* others. Indeed, friendships grounded in *agape* provide a platform for us to know how God himself feels.

True friendship *"hopeth all things, endureth all things."* True friendship forgoes the temptation to feel sorry for oneself and resists the lure of self-pity. I do not think God assigns blame to others for the depressed, lonely feelings of some of his children. Depression, loneliness, feelings of social inadequacy emanate from the environment of our fallen world. But it seems to me that God does expect his disciples to help change the miserable circumstances of others (see Matthew 25:31–40). And he expects that all individuals invest something of themselves in changing their own miserable circumstances.

In a much appreciated self-disclosure, Elder Scott discussed ways to overcome feelings of aloneness and enjoy the blessings of friendship. Of his youth, he said he participated in social activities but always felt he was on the periphery, on the sidelines, watching others enjoying themselves but personally left out, alone, and unwanted. It wasn't until later in life he realized it was largely his own fault:

> I have since learned that one cannot demand love and respect or require that the bonds of friendship and appreciation be extended as an unearned right. These blessings must be earned. . . . Sincere concern for others, selfless service, and worthy example, qualify one for such respect. All my rationalization, that others had formed select groups and knowingly ruled out my participation, was largely a figment of my imagination. Had I practiced correct principles, I need not have felt alone.[31]

FRIENDSHIP AND SACRIFICE

Of the many requirements of true, loyal, and lasting friendship, one thing may well be the most important, though it is not mentioned explicitly by Mormon. However, it underlies all the other attributes of charity as well as friendship. True friendship requires its practitioners to make sacrifices. As Jesus reminds us, love is at the heart of friendship, and love increases where sacrifices are made. In this regard, Jesus is both our greatest teacher and our greatest exemplar.

On the eve of his great suffering in Gethsemane, Jesus took time to talk about friendship with his Apostles. Presumably, these men were some of his closest associates in mortality. On that emotionally charged night, after the Last Supper had concluded, Jesus paid the highest personal compliment to the Apostles that we find in the four Gospels. Here are his words taken from the fifteenth chapter of John:

> As the Father hath loved me, so have I loved you: continue ye in my love.
>
> If ye keep my commandments, ye shall abide in my love; even as I have kept my Father's commandments, and abide in his love.
>
> These things have I spoken unto you, that my joy might remain in you, and that your joy might be full.
>
> This is my commandment, That ye love one another, as I have loved you.
>
> Greater love hath no man than this, that a man lay down his life for his friends.
>
> Ye are my friends, if ye do whatsoever I command you.
>
> Henceforth I call you not servants; for the servant knoweth not what his lord doeth: but I have called you friends; for all things that I have heard of my Father I have made known unto you.
>
> Ye have not chosen me, but I have chosen you. (John 15:9–16)

What messages do we see embedded in Jesus' words? I suggest at least the following: first, significantly, the original Greek words in this passage that are translated as "love" are all *agape*, or a form of it, the same word that is rendered as "charity" in 1 Corinthians 13. "Friends" is translated from the now familiar (and common) *philōn*. Friendship and charity are officially and inextricably linked by Jesus in this post–Last Supper discourse. In Jesus' view, eternal *philōn* and *agape* are cut of the same cloth. Jesus' friendship is born of *agape*. The kind of friendship Jesus extends to his disciples, and expects them to practice, is bound up with the highest, most ennobling and selfless form of love we can contemplate. (There is another kind of love found in Greek literature that is never mentioned in the New Testament—that is *eros*. Erotic love is not of any interest to Jesus Christ, nor of importance in understanding the doctrines of friendship or eternal life.)

Second, Jesus tells his disciples that the foundation of the relationship between himself and all other people is *agape*, or charity. As the Father loved him, so he loves us with the purest and deepest love of all. Charity is not only the pure love of Christ but the pure love of the Father.

Third, because Jesus loves his disciples, he expects them to love each other—to cultivate *agape* for one another. It is a commandment. Even after the Resurrection Jesus continued to try to teach Peter and the others about the demands of *agape*. This was one of the reasons Jesus undertook his forty-day post-Resurrection ministry. The last recorded episode in John's Gospel seems to indicate that Peter did not yet fully grasp the lessons of *agape*. He and his associates had gone fishing in Galilee but caught nothing until a man on the shore told them where to fish. They finally recognized their Master, went to the shore, and found him preparing a fire and warm meal because they were cold, tired, and hungry.

Jesus had already performed an eternity's worth of service through his atoning sacrifice. But now he *showed* them through seemingly mundane acts the true nature of *agape*. He demonstrated his continuing concern for their economic and temporal welfare by helping them fish successfully. Then he stooped to cook dinner and care for their immediate physical comfort. He again sacrificed for them. When he finished feeding them physically, he fed them spiritually—teaching them about *agape*. Turning to Peter, he asked the chief Apostle if he loved (*agapas*) Jesus (see John 21:15). Peter responded not by declaring his own *agape* (pure love) for Jesus but his *philō* (affection and fondness). Jesus asked again, "Lovest [*agapas*] thou me?" (21:16) Peter again responded by declaring his *philō*. It is instructive that Jesus asked Peter a third time, but, at this point seems to have lowered expectations, perhaps to begin at Peter's level, by asking the chief Apostle, "Lovest [*phileis*] thou me?" or "Are you fond of me?" (21:17). Peter was grieved over the same kind of question. But it was not exactly the same question, and Peter seemed oblivious to its intent.

Was Jesus attempting to get Peter to perceive the difference between *agape* and *phileo*, even asking a less-intense question when Peter could not see the difference? Perhaps. Whatever the case, we may rest assured that Peter would come to understand fully the demanding nature of *agape* and would act accordingly. Peter would indeed "follow" Jesus, even to the point of suffering death for his Master's sake (see John 21:18–19). *Agape*, true friendship, the kind of friendship Jesus spoke of, demands much (even everything?) of all who profess the deepest kind of love for the Savior.

Fourth, the greatest testament of Jesus' love (*agape*, or charity) for others is the sacrifice of his perfect life. Willingly giving up his life is the great exhibition or demonstration of his love or charity toward others. Of this, Elder Holland made an arresting statement. He said we are to "cherish" charity. "That is, all Christians should try to love as the Savior loved, showing pure, redeeming compassion for all." Interesting. *We* are to demonstrate pure, redeeming compassion. It isn't just the Savior who does that; we are supposed to do that as well. It is only on this basis that true, faithful, and lasting friendship with Jesus Christ is actually possible. However, and here is the bombshell, "Unfortunately few, if any, mortals have been entirely successful in this endeavor. . . . *True* charity has been known only once." To repeat, true charity has been known only once! Yet "this does not in any way minimize the commandment that we are to try to acquire this kind of love for one another."[32]

Ironically, the pure love of Christ, which is precisely that—Christ's own love—is also that which aids us, assists, complements and strengthens our sometimes weak or flagging quest to acquire the pure love of Christ. Such bestowals of his love to assist us in the very acquisition of his love are part of the grace of Christ—the enabling power to allow us to "do all things through Christ which strengtheneth [you and] me" (Philippians 4:13).

Fifth, the disciples and, by extension, all individuals may become the friends of the Savior *if* they keep his commandments and honor his sacrifice. Jesus' friendship is an extension of his love, but it is *not* automatic. Jesus does the choosing as to whom his friends will be. We do not choose him to be our friend; he chooses us—which leads to the last point.

Sixth, while Jesus' love is constant, his friendship is not. There is a special relationship with Jesus that is reserved for those who keep his commandments (or who seek to do so). That special relationship is founded on righteousness and is called friendship with the Savior.

The prophet Nephi summarized this last point using different words, but one believes the meaning is the same: "Behold, the Lord esteemeth all flesh as one; [but] he that is righteous is favored of God" (1 Nephi 17:35).

I believe that the aggregate of the Savior's words found in the New Testament, as well as his whole life, show that he loves us and constantly desires to help us; he wishes all people would think enough of him to desire his friendship. But I also believe that his friendship, which by definition is an eternal relationship since he is eternal (see D&C 19:10), is not handed out cheaply! His friendship demands something, and it means something—it is worth something. What it demands from mortals is allegiance enough to be strictly obedient, to love others as Jesus loves. What that is worth is nothing less than the offer to enjoy the greatest of all the gifts of God, eternal life, also called the riches of eternity (see D&C 14:7; 6:7; 38:39). In other words, the Savior's *friendship* is synonymous with *eternal life*.

Space does not permit us to examine in depth all of the passages that help us appreciate what it cost the Savior to *be* our Savior and extend his unique friendship to us. But we may rest assured that

> all the negative aspects of human existence brought about by the Fall, Jesus Christ absorbed into himself. He experienced vicariously in Gethsemane [and on the cross] all the private griefs and heartaches, all the physical pains and handicaps, all the emotional burdens and depressions of the human family. . . . Having personally lived a perfect life, he then chose to experience our imperfect lives. In . . . Gethsemane and on the Cross . . . he lived a billion billion lifetimes of sin, pain, disease, and sorrow. God has no magic wand with which to simply wave bad things into non-existence. The sins that he remits, he remits by making them his own and suffering them. The pain and heartache that he relieves, he relieves by suffering them himself. These things can be transferred, but they cannot be simply wished or waved away. They must be suffered. Thus we owe him not only for our spiritual cleansing from sin, but for our physical, mental and emotional healings as well, for he has borne these infirmities for us also.[33]

This great transfer, great substitution (see 2 Corinthians 5:21), is at the heart of Jesus Christ's offer of friendship. His personal and infinite sacrifice is an infinite gift, infinitely superior to any other gift given by one friend to another. This great substitution was well expressed by the church father Athanasius of Alexandria (296–373): "For He [God] was made man that we [man] might be made God."[34]

Summary and Conclusions

To sum up, we return to where we began our discussion, to the statement made by the Prophet Joseph Smith about the place of friendship in Mormonism. But let us quote it within its context. In July of 1843, less than a year before his martyrdom, Joseph said:

> Let me be resurrected with the Saints, whether I ascend to heaven, or descend to hell, or go to any other place. And if we go to hell, we will turn the devils out of doors and make a heaven of it. Where this people are, there is good society. What do we care where we are, if the society be good? I don't care what a man's character is; if he's my friend—a true friend, I will be a friend to him, and preach the Gospel of salvation to him, and give him good counsel, helping him out of his difficulties. Friendship is one of the grand fundamental principles of Mormonism [designed] to revolutionize and civilize the world, and cause wars and contentions to cease and men to become friends and brothers.[35]

Perhaps like me, many readers have heard or read that statement many times. And perhaps, like me, many have not paid attention to what follows it. But here is how the Prophet ended this particular discussion on friendship: "Even the wolf and the lamb shall dwell together, the leopard shall lie down with the kid, the calf, the young lion and the fatling; and a little child shall lead them, the bear and the cow shall lie down together, and the sucking child shall play on the hole of the asp [viper], and the weaned child shall play on the cockatrice's den; and they shall not hurt or destroy in all my holy mountain, saith the Lord of hosts."[36]

This last statement is almost an exact quotation from Isaiah 11:6–9, and is a clear reference to the conditions that will exist during the Millennium. Because of it, I now see something else behind the Prophet's discussion of the concept of friendship. I believe that Joseph Smith saw a connection between the principle or doctrine of friendship and the environment that will exist during the Millennium. The atmosphere of the millennial reign of Christ on earth is the same that forms the core of true and loyal friendships. Bluntly stated, true, loyal, and righteous friendship is the vehicle provided to prepare us to enjoy the environment of the Millennium and, beyond that, the environment of the celestial kingdom, where the needs of all are met. That is the environment of charity, or the pure love of Christ. Friendship is part of a schooling process that molds us and prepares us for the environment of the Millennium and the celestial kingdom, where all will enjoy the friendship of the Lord Jesus Christ—and then God the Father. In fact, it is friendship that will maintain the righteous environment of the Millennium for a thousand years and the celestial kingdom for eternity.

Our friendships as mortals not only bless our lives here and now but are also a way for Deity to see if we can and will prepare ourselves to become the kind of beings fit to enjoy millennial and celestial environments and be worthy of the friendship of the Gods. Friends of the kind described in prophetic discourses are to be united in one overarching purpose: to help each other prepare for exaltation; they are to be "united according to the union required by the law of the celestial kingdom" (D&C 105:4). This, I submit, is the mind and will of God as it relates to friendship.

It is now clear to me that, indeed, friendship is one of the grand, fundamental principles of the restored gospel of Jesus Christ, as Joseph Smith stated from his expansive perspective. The reach of friendship extends far and its influence deep. Little wonder that President Gordon B. Hinckley stated that all members of The Church of Jesus Christ of Latter-day Saints need three critical things in their lives in order for their associations with the Church to remain vibrant: a friend, a responsibility, and nourishment by the good word of God.[37] Should we not seek to cultivate the kind of friendship Mormon's instruction comprehends? After all is said and done, aren't we nothing in the Lord's eyes if we do not possess the qualities and characteristics upon which eternal friendship is predicated (see Moroni 7:46)?

Notes

1. Manuscript History of the Church of Jesus Christ of Latter-day Saints, July 23, 1843, vol. E-1, 1680, Church History Library, Salt Lake City (hereafter cited as Manuscript History of the Church).
2. Manuscript History of the Church, July 23, 1843, vol. E-1, 1680.
3. Manuscript History of the Church, August 16, 1842, vol. D-1, 1372.
4. Manuscript History of the Church, August 22, 1842, vol. D-1, 1381–82.
5. William Shakespeare, *Julius Caesar*, act 4, scene 3, line 89.
6. Mark Water, comp., *The New Encyclopedia of Christian Quotations* (Grand Rapids, MI: Baker Books, 2000), 385.
7. Water, *The New Encyclopedia of Christian Quotations*, 385.
8. Benjamin F. Johnson to George F. Gibbs, 1903, 6–8, Benjamin Franklin Johnson Papers, 1852–1911, Church History Library, Salt Lake City.
9. Manuscript History of the Church, August 23, 1842, vol. D-1, 1383.
10. Joseph Smith to Emma Smith, November 12, 1838, Community of Christ Library and Archives, Independence, Missouri.
11. *Discourses of Brigham Young*, sel. John A. Widtsoe (Salt Lake City: Deseret Book, 1971), 271–73.
12. David O. McKay, in Conference Report, April 1940, 116.
13. Aristotle, *Nicomachean Ethics*, trans. Martin Ostwald (Englewood Cliffs, NJ: Prentice Hall, 1962), 214.
14. Aristotle, *Nicomachean Ethics*, 215. The quotation from Homer is found in *Iliad* X, 224.
15. Aristotle, *Nicomachean Ethics*, 214n1.
16. It is really only after the time of the early Greek poet Hesiod that "friendship" becomes an equal partner with love as a definition for *philia*. See Aristotle, *Nicomachean Ethics*, 214n1.
17. Aristotle, *Nicomachean Ethics*, 214n1.
18. Aristotle, *Nicomachean Ethics*, 214n1.
19. *A Lexicon Abridged from Lidell and Scott's Lexicon* (Oxford: Clarendon Press, 1976), 3.
20. Aristotle, *Nicomachean Ethics*, 217.
21. Aristotle, *Nicomachean Ethics*, 217–19.
22. Aristotle, *Nicomachean Ethics*, 219.

23. Ben Witherington, *A Week in the Life of Corinth* (Downers Grove, IL: IVP Academic, 2012), 39.
24. Richard G. Scott, "The Comforting Circle of True Friendship," *Ensign*, July 1983, 65. This essay was originally presented as a devotional address given at Brigham Young University, August 10, 1982.
25. See, for example, Megan McKenna and Tony Cowan, *Keepers of the Story* (Maryknoll, NY: Orbis Books, 1997), 79–80.
26. Burton Feldman, *Einstein's Genius Club* (New York: Arcade Publishing, 2011).
27. John Shelton, "When I Work with You We Both Succeed," *Lindon Character Connection*, January 2010, 1.
28. Neal A. Maxwell, "Meekness—A Dimension of True Discipleship," *Ensign*, March 1983, 71–72.
29. Aristotle, *Nicomachean Ethics*, 218–19.
30. Jeffrey R. Holland, "Laborers in the Vineyard," *Ensign*, May 2012, 33.
31. Richard G. Scott, "The Comforting Circle of True Friendship," 64.
32. Jeffrey R. Holland, *Christ and the New Covenant* (Salt Lake City: Deseret Book, 1997), 336.
33. Stephen E. Robinson, remarks at Religious Education prayer meeting, February 12, 1992.
34. Athanasius, *On the Incarnation*, section 54.
35. Manuscript History of the Church, July 23, 1843, vol. E-1, 1680.
36. Manuscript History of the Church, July 23, 1843, vol. E-1, 1680.
37. Gordon B. Hinckley, "Converts and Young Men," *Ensign*, May 1997, 47. It is interesting that most scriptural and prophetic instruction on friendship does not link it directly to marriage. A significant exception is Elder Marlin K. Jensen, "Friendship: A Gospel Principle," *Ensign*, May 1999, 64–65.

"The Work of Translating"
The Book of Abraham's Translation Chronology[1]

Kerry Muhlestein and Megan Hansen

One of Joseph Smith's great gifts was translation. While millions have benefitted from his translation efforts, we understand very little of the process. This is particularly true of the Book of Abraham. Here we will investigate how much of the Book of Abraham was translated in Kirtland and how much in Nauvoo. Understanding this chronology will allow us to better perceive doctrinal developments within the Church and to more fully understand Joseph Smith's revelatory process.

We wish to note at the outset that we have not been able to reach a firm conclusion about this chronology. There are scholars who feel strongly about various possible timelines, and initially we were among these. We expected that the evidence would allow us to make a firm conclusion. Yet, as we followed the evidence, it became clear that the evidence is ambiguous. It may be stronger for one theory than others, but not enough to end debate. Therefore, we do not take a stand that is stronger than the evidence allows, but rather acknowledge that sometimes historical information forces us to live with a degree of ambiguity.

"THE WORK OF TRANSLATING"

Early Translation Efforts

On July 3, 1835, Michael Chandler arrived in Kirtland with four mummies and several pieces of papyrus, including two scrolls. Chandler invited Joseph Smith to examine the artifacts, which Joseph did the next morning; Chandler then allowed him to take the papyri home for a more thorough examination.[2] Joseph apparently completed some translation by Sunday, July 5, because on that day Oliver Cowdery read to Chandler from some leaves the Prophet had translated.[3] Joseph Smith felt they needed to acquire the papyri, so he raised $2,400 for the purchase.[4] He immediately began translation. About this time they learned the papyri contained records of Abraham and Joseph of Egypt.[5] If it was not until after they acquired the papyri that they made this discovery, it is not clear what Joseph translated on July 4 or 5 that convinced him to purchase the papyri. It seems more likely that they discovered this before purchasing the papyri and that the date for discovering it was misremembered when making later historical notes.

Assisted by his companions, the Prophet spent the rest of July "translating an alphabet of the Book of Abraham and arranging a grammar of the Egyptian language."[6] It is difficult to tell how much of the Book of Abraham itself was translated during that month. We have no record of translation in August or September. Moreover, Joseph spent much of August traveling to Michigan, and he spent a week in September at a Church conference in Portage, Ohio. William W. Phelps also noted in mid-September that they had not translated recently.[7] All of this suggests that the papyri lay virtually untouched during August and September.

That changed on October 1, when Smith, Phelps, and Cowdery were working on an Egyptian alphabet, and "the system of astronomy was unfolded" to them.[8] On October 7, Joseph "recommenced translating the ancient records."[9] The most intense period of translation, however, apparently occurred in November. On both November 19 and 20, Joseph "spent the day in translating the Egyptian records,"[10] making "rapid progress."[11] On November 24, Joseph translated in the afternoon,[12] and the following day he spent the whole day translating.[13] On November 26, Joseph's journal included this entry: "We spent the day in transcribing Egyptian characters from the papyrus."[14] In December, the study of Hebrew suddenly eclipsed any efforts to translate from the papyri or work on an Egyptian grammar. Thereafter, we have no record of translating from the papyri until 1842.

Later Translation Efforts

The Prophet retained an interest in the translation between 1835 and 1842, despite apparently not actively translating. In December of 1835, he noted that he was preparing a room for translation near the place he intended to store and display the papyri.[15] Nearly two years later the Kirtland high council received a request to appoint Willard Richards and Reuben Hedlock to assist in translating and printing the papyri.[16] While the motion was approved, the result was not realized for several years. Soon after this vote the antiquities were hidden and then secreted away to Far West, Missouri, because someone attempted to steal the mummies. Joseph Smith's incarceration in Missouri—from late 1838 to early 1839—forestalled continued translation. Only after he was freed, helped establish a new city in Illinois, and obtained a measure of peace would he again take up the Book of Abraham translation.

In mid-1840, Joseph again brought up translation with a high council, this time in Nauvoo, asking to be relieved from meeting his temporal needs so he could "commence the work of translating the Ejyptian records."[17] Just over a year later, Joseph instructed the Quorum of the Twelve to take over more of the affairs of the kingdom so he could attend to the "business of translating."[18]

It was not until early 1842 that efforts to publish the Book of Abraham began to bear fruit. Under the direction of Brigham Young, a call was issued to Church members asking them to pay their tithes so Joseph might have time to publish his translation of the Bible and the "record of Father Abraham."[19]

About this same time Joseph Smith took over editorship of the *Times and Seasons*. He intended to use this venue to publish the Book of Abraham in the March 1, 1842, edition, the first over which he would have full editorial control.[20] Thus, on February 23 and March 1, he worked with Reuben Hedlock to create the carving for Facsimile 1.[21] The March 1 edition of *Times and Seasons* contained Facsimile 1 and Abraham 1:1–2:18.

Joseph and his coeditors immediately began to prepare a second installment of the Book of Abraham. On March 4, the Prophet collaborated with Hedlock on the carving for Facsimile 2.[22] On March 8, the Prophet "Commenced Translating from the Book of Abraham, for the 10 No of the Times and seasons."[23] On the next day Joseph continued translating.[24]

On March 15, Facsimile 2 and additional text from the Book of Abraham were printed in *Times and Seasons*. On May 1, Facsimile 3 was printed. Although there were plans to publish more of the Book of Abraham,[25] that never happened.

WHAT WAS TRANSLATED WHEN?

The question remains open as to how much of the Book of Abraham Joseph translated by the end of 1835 and whether he translated a significant amount in 1842 while preparing the manuscripts. The earliest attested manuscripts of the Book of Abraham, however, make this question quite difficult to answer. Three manuscripts created in 1835 still survive, along with one that was begun in 1835 but finished in 1842.[26] None are the original translation manuscript, none are the same, and none of the 1835 documents go past Abraham 2:18.[27] Because the first *Times and Seasons* installment only published through Abraham 2:18, and because the Prophet's journal says he engaged in translation on two days between that installment and the second, it can be argued that Joseph Smith only translated up through Abraham 2:18 by the first publication and spent two days frantically translating in order to publish Abraham 2:19–5:21 in the next edition of the newspaper. This hypothesis explains why the ending points in one of the 1835 manuscripts and the 1842 first installment of publication match. This is fairly convincing, yet poses a few problems.

First, this hypothesis is based on an argument of silence. It is not clear what the 1835 manuscripts represent. That none are identical suggests that none of them represent a complete copy of what Joseph translated to that point. One contains a translation up to verse 18 of chapter 2, but the others do not make it that far. If we had not found the former manuscript, would we be justified in suggesting that Joseph translated only through Abraham 2:6 (the furthest verse present in the other 1835 manuscripts) and quickly translated verses 7–18 just before publishing the March 1 edition of the *Times and Seasons*? Clearly that suggestion would be incorrect, but we know that only because we found another manuscript showing otherwise.

A second problem with this argument lies in the amount of material translated. The latter part of 1835 was clearly the most intense time for translating the Book of Abraham, both in terms of time spent translating and in terms of how much the antiquities seemed to occupy the Prophet's thoughts and journal entries. While we cannot tell how much time was spent translating in July, we know of at least three days wherein he did some translating (it was likely more), and if we count the day that the "principles of astronomy were unfolded," as well as the other days we know he spent on translating, Joseph spent at least eight and a half days translating in the latter half of 1835. If we were to suppose that he translated from Abraham 1:1 through Abraham 2:18 during that time, that would mean that he translated 49 verses, or 2,149 words, averaging almost 6 verses or 253 words a day.[28]

In contrast, with much fuller journal coverage for the first part of 1842, there are only one and a half days where Joseph Smith noted that he was translating. Because of the fairly robust journals from those months and since the March 8 entry notes that he "commenced" translating,[29] we can be reasonably sure he did not do any translating before this; moreover, given the journal notations afterwards, we can also be fairly sure he did not translate anything afterwards. If we were to suppose that on these days he translated Abraham 2:19–5:21, then during that day and a half he translated 88 verses, or 3,340 words, averaging just over 58 verses or 2,226 words a day. This would suggest he translated about 9 times faster in 1842 than 1835. This seems unlikely. Yet, because all things are possible with God and because it is worthwhile to more fully develop a picture of Joseph's translation efforts, we will examine other kinds of evidence.

Sometime before September 29, 1835, Oliver Cowdery recorded, "We diligently sought for the right of the fathers, and the authority of the holy priesthood, and the power to administer the same; for we desired to be followers of righteousness, and in the possession of greater knowledge, even the knowledge of the mysteries of the kingdom of God."[30] The language clearly draws from the first few verses of the Book of Abraham. Because no translation was performed in August and September, this indicates that at least some was performed in July.

Similarly, between 1835 and 1842, a number of writings mention topics that seem to arise from the text of Abraham 3–5. Because no translation activity seems to have taken place between December 1835 and March 1842, any evidence of material from Abraham 3–5 between those dates suggests that Joseph translated those chapters in 1835.

For example, in the "Grammar and Alphabet of the Egyptian Language" (GAEL), which seems to have been created during the latter half of 1835, appears the line "The first Being—supreme intelligence."[31] This is evocative of the language in Abraham 3:19. This does not necessitate that Abraham 3:19 had been translated by the time GAEL 3 was created,[32] but it strongly suggests it. Likewise, a few pages later in the grammar a discussion of Abraham being foreordained and chosen to go to Egypt to preach the gospel appears.[33] These are concepts found only in Abraham 3, again strongly suggesting the translation had proceeded at least that far before the end of 1835. These last two attestations are important because, unlike many other references to astronomy that could come from either Facsimile 2 or Abraham 3, these two phrases appear only in Abraham 3. This strengthens the likelihood that other astronomical references were linked to Abraham 3, again indicating that the translation had reached that stage by the end of 1835.

Similarly, the word "Shinehah" is attested in Abraham 3:13, where it is part of the astronomical explanation given there.[34] However, in section 86 of the 1835 edition of Doctrine and Covenants,[35] the word "Shinehah" is used as a code for "Kirtland."[36] This happens again in the heading of section 96,[37] as well as three times in section 98.[38] While it is possible that this was a code word that Joseph randomly created and then later inserted into Abraham 3, it seems more likely that he translated through Abraham 3 and then borrowed a word from that text. If this assumption is correct, then, again, Joseph had translated Abraham 3 before the end of 1835.

As mentioned above, in early October the principles of astronomy were unfolded to Smith and others while working on a grammar.[39] We cannot be certain this is tied directly to any text from the Book of Abraham, but it seems most likely that either an understanding of Facsimile 2 or a translation of Abraham 3 was provided at this time. Given the references to chapter 3 in the Grammar, that text is the likely referent. Further evidence strengthens this supposition, as is evident when we examine the principles of astronomy outlined in Abraham 3 and alluded to in Facsimile 2, which were frequently employed by Joseph in following years.

As a case in point, when Wilford Woodruff was set apart as a member of the First Quorum of the Seventy, he was told "that [he] should visit COLUB."[40] Later, in December of 1838, Woodruff again spoke of "COLOB."[41] Both of these journal entries make it clear that Joseph's colleagues were familiar with Kolob. Given the paucity of other or earlier references to Kolob in the documentary record, these mentions in Woodruff's journal likely serve as evidence of familiarity with Facsimile 2 or Abraham 3, indicating that knowledge of Kolob arose in 1835.

A similar example comes from a May 6, 1838, record of a Joseph Smith sermon: "This day, President Smith. delivered a discourse. to the people. . . . He also instructed the Church, in the misteries of the Kingdom of God; giving them a history of the Plannets &c. and of Abrahams writings upon the Plannettary system &c."[42] The specific phrase "writings upon the Plannettary system" strongly suggests that the Prophet was preaching about Abraham 3; nothing else in his revelations match that description. Despite this language, the entry could be referring to Joseph's understanding of Facsimile 2. It may also be that while looking at the papyri the Prophet received clear enough impressions about what the Book of Abraham contained that he could preach about text he had not yet actually translated. Still, the most straightforward reading of this journal entry is that Joseph Smith had read Abraham's writings about astronomy. Only Abraham 3 fits this description. Because this is the most straightforward reading, it should be assumed that Joseph translated Abraham 3 during 1835.

During the Prophet's 1839 imprisonment in Liberty Jail, he wrote an "Epistle to the Church" wherein he employed language found in the Book of Abraham. Part of his letter describes:

> a time to come, in the which nothing shall be withheld whether there be one God or many Gods they shall be manifest all thrones and dominions, principalities and powers, shall be revealed and set

> forth upon all who have endured valiantly for the Gospel of Jesus Christ, and also if there be bounds set to the Heavens, or to the Seas, or to the Dry Land, or to the Sun Moon or Stars, all the times of their revolutions, all the appointed days, months and years, and all the days of their days, months and years, and all their glories, laws, and set times shall be revealed in the days of the dispensation of the fulness of times according to that which was ordained in the midst of the Council of the Eternal God of all other Gods, before this world was.[43]

The above references to multiple Gods could reflect the use of the term "gods" in Abraham 4, a concept that will be discussed further below. The word "revolutions" used in reference to astronomical bodies occurs in the scriptures only in Abraham 3:4 and in D&C 121. While not unique to the Book of Abraham, the use of the word "appointed" when referring to time occurs in Abraham 3:4.[44] The phrase "set times" (or slight variations of it) occurs in Abraham 3:6, 7, and 10.[45] The final reference in this paragraph of the letter that seems to refer to the Book of Abraham is the mention of "the Council of the Eternal God of all other Gods, before this world was." Abraham 3:22–28 describes the council held in the premortal existence. Abraham 4 and 5 further discuss a multiplicity of gods being part of creation. Although many of these phrases are found throughout the scriptures, the use of all of them together in one paragraph seems to link this excerpt with the last three chapters of the Book of Abraham.

A similar possibility is attested in Joseph Smith's teachings from January of 1841, when he taught that the phrase "'without form and void' was better translated 'empty and desolate.' The word 'created' should be 'formed and organized'. . . . Spirits are eternal."[46] While this language evokes that of Abraham 4:1–2, it may be that the Prophet's study of Hebrew evoked both (as further discussed below). This same sermon continues to discuss elements of a premortal council that are similar to Abraham 3:27–28, which is not associated with the Prophet's Hebrew studies. The idea of a premortal council is present in earlier revelations, such as the Book of Moses, but the language in the sermon is more similar to Abraham 3, again suggesting an 1835 translation of Abraham 3.[47]

Had They Translated Beyond What We Now Have?

While our examination thus far suggests that by the end of 1835 Joseph translated through Abraham 5—everything we have in the current text of the Book of Abraham—there is some evidence suggesting he translated even further. For example, Anson Call saw the Book of Abraham manuscript arrive in Far West in 1838 and helped take it to the Prophet's office, where the Prophet said, "'Sit down and we will read to you from the translations of the Book of Abraham' Oliver Cowdery then read until he was tired when Thomas Marsh read making altogether about two hours."[48] The current text of the Book of Abraham can be easily read aloud in under half an hour. Even if half of the "reading" was really discussion, it would still imply that by 1838 they already had twice as much of the Book of Abraham as we now have. Yet Call's wording indicates they did not discuss but actually read from the text the entire time—connoting that they had already translated four times as much as we now have.

Of course, we must be careful in using sources created some time after the event, and we cannot be certain Call was fully accurate in knowing how long the reading lasted. His writing seems to have taken place sometime afterwards, yet his ability to give a precise date suggests he was consulting a diary. The accuracy of the account is questioned by the claim that Oliver Cowdery was part of the group present. Cowdery had been excommunicated some months earlier and was not in Far West at this date. Yet, while Call may have misremembered who did the reading, it is still likely that he accurately recalled that the reading took more than an hour. This source strongly suggests that the Book of Abraham had been translated beyond Abraham 5 before the end of 1835. It would take fairly strong evidence to discard this historical source, as problematic as it is.

Before the end of 1835, Oliver Cowdery wrote a description of the papyri, mentioning that it seemed to contain information about the Creation and the Fall.[49] The current Book of Abraham does not contain material about the Fall. While it could be assumed this means they had already translated up to Abraham 5 and beyond, it is also quite possible that Cowdery was either recording their impressions of what they would eventually translate or

"THE WORK OF TRANSLATING"

his impressions of the meaning of the drawings on the papyri. Because he also wrote that some of those drawings were about the Fall, the latter seems quite likely.

Within the next few years, William West visited Kirtland, saw the mummies and papyri, and wrote of the experience in an anti-Mormon pamphlet, which he published in 1837. He wrote, "The records are those of Abraham and Joseph, and contain important information respecting the creation, the fall of man, the deluge, the Patriarchs, the book of Mormon, the lost tribes, the gathering, the end of the world, the judgment, &c. &c. This is as near as I can recollect; if there is an error I hope some of the Mormons will point it out, and I will recall it."[50] West is explicit that he was not absolutely sure if he remembered the topics covered in the papyri correctly. Yet, if he was correct, he was at least told the papyri contained a creation account, such as is found in Abraham 4 and 5, as well as information about things not mentioned in the current Book of Abraham, such as the deluge and lost tribes. Even if West recalled correctly and if he had been told accurately what Joseph Smith had said were in the papyri, this could merely represent the impressions of the Prophet regarding what was in the papyri as opposed to his having specifically translated passages about those topics. The same is true of other accounts that mention the papyri containing accounts of topics not in the published version of the Book of Abraham, such as Albert Brown's recollection that the writings of Jacob were on the papyri,[51] William Appleby's account of the Fall and Creation,[52] or Josiah Quincy's recollection of the writings of Moses and Aaron being on the papyri.[53] Even if we should accept the accuracy of all of these accounts without question, which does not seem reasonable, they do not demonstrate anything beyond an impression of what could be on the papyri.

The evidence considered thus far is mixed. Most of it could be taken to mean that all of the current Book of Abraham, and perhaps more, was translated before 1835. Some of the evidence examined makes this same suggestion somewhat strongly and requires intentionally understanding the evidence differently than its most obvious reading in order to avoid such a conclusion. Now let us look at information that may give cause to read these documents differently.

Evidence for an 1842 Translation of Abraham 3–5

Besides the weak evidence that the 1835 Book of Abraham manuscripts contain material only up through Abraham 2:18, there is some additional evidence that may indicate Abraham 3–5 was not yet translated in 1835. We must also examine the recorded events during the 1842 publication of the Book of Abraham and analyze the influence Joseph Smith's study of Hebrew had on that publication.

As was noted above, the first *Times and Seasons* installment of the Book of Abraham published the same material present in one of the four earliest manuscripts. The precision of that break, at Abraham 2:18, seems to go beyond coincidence. Furthermore, the Prophet's journal does not record him "translating" in preparation for that first publication, but it does record him doing so for a day and a half before the next installment. No further mention of translation occurs, and even though another facsimile was later published, no further publication of the text took place either. One would think that if more of the text had been translated it would have been published alongside Facsimile 3. Clearly there was a desire to publish more, and obviously the paper had the time and capacity to do so. The story that most easily explains those historical facts could be hypothesized thus: as Joseph was eager to publish from the Book of Abraham in his first full edition as editor of the *Times and Seasons*, he quickly published up through Abraham 2:18, which was all that he had translated up to that point. Still eager to publish more of the ancient record, he spent more time frantically translating, and in the next edition of the paper he published the new material he had translated during those few days. While wanting to translate more, he did not, and thus he half-heartedly kept up with his desire by publishing another facsimile and its explanation. A year later the paper promised that he intended to publish more, but because he never translated more, further publications didn't occur.

While we have no way of verifying that narrative, it does fit many of the facts well. On the other hand, it is reasonable to suppose that when Joseph said he was "translating" between the first and second installments of publication, he was actually revising. We know that the Prophet did make inspired revisions in most, if not all, of his other revelations. Calling these changes "translation" is perfectly in keeping with his broader translation and publication patterns. Yet such a scenario fails to explain why the break after the first installment matches so well the break in one of the 1835 manuscripts or why no more of the Book of Abraham was published, either along with Facsimile 3 or at any point thereafter.

Further evidence comes from examining Hebrew aspects of the Book of Abraham. Chapter 3 is full of Hebrew transliterations that match perfectly with the Hebrew grammar, lexicon, and lessons that Joseph began after he stopped translating Egyptian at the end of 1835. For example, transliterations such as "Kokob" and "Kokaubeam" are clearly influenced by the Hebrew grammars Smith was studying.[54] On the surface, this suggests Joseph translated these phrases after he began his study of Hebrew and that his transliterations were influenced by his grammar book. Yet it seems equally as likely that these are glosses, the "translation" efforts of 1842 were actually Joseph editing translated text and that this editing included inserting newly acquired Hebrew phrases.[55]

The influence of Joseph's grammar, authored by Rabbi Seixas, is also evident in the creation account portrayed in Abraham 4 and 5. Phrases like "organized and formed" (Abraham 4:1) instead of "created,"[56] "expanse," instead of "firmament,"[57] "heavens" (Abraham 4:1) instead of "heaven,"[58] and "empty and desolate" (Abraham 4:2) as opposed to "without form and void"[59] are all phrases Joseph likely picked up from his Hebrew study and some of which he referenced elsewhere. Even an apparent use of the Hebrew *hiphil* verb form is present in Abraham 4:4. Various words and phrases which were clearly influenced by Joseph Smith's Hebrew studies are used throughout the entire narrative of chapters 4 and 5.[60] The same is true of representing creation being brought about by "gods" instead of "God," something that Joseph Smith argued could be demonstrated in the Hebrew name for God.[61] These elements are so thoroughly interwoven in the text of Abraham 4 and 5 that it is difficult to imagine them as glosses. Rather, they seem to represent integral features of the text. This is fairly convincing evidence that at least Abraham 4 and 5 were translated after 1835.

There is another issue to consider here. While phrases such as "organize" and "desolate" seem to argue for the influence of the Prophet's study of

Hebrew, his use of "gods" throughout chapters 4 and 5 may actually argue against it. This bears further examination.

While it is true that *Elohim* is a plural form of the word for "god" in Hebrew, it is not the standard plural form, which would be *elim*. It is almost certainly during his study of Hebrew at the end of 1835 and the beginning of 1836 that Joseph first saw any linguistic evidence in Hebrew that supported the notion of a plurality of gods. Yet the way he would have encountered this does not seem like it would have propelled him towards that interpretation. The word *Elohim* first appears in the Seixas grammar on page 34, but there it is only mentioned; it is not explained at all. On page 85 the explanation for this word is "God; a sing. noun with a plur. form."[62] It then refers the reader to *Elo'ah* in the lexicon. The lexicon referred to is the Gibbs lexicon, which contains a definition for *Elo'ah* on page 12. Under that entry is a subentry on *Elohim*: "A god, by way of eminence, the true God, Jehovah. (1) as the ordinary plural, gods; also spoken of kings, princes, magistrates, or judges, and perhaps angels." The definition speaks of the word being applied to gods, but "preeminently to the true God, Jehovah, also a godlike form or apparition. This *pluralis excellentiae* is generally construed with singular adjectives and verbs, but there are many exceptions."[63] Both of these definitions certainly leave open the possibility of a plural interpretation of the word, but they are both clear that it is not normally to be interpreted that way, and grammatically it does not normally function that way. In other words, they teach that, unless there is a reason to do so, the word should be construed as singular. Similarly, the other grammar Joseph had access to defined the word thus: "For the sake of emphasis, the Hebrews commonly employed most of the words which signify Lord, God, etc. in the plur. form, but with the sense of the singular. This is called *pluralis excellentiae*."[64]

While we cannot read Joseph's mind, he likely would have taken these entries at face value without an *a priori* reason to do otherwise, meaning that unless something he already encountered caused him to disagree, Joseph would probably rely on what these three publications said, and take *Elohim* as used in Genesis 1, which is paired with a singular verb, suggesting a singular noun in a majestic form. Yet he did not do so and in fact argued with his Jewish Hebrew teacher, whom he greatly respected, about this very point. Years later he would say, "I once asked a learned Jew, 'If the Hebrew language compels us to render all words ending in *heim* in the plural, why not render the first *Eloheim* plural?' He replied, 'That is the rule with few exceptions; but in this case it would ruin the Bible.' He acknowledged I was right."[65] The Prophet is probably referring to Rabbi Seixas, with whom he was studying Hebrew, who, it seems, when pressed by Joseph, acknowledged that the noun was plural, but did not agree with translating it that way. The Prophet would probably not have disagreed with his respected teacher, his teacher's grammar book, and the other Hebrew books he was using, if he had not already come to believe that there was more than one god at work in the creation story.

Clearly Joseph Smith already knew that God the Father and his Son, Jesus Christ, were two separate beings. Visions had made that clear to him, and he had spoken of it before. Yet nothing he saw, revealed, or taught before 1835 would have pushed him so forcefully towards the idea that there was a plurality of gods acting in the creation. By far the most likely explanation for his determination to use his nascent Hebrew skills to say there were multiple gods at work, and to continue to use those skills to verify and justify such teachings, is that he had already translated Abraham 4 and 5. Surely other revelations and teachings that we may not know of could have brought him to this point, but the most forthright explanation is that Joseph learned of a multiple-god creation when translating Abraham 4 and 5 and then saw a confirmation of this in a less-likely but possible use of Hebrew. It is difficult to construe this particular use of Hebrew elsewise.

If this is true, then Joseph's other uses of seemingly Hebraic-influenced phrases had also been translated *before* his study of Hebrew. In this case his Hebrew study must have also heavily influenced the way he reworded his translation of the Book of Abraham as he prepared it for publication. This would also explain why he spent time "translating" before the second installment of the Book of Abraham and not the first. It is in that second installment he would need to so thoroughly rework the text in order to incorporate the Hebrew-influenced phrases that said so well what he already learned when he first translated the text. We have tried writing the text of Abraham 4 and 5 using conventional language and then reworking it using new phrases that could arise from studying

Hebrew. We found that while it is extensive, it is not overly so; nor does it require more than a very heavy job of editing, the kind of editing that might take a day and a half. There are about 150 words that would be changed due to Joseph's understanding of Hebrew. These changes are repetitive, coming from less than a dozen words, phrases, or ideas. By far the most common change would have been changing nouns, pronouns, and verbs incumbent with representing a plurality of gods, since these changes represent almost half of the possibly Hebrew-influenced phraseology. If the plurality of gods was already present in the Abraham 4–5 text, as it seems, then there are around 80 other phrases the Prophet may have edited in order to better reflect his Hebrew-enhanced understanding of the creation. This certainly would require a somewhat extensive rewriting, but not an unusual amount, and it is not difficult to work in such changes to an already existing text. Because the Prophet would have been consulting his Hebrew grammars and lexicon during this process, he would be all the more likely to use the phrase "translate." In summary, this hypothesis purports that Joseph translated at least through Abraham 5 by the end of 1835 and then heavily edited the last three chapters in 1842 to reflect more fully both his Hebrew learning and any fuller understanding of the gospel he had developed since his 1835 translation.

Conclusion

This last theory can account for almost all of the evidence (summarized in the chart below). Subscribing to this theory means there is no blaring discrepancy between the translation speed of 1835 and 1842. It incorporates all evidence from writings and sermons that suggest Joseph translated through Abraham 4 and 5 by the end of 1835. It explains the two hours it took to read the translation in 1838. It also accounts for the varying ways Hebrew was incorporated into the text. Yet it does not account for the twice-repeated break at Abraham 2:18, which is a weak but important piece of evidence. Nor does it account for the fact that the Prophet seems to have wanted to publish more of the Book of Abraham but did not. This last fact remains best explained by the notion that he wanted to publish more but had not yet translated more.

"THE WORK OF TRANSLATING"

Evidence	Suggests	Strength of suggestion based on this evidence
The earliest Book of Abraham manuscripts end at either Abraham 1:3, 2:2, 2:6, or 2:18.	Only up through Abraham 2:18 was translated in Kirtland.	Weak
The one and a half days of translation in 1842 do not allow much time to translate Abraham 2:19–5:21.	More than Abraham 2:18 had been translated in Kirtland.	Fairly strong
GAEL 3 uses language very similar to Abraham 3:19.	Abraham 3 was translated in Kirtland.	Strong
GAEL 6 uses language similar to Abraham 3:22.	Abraham 3 was translated in Kirtland.	Strong
Principles of astronomy were unfolded in October 1835.	Either Abraham 3 or an understanding of Facsimile 2 was revealed in Kirtland, perhaps just a revelatory impression.	Fairly strong
"Shinehah" is used as a code word in the 1835 D&C.	Abraham 3 had been translated by then.	Fairly strong
Wilford Woodruff mentions Kolob in 1837 and 1838.	Either Abraham 3 or an understanding of Facsimile 2 was revealed in Kirtland.	Strong
"Shinehah" is used in D&C 117:8.	Abraham 3 was translated in 1835.	Weak

Evidence	Suggests	Strength of suggestion based on this evidence
In 1839 Joseph Smith talks about astronomy and where God resides.	Either Abraham 3 or an understanding of Facsimile 2 was revealed in Kirtland.	Fairly strong
In 1838 Joseph Smith speaks on Abraham's astronomical writings.	Abraham 3 was translated in 1835.	Strong
In 1839 Joseph Smith teaches about premortal council and organization of man.	Abraham 3 was translated in 1835.	Fairly strong
In 1839 Joseph Smith writes about plurality of gods and revolutions of planets and a council of the gods.	Abraham 3 and 4 were translated in 1835.	Moderate
In 1841 Joseph Smith speaks of Adam's death taking place in a 1,000-year "day."	Abraham 5 was translated in 1835.	Moderate
In 1828 Anson Call remembers reading out loud from the Book of Abraham for two hours.	More of the Book of Abraham was translated than we now have.	Strong
In 1835 Oliver Cowdery says the papyri contains information about the Fall.	More of the Book of Abraham was translated than we now have.	Weak

"THE WORK OF TRANSLATING"

Evidence	Suggests	Strength of suggestion based on this evidence
William West says he heard that the papyri contained information about the Fall, Flood, Patriarchs, and lost tribes in 1836 or 1837	More of the Book of Abraham was translated than we now have.	Weak
Albert Brown speaks of the papyri containing information about Jacob.	More of the Book of Abraham was translated than we now have.	Weak
William I. Appleby speaks of the papyri containing information about the Fall.	More of the Book of Abraham was translated than we now have.	Weak
Josiah Quincy speaks of the papyri containing information about Moses and Aaron.	More of the Book of Abraham was translated than we now have.	Weak
Joseph Smith says he was translating in between the first and second publications installments of the Book of Abraham.	The material after Abraham 2:18 had not yet been translated.	Moderate
Though Joseph Smith clearly intended to publish more of the Book of Abraham, he never did.	All that had been translated was published in 1842.	Fairly strong

Evidence	Suggests	Strength of suggestion based on this evidence
Abraham 3 contains Hebrew phrases influenced by the 1836 study of Hebrew.	Abraham 3 was translated after 1835, which means it was translated in 1842.	Weak
Phrases influenced by the Prophet's study of Hebrew are thoroughly interwoven in Abraham 4 and 5.	Abraham 4 and 5 were translated in 1842.	Strong
The translation of "Elohim" as "gods" seems to rely on an already formed idea that there was a plurality of gods.	Joseph Smith had already translated Abraham 4 (and probably 5) by the end of 1835.	Fairly strong

At this point, there is no theory that accounts for all of the evidence. Clearly, either we need to find more evidence or create another model. Such is not surprising when dealing with a process so heavily influenced by the Divine and so scattered or absent in the historical record. For the time being, the most we can do is say that it seems likely Joseph Smith translated all of the text of the Book of Abraham we now have, and perhaps even more, by 1835. While such a theory is plausible, it remains problematic because it is simultaneously incomplete *and* the most probable of the theories proposed thus far.

Notes

Editorial note from Kerry Muhlestein: Professor Robert Millet has had a profound impact on thousands, including me. He inspired me to work towards my current profession and has served as a model to which I aspire as a religious educator. His wisdom and foresight have helped chart the course of Religious Education at BYU in the broadest sense. Brother Millet is a great teacher of the Pearl of Great Price and understands the teachings of Joseph Smith better than anyone else I know. Because he and I often spoke of Joseph Smith's translation of the Book of Abraham, and because of his interests in that book and the teachings of the Prophet, an article that combines these subjects seems fitting for a volume honoring him.

1. The title is taken from a phrase in which Joseph Smith asked for time to engage in the "work of translating" the papyri. See Joseph Smith, "Memorial to High Council," June 18, 1840, Letterbook 2, Joseph Smith Collection, Church History Library, Salt Lake City.
2. "Dr. John Riggs," *Tullidge's Quarterly Magazine* 3, no. 3 (1884): 282.
3. "Dr. John Riggs," 282.
4. Joseph Coe, letter to Joseph Smith, January 1, 1844, L. Tom Perry Special Collections, Harold B. Lee Library, Brigham Young University, Provo, UT.
5. Manuscript History of the Church, B-1, 596, Church History Library, Salt Lake City. The entries for July 1835 seem to be written by Willard Richards, probably assisted by W. W. Phelps, in 1843.
6. Manuscript History of the Church, B-1, 596.
7. W. W. Phelps, letter to Sally Phelps, September 11, 1835, in Bruce A. Van Orden, ed., "Writing to Zion: The William W. Phelps Kirtland Letters," *BYU Studies* 33, no. 3 (1993): 563.
8. Dean C. Jessee, Mark Ashurst-McGee, and Richard L. Jensen, eds., *Journals, Volume 1: 1832–1839*, vol. 1 of the Journals series of *The Joseph Smith Papers*, ed. Dean C. Jessee, Ronald K. Esplin, and Richard Lyman Bushman (Salt Lake City: Church Historian's Press, 2008), 67 (hereafter *JSP*, J1).
9. *JSP*, J1:71.
10. *JSP*, J1:107.
11. *JSP*, J1:107.
12. *JSP*, J1:109.
13. *JSP*, J1:110.
14. *JSP*, J1:110–11.
15. *JSP*, J1:140.
16. Minute Book 1, or the Kirtland High Council Minute Book, December 1832– November 1837, MS 11871, folder 1, volume 1, CHL, Salt Lake City.

17. Joseph Smith, "To the honorable the High Council of the Church of Jesus Christ of Latter Day Saints" June 18, 1840, Joseph Smith Collection, MS 155, box 2, folder 4, Church History Library, Salt Lake City.
18. "Conference Minutes," *Times and Seasons*, September 1, 1841, 522.
19. Brigham Young and Willard Richards to the recorder's office, February 21, 1842, in *Times and Seasons*, March 1, 1842, 715.
20. See Joseph Smith, "To Subscribers," *Times and Seasons*, March 1, 1842, 710.
21. Andrew H. Hedges, Alex D. Smith, and Richard Lloyd Anderson, eds., *Journals, Volume 2: December 1841–April 1843*, vol. 2 of the Journals series of *The Joseph Smith Papers*, ed. Dean C. Jessee, Ronald K. Esplin, and Richard Lyman Bushman (Salt Lake City: Church Historian's Press, 2011), 36, 39 (hereafter *JSP*, J2).
22. *JSP*, J2: 40.
23. *JSP*, J2:42.
24. *JSP*, J2:42. See also Joseph Smith to Edward Hunter, March 9, 1842, in Dean C. Jessee, ed., *Personal Writings of Joseph Smith* (Salt Lake City: Deseret Book, 2002), 549–50.
25. "Notice," *Times and Seasons*, February 1, 1843, 95.
26. On these manuscripts, see Brian M. Hauglid, *A Textual History of the Book of Abraham: Manuscripts and Editions* (Provo, UT: Neal A. Maxwell Institute for Religious Scholarship, 2010).
27. One manuscript covers up to Abraham 1:3, another up to Abraham 2:2, another to Abraham 2:6, and one to Abraham 2:18. See Hauglid, *Textual History*, 6. Only the first of these contains the first few verses of Abraham 1.
28. Because we have probably underestimated the amount of time he spent translating, the average is probably lower than these numbers, but they represent an accurate enough figure for comparative purposes.
29. *JSP*, J2:42.
30. Oliver Cowdery, Patriarchal Blessing Book, 2 October 1835, cited in Joseph Fielding Smith, "Restoration of the Melchizedek Priesthood," *Improvement Era*, October 1904, 942–43; and H. Michael Marquardt, comp., *Early Patriarchal Blessings of The Church of Jesus Christ of Latter-day Saints* (Salt Lake City: Smith-Pettit Foundation, 2007), 3.
31. *Grammar and Alphabet of the Egyptian Language* (GAEL), Kirtland Egyptian papers circa 1835–1836, MS 1295, folder 1, CHL, Salt Lake City. 3.

32. GAEL 3 and 6 were likely created before October 1, 1835, but certainly before the end of 1835.
33. GAEL 6.
34. We are grateful to Matt Roper for pointing out the references to "Shinehah" and for general help in working through the ideas presented in this article. See also Hauglid, *Textual History*, 2.
35. Section LXXXVI in this edition corresponds with section 82 in the current edition.
36. This happens twice on page 220 of the 1835 edition.
37. Page 224 of the 1835 edition, corresponding to section 96 in the current edition.
38. Pages 241–43 of the 1835 edition, corresponding to section 104 of the current edition.
39. *JSP*, J1:67.
40. Scott G. Kenney, ed., *Wilford Woodruff's Journal: 1833–1898 Typescript* (Midvale, UT: Signature Books, 1983), 1:119.
41. Kenney, *Woodruff Journal*, 309.
42. *JSP*, J1:266.
43. Manuscript History of the Church, November 2, 1838–July 31, 1842, vol. C-1, 904[b], CHL, Salt Lake City.
44. Daniel 11:35, Galatians 4:2, and Alma 40:4 are other scriptural instances of variations of the phrase "appointed time."
45. "And the Lord said unto me: Now, Abraham, these two facts exist, behold thine eyes see it; it is given unto thee to know the times of reckoning, and the set time, yea, the set time of the earth upon which thou standest, and the set time of the greater light which is set to rule the day, and the set time of the lesser light which is set to rule the night. Now the set time of the lesser light is a longer time as to its reckoning than the reckoning of the time of the earth upon which thou standest. . . . And it is given unto thee to know the set time of all the starts that are set to give light, until thou come near unto the throne of God." (Abraham 3:6, 7, 10)
46. Andrew F. Ehat and Lyndon W. Cook, *The Words of Joseph Smith: The Contemporary Accounts of the Nauvoo Discourses of the Prophet Joseph Smith* (Provo, UT: Religious Studies Center, 1980), 27–28.
47. Similarly, in March of 1841 Joseph Smith taught: "Now as to Adam the Lord said in the day thou Shalt Eat there of thou shalt shurely Die Now the Day the Lord has Refferance too is spoken of By Petter a thousand of our years is with the Lord as one Day &c at the time the Lord said this to adam—there was No

mode of Counting time By Man, as man Now Counts time." William P. McIntire notebook, 15, March 9, 1841, MS 1014, folder 1, CHL, Salt Lake City. While there are a number of places wherefrom the notion that God measures time differently than man could arise, the language of this sermon most closely resembles Abraham 5:13. Again, the most straightforward explanation would be that the translation of Abraham 5 influenced the Prophet's sermon, but it could instead be that the concepts he gained elsewhere and expressed in this sermon influenced the language he employed when later translating Abraham 5. Still, without good contrary evidence, the *most likely* harmonization of the evidence gathered thus far is that the Prophet had translated through Abraham 5 before 1842.

48. Anson Call, journal of Anson Call, handwritten copy dated February 1879, MS 270.1 C156L 1987, CHL, Salt Lake City.

49. "Egyptian Mummies Ancient Records," *Latter Day Saints' Messenger and Advocate*, December 22, 1835, 236.

50. William S. West, *A Few Interesting Facts Respecting the Rise Progress and Pretensions of the Mormons* (Ohio: self-published, 1837), 4–5. Because West saw the mummies in the temple we can date his visit to either 1836 or 1837.

51. Albert Brown to Mr. James Brown, November 1, 1835, cited in Christopher C. Lund, "A Letter Regarding the Acquisition of the Book of Abraham," *BYU Studies* 30, no. 4 (Fall 1990): 1.

52. *William I. Appleby Autobiography and Journal*, July 6, 1848, MS 1401, folder 1, CHL, Salt Lake City, 72–73.

53. Josiah Quincy, *Figures of the Past from the Leaves of Old Journals* (Boston: Roberts Brothers, 1892), 386.

54. See Louis C. Zucker, "Joseph Smith as a Student of Hebrew," *Dialogue: A Journal of Mormon Thought* 3 (1968): 51. See also Karl C. Sandberg, "Knowing Brother Joseph Again: The Book of Abraham and Joseph Smith as Translator," *Dialogue: A Journal of Mormon Thought* 22, no. 4 (1989): 31.

55. On Joseph Smith "showing off" his Hebrew knowledge in the published text of the Book of Abraham, see Michael T. Walton, "Professor Seixas, the Hebrew Bible, and the Book of Abraham," in *Sunstone* 6 (1981): 42.

56. For example, see the first lexicon Joseph consulted: Josiah W. Gibbs, *A Manual Hebrew and English Lexicon, Including the Biblical Chaldee. Designed Particularly for Beginners* (New Haven: Hezekiah Howe, 1832), 36, where the word often translated as "create" has "to form" as the first meaning and "create" as the third possibility.

57. See the grammar book most used by Joseph Smith: J. Seixas, *Manual Hebrew Grammar, for the Use of Beginners* (Andover: Gould and Newman, 1834), 12, 21, 32. The pronunciation is on p. 12, and definitions and use are on pp. 21, 32.
58. See Seixas, *Manual Hebrew Grammar*, 22. We are grateful to Matt Grey, who pointed out this and other references to us and who has graciously talked through these issues with us.
59. See Gibbs, *A Manual Hebrew and English Lexicon*, 229 and 27, where the definitions match precisely how Joseph Smith used them in Abraham 4.
60. Matthew Grey is doing a more thorough study of this than we are undertaking here. We are grateful to him for his help and ideas as we prepared this paper.
61. See Joseph Smith's June 16, 1844, sermon in the Grove at Nauvoo. Ehat and Cook, *Words of Joseph Smith*, 379.
62. Seixas, *Manual Hebrew Grammar*, 85.
63. Gibbs, *A Manual Hebrew and English Lexicon*, 11.
64. Moses Stuart, *A Grammar of the Hebrew Language* (Andover: Gould and Newman), 180.
65. Joseph Smith's sermon in the Grove in Nauvoo. Ehat and Cook, *Words of Joseph Smith*, 379.

Was Noah's Flood the Baptism of the Earth?

Paul Y. Hoskisson and Stephen O. Smoot

> "I am the Earth,
> Thy mother; she within whose stony veins,
> To the last fibre of the loftiest tree
> Whose thin leaves trembled in the frozen air,
> Joy ran, as blood within a living frame,
> When thou didst from her bosom, like a cloud
> Of glory, arise, a spirit of keen joy!"[1]

The people who joined the Restoration in the second quarter of the nineteenth century were not *tabulae rasae*. Most, with some exceptions, came out of a Protestant background.[2] Therefore, it is to be expected that at least some Protestant understandings would find their way into the Restoration and remain in the Church. But the Restoration was much more than simply a rearranging of Protestant tenets or a reshuffling of contemporary ideas. In many ways, Latter-day Saint discourse ranged beyond its environment. Such is the case with Latter-day Saint understandings of the doctrinal significance of the Flood in Genesis.

This essay begins with a limited survey of traditional Protestant interpretations of the Flood. These traditional interpretations formed an interpretative backdrop for Latter-day Saints joining the Restoration. Latter-day Saint discourse, hesitatingly at first, soon blazed new trails and presented uniquely LDS understandings. One of these innovative understandings—namely, that the Flood was the baptism of a sentient earth—is based on a debatable reading of the nineteenth-century Mormon sources and can lead to questionable conclusions. Therefore, we argue for a nuanced understanding of these Restoration accretions that departs from the popular understanding that has been offered by some LDS scriptural exegetes.

Protestant Interpretations

The most prevalent nineteenth-century Protestant understandings of the Flood of Noah viewed it as a symbol of baptism—that is, the Flood was a type or symbol of Christian baptism and its cleansing nature. First Peter 3:18–21 provided the proof text for Protestant (as well as Latter-day Saint) commentators.

A sampling of nineteenth-century commentaries reveals a relatively uniform understanding that the Flood in the Old Testament cleansed the earth of wickedness. Just as Christian baptism cleanses individuals from sin, William Trollope wrote in 1835, "The preservation of Noah and his family in the ark from perishing by water is emblematic of baptism, inasmuch as it is only by baptism that Christians are admitted into the Church."[3] Henry Alford similarly reasoned that "the few in Noah's day were saved by water; we also are saved by water. The antitype to that water on which the ark floated, saving its inmates, is the water of baptism."[4]

Even C. F. Keil and F. Delitzsch, two highly influential German Protestant scholars of the second half of the nineteenth century, in a sophisticated analysis of 1 Peter 3, opined that the Flood of Noah contained dual symbolism. On the one hand, according to Keil and Delitzsch, the Flood represented "a judgment of such universality and violence as will only be seen again in the judgment at the end of the world," yet on the other, the Flood was also "an act of mercy which made the flood itself a flood of grace, and in that respect a type of baptism (1 Pet. iii. 21), and of life rising out of death."[5]

Even late in the nineteenth century, Protestant scholarly commentary perpetuated these themes. Edward Hayes Plumptre, in a Bible commentary published by Cambridge, observed, "At first it seems hard to see the parallelism between the flood which destroyed and the baptism which saves, but reflection will show that the Apostle may well have thought of the deluge as burying the old evils of the world and giving the human race, as it were, a fresh start, under new and better conditions, a world, in some sense, regenerated or brought into a new covenant with God, and therefore new relations to Him."[6]

This sampling of Protestant commentaries on the Flood narrative in Genesis and in 1 Peter 3 is representative of a persistent nineteenth-century Christian understanding of the Flood as, at the very least, symbolic of baptism. Though they stopped short of labeling the Flood a literal ordinance (*sacrament* in traditional Christian language),[7] they clearly thought of the Flood as accomplishing the same end for the earth that baptism does for mortals.[8]

Early Latter-day Saint Teachings Concerning the Flood as Baptism of the Earth

As would be expected, there is considerable overlap between nineteenth-century Latter-day Saint and Protestant understandings of the Flood as a cleansing of the earth of wickedness and therefore a symbolic prefiguring of Christian baptism. Yet Latter-day Saints seemed much more invested than Protestants in interpreting the Flood as a literal ordinance, perhaps because the Restoration presents stronger forms of sacramentalism than Protestantism does. This Latter-day Saint penchant for ordinances, as we will see, would bring its own set of complex issues into the discourse. First, though, before considering those complexities, we need to briefly outline the development of the Latter-day Saint argumentation.[9]

Apparently the first public Latter-day Saint comment came in the form of an 1832 unsigned editorial, under the nominal editorship of

W. W. Phelps, in *The Evening and the Morning Star*. "Every man lives for himself," the editorial reads. "Adam was made to open the ways of the world, and for dressing the garden. Noah was born to save seed of every thing, when the earth was washed of its wickedness by the flood; and the Son of God came into the world to redeem it from the fall."[10] For all intents and purposes, the language and thought of this declaration, while containing other interesting concepts, does not vary from standard Protestant Flood interpretation.

The beginnings of variance, however, were not long in coming. In the first of two sequential 1835 editorials in the Church's *Latter Day Saints' Messenger and Advocate*, Phelps, this time as acknowledged author, wrote about the Flood in terms of it being an instrument of cleansing. In the first of these editorials, Phelps wrote that "when the flood abated . . . the world was cleansed from iniquity."[11] In the second article, Phelps's language anticipates later steps beyond Protestant interpretations toward a uniquely Latter-day Saint understanding: "After the earth had been baptized by a flood, for a remission of her sins . . . [the Lord] blessed Noah and his sons."[12] Here Phelps mentions both a baptism and a cleansing of the earth from "her sins." While these may have been merely rhetorical moves, Phelps can also be seen as introducing, however preliminarily and unintentionally, an ambiguity into the discussion that still besets Mormon discourse. That is, though by "her sins" he likely referred to sins committed by mortals living on the earth, subsequent developments make his usage notable because it can be read as positing a sentient earth.[13] This ambiguity, it turns out, would continue throughout the twentieth century in much of the Latter-day Saint discourse about the Flood.

For Latter-day Saints, the distinction between a formal, literal ordinance and a symbolic immersion is important. Simple immersion in water does not constitute an ordinance. First, the baptismal ordinance must be a complete immersion in water performed by a priesthood holder who has the requisite authority and commission. In addition, the person being baptized must have been found worthy to be baptized.[14] Otherwise, the baptism is just an immersion, or a sprinkling, or a washing with no salvific efficacy, though perhaps symbolically significant. If the Flood constituted a literal baptism, in other words, it would raise significant questions for Latter-day Saints.[15]

Phelps was not the only early Latter-day Saint to speak of the Flood as a baptism. While serving as a missionary in England in 1841, Elder Lorenzo Snow published an important missionary tract on the foundational principles of the gospel in which he called the Flood of Noah "typical" of Christian baptism: "The destruction of the Antediluvian world, by water, was typical of receiving remission of sins through baptism. The earth had become clothed with sin as with a garment; the righteous were brought out and saved from the world of sin, even by water; the like figure, even baptism, doth now *save* us, says Peter (1 Peter iii. 21)." With wording and theological reasoning that would have found ready home in contemporary Protestantism, Snow went on to state that "Noah and family were removed, and disconnected from sins and pollutions, by *means* of water; so baptism, the like figure, doth now remove our souls from sins and pollutions, through faith on the *great* atonement made upon Calvary."[16] Though Snow did not follow Phelps in arguing that the earth was literally baptized, in returning to 1 Peter 3, Snow put the Flood in the context of the ordinance of baptism: "Peter, when speaking of Noah and family being saved by water, would have said, The like figure whereunto even baptism doth now save us;—1st Peter iii.21."[17]

As Church members migrated west, the idea of the Flood being the earth's baptism came with them. Elder Orson Pratt began as early as 1851 to follow Phelps in framing the Flood as a literal baptismal ordinance, with all that might mean for Latter-day Saints. "The first ordinance instituted for the cleansing of the earth, was that of immersion in water," Elder Pratt explained. "It was buried in the liquid element, and all things sinful upon the face of it were washed away. As it came forth from the ocean flood, like the new-born child, it was innocent, it arose to newness of life; it was its second birth from the womb of mighty waters—a new world issuing from the ruins of the old, clothed with all the innocency of its first creation."[18]

Important questions, however, were left unaddressed: Why would wicked inhabitants necessitate a literal baptism of the earth rather than their own repentance? Was the earth's baptism *necessary*, that is, salvific, or was it both more literal than the Protestants had provided for and yet still symbolic in some way? Such unanswered questions can easily lead to creative interpretation and perhaps misunderstanding, as will be seen.[19]

Pratt would teach this same doctrine a number of times during his tenure as an Apostle. During his missionary experience in Europe, he published a series of tracts that touched on the first principles and ordinances of the gospel. In his tract on the subject of "Water Baptism," Pratt again reiterated his ideas about the Flood as the baptism of the earth. "Even the very earth itself was Baptized in the mighty flood," Pratt wrote. "The Baptism of the earth, to wash away its sins, was a literal representation of the baptism of all penitent believers to wash away their sins." Pratt concluded his argument by citing 1 Peter 3:20–21 as a proof text.[20]

On another occasion, Pratt, after detailing a litany of sins committed by the antediluvians, with no mention of sins the earth might have committed, explained that the waters of the Flood "then made an entire sweep of the wicked, they were laid low, and the earth was cleansed. We might, in other words, call it a baptism of the earth by water, or a cleansing of it from sin. You know that baptism is intended for the remission of sins; it is the ordinance through which our heavenly Father forgives the sins of those who believe in his Son Jesus Christ."[21]

Finally, in a sermon delivered in 1880, Pratt's words evidenced the persistent ambiguity introduced into Latter-day Saint Flood discourse by Phelps. In this sermon he again explicitly taught that the earth "was baptized by water." This, Pratt explained, was because "God requires the children of men to be baptized. What for? For the remission of sins. So he required our globe to be baptized by a flow of waters, and all of its sins were washed away, not one sin remaining."[22] Again, Pratt offered no sustained explanation of why the earth would require a baptism over and against the cleansing effect the Flood ostensibly represented in removing wicked inhabitants. Moreover, his usage of phrases such as "its sins" left open the question for later commentators of whether or not the earth itself might be viewed individualistically, even animistically, in Mormon theology.

Presidents of the Church in the nineteenth century tended to affirm the Flood as a baptism, even as they too avoided some of the complexities inherent in such a characterization. In his usual forthright style, President Brigham Young taught:

> The Lord said, "I will deluge (or immerse) the earth in water for the remission of the sins of the people;" or if you will allow me to express myself in a familiar style, to kill all the vermin that were nitting and breeding, and polluting its body; it was cleansed of its filthiness; and soaked in the water, as long as some of our people ought to soak. The Lord baptized the earth for the remission of sins and it has been once cleansed from the filthiness that has gone out of it which was in the inhabitants who dwelt upon its face.[23]

In a subsequent sermon, President Young used words associated with human baptism to describe the immersion of the earth: "This earth . . . has been baptized with water, will be baptized by fire and the Holy Ghost, and by-and-by will be prepared for the faithful to dwell upon."[24] Perhaps because President Young's language can easily be construed to be analogous to priesthood ordinances for mortals, the quotes that follow below will demonstrate, using Pratt and Young's words as their source, that many Latter-day Saint writers speak of the baptism of the earth as a literal ordinance, and one pertaining to the earth's own destiny at that.

President John Taylor, who would succeed President Young as the prophet, did not impute any sins to the earth, but he continued to speak of the Flood as the earth's literal baptism. For example, he taught that at the time of the Flood "the earth was immersed," and this was, accordingly, "a period of baptism."[25]

A turn-of-the-century Apostle, Elder Orson F. Whitney, built on these foundations to establish another layer of interpretation about the Flood. On at least three occasions, Whitney added his voice to that of these earlier commentators in teaching that the earth received its baptism by means of the Flood, and these teachings were widely dispersed over his lifetime. In his first sermon mentioning the Flood, delivered more than twenty years before he became an Apostle, he stated, "The earth underwent a baptism by being immersed in water, for the remission of sins, the washing away of its iniquities. 'As it was in the days of Noah, so shall it be in the days of the coming of the Son of Man' [Luke 7:26]. . . . Not only man, but the earth itself, which is a living creature, must undergo this ordinance."[26]

The parallels he drew between the baptism of the earth "in water, for the remission of sins" to the ordinance of baptism for "man" could certainly leave the impression that the earth had sinned and therefore needed "its iniquities" washed away in an ordinance. This impression is reinforced by Whitney's mention that the earth "is a living creature." Though the concept taught by Brigham Young and others that the earth has a spirit (see below) could stand behind Whitney's comment, calling the earth "a living creature" goes beyond saying the earth has a spirit. It implies that as a "living creature" which "must undergo" baptism, the earth could sin.

After becoming an Apostle, Whitney continued to speak of the baptism of the earth in subsequent general conference addresses. In 1908 he stated that in Noah's day "the earth was baptized with water."[27] Then, more than forty years after he first mentioned the baptism of the earth, he taught in 1927: "Baptized with water in the days of Noah, the earth will yet be baptized with fire and with the Holy Ghost."[28] These three Whitney sermons feature three strands that would enliven twentieth-century Latter-day Saint commentaries: that the Flood was the earth's literal baptism, that the earth constitutes an individualized living being, and that baptism is somehow central to its eschatological destiny. While he hardly brought all three together in any meaningful way at any one given time, his statements form a kind of pivot from the ambiguous and ambivalent nature of nineteenth-century utterances and the more speculative systematizers of the twentieth century.

Later Latter-day Saint Teachings Concerning the Flood as Baptism

Far from being an archaic teaching found only in its developmental stage, the teaching that the Flood was an immersion analogous to a salvific ordinance can be found in more recent Latter-day Saint discourse. For instance, Elder John A. Widtsoe, in his popular compendium first published in 1943, articulated what has become something of the codified understanding of Noah's Flood in the minds of many Church members: "Latter-day Saints look upon the earth as a living organism, one which is gloriously filling 'the measure of its creation.' They look upon the flood as a baptism of the earth, symbolizing a cleansing of the impurities of the past, and the beginning of a new life. This has been repeatedly taught by the leaders of the Church. The deluge was an immersion of the earth in water."[29]

Widtsoe took pains to point out that the earth was completely covered by water. This concept of total immersion, combined with his use of the term *baptism*, would suggest to Latter-day Saint readers the priesthood ordinance. Yet readers should note that Widtsoe was careful to stop short of equating the Flood with the baptismal ordinance for mortals by his use of words such as "as a baptism" and "symbolizing a cleansing."

Elder Joseph Fielding Smith wrote more forcefully: "Now a word as to the reason for the Flood. *It was the baptism of the earth, and that had to be by immersion*. If the water did not cover the entire earth, then it was not baptized, for the baptism of the Lord is not pouring or sprinkling."[30] By declaring that "the entire earth" was immersed in water, Smith not only validated the Latter-day Saint mode of baptism, but he also staked claim for a literalist approach to biblical interpretation. Likewise, Elder Bruce R. McConkie explained, "In the days of Noah the Lord sent *a universal flood* which completely immersed the whole earth and destroyed all flesh except that preserved on the ark. . . . This flood was the baptism of the earth."[31] Both Joseph Fielding Smith and Bruce R. McConkie come close to equating the Flood with baptism for mortals, implying that the Flood was an ordinance.

Understandably, commentators publishing in official organs of the Church followed the lead of these General Authorities. In a 1980 article in the *Ensign*, F. Kent Richards wrote: "The worldwide flood of Noah's time has been accepted as a benchmark historical event by Jews and Christians for thousands of years. . . . The worldwide flood of Noah's time, so upsetting to a restricted secular view, fits easily into place. It is the earth's baptism."[32] Likewise, in a 1998 article in the *Ensign*, Donald W. Parry stated, "Latter-day prophets teach that the Flood or the total immersion of the earth in water represents the earth's required baptism."[33] His use of the words "required baptism" unequivocally puts the Flood in the category of a salvific ordinance. One month later the *Ensign* printed an article on Noah by Joseph B. Romney, wherein Romney remarked, "Modern revelation teaches that God indeed suffered great sorrow over the Flood, which served as the baptism of the earth."[34]

The Church's 1957 Melchizedek Priesthood study manual, written by Hugh Nibley, spoke of a certain "Jewish tradition that tells of how the baptism of the earth by water in the days of Noah, purging it from wickedness, was later followed by a baptism of wind, to be followed in turn at the end of the world by a baptism of fire."[35] The Church's institute manual on the Old Testament, in its discussion of the significance of the Flood, teaches that the Flood was the earth's baptism by quoting the statements by Young, Taylor, and Pratt examined above.[36] Finally, a recent statement on the Church's website affirmed that "during Noah's time the earth was completely covered with water. This was the baptism of the earth and symbolized a cleansing (1 Peter 3:20–21)."[37]

The idea that the Flood was the baptism of the earth is likewise found in popular Latter-day Saint literature. W. Cleon Skousen, writing in the 1950s, opined, "The great flood is spoken of as the 'baptism' of the earth or burial of the earth in water."[38] Skousen has been followed by Victor L. Ludlow, who wrote that "the earth itself was a living entity and desired a rest from wickedness . . . [and] needed to go through its own baptism of water preparatory for a later baptism of fire and eventual celestialization."[39]

More recently, D. Kelly Ogden and Andrew C. Skinner have not only written that the Flood was the earth's baptism but also that the earth is a sentient, living entity. "It is apparent from Ether 13:2 that the Flood was not just a local phenomenon but covered all of earth's lands." Ogden and Skinner continue, "The Flood, as the earth's baptism by water, was a complete immersion." After quoting Elders Mark E. Petersen and Joseph Fielding Smith on the Flood constituting the earth's baptism, Ogden and Skinner argue, "The earth is a living entity, and Enoch had heard Mother Earth yearn for a cleansing of 'the filthiness which is gone forth out of me' (Moses 7:48). The Flood removed that filthiness or wickedness, just as baptism removes sin from human beings."[40]

As this sampling of literature shows (and we have by no means exhausted the sources),[41] there has been a general continuity of thought among modern Latter-day Saint leaders and writers on this subject.[42] Beginning in the early days of the Church down to the present, many Latter-day Saints have understood that the Flood of Noah constituted the baptism of the earth. Even so, no Latter-day Saint author has made an attempt to distinguish between the purpose and result of the immersion of a mortal and the cleansing of the earth in water. In fact, all the Latter-day Saint comments we have quoted that speak of the baptism of the earth have done so without indicating exactly what they mean by *baptism*. As mentioned above, unless further explanation is given, for most Latter-day Saints the immediate connotation is the salvific priesthood ordinance of immersion for the remission of personal sin.[43]

Although the understanding of Noah's Flood as a salvific ordinance for a sentient earth, parallel to baptism for mortals, has become popular among some members of the Church, we feel a different reading of the nineteenth-century sources is in order. We believe that a distinction must be made between baptism for mortals and any cleansing of the earth by water, and that the distinction should be made explicit to clarify doctrine, eliminate potentially problematic ideas, and provide a more nuanced understanding.

The first step to bringing the problematic issues into sharper focus is to discuss why Latter-day Saint commentators have drawn attention to what we believe is a doctrinal red herring, namely, that the earth is alive or that the earth has a spirit. This assumption allows "many Latter-day Saints and students of our theology [to] make us out to be animists who believe the earth to be a living thing and therefore in need of baptism."[44] We will dissect this red herring along two lines: First, we will analyze the statements that the earth is alive. And second, we will discuss the issue of the earth needing baptism. As we will discuss below, part of the issue hinges on whether the scriptures are read literally or metaphorically. We will suggest that reading some scriptures exclusively literally can lead to questionable conclusions.

Is It a Living Earth?

The unique Latter-day Saint discourse about the earth as a living entity[45] would seem to require a formal, salvific immersion of the earth. We have seen this idea mentioned already by Whitney in 1885, Widtsoe in 1943, Ludlow in 1981, Ogden and Skinner in 2013, and many others. In fact, the idea that the earth is a living entity is mentioned so often in conjunction with the earth's baptism that it seems to be the cornerstone of the Latter-day Saint belief that the earth was required to undergo a salvific ordinance analogous to baptism for mortals.

Though we cannot pinpoint the time and place of the origin of the idea of a sentient earth, we believe the concept could have found its origins in what would later become canonized scripture, the Book of Moses. The relevant passage reads as follows:

> And it came to pass that Enoch looked upon the earth; and he heard a voice from the bowels thereof, saying: Wo, wo is me, the mother of men; I am pained, I am weary, because of the wickedness of my children. When shall I rest, and be cleansed from the filthiness which is gone forth out of me? When will my Creator sanctify me, that I may rest, and righteousness for a season abide upon my face?
>
> And when Enoch heard the earth mourn, he wept. (Moses 7:48–49)

Extracts of the Book of Moses, including the words of these verses, were published as early as 1832 in *The Evening and the Morning Star* and again in the *Times and Seasons* in 1840 and in 1843.[46] Given the frequency of the publication of this passage, it is likely that many Latter-day Saints were aware of its content even before its inclusion in the 1851 Liverpool publication of the Pearl of Great Price. A literal interpretation of the scriptures, if imposed on Moses 7:48, would certainly make it easy to view the earth as a living entity, and female at that. Certainly, a talking, feeling, tired, mourning earth sounds like it may be alive. But there are other ways of looking at these verses.

Although it is tempting to view this passage literally, it is more likely that the passage is speaking poetically, employing figurative language to personify the earth.[47] There are indications in the pericope itself that metaphor, hyperbole, and symbolism are at play. For example, Moses 7:41 waxes poetic when it states that when Enoch beheld the wickedness on the earth "his heart swelled wide as eternity." No one would take literally the phrase "his heart swelled wide as eternity." It is, simply put, poetically and beautifully symbolic of Enoch's love and compassion for the earth's inhabitants.

Of particular importance is the statement in verse 48 that the earth is "the mother of men." If mortals were actually fashioned from the dirt or clay of this earth, and had their beginning here in this physical world, it might be possible to believe that "the mother of men" literally applies to the earth. But for Latter-day Saints the earth is not the literal "mother of men."[48] The earth can only be the "mother of men" in a symbolic manner.[49] These examples make it clear that symbolism and metaphor are part and parcel of this passage in which the earth is said to bemoan the "the filthiness which is gone forth out of" it. Therefore, it seems likely that a speaking earth is a symbolic personification, a beautiful and poignant poetic expression of the earth's condition in the days of Noah.

In addition to Moses 7:48–49, another early Latter-day Saint scripture could be used to posit a living earth. D&C 88:26, given as part of a revelation to the Prophet Joseph Smith on December 27, 1832, reads in part, "[The earth] shall die, it shall be quickened again, and shall abide the power by which it is quickened." Reading the verse literally, as if it were speaking of a mortal, would suggest that if the earth will "be quickened again" (the verb *quicken* means to be made alive), it will have to die. Just as with Moses 7:48–49, D&C 88:26 can be read poetically rather than literally. If taken literally, it would suggest that the earth has a distinct, particular spirit of its own that can die. While this is possible, Orson Pratt, in speaking about the earth being alive, made the interesting statement, "That which quickens the earth is the Spirit of God."[50] In other words, if the Spirit of God makes the earth alive, then when God withdraws his Spirit from the earth, it in essence "dies." That is, as long as the Spirit of God is present, the earth may be said to be alive. The quotes about the earth being alive and dying at some time in the future can be understood to mean that God will withdraw his Spirit and the earth will cease to sustain life as we know it. Then the earth will be quickened again as if, speaking metaphorically, from the dead and made capable of supporting celestial life. In other words, just as the separation of spirit and body define mortal death for humans, the separation of the Spirit of God from the earth would define the earth's death.

WAS NOAH'S FLOOD THE BAPTISM OF THE EARTH?

We have demonstrated that both passages of scripture that appear to imply that the earth is alive and has a distinct and sentient spirit can be read symbolically and metaphorically and need not be interpreted literally. With the symbolic nature of Moses 7:48–49 and D&C 88:26 in mind, we now turn to the words of Latter-day Saints who speak of the earth being alive. We believe that a careful reading of their words does not imply that the earth has a distinct, sentient spirit that quickens the earth. Rather, as can be understood from Orson Pratt's statement quoted above, the earth is alive because the Spirit of God quickens it.

The first public Latter-day Saint sermon we could find where the earth is declared to be alive was given by Orson Pratt in 1852. In this sermon, rather than reading Moses 7:48 or D&C 88:26, Pratt quoted Isaiah 51:6 and interpreted Isaiah's poetry quite literally:

> The earth itself, as a living being, was immortal and eternal in its nature. "What! is the earth alive too?" If it were not, how could the words of our text be fulfilled, where it speaks of the earth's dying? How can that die that has no life? "Lift up your eyes to the heavens above," says the Lord, "and look upon the earth beneath; the heavens shall vanish away like smoke, and the earth shall wax old like a garment, and they that dwell therein shall die in like manner" [Isaiah 51:6]. In like manner! What! The earth and the heavens to die? Yes, the material heavens and earth must all undergo this change which we call death; and if so, the earth must be alive as well as we.[51]

Pratt is consistent when he states that the earth is alive, but not as some would understand him.[52] In the quote cited earlier, given more than a quarter century after the quote immediately above, he defines what he means for the earth to be alive, and his full statement is worth quoting: "What is it that will make the earth die? It will be the withdrawing of the spiritual portion from it, that which gives it life—that which animates it, and causes it to bring forth fruit; that which quickens the earth is the Spirit of God."[53] Thus it is reasonable to conclude that the Spirit of God makes the earth capable of sustaining life, that the earth will eventually die when the Spirit of God is removed, and that the earth will be resurrected to a new level of life-sustaining existence.

Other Latter-day Saint authorities have also spoken of the earth being alive, but note how Pratt's statement about the Spirit of God making the earth alive colors the sense of these statements. In 1856, about four years after Pratt first spoke of an earth that is alive, Brigham Young also taught that the earth is a living entity with a spirit: "There is life in all matter, throughout the vast extent of all the eternities; it is in the rock, the sand, the dust, in water, air, the gases, and, in short, in every description and organization of matter, whether it be solid, liquid, or gaseous, particle operating with particle."[54] Besides insisting that all matter has life, President Young also evidently believed that a living spirit inhabited all matter:

> The spirit constitutes the life of everything we see. Is there life in these rocks, and mountains? There is. Then there is a spirit peculiarly adapted to these rocks and mountains. We mark the progress of the growth of grass, flowers, and trees. There is a spirit nicely adapted to the various productions of the vegetable kingdom. There is also a spirit to the different ores of the mineral kingdom, and to every element in existence. And there is a spirit in the Earth.[55]

Besides expressing ideas similar to Orson Pratt's claim that the earth is alive, Brigham Young also took the next step beyond Pratt and proclaimed that "there is a spirit in the Earth."

Heber C. Kimball, counselor to Brigham Young, also taught that a living spirit inhabited all matter, including the material earth. "Some say the earth exists without spirit; I do not believe any such thing; it has a spirit as much as anybody has a spirit. How can anything live, except it has a living spirit? How can the earth produce vegetation, fruits, trees, and every kind of production, if there is no life in it?"[56]

While some have seen Pratt, Young, and Kimball as moving in animistic directions with these statements, it should be noted that it remains unclear whether each was working within a framework of universal "intelligence" or a universal "light of Christ," both posited in Joseph Smith's revelations. It is far from clear what each metaphysically intended with these teachings.

Especially if their statements are taken together, it seems clear to us that no single view of the earth's spirit existed among early Church leaders.

The bottom line is that comments about the earth having a spirit need not be interpreted *a priori* to mean that the earth has its own particular, discrete, and sentient spirit and therefore needs baptism. While this argument works for mortals, it does not necessarily work for the earth. This brings us to the second part of our dissection of the red herring: the earth's need of baptism.

WHY WAS THE EARTH CLEANSED BY IMMERSION?

If, as we've argued, the "spirit" of the earth, whatever its nature, does *not* make it truly sentient like a human being, then why would the earth need to undergo a salvific ordinance? This is essentially the critique that has been made by a number of recent Latter-day Saint authors. We begin by calling attention to the points raised by Duane E. Jeffery a decade ago.[57] Jeffery, in his article exploring the discussion of the Flood of Noah being a global versus a local event, examines the rationale given for the Flood being the salvific baptism of the earth. After reviewing a few of the statements of past General Authorities on this topic, Jeffery correctly observes, as we have quoted above, that "many Latter-day Saints and students of our theology make us out to be animists who believe the earth to be a living thing and therefore in need of baptism."[58] This, it seems, was clearly the belief of a number of modern interpreters quoted above. Given this, Jeffery continues to articulate what he thinks are problematic aspects of this belief. "By this logic," Jeffery concludes,

> then every living thing needs to be baptized. I'm not sure we'd want to take that on. If we choose to argue in some fashion that the earth needs baptism because it is a sentient entity with some capability of moral decision-making like that of humans, we run into further difficulty. Just for the sake of clarification, many animals have sentience far beyond anything we could likely adduce for the earth. Latter-day Saints also have a longstanding ecclesiastical policy that humans who lack the ability to make and exercise genuine moral decisions (i.e., those who are mentally handicapped or under eight

years of age) do not need baptism. But many such persons surely have sentience beyond anything we could likely identify for the earth as a planet.[59]

Jeffery is not alone in raising these important points. Ben Spackman, an independent Latter-day Saint scholar with graduate training in ancient Near Eastern studies, also recognizes that the insistence that the earth needed to be baptized raises further questions of what else might need to be baptized. With tongue firmly in cheek, Spackman asks, "Why does the planet need baptism? Do dogs? Plants? Can it make decisions, or repent? Did someone lay hands on it? What sins had it committed? Is it now a member of the church?"[60] All things considered, Spackman concludes, the rationale behind this teaching leaves much to be explained.

These questions should be considered by anyone arguing that a sentient earth is culpable for its conjectured sins. However, a different reading of the nineteenth-century sources avoids the problems raised by Jeffery and Spackman.

If the earth does not have a separate, sentient spirit, but is quickened by the Spirit of God, why should it be baptized? The first point to be made is that the earth was not baptized for any sins it committed. As was pointed out above, Brigham Young clearly made the claim that mortals befouled the earth with their sins. Yet the statements of Pratt, Young, Kimball, and others clearly declare that the earth was washed clean, as if its baptism were an ordinance.[61]

The fundamental question is, if the earth committed no sins, what is the relationship of its immersion to the baptism of mortals who have sinned? Obviously, there are parallels. But we suggest that the parallels are more analogous than functional. Orson Pratt, as quoted earlier, stated, "The earth is to die; it has already received certain ordinances, and will have to receive other ordinances for its recovery from the fall."[62] As Elder McConkie wrote, "The earth itself is subject to certain laws of progression and salvation because of which it eventually will become a fit abode for exalted beings. This earth was created as a living thing, and the Lord ordained that it should live a celestial law. It was baptized in water and will receive the baptism of fire; it will die, be resurrected and attain unto a state of celestial exaltation."[63]

More recently, Elder Tad R. Callister restated this concept, with an explicit parallel drawn between the plan for God's children and the plan for the earth:

> The consequences affecting the earth following the Fall [of Adam] mirrored the consequences that came upon man. . . . Both are subject to death, both will be resurrected, both fell from the presence of God, both need to be born of water to be cleansed (i.e., the earth being baptized at the time of Noah), both need to be cleansed by fire (i.e., the earth being baptized by fire at the Second Coming and also prior to its final judgment), and both seek the day of their celestialization and return to God's presence.[64]

Just as there is a plan for the Creation, Fall, and Atonement for God's children, so this line of argumentation goes, there is also a plan for the earth that was laid out from the beginning and that shares some common external features with the plan of salvation, including analogs of what are salvific ordinances for God's children. Given that the earth's cleansing by water is analogous to baptism, it would be easy to posit a dichotomy: either the Flood constituted a salvific and therefore necessary ordinance for the earth, or the Flood was a magnificent symbol of cleansing and nothing more. But there may be an alternative explanation.

Perhaps There Is an Alternative

As we have interpreted the evidence, the Spirit of God quickens the earth, giving it life. The earth received and is guided by laws, and a path was laid out for it to follow. As a thing to be acted upon,[65] it has followed that path without variance and will continue to move along that prescribed path. In short, the cleansing of the earth with water was a necessary and foreordained event in its chain of becoming our celestial abode but not a baptism for remission of any sins it committed. How, then, do we explain the discourse about the earth being baptized? As we have emphasized above, one of the Lord's most often used and inspired teaching methods employs symbols, types, shadows, similes, metaphors, and similitudes. Because "all things denote there is a God; yea, even the earth, and all things that are upon the face of it" (Alma 30:44), we suggest that the path laid out for the earth from its creation to its celestialization is designed to teach us about and to bear witness of the great plan of salvation that we mortals must follow.

Returning specifically to the immersion of the earth, that it was cleansed from others' sins rather than its own is not without precedence. In like symbolism, the Book of Mormon prophet Jacob told his people, "Behold, I take off my garments, and I shake them before you . . . that the God of Israel did witness that I shook your iniquities from my soul, and that I stand with brightness before him, and am rid of your blood" (2 Nephi 9:44). Note that Jacob was not concerned publicly with his own sins and transgressions. He was worried about the sins of others making him unclean. King Benjamin also performed the same ritual: "I say unto you that I have caused that ye should assemble yourselves together that I might rid my garments of your blood, at this period of time when I am about to go down to my grave, that I might go down in peace, and my immortal spirit may join the choirs above in singing the praises of a just God" (Mosiah 2:28). Like Jacob, Benjamin was worried about being soiled with others' sins. Moroni expressed the same sentiment in one of his last homilies, namely, that the Book of Mormon was "written that we may rid our garments of the blood of our brethren" (Mormon 9:35).[66]

It would also seem that prophets are not the only individuals who must become clean from the wickedness in their environment. In the early years of the Restoration, the Lord told the "first laborers in this last kingdom" to "assemble yourselves together, and organize yourselves, and prepare yourselves, and sanctify yourselves; yea, purify your hearts, and cleanse your hands and your feet before me, that I may make you clean; that I may testify unto your Father, and your God, and my God, that you are clean from the blood of this wicked generation" (D&C 88:74–75).

Though the Lord was surely concerned that the "first laborers in this last kingdom" repent of their personal faults and sins, this passage seems to suggest the same concept that Jacob, Benjamin, and Moroni expressed. As Elder McConkie explained, "Thus through their faithfulness the elders have power to become clean from the blood and sins of this generation."[67]

It is possible that the earth, in like manner and in preparation for eventual celestialization, was physically washed and symbolically cleansed so that it could become free from the blood and sins of the mortals who polluted its surface. So might the earth, like King Benjamin, metaphorically sing the praises of a just God for the Flood of Noah that washed away the blood and sins of the generations who inhabited or will inhabit this earth.

Notes

1. Percy Bysshe Shelley, *Prometheus Unbound*, act 1, lines 152–58.
2. David Holland has tangentially explored Mormonism's relationship to nineteenth-century evangelicalism, including the Methodist background of some of its early converts. See David Holland, *Sacred Borders: Continuing Revelation and Canonical Restraint in Early America* (New York: Oxford University Press, 2011), 141–57.
3. William Trollope, *Analecta Theologica: A Digested and Arranged Compendium of the Most Approved Commentaries on the New Testament* (London: T. Calldel, 1835), 2:625.
4. Henry Alford, *The New Testament for English Readers, Volume II: The Epistle to the Hebrews, the Catholic Epistles, and the Revelation* (London: Deighton, Bell, and Co., 1866), 816.
5. C. F. Keil and F. Delitzsch, *Biblical Commentary on the Old Testament, Volume I: The Pentateuch*, trans. James Martin (Edinburgh: T & T Clark, 1866), 141.
6. Edward Hayes Plumptre, *The General Epistles of St. Peter and St. Jude* (Cambridge: Cambridge University Press, 1890), 136.
7. For most traditional Christians, the words *sacrament* and *ordinance* are somewhat interchangeable, though some congregations prefer one or the other. In this paper, we will consistently follow Latter-day Saint practice of speaking of all Christian sacraments as ordinances.
8. It must be added parenthetically that, though important to some, for many Christian groups the distinction between symbolic immersion and sacramental baptism is purely academic.
9. We want to thank Spencer Fluhman for suggesting some of the ideas in this paragraph.

10. "To the Honorable Men of the World," *The Evening and the Morning Star,* August 3, 1832, 21.
11. W. W. Phelps, "Letter No. 4," *Latter Day Saints' Messenger and Advocate*, February 1835, 67.
12. W. W. Phelps, "Letter No. 9," *Latter Day Saints' Messenger and Advocate*, July 1835, 146.
13. In fact, most of the statements we review about the "sins of the earth" being washed away in the Flood are ambiguous. The straightforward reading would be that "her sins" were sins the earth had committed. However, in each case, a more nuanced reading would be that earth was cleansed of human sins.
14. See, for example, the beliefs outlined already in Mosiah 18:12–14 and Moroni 6:2–3.
15. Without mentioning "remission of her sins," Phelps again spoke in similar terms in his 1844 pamphlet for Joseph Smith's presidential platform: "God . . . cleansed the violence of the earth with a flood." W. W. Phelps, "Gen. Smith's Views on the Government and Policy of the U.S.," *Times and Seasons*, May 15, 1844, 532. This piece was initially published in pamphlet form as *General Smith's Views on the Powers and Policy of the Government of the United States* (Nauvoo, IL: John Taylor, 1844), 8. Although authorship of this piece is attributed to Joseph Smith, it was in fact ghostwritten by Phelps. See Michael Hicks, "Joseph Smith, W. W. Phelps, and the Poetic Paraphrase of 'The Vision,'" *Journal of Mormon History* 20, no. 2 (Fall 1994): 74; Samuel Brown, "The Translator and the Ghostwriter: Joseph Smith and W. W. Phelps," *Journal of Mormon History* 34, no. 1 (Winter 2008): 47–48.
16. Lorenzo Snow, *The Only Way to Be Saved* (London: D. Chalmers, 1841), 3–4; italics in original.
17. Snow, *The Only Way to Be Saved*, 6–7.
18. Orson Pratt, in *Journal of Discourses* (London: Latter-day Saints' Book Depot, 1854–86), 1:331.
19. Pratt does discuss this issue more fully in this speech (on the same page, 331) but only in that he says the earth was polluted by the "sins of the posterity of Adam." He generally leaves the impression implicitly that the baptism of the earth was the same priesthood ordinance performed for mortals.
20. Orson Pratt, *Water Baptism* (Liverpool: L.D.S. Book and Star Depot, 1856), 37.
21. Orson Pratt, in *Journal of Discourses*, 16:314.
22. Orson Pratt, in *Journal of Discourses*, 21:323.

23. Brigham Young, in *Journal of Discourses,* 1:274.
24. Brigham Young, in *Journal of Discourses,* 8:83.
25. John Taylor, in *Journal of Discourses,* 26:74–75.
26. Orson F. Whitney, in *Journal of Discourses,* 26:266.
27. Orson F. Whitney, in Conference Report, April 1908, 91.
28. Orson F. Whitney, in Conference Report, April 1927, 100.
29. John A. Widtsoe, *Evidences and Reconciliations* (Salt Lake City: Bookcraft, 1960), 127.
30. Joseph Fielding Smith, *Doctrines of Salvation,* comp. Bruce R. McConkie (Salt Lake City: Bookcraft, 1955), 2:320; emphasis in original. One year earlier, in an antievolution polemic, Smith made this same point, with the same citations of Young and Pratt as his support. See Joseph Fielding Smith, *Man: His Origin and Destiny* (Salt Lake City: Bookcraft, 1954), 433–36.
31. Bruce R. McConkie, *Mormon Doctrine,* 2nd ed. (Salt Lake City: Bookcraft, 1966), 289; italics in original. McConkie made similar remarks on this subject in his commentary on the life of Jesus. See Bruce R. McConkie, *The Mortal Messiah: From Bethlehem to Calvary, Book II* (Salt Lake City: Deseret Book, 1980), 356.
32. F. Kent Nielsen, "The Gospel and the Scientific View: How Earth Came to Be," *Ensign,* September 1980, 67.
33. Donald W. Parry, "The Flood and the Tower of Babel," *Ensign,* January 1998, 41.
34. Joseph B. Romney, "Noah, The Great Preacher of Righteousness," *Ensign,* February 1998, 22.
35. The quote is from the updated publication of the original book, Hugh Nibley, *An Approach to the Book of Mormon,* 3rd ed. (Provo, UT: FARMS, 1988), 333.
36. *Old Testament Student Manual: Genesis–2 Samuel* (Salt Lake City: The Church of Jesus Christ of Latter-day Saints, 2003), 55.
37. "Flood at Noah's Time," online at http://www.lds.org/scriptures/gs/flood-at-noahs-time. See also "Noah," online at https://www.lds.org/topics/noah?lang=eng. "In the New Testament, Peter explained that the flood was a 'like figure' or symbol of baptism (1 Peter 3:20–21). Just as the earth was immersed in water, so we must be baptized by water and by the Spirit before we can enter the celestial kingdom." The use of the word *cleansing* in this quote makes the Flood at least a symbol but not necessarily an ordinance.
38. W. Cleon Skousen, *The First 2,000 Years* (Salt Lake City: Bookcraft, 1953), 217.

39. Victor L. Ludlow, *Unlocking the Old Testament* (Salt Lake City: Deseret Book, 1981), 9.
40. D. Kelly Ogden and Andrew C. Skinner, *The Old Testament Verse By Verse: Volume One, Genesis through 2 Samuel, Psalms* (Salt Lake City: Deseret Book, 2013), 76–77.
41. For other recent and similar commentary, see Susan Easton Black, *400 Questions & Answers about the Old Testament* (Salt Lake City: Covenant Communications, 2013), 38. See also Ronald P. Millett, "In Defense of the Prophet Noah and the Great Flood," *Meridian Magazine*, posted on March 12, 2014, online at http://www.ldsmag.com/article/1/14059. Somewhat surprisingly, given the recent trend, BYU religion professor Kerry Muhlestein does not include a discussion of the Flood being the earth's baptism in his recent commentary. See Kerry Muhlestein, *The Essential Old Testament Companion* (Salt Lake City: Covenant Communications, 2013).
42. As we will mention later, some Latter-day Saint scholars have objected to this general view.
43. However, this un-nuanced connotation may not always be intended. For example, President Taylor's quote cited above, speaking of the time "the earth was immersed" as "a period of baptism," may mean nothing more than that the earth was symbolically cleansed by water. Or, he could have meant an ordinance involving immersion that was necessary for the earth's salvation. Without more clarification, readers are left to their own interpretation. *Journal of Discourses,* 26:74–75. His words could be construed as a tautology, since *baptism* can mean *immersion*: "the earth was immersed," and this was, accordingly, "a period of immersion."
44. Duane E. Jeffery, "Noah's Flood: Modern Scholarship and Mormon Traditions," *Sunstone*, October 2004, 36.
45. We have been unable to locate anything akin to this in mainstream nineteenth-century Protestant teaching, though no doubt there were spiritualists who saw living spirits in inanimate objects and Romantic thinkers like Goethe—as well as the seventeenth-century philosopher and pantheist Spinoza—who saw various levels of some kind of "divine" nature in all objects.
46. *The Evening and the Morning Star*, August 1832, 18; "Extract from the Prophecy of Enoch," *Times and Seasons*, November 1840, 193–96; "Extract from the Prophecy of Enoch," *Times and Seasons*, October 1843, 336–38.

47. Since in older English, before grammatical genders were dropped for nouns, the word *earth* was construed as feminine, and since both words in Hebrew for *earth* are grammatically feminine, it would not have been as anachronistic (least of all as poetic license) to speak of the earth as female. For example, note the use of the feminine pronoun *her* in a scripture that was familiar to nineteenth-century Bible readers, "And now *art* thou cursed from the earth, which hath opened her mouth to receive thy brother's blood from thy hand" (Genesis 4:11). Even today many people lovingly call the earth and its environments "Mother Nature."

48. Brigham Young explained, "Adam was made from the dust of an earth, but not from the dust of this earth. He was made as you and I are made, and no person was ever made upon any other principle." *Journal of Discourses*, 3:316. That is, as he said on another occasion, "When you tell me that father Adam was made as we make adobies from the earth, you tell me what I deem an idle tale. When you tell me that the beasts of the field were produced in that manner, you are speaking idle words devoid of meaning. There is no such thing in all the eternities where the Gods dwell. Mankind are here because they are the offspring of parents." *Journal of Discourses*, 7:285. Similarly, in verse 43, in speaking of saving Noah in the ark, the text states that the Lord "held it [the ark] in his own hand." It would be absurd to assume the verse is saying that God literally held the ark in his hand during the Flood. Instead, the image of God holding something "in His own hand" is a beautiful metaphor for his watchful care and particular protection, much like the poetic image of God protecting Isaiah "in the shadow of his hand" (Isaiah 49:2). The same is true of the phrase in verse 47: "the Lamb is slain from the foundation of the world." There is no literal ovine lamb that will be offered as sacrifice for the sins of the whole world. Literal lambs were offered only in similitude of the one salvific offering of the Savior, who is symbolized by the "lamb without blemish" (1 Peter 1:19; cf. Leviticus 23:12; Exodus 12:5).

49. See also the poetic symbolism in the Doctrine and Covenants 88:45, "The earth rolls upon her wings."

50. Orson Pratt, in *Journal of Discourses*, 21:199.

51. Orson Pratt, in *Journal of Discourses*, 1:281–82.

52. Orson Pratt makes a philologic leap that may not be justified when he interprets Isaiah. Isaiah does not say the earth will die, only that it will "wax old." Without going too much into Isaiah's meaning, the Hebrew word for *wax old* is *bālāh*, "to be used up, to be worn out." Ludwig Kohler and Walter Baumgartner, *The Hebrew*

and Aramaic Lexicon of the Old Testament (Leiden, Netherlands: Brill, 2001), 1:132. The word carries the connotation not of dying but rather of reaching the condition where the object is no longer useful. For example, Isaiah's word that is translated "wax old" is the same word that is used in Genesis 18:12 to describe Sarah, who is too old to have children. Sarah was certainly not dead, though she considered herself "waxed old," that is, "worn out." Nevertheless, even though we believe that questionable proof texting is involved, Orson Pratt is correct when he states that the earth is alive, but not in the sense of having a separate, sentient spirit. It is alive in that it sustains life, will cease to sustain life, and will again be raised to a life of service.

53. Orson Pratt, in *Journal of Discourses*, 21:199. In an article in the *Seer*, Orson Pratt gave a more lengthy explanation of what he believed: "Unintelligent materials are incapable of being endowed with any kind of powers, much less with the wise and intelligent powers that characterize the workings of the universe. God is every moment in nature, and every moment acts upon nature, and through nature. . . . If God should withdraw himself from nature or should cease to act upon it, that portion of it without life or intelligence, (if there be any such portion) would immediately cease all action . . . or in other words unintelligent nature would be entirely dead." Orson Pratt, "Powers of Nature," *The Seer*, March 1854, 227.

54. Brigham Young, in *Journal of Discourses*, 3:277.

55. Fred C. Collier, comp., *The Teachings of President Brigham Young, vol. 3: 1852–1854* (Salt Lake City: Collier's Publishing, 1987), 240–41.

56. Heber C. Kimball, in *Journal of Discourses*, 5:172.

57. Jeffery, "Noah's Flood," 27–45.

58. Jeffery, "Noah's Flood," 36.

59. Jeffery, "Noah's Flood," 36–37.

60. Ben Spackman to Stephen O. Smoot, email. Some of Spackman's work on Latter-day Saint topics includes the following: "Swimming in Symbols," *FARMS Review* 16, no. 2 (2004): 329–36; "Negative Questions in the Book of Mormon," *Insights* 26, no. 4 (2006): 2–3; "The Story of Judah and Tamar," *Religious Educator* 11, no. 1 (2010): 65–76; "Why Bible Translations Differ: A Guide for the Perplexed," *Religious Educator* 15, no. 1 (2014): 31–66.

61. As Pratt stated it, "It has seemed good unto the great Redeemer to institute ordinances for the cleansing of the earth, not from the original sin, but from the sins of the posterity of Adam." *Journal of Discourses*, 1:331.

62. Orson Pratt, in *Journal of Discourses,* 1:290.
63. Bruce R. McConkie, *Mormon Doctrine,* "Earth," 210.
64. Tad R. Callister, *The Infinite Atonement* (Salt Lake City: Deseret Book, 2000), 86.
65. Perhaps 2 Nephi 2:14 applies to the earth, insomuch as the earth is a thing "to be acted upon."
66. See also Acts 18:6 and Ezekiel 3:20; 33:6, 9.
67. McConkie, *Mormon Doctrine,* "Cleanliness," 147.

The "Spirit" That Returns to God in Ecclesiastes 12:7

Dana M. Pike

Ecclesiastes 12:7:

Then shall the dust return to the earth as it was: and **the spirit** shall return unto God who gave it. (King James Version, hereafter cited as KJV)

and the dust returns to the earth as it was, and **the breath** returns to God who gave it. (New Revised Standard Version, hereafter cited as NRSV)

and the dust returns to the earth as it was, and **the life's breath** returns to God who gave it. (New English Translation, hereafter cited as NET)[1]

Influenced by the Restoration doctrine of premortality, some Latter-day Saints have employed the KJV translation "the spirit" in Ecclesiastes 12:7 to support the doctrine that spirit personages leave their mortal bodies at death. Furthermore, Latter-day Saints have sometimes asserted, again citing Ecclesiastes 12:7, that a premortal spirit being can only "return" to God because it previously came from him. This verse has thus become one of several in the Old Testament that some Latter-day Saints have employed as support for premortal existence, a doctrine that is so important in the broader plan of salvation.[2]

Although the doctrine itself is not in question, this paper does question whether "the spirit" in Ecclesiastes 12:7 refers to individual spirit personages and considers the validity of employing this verse as biblical support of premortal existence. In order to determine whether Ecclesiastes 12:7 can bear the interpretation placed on it by many Latter-day Saints, I will (1) review what Latter-day Saints have claimed about the content of this verse, (2) consider 12:7 in the context of Ecclesiastes, especially chapter 12, and (3) analyze the language and meaning of 12:7 in its biblical context.

Latter-day Saint Views on Ecclesiastes 12:7

Latter-day Saint Church leaders and authors have often employed Ecclesiastes 12:7, without making a specific connection to premortality, to emphasize that our individual "spirits" return to God at death. For example, in the past decade, Apostles James E. Faust and Russell M. Nelson each employed this verse in the notes of a general conference address for such support.[3] And commentators D. Kelly Ogden and Andrew C. Skinner have claimed that "the Preacher's comment that 'the spirit shall return unto God who gave it' parallels the teaching in Alma 40:11 that 'the spirits of all men . . . are taken home to that God who gave them life.'"[4] When so employed, the "spirit" mentioned in Ecclesiastes 12:7 is regularly assumed by Latter-day Saints to be an individual spirit personage that was created by God in premortality and that inhabits every human's mortal body.[5]

Using Ecclesiastes 12:7 to emphasize a different doctrinal dimension, a number of Latter-day Saint church leaders have taught something similar to President Harold B. Lee, who, when referring to the premortal existence of our spirits, quoted Ecclesiastes 12:7 and stated, "Obviously we could not return to a place where we had never been, so we are talking about death as a process as miraculous as birth, by which we return to 'our Father who art in heaven.'"[6] Elder Orson Pratt seems to have been among the first Latter-day Saint authorities to employ this logic to provide biblical support for the doctrine of premortality. In 1852 he taught: "We have ascertained that we have had a previous existence. We find that Solomon, that wise man [and traditionally viewed as the author of Ecclesiastes], says that when the body returns to the dust the spirit returns to God who gave it [Ecclesiastes 12:7]. Now all of this congregation very well know, that if we never existed *there* we could not *return* there. I could not return to California. Why? Because I never have been there. . . . But if we have once been there [premortal existence in God's presence], then we can see the force of the saying of the wise man, that the spirit returns to God who gave it—it goes back where it once was."[7] In more recent times, Elder Hugh B. Brown stated, "At a time far antedating Eden, the spirits of all men had a primeval existence and were intelligences with spirit bodies of which God was universal Father. In the Bible we read, 'Then shall the dust return to the earth as it was: and the spirit shall return unto the God who gave it' (Eccl. 12:7)."[8] And Elder Boyd K. Packer taught, "Before we came into mortal life, we lived as spirit children of our Father in Heaven," for which he cited Ecclesiastes 12:7 as support.[9]

Church-produced materials, when they specifically mention this verse, have regularly followed this interpretive approach. For example, the Topical Guide cites Ecclesiastes 12:7 among other scriptures under the entry "Man, a Spirit Child of Heavenly Father."[10] Likewise, 12:7 is cited under the entry "Premortal Life" in Guide to the Scriptures.[11] Interestingly, the Church's Sunday School, seminary, and institute manuals provide little comment on this verse and thus do not connect it with the doctrine of premortality.[12]

Notwithstanding periodic mention by Church leaders and references in Church materials, Latter-day Saint commentators have not generally given much attention to Ecclesiastes 12:7. If they note the verse at all, they understand "the spirit" to be a spirit personage. For example, Daniel H. Ludlow quoted President Harold B. Lee (cited above) in support of his own similar view of this verse.[13] Ellis Rasmussen merely commented, "The 'spirit' lives on and does return to God when the mortal body returns to its constituent 'dust' (Eccl 12:7)."[14] In their brief overviews of Ecclesiastes, neither Victor L. Ludlow, David R. Seely, nor Kerry Muhlestein commented on 12:7.[15] As noted above, Ogden and Skinner provided a relatively extended comment on Ecclesiastes 12:7, seeing in it support for "a duality to the human soul, . . . the concept of an ongoing, living spirit of man after the body's death."[16]

Ecclesiastes 12:7 in Its Broader Context

Before analyzing the verse in question, it is important to understand its context. The Hebrew name of Ecclesiastes is Qohelet, which is the title of the person who is speaking, as found in 1:1, 2, 12, and elsewhere in the book. The KJV and some other English translations render this Hebrew term (*qōhelet*) as "Preacher," but other possibilities include "Assembler" and "Teacher." The English title "Ecclesiastes" derives from the Greek rendition of *qōhelet* in the Septuagint (*Ekklēsiastēs*). Authorship of Ecclesiastes is traditionally ascribed to Solomon, and certain phrases in the early chapters of the book are intended to imply such a connection (for example, 1:1, 12, 16; 2:7, 9). However, his name is never actually mentioned in Ecclesiastes, some passages argue against Solomonic authorship, and the style and language of the book are generally seen as deriving from later in Israelite history. Thus biblical scholars tend to attribute the authorship of Ecclesiastes to some unknown individual living five to seven centuries after Solomon.[17]

Ecclesiastes belongs, along with Job and Proverbs, to the genre of "wisdom literature" found in the Bible and other ancient Near Eastern texts.[18] Wisdom literature generally presents life lessons learned through experience and observation, with the view that "wise" and principled living brings happiness, contentment, and prosperity. Ecclesiastes, however, more than other biblical literature, rather pessimistically emphasizes the challenge and frustration of finding meaning in mortal life, which seems somewhat futile to the Teacher (for example, 2:17–23; 6:7–12; 8:7; 9:12; 10:14). The one certainty, so it is claimed, is death, which will impact everyone and everything (for example, 3:19–20; 12:7). So, while Ecclesiastes does indicate that God is in control (for example, 3:9–18; 7:13–14), the inscrutability of God and his ways in this difficult world is repeatedly underscored.

After ranging through a variety of topics in the first eleven chapters of the book, including the encouragement to enjoy life, especially in one's youth (11:9–10), the closing words from the Teacher, in Ecclesiastes 12:1–7, emphasize the long, dark days of misery encountered in old age and the inevitability of the grave. Ultimately, for the Teacher, "all is vanity"—unsubstantial, transitory, meaningless—in this fallen world (12:8). Although scholars disagree on whether this pericope ends with verse 8 or whether verse 8 begins the epilogue that follows, verse 7 highlights the inevitable conclusion to mortal life: "Then shall the dust return to the earth as it was: and the spirit shall return unto God who gave it." The finality of this termination comes after the lamentable burdens of those who live to older age, in which there is "no pleasure" (12:1). Thus life comes to an end, and "man goeth to his long home [the grave], and the mourners go about the streets" (12:5), and "the spirit shall return unto God who gave it" (12:7).

What follows in 12:8–14 is not presented as the Teacher's words.[19] Scholars regularly suggest this epilogue was added by a later author or editor whose tone seems more positive than that of the text attributed to the Teacher. Verses 9–10 describe the Teacher as a sage, while verses 11–14 provide summary instruction and encouragement from the later author or editor.[20]

Remains of only two copies of Ecclesiastes were discovered at Qumran, part of the cache of documents called the Dead Sea Scrolls. Both were found in cave 4, but nothing beyond chapter 7 survives.[21] The Greek text of 12:7 in the Septuagint is similar to the Hebrew in the Masoretic Text.[22] We are thus dependent upon the traditional Masoretic Text when analyzing this verse. However, this is not problematic, since there are no unusual features attested in the verse. The comments that follow, therefore, utilize the traditional Hebrew text of the Bible.

Analyzing Ecclesiastes 12:7

As is evident from reviewing the three translations of the Bible quoted above, translating the first portion of Ecclesiastes 12:7 is a straightforward matter; most English versions render the Hebrew quite similarly ("Then shall the dust return to the earth as it was"). The second half of the verse, however, is another matter, and it is this latter portion to which attention is now given. According to 12:7, when a person dies, something—"the *rûaḥ*"—returns to God "who gave it."

The real challenge to understanding this verse is determining to what the Hebrew noun *rûaḥ* refers. The broad semantic range of *rûaḥ* in biblical Hebrew is evident by the fact that it can be translated as "breeze, wind, breath, life breath, or spirit." And "spirit" can designate a person's life force and internal power, as well as the "spirit of the Lord," the "spirit of God," the "holy Spirit," an evil spirit, and a heavenly spirit personage. This latter use is rare in the Hebrew Bible and is perhaps best illustrated in 1 Kings 22, in a passage in which the prophet Micaiah proclaimed to an Israelite king: "Hear thou therefore the word of the Lord: I saw the Lord sitting on his throne, and all the host of heaven standing by him on his right hand and on his left. And the Lord said, Who shall persuade [King] Ahab, that he may go up and fall [in battle] at Ramoth-gilead? . . . And there came forth a spirit [*hārûaḥ*, literally "the spirit"] and stood before the Lord, and said, I will persuade him" (1 Kings 22:19–21; see also 2 Chronicles 18:20).[23]

Ezekiel 37:9–10 illustrates well the challenge translators face when rendering the noun *rûaḥ* into English. In this passage the Lord taught Ezekiel about the future gathering of Israel using the imagery of a great army of dead soldiers coming back to life.

> KJV: Then said he unto me [Ezekiel], Prophesy unto the **wind** [*rûaḥ*], prophesy, son of man [a title used for Ezekiel meaning "human"], and say to the **wind** [*rûaḥ*], Thus saith the Lord GOD; Come from the four winds [*rûḥôt*], O breath [*rûaḥ*] and breathe [*pěḥî*] upon these slain, that they may live. So I prophesied . . . and the breath [*rûaḥ*] came into them, and they lived.

> NRSV: Then he said to me, "Prophesy to the **breath** [*rûaḥ*], prophesy, mortal, and say to the **breath** [*rûaḥ*]: Thus says the Lord GOD: Come from the four winds [*rûḥôt*], O breath [*rûaḥ*], and breathe [*pěḥî*] upon these slain, that they may live." I prophesied . . . and the breath [*rûaḥ*] came into them.

According to translators of both the KJV and the NRSV, the divinely commanded "breath" (*rûaḥ*) arrived to bring life to the collective dead.

Another passage pertinent to this discussion is Ecclesiastes 3:19–21, which contains three of the several attestations of *rûaḥ* in Ecclesiastes.

> KJV: For that which befalleth the sons of men befalleth beasts; even one thing befalleth them: as the one dieth, so dieth the other; yea, they have all one breath [*rûaḥ*]; so that a man hath no preeminence above a beast: for all is vanity. All go unto one place; all are of the dust, and all turn to dust again. Who knoweth the spirit [*rûaḥ*] of man that goeth upward, and the spirit [*rûaḥ*] of the beast that goeth downward to the earth?
>
> NRSV: translated similarly where *rûaḥ* occurs.

After observing the lack of justice in mortal life (3:16) but finding some consolation in God's eventual just judgment (3:17), the Teacher turns to the resolute nature of death (3:18). People, like animals, will die. Ecclesiastes 3:19–21 is fairly analogous to 12:7, teaching that when people, and in this case animals as well, die, their bodies decay and turn to dust (see similarly, Psalm 49:12 [Heb., 49:13]). And the spirit [*rûaḥ*] of people (Heb., *benêy-hā'ādām*) goes "upward," presumably meaning to God. However, 3:21 also claims that people and animals "all have one breath [*rûaḥ*]."

Significantly, the *rûaḥ* of animals and of people is represented in this passage with a singular term, not a plural one (not "spirits of," as occurs in Numbers 16:22 and 27:16).[24] Thus the KJV and most modern English translations render the occurrence of *rûaḥ* in Ecclesiastes 3:19 with "breath." The rendering of the additional occurrences of *rûaḥ* in 3:21 with "spirit" is intended to parallel "breath," with *rûaḥ* in all three instances designating the life breath or animating essence that all humans and animals have until death—"they all have one *rûaḥ*."[25] Although it is not always possible to confidently know what translators and commentators intend when they use the word "spirit," it is clear that in this passage *rûaḥ* was not used to indicate spirit personages.

In fact, in none of the 23 occurrences of *rûaḥ* in Ecclesiastes, not counting 12:7, does *rûaḥ* convincingly have the meaning of spirit personage. Sometimes it clearly refers to the wind (for example, 1:6; 11:4). And it occurs (nine times) in the expression "vexation of spirit" (KJV; *rĕʿût rûaḥ*; for example, 1:14, 17; 4:4), which is now often rendered as "striving after wind" (NET and the English Standard Version; the NRSV has "chasing after wind").

In addition to 3:19–21, another passage in Ecclesiastes that deserves attention in discussing 12:7 is 11:5. Again, context provides a helpful guide. Ecclesiastes 11:3 mentions what appear to be matter-of-fact outcomes in the natural world such as, "If the clouds be full of rain, they empty themselves upon the earth." And verse 4 counsels against letting the forces of nature unduly impact what needs to be accomplished in life: "He that observeth the wind [*rûaḥ*] shall not sow; and he that regardeth the clouds shall not reap." Verse 5 further highlights the uncertain nature of life: "As thou knowest not what is the way of the spirit [*rûaḥ*], nor how the bones do grow in the womb of her that is with child: even so thou knowest not the works of God who maketh all." The Teacher concludes this concept in verse 6 by counseling us to proceed with what needs to be done, despite life's uncertainties.

The expression "the way of the spirit [*derek hārûaḥ*]" (KJV) in 11:5 has provoked two main interpretations, as exhibited in ancient and modern translations of the Hebrew text: (1) *rûaḥ* refers to the wind, which makes sense, given the reference to clouds and wind (*rûaḥ*) in the previous verse; and (2) *rûaḥ* refers to the spirit or breath that gives life, which makes sense given the reference to the growth of a fetus in a mother's womb in the latter part of verse 5.[26] Given the historical uncertainty of how to render the phrase "the way of the spirit/*rûaḥ*" in 11:5, it is problematic to use it as support for interpreting the occurrence of *rûaḥ* in 12:7. And given the theological orientation of those involved in producing the ancient and the modern translations of the Hebrew text, Latter-day Saints can be certain that those who rendered *rûaḥ* as "spirit" were thinking of the divinely given animating spirit in all creatures (see the above discussion of Ezekiel 37:9–10 and Ecclesiastes 3:19–21), not spirit personages created by God.

The traditional *non*–Latter-day Saint understanding of Ecclesiastes 12:7—"Then shall the dust return to the earth as it was: and the spirit shall return unto God who gave it" (KJV)—and particularly of *rûaḥ* as "spirit"/life breath/life force, as opposed to spirit personage (a use rarely attested in the Old Testament), correlates terminologically and conceptually with passages in the biblical accounts of creation and the Flood, at least as understood traditionally by non–Latter-day Saints. Genesis 2:7 reads, "And the Lord God formed man of the dust of the ground, and breathed into his nostrils the breath of life; and man became a living soul."[27] The phrase "breath [*nišmat*] of life" here employs *nĕšāmâ*, "breath, life force," rather than *rûaḥ*. But *nĕšāmâ* and *rûaḥ* are sometimes used in conjunction with each other, and can function synonymously (such as in Genesis 7:22; Job 33:4; and Isaiah 42:5).

As an aside, the correlated occurrence of *rûaḥ* and *nĕšāmâ* in Job 27:3 is instructive for this study. Amidst his heartbreaking challenges, Job exclaims that although God has vexed his soul, "All the while my breath [*nišmātî*] is in me, and the spirit [*rûaḥ*] of God is in my nostrils." These two phrases convey essentially the same meaning: despite his difficulties Job still lives. Since the "*rûaḥ* of God" was still in his "nostrils," this use of *rûaḥ* cannot easily refer to Job's premortal spirit being but must be understood as the life breath in all living creatures, the traditional understanding of the "breath of life" mentioned in Genesis 2:7 and elsewhere. The "*rûaḥ* of God," not Job's own spirit, was still in his body.[28]

After Genesis 2:7, the phrase "breath of life" next occurs in Genesis 6:17, where God indicated to Noah, "I, even I, do bring a flood of waters upon the earth, to destroy all flesh [in this context, human and animal flesh], wherein is the breath [*rûaḥ*] of life, from under heaven; and every thing that is in the earth shall die." Here *rûaḥ* is used instead of *nĕšāmâ* (as found in Genesis 2:7), although the translation and meaning of the phrase is clearly the same. The divinely originating animating force or life breath is withdrawn at the end of mortality, from animals as well as from people; this is what is taken back by God (figuratively or literally) at death. The expression "breath of life" only occurs two more times in the Old Testament, Genesis 7:15 and 7:22, and *rûaḥ* occurs in both instances.

As already emphasized above in relation to Ezekiel 37:9–10 and Ecclesiastes 3:19–21, *rûaḥ* is also singular in the verses just reviewed. The "*rûaḥ* of God" was in Job's nostrils (Job 27:3), and the "the *rûaḥ* of life" was found "in all flesh" (Genesis 6:17; 7:22). These biblical passages emphasize *a* spirit or life breath in all living creatures, not individual spirits housed in each creature. There is thus a marked distinction between the use of this biblical language and imagery, which is first found in Genesis 2 and which occurs multiple times in the Hebrew Bible, and between the plural form "spirits" in Alma 40:11 ("the spirits of all men . . . are taken home to that God who gave them life").[29]

Summarizing this analysis, the Hebrew Bible (Old Testament) uses the term *rûaḥ* in a variety of related meanings. It rarely occurs therein to designate a spirit being or personage. The occurrence of *rûaḥ* in Ecclesiastes 3:21 and 12:7, in the context of addressing what happens to the physical body and the *rûaḥ* at death, appears in harmony with statements in Genesis 2:7 (with *nĕšāmâ*) and 6:17; 7:15, 22. Such usage is traditionally understood as referring to the animating "breath" God has given to all humans and animals (again, see Ezekiel 37:9–10; Job 27:3).

Although Latter-day Saints have not consistently dealt with the meaning of the phrase "the breath of life," a review of that topic is too large an undertaking for inclusion in this study.[30] Suffice it to say, a study of Latter-day Saint approaches to the meaning of "the breath of life" does not change *my* view of the meaning of *rûaḥ* in Ecclesiastes 12:7 as presented in this study.

Concluding Thoughts

As the above review of Latter-day Saint approaches to Ecclesiastes 12:7 illustrates, some Church leaders and commentators have employed the KJV rendering "the spirit" to refer to a spirit personage; additionally, some have utilized the verse as support for the doctrine of premortal life.

Given the nonacceptance of premortal life in what became traditional Jewish and Christian theology, it is not surprising that non–Latter-day Saint scholars and theologians do not connect that doctrine with Ecclesiastes 12:7. Furthermore, given the uses and semantic range of the Hebrew term *rûaḥ* and given the whole of the evidence in the Hebrew Bible *as it has come down to us*, there is no biblical support for claiming that "the spirit" that returns to God in 12:7 is a reference to our individual spirit personages.

My understanding of Ecclesiastes 12:7 is that mortal bodies return to the dust, and, to use a poetic figure of speech, a divinely originating *rûaḥ*, a life breath or life force, leaves the body. This animating power, perhaps the Light of Christ,[31] "returns to God" at mortal death. The three translations of 12:7 quoted at the beginning of this paper—KJV, NRSV, and NET— each intended to convey this perspective, whether *rûaḥ* was rendered as "the spirit," "the breath," or "the life's breath." And the combined range of biblical evidence supports this understanding.

Thus, in my opinion, the desire to support with biblical passages the doctrine of all people's premortality, perhaps coupled with an awareness of Alma 40:11 ("the spirits of all men . . . are taken home to that God who gave them life"), has led some Latter-days Saints to utilize "the spirit" in Ecclesiastes 12:7 ("the spirit returns to God") to teach something about individual "spirits." In a case of *application*, rather than interpretation, an uncritical use of the KJV language in 12:7 has been employed to support the true doctrine of spirit beings and their premortality. But the biblical verse itself (12:7) does not teach that doctrine.[32] This does not detract from the reality of spirit persons created by God and of the premortal existence of these spirits. It just means that support for such realities must be sought elsewhere.

Notes

It is a pleasure to contribute to this collection of essays dedicated to Bob Millet. Bob has been a friend and an informal mentor to me in Religious Education at BYU for more than two decades. I appreciate his support, his inquisitiveness, and his enthusiasm for teaching the gospel.

1. The King James Version was published in 1611, the New Revised Standard Version in 1989, and the New English Translation in 2005. Quotations from the Bible in this paper are from the KJV unless otherwise noted.
2. Other verses in the Old Testament employed by Latter-day Saints to support the doctrine of premortal life include Jeremiah 1:5 and Numbers 16:22. For comments on these, see Dana M. Pike, "Before Jeremiah Was: Divine Election in the Ancient Near East," in *A Witness for the Restoration: Essays in Honor of Robert J.*

Matthews, ed. Kent P. Jackson and Andrew C. Skinner (Provo, UT: Religious Studies Center, 2007), 33–59, and Dana M. Pike, "Exploring the Biblical Phrase 'God of the Spirits of All Flesh,'" in *Bountiful Harvest: Essays in Honor of S. Kent Brown*, ed. Andrew C. Skinner, D. Morgan Davis, and Carl Griffin (Provo, UT: Neal A. Maxwell Institute for Religious Scholarship, 2011), 313–27.

3. James E. Faust, "Where Do I Make My Stand?," *Ensign*, November 2004, 19; Russell M. Nelson, "Thanks Be to God," *Ensign*, May 2012, 80.

4. D. Kelly Ogden and Andrew C. Skinner, *Verse by Verse: The Old Testament* (Salt Lake City: Deseret Book, 2013), 2:109.

5. Ogden and Skinner quote statements that George Q. Cannon and Joseph Fielding Smith Jr. made in reference to Alma 40:11, explaining that we move into the spirit world at death, not literally into God the Father's presence, as the phrase "taken home to that God" at death might imply. I will not discuss this question further in this paper. For the quotations, see Ogden and Skinner, *Verse by Verse*, 2:109. See also Brigham Young's statement, "You read in the Bible that when the spirit leaves the body it goes to God who gave it [Ecclesiastes 12:7]. Now tell me where God is not, if you please; you cannot. . . . The Lord Almighty is here by His Spirit, by His influence, by His presence. . . . It reads that the spirit goes to God who gave it. Let me render this Scripture a little plainer; when the spirits leave their bodies they are in the presence of our Father and God, they are prepared then to see, hear and understand spiritual things. But where is the spirit world? . . . It is on this earth that was organized for the people that have lived and that do and will live upon it." In *Journal of Discourses* (London: Latter-day Saints' Book Depot, 1854–86), 3:368, 372.

6. Harold B. Lee, "Understanding Who We Are Brings Self-Respect," *Ensign*, January 1974, 4. I presume President Lee was speaking loosely when he stated, just before quoting Ecclesiastes 12:7, "So the Old Testament prophets declared with respect to death. . . ."

7. Orson Pratt, in *Journal of Discourses*, 1:56a; emphasis in original. O. Pratt returned to Ecclesiastes 12:7 and this same line of reasoning in 1871 and 1872; see *Journal of Discourses*, 14:240–41 and 15:244, respectively. See similarly, John Morgan, "Restitution of All Things—Pre-Existence of Man—First Principles of the Gospel," in *Journal of Discourses*, 20:279.

8. Hugh B. Brown, in Conference Report, October 1963, 92.

9. Boyd K. Packer, "The Standard of Truth Has Been Erected," *Ensign*, November 2003, 24. He also cited Numbers 16:22 and Hebrews 12:9, two other biblical

passages that are often cited by Latter-day Saints, in addition to Jeremiah 1:5 and Ecclesiastes 12:7, in support of premortality. See similarly, N. Eldon Tanner, in Conference Report, October 1969, 50.

10. See Topical Guide, "Man, a Spirit Child of Heavenly Father," at https://www.lds.org/scriptures/tg/man-a-spirit-child-of-heavenly-father?lang=eng. Ecclesiastes 12:7 is also listed in the Topical Guide under the entry "Man, Antemortal Existence of."

11. See Topical Guide, "Premortal Life," at https://www.lds.org/scriptures/gs/premortal-life?lang=eng&letter=p. See also Gayle Oblad Brown, "Premortal Life," in *Encyclopedia of Mormonism*, ed. Daniel H. Ludlow, 4 vols. (New York: Macmillan, 1992), 3:1123, who cited Ecclesiastes 12:7 and Jeremiah 1:5 as biblical support for the doctrine of premortal existence.

12. See the pertinent manuals at https://www.lds.org/manual?lang=eng.

13. Daniel H. Ludlow, *A Companion to Your Study of the Old Testament* (Salt Lake City: Deseret Book, 1981), 279–80.

14. Ellis T. Rasmussen, *A Latter-day Saint Commentary on the Old Testament* (Salt Lake City: Deseret Book, 1993), 494. Rasmussen further noted that "life endures in the spirit" (495) and seems to suggest Ecclesiastes 12 presents legitimate revelation when he claims, "it was revealed to the Preacher that . . ." (494). This is a position few if any other commentators have taken. This is not to say that Ecclesiastes 12 does not contain true doctrine, just that neither the book itself nor commentators claim it is revelation in the same sense that prophetic books make that claim about their content.

15. Victor L. Ludlow, *Unlocking the Old Testament* (Salt Lake City: Deseret Book, 1981), 140–41. See also David Rolph Seely, "Ecclesiastes," in *Studies in Scripture*, vol. 4: *1 Kings to Malachi*, ed. Kent P. Jackson (Salt Lake City: Deseret Book, 1993), 4:463–66; Kerry Muhlestein, *The Essential Old Testament Companion* (American Fork, UT: Covenant Communications, 2013).

16. Ogden and Skinner, *Verse by Verse*, 2:109.

17. For introductory comments on Ecclesiastes, see, for example, Antoon Schoors, *Ecclesiastes*, Historical Commentary on the Old Testament (Walpole, MA: Peeters, 2013), 1–25; Stephen Garfinkel, "Ecclesiastes," in *The Oxford Encyclopedia of the Books of the Bible*, ed. Michael D. Coogan (New York: Oxford, 2011), 1:215–23; Augustinus Gianto, "Ecclesiastes, Book of," in *The New Interpreter's Dictionary of the Bible*, ed. Katharine Doob Sakenfeld (Nashville: Abingdon, 2007), 2:178–85; Tremper Longman III, *The Book of Ecclesiastes* (Grand Rapids,

MI: Eerdmans, 1998), 1–40, but especially 1–15; and M. V. Fox, *A Time to Tear Down and a Time to Build Up: A Rereading of Ecclesiastes* (Grand Rapids, MI: Eerdmans, 1999). Among Latter-day Saint commentators, Seely ("Ecclesiastes," 463–64) and Ludlow (*Unlocking*, 140–41) imply it is unlikely that Solomon wrote Ecclesiastes.

18. For general comments on this genre, with examples, see Richard Neitzel Holzapfel, Dana M. Pike, and David Rolph Seely, *Jehovah and the World of the Old Testament* (Salt Lake City: Deseret Book, 2009), 238–40.

19. Commentators differ somewhat on how these final verses should be divided, with some grouping 12:8 with the previous seven verses, and others (including me) seeing verse 8 as the beginning of the epilogue (1:12–12:7 are presented as the first person musings of the Teacher). Also, different commentators attribute this epilogue to one or to two different authors or editors. Those interested in such details are encouraged to consult the works on Ecclesiastes cited in previous notes of this paper.

20. The secondary nature of 12:8–14, and the consequent impact this has on the interpretation of Ecclesiastes as a whole is rarely addressed by Latter-day Saint commentators on this book.

21. See Eugene C. Ulrich, *The Biblical Qumran Scrolls: Transcriptions and Textual Variants* (Boston: Brill, 2010), 746–48; Martin G. Abegg, Peter W. Flint, and Eugene C. Ulrich, *The Dead Sea Scrolls Bible: The Oldest Known Bible* (San Francisco: HarperSanFrancisco, 1999), 619–21.

22. See Albert Pietersma and Benjamin G. Wright, eds., *A New English Translation of the Septuagint* (New York: Oxford, 2007), 656, which renders Ecclesiastes 12:7, "and the dust returns to the earth as it was and the spirit returns to the God who gave it."

23. The spirit in question here is part of the heavenly host. There is nothing in this passage that suggests this or any other spirit personage in that category would inhabit mortal flesh. The focus of the passage is on Israel's God, surrounded by his heavenly host, and his intent to overthrow Ahab, a king of Israel who had departed from the faith as taught by Israelite prophets. This is not to say that the spirit in 1 Kings 22:21 is not a premortal spirit child of God the Father, just that such a doctrine is not evident in the biblical passage itself.

24. For a study of these two verses, see Pike, "Exploring the Biblical Phrase 'God of the Spirits of All Flesh,'" 313–27.

25. See further the comments on this passage in Longman, *The Book of Ecclesiastes*, 130; see also his comments on 6:10, on pages 176–77.

26. For further details, see for example, *The NET Bible Notes* (Biblical Studies Press, 2005; www.netbible.com, version 5.830), Translator's Note 11, s.v., Ecclesiastes 11:5: "There is debate whether [the Hebrew *mah-derek hārûaḥ*] refers to the wind ('the path of the wind') or the human spirit of a child in the mother's womb ('how the spirit comes'). The LXX [Greek Septuagint] understood it as the wind: 'the way of the wind' (. . . *hē hodos tou pneumatos*); however, the Targum [Aramaic] and Vulgate [Latin] take it as the human spirit. The English versions are divided: (1) spirit: 'the way of the spirit' (KJV, YLT, Douay); 'the breath of life' (NAB); 'how a pregnant woman comes to have . . . a living spirit in her womb' (NEB); 'how the lifebreath passes into the limbs within the womb of the pregnant woman' (NJPS); 'how the spirit comes to the bones in the womb of a woman with child' (RSV); 'how the breath comes to the bones in the mother's womb' (NRSV); and (2) wind: 'the way of the wind' (ASV, RSV margin); 'the path of the wind' (NASB, NIV [and NET]); and 'how the wind blows' (MLB, Moffatt)."

27. The teaching that human flesh will return to the dust at death was first announced by God to Adam in Genesis 3:19 ("for dust thou art, and unto dust shalt thou return"), but that passage says nothing about spirit/breath. The first portion of Ecclesiastes 12:7 obviously employs this concept—"the dust returns to the earth as it was."

28. See similarly, Job 32:8, "But there is a spirit [*rûaḥ*] in man: and the inspiration [*nišmat*] of the Almighty giveth them understanding" (KJV). Most modern English translations render *rûaḥ* here as "breath," in harmony with the sense of Genesis 2:7. This passage deserves its own treatment some other time.

29. I here disagree with Ogden and Skinner, cited in note 5, above, who claim that the content of Ecclesiastes 12:7 "parallels the teaching in Alma 40:11."

30. I originally intended to provide in this study an excursus on Latter-day Saint approaches to the meaning of "the breath of life." It became apparent, however, that such a treatment would be too long and too distracting from the main point of this study to profitably include herein. I plan to publish a separate study of "the breath of life" elsewhere in the future.

31. After having originally considered this connection, I was interested to find it suggested in Draper, Brown, and Rhodes, *The Pearl of Great Price, A Verse-by-Verse*

THE "SPIRIT" THAT RETURNS TO GOD IN ECCLESIASTES 12:7

Commentary, 223, with a link to D&C 88:13: "the light which is in all things, which giveth life to all things."
32. In light of this assessment, I obviously support the excision of Ecclesiastes 12:7 from Latter-day Saint publications dealing with premortal life.

Unveiling Revelation and a Landmark Commentary Series

Craig L. Blomberg

The one major book of the New Testament on which John Calvin never wrote a commentary was the Book of Revelation.¹ Historians believe that he was unsure how to interpret it.² Many writers over the centuries who did pontificate dogmatically about the last book in the Bible might have done better to follow in Calvin's footsteps. Today, however, as is true with almost every book of the New Testament, there are a plethora of outstanding commentaries on John's Apocalypse, from the most scholarly of works to the most devotional.³ Robert Millet, to whom this Festschrift is dedicated, has himself a very short but clear exposition of Revelation.⁴ But now a landmark set of commentaries has begun to appear, the BYU New Testament Commentary Series. In what may be an unprecedented sequence of releasing volumes in a commentary series, the initial offering to appear is on the book of Revelation. Richard D. Draper and Michael D. Rhodes have coauthored the work, which was released first for Kindle in 2013 and presumably will be coming out in hard copy soon.⁵

If Draper and Rhodes's work is any indication of what the rest of the volumes in the collection will look like, this will be the most ambitious, detailed, and scholarly commentary series on a portion of the Bible ever produced by Latter-day Saints. Perhaps even more noteworthy is the use of the full range of scholarly sources. A substantial majority of the items in the bibliography are non-Mormon; within the footnotes, close to half of the citations represent sources authored by non–Latter-day Saints. Of course, a work that utilizes a wide cross-section of previously published commentaries will inevitably draw on a full range of theological traditions, given the comparative paucity of formal Mormon commentaries on individual books of the Bible. Particularly encouraging to me, though, were the number of major evangelical commentaries consulted. Of the 2,249 footnotes in Draper and Rhodes's volume, 243 cited Greg Beale's massive *New International Greek Testament Commentary*,[6] 220 referenced David Aune's three-volume *Word Biblical Commentary*,[7] and 95 mentioned Robert Mounce's *New International Commentary on the New Testament*.[8] The next most commonly cited non–Latter-day Saint commentators were individuals who are not distinctively evangelical, and the numbers dropped off considerably in frequency of appearance: R. H. Charles with 68 occurrences,[9] George Caird with 48 references,[10] and J. Massyngberde Ford with 45.[11]

Undoubtedly to assuage Mormon readers who might fear that the result of this broad-ranging use of sources had compromised the Mormonism of the end product, the authors explain in their preface:

> This study is not a compendium of statements about the book of Revelation nor is it a study of the last days. It is a complete examination of every verse in Revelation within its historical setting. Though a person may enjoy Shakespeare without any knowledge of Elizabethan England, both understanding and appreciation are greatly increased by background knowledge. The same holds for the whole of the New Testament, including Revelation. Therefore, we have studied the most important Jewish and Christian apocalypses and other historical, apocryphal and pseudepigraphical materials from the first and early second centuries AD. Also we have consulted and drawn from scholars both in and out of the LDS community. Of all our sources, however, none trump [*sic*] the information that has come from the Restoration. The inspiring words and insights from latter-day scripture and general authorities have anchored this volume in the

teachings of the Restoration. In all of this, our intent has been to bring John's writing into its fullest light.¹²

What they mean by this is that if non-Mormon authors present evidence from the historical or literary contexts, or from the meaning of the words or grammar of a certain passage in Revelation, which might call into question Latter-day Saint doctrine or statements from General Authorities, that material will not appear in the commentary except on very rare occasions.

This creates an interesting read for the non-Mormon scholar. Early on I recognized that every time the Joseph Smith Translation diverges significantly from the King James Version, Draper and Rhodes will tell us and will find a way to defend the JST. Almost every time Joseph Smith, Brigham Young, or one of a host of other Church leaders made some well-known pronouncement about a certain verse or text in Revelation, their statements will be quoted as the definitive interpretation of that passage. So I was curious to see whether or not the commentary would hang together as a coherent whole at these junctures. Some of the time it does, and evangelical scholars who were given an excerpt from Draper and Rhodes without knowing who wrote it could easily imagine it was someone from their own community. For example, in explaining Revelation 10:6, the authors note that while the KJV renders *hoti chronos ouketi estai* as "that time shall be no longer," in context a more accurate translation (as in the BYU rendition) would be "that there will be no further delay."¹³ Almost all modern translations agree, though the JST merely followed the KJV. Or again, in illuminating the identity of the great whore in chapter 17, we read, "It is easy to see that Rome, like Babylon of old in all her glory and decadence, was an excellent symbol of the corrupt godless societies that had arisen and would arise over the years, more particularly during the last period of earth's history."¹⁴ Few evangelicals would disagree.

On other occasions, the informed non-Mormon scholar would recognize that the source of a certain piece of commentary was Mormon but also see how the believing Mormon could understand it to flow naturally from the text at hand. For example, in speaking of the Greek word *prōtotokos* in Revelation 1:5, usually translated "firstborn," Draper and Rhodes remark that the term "in its literal sense . . . was used to designate either the firstborn or the only son in a household," while "in a figurative sense, it referred to one with rank and dignity. It also carried both messianic and royal nuances."[15] From the context and the Old Testament background, we can clearly see the regal use; from Doctrine and Covenants 93:21 we see the filial use. No logical contradiction is involved in affirming with our authors that both meanings are present in Revelation 1:5, though those who do not accept Joseph Smith's writings as divine revelation would undoubtedly point out that nothing in Revelation itself or its historical background would ever suggest that "Jesus is the firstborn spirit child of Elohim."[16]

In still other places, however, the quote from the Church leader does not merely supplement but seems to conflict with the meaning of the text arrived at through historical-grammatical methods of interpretation. As mentioned above, often the reader of Draper and Rhodes's commentary would not know this unless they do some of their own exegetical homework or are familiar with non-Mormon scholarship. An excellent example of this is the treatment of the seven seals as seven millennia from the creation of the earth to the Lord's Second Coming, a topic to which we will return shortly.

In a few places, Draper and Rhodes themselves offer sufficient exegetical data to show the historical-grammatical interpretation of the text to be at odds with later Mormon commentary and give no indication how they hold the two approaches together. As an illustration, the Greek of Revelation 1:6 includes the words *tō theō kai patri autou*. Apart from any context, they could be translated "to God and his father," as the KJV misleadingly renders them. In context, however, this interpretation is virtually impossible. Verse 5 has just mentioned Christ, who in verse 6 we learn is the one who loves us and who freed us from our sins by his blood and made us a "kingdom" and "priests." Given the frequency with which John in his other writings refers to God as Jesus' Father, and given that the standard *koinē* Greek way of expressing the concept of a possessive adjective governing two nouns was to use the genitive of the personal pronoun placed immediately after the second noun, the phrase would normally mean "to his [Jesus'] God and Father."[17] In fact, this is precisely how the BYU New Testament rendition translates it.[18]

We can state the matter even more strongly. Granville Sharp's rule, formulated by the polymath by that name, also a fighter of the British slave trade with his contemporary William Wilberforce, articulated a pattern for which he found no exceptions in Hellenistic Greek, and even today with sophisticated searchable databases of all extant ancient Greek, remarkably no exception has ever been found. When a single article governs a pair of nouns in an "x and y" construction (that is, "the x and y" rather than "the x and the y"), the two nouns are always closely linked together. But when those nouns are singular, personal and nonproper (including words like "God" and "Father") they always refer to the identical person.[19] In other words, "God" and "Father" in Revelation 1:6 simply cannot refer to two separate individuals, as if God had a Father. Grammatically, the sentence can only mean that the God of Jesus Christ is also his Father.

Draper and Rhodes observe that the JST also translated it this way, but that ten years after Joseph Smith completed his translation, he claimed to have received revelation that his understanding of the KJV was right because "John discovered that God the Father of Jesus Christ had a Father, [and] you may suppose he had a father also."[20] Of course, if that is what the KJV meant in its Elizabethan English, then English-speaking Christians would have been teaching that doctrine widely in between 1611 and the Restoration, but they did not. The KJV translators took *tō theō kai patri autou* to mean "to God, even his [Jesus'] Father,"[21] but rendered it awkwardly, so that Joseph Smith, as he increasingly departed from the more orthodox faith of his earlier years in Mormonism, later misinterpreted it as meaning that God himself had a Father. Or at least he posited a revelation that would trump the historical-grammatical meaning of the text.[22] So it is mystifying to a non-Mormon how Draper and Rhodes can supply sufficient data for concluding that this passage does *not* teach "a plurality of Gods" but then go on to assert that it does indeed promulgate precisely that doctrine.[23] It is time for Latter-day Saints to invert the hermeneutical principle that the later Joseph Smith always trumps the earlier Joseph Smith even when he is demonstrably wrong, at least if words and grammar are allowed to mean what they normally mean. Often the earlier Smith should be allowed to trump the later Smith by a "back-to-our-oldest-roots" hermeneutic.[24] And if this approach isn't *ever* permitted, then that means the JST is wrong in at least this one place, since Smith later changed his understanding. So why should Draper and Rhodes follow the JST so slavishly elsewhere in the commentary?

One early online reviewer of the commentary, David Tayman, who describes himself as "an active and believing Latter-day Saint who might be considered an informed nonscholar," had almost the identical reaction to Draper and Rhodes's attempt to wed large segments of non-Mormon scholarship together with past pronouncements by Latter-day Saint leaders and to allow the JST consistently to trump the original Bible. He writes:

> At times, a selection of LDS traditions surrounding a passage are [*sic*] indeed presented, as they should be. But I noticed times when a passage of modern LDS scripture or modern doctrinal concept is expressed as interpretively authoritative or preferred, with a single authoritative interpretation of the selected quote being presented, and the discussion is then considered resolved. Even non-scriptural texts, such as ideas from the Lectures on Faith, curiously "trump" other concepts without much discussion.[25]

After giving his own examples of this practice, he reaffirms that, "to be clear, I do not find the *existence* of connection and exploration of the uniquely Mormon concepts connected with the text to be incorrect, wrong, or even problematic." He acknowledges that doing so can be "a very important part of helping Latter-day Saints find many roads of relevance and resonance to these texts, and exploring our rich history seeking to find meaning from them." But he then adds that what frustrated him personally "was the way in by which, in *practice*, certain doctrinal ideas tended to 'trump' other options seemingly only by virtue of them being more in line with the author's preferred school of conservative Mormon thought."[26]

One example where Draper and Rhodes offer an alternative interpretation to that of a General Authority might point the way to what they could have done much more often. In discussing the choice of the seven churches to which John had his writing delivered, they first note that Elder James Talmage "suggested that the seven congregations were the last bastions of faith, the great apostasy having engulfed all the other areas."[27] But then they add, "John's symbolic use of numbers, however, should not be overlooked. From early times the number seven connoted that which was full or complete and, therefore, could show that John's message was universal, that is, for all branches of the Church, even those outside of

Asia Minor and those beyond."[28] Draper and Rhodes's option is far more likely than Talmage's, given the very limited and very gradual departure of second-century Christianity from the various forms of the early church in the first century, to which the sizable majority of primary sources point. There never was one moment or even one century when everyone "turned the lights out," turning them on again only to discover a radically different form of Christianity.[29] Draper and Rhodes recognize this, but they present Talmage's view respectfully and do not directly challenge or contradict it, while nevertheless showing us a still more excellent way. One could hope that future volumes in the BYU New Testament Commentary series will acknowledge this kind of diversity of perspectives, even *within* Mormon thought, much more often.

It would be easy to spend this entire short essay focusing just on the key places in Draper and Rhodes's commentary where I disagreed—not with their historical-grammatical exegesis, which rarely ever misleads, but where they rushed too quickly to cite some Latter-day Saint authority, especially outside of the standard works, whose perspective just doesn't fit the culture or context of the Apostle John and his audiences in Asia Minor in the late first century. What I would prefer to do with the rest of this essay, however, is to highlight a cross-section of the many marvelous points of agreement between the commentary and non-Mormon scholarship, especially evangelical Christian scholarship.

I begin with Draper and Rhodes's thorough introduction.[30] Like many conservative Protestants and Catholics, but against the rest of the guild, Draper and Rhodes argue that the case for authorship by the Apostle John is the strongest of the alternative proposals. John was exiled to the island of Patmos in the mid-90s under the emperor Domitian. While actual persecution at this time has sometimes been overestimated, it did exist, even if it wasn't all from Rome or generated by imperial decree. With references to a "synagogue of Satan," Revelation 2:9 and 3:9, in particular, show how deeply seated local Jewish hostility could become. Draper and Rhodes present the four main interpretive approaches to the Apocalypse—preterist, historicist, idealist and futurist—complete with each other, along with their various strengths and weaknesses. They distinguish between "dispensational futurism" and "modified futurism,"[31] which correspond roughly to what is more commonly called dispensational premillennialism and historic (or sometimes "classic") premillennialism. It would appear that Joseph Smith was a historic premillennialist, arguably the most common viewpoint among second- through fourth-century Christians prior to Augustine's *City of God*, which catapulted amillennialism into the prominence it would maintain for the next thousand years in Roman Catholicism.[32] In other words, Smith looked for a literal future millennial reign of Christ on earth but did not exempt the Saints from living through the horrors of the tribulation that unfolds just before Jesus' return.[33] Draper and Rhodes do not, however, discuss pre-, mid- and post-tribulationism *per se*. They do, however, opt for modified futurism with a touch of idealism—the view that the Apocalypse presents timeless behaviors of God throughout history with respect to both his people and his enemies, an approach I have defended myself.[34]

In ways I similarly applaud, Draper and Rhodes go on to discuss the significance of Revelation embodying elements of three literary genres—apocalypse, prophecy, and epistle. They accurately survey the historical background of events at the end of the first century, even if they considerably exaggerate the amount of heresy and apostasy that was occurring.[35] Very helpfully, they highlight those verses and portions of Revelation that have been most stressed by key Church leaders, beginning with Joseph Smith, and nicely summarize their emphases.

I next turn to the commentary proper. At the beginning of each section of text into which our authors subdivide Revelation, they present the Greek text according to the 27th edition of the Nestlé-Aland Greek New Testament,[36] the official Latter-day Saint–approved King James Version in English, and a brand new translation that largely follows the best textual evidence (even when the KJV doesn't) and that remains very formally equivalent in its translation theory but is up to date in its use of twenty-first-century English. Instead of calling it a translation, however, it is labeled the BYU New Testament rendition, even though it is very much a translation in all the ways that the JST is not! This portion of the commentary alone could be of great help to Latter-day Saints, especially those who may be wary of modern translations of the Bible outside the Church and nevertheless find the Elizabethan English of the KJV increasingly difficult to navigate. The commentary portion of the treatment of each pericope is divided into two main sections, "Translation Notes and Comments" (the bulk of each section), which proceeds phrase-by-phrase through the text, and a much briefer "Analysis and Summary" that crystallizes the fundamental meaning of the passage and often reflects on the contemporary significance of its main ideas.

After the Apostle's description of his initial vision in Revelation 1, the commentary which we have already cited several times, John pens the letters to the seven churches, which span all of chapters 2 through 3. Here Draper and Rhodes give excellent historical information about each of the seven cities in which the churches were located, often noting how the choice of metaphors used to describe the spiritual health of the congregations draws directly on details of local history and current events. Particularly important is the recognition that the water supply for Laodicea came either from the cold, clear mountain springs near Colossae or the therapeutic hot spring at Hierapolis. By the time the aqueducts reached Laodicea, however, the water was tepid and hard to drink. Little wonder Christ threatens to spew the lukewarm churches, like their city's water, out of his mouth (see Revelation 3:16). Maybe the Latter-day Saints have not been afflicted with the teaching popular in other Christian circles that "hot" is good and "cold" is bad when Christ declares he wishes the Laodiceans were either hot or cold, as if staunchly resisting the gospel were somehow better than being right on the threshold of making a clear-cut stand for Christ! But Draper and Rhodes recognize that this cannot be, in light of the context in which both cold and hot water are considered good.[37]

Chapters 4 and 5 are nicely summarized by our authors with this introduction: "The throne room theophany provided the seven churches with the reason why they should put their trust in the Eternal God. The rest of the vision gives additional support for that trust. It reveals the power, majesty, and omnipotence of God and the Lamb and also discloses their work as they prepared for the salvation of the faithful."[38]

When we come to chapter 6, Draper and Rhodes apparently have no choice but to adopt the interpretation of Doctrine and Covenants 77:7 that each seal represents a thousand years of world history. Had Joseph Smith heard of the historicist approach of interpreting the seven churches as seven periods of church history and decided to try out the same approach on the seven seals?[39] Of course, conquest,[40] warfare, famine, and death are common enough in any era of world history, so one can make the interpretation work—very broadly and vaguely and by ignoring all the other events that occurred in each era. But what in the context of the Apocalypse or of the end of the first century would ever lead to equating a *seal* with a thousand years, much less requiring the otherwise unbroken chronological progression of events (except for chapter 12) to be ruptured, returning instead to the beginning of world history, a history which we now also know long predated 4000 BC? Texts like Doctrine and Covenants 77, even though they appear in the standard works, are those that reinforce the non-Mormon conviction that we have merely one man's opinion here, not divine revelation.[41]

Joseph Smith's take on the seven seals, nevertheless, is superior to most of the other Christian schemas in that he recognizes that the seals represent what must be removed before one can read the scroll of God's final judgments against humanity. Thus they do not constitute something that happens only right before Christ's return or which occurred only in the first century. Instead, they refer to preparatory events that are not unique to the period of intensified horrors which John calls the "great tribulation" (7:14).[42] They closely resemble the features of life in this fallen world that Jesus taught in his Olivet Discourse would characterize the forty-year period between his death and the destruction of temple in AD 70 (see Matthew 24:1–14), as the preterist stresses. Yet, as the idealist interpreter observes, they have been repeated throughout church history many times over. Finally, as the futurist suspects, they may well characterize the generation before Christ's Second Coming as well.[43]

Interpretations of the relationships among the seal, trumpet, and bowl judgments have historically divided into three main camps. The most straightforward is the strictly chronological, in which all twenty-one judgments follow one another in strict sequence, though not necessarily with identical intervals in between them. This approach fails to account for why the sixth seal and the sixth trumpet appear to bring us to the very threshold of the end, after which the cosmos as we know it cannot continue. And yet it does. A second main view, therefore, is the recapitulative perspective, by which each series of seven judgments covers the same chronological ground but from different vantage points. The sixth of each series then *does* bring us very close to the end of human history as we know it. But this view doesn't adequately explain the intensification from one-fourth of the earth affected during the seal judgments, to one-third during the trumpet judgments, to the entire world during the bowls (or "vials of God's wrath" as the KJV memorably rendered it). The third approach is sometimes called the telescopic view. Here the seventh seal when looked at closely turns out to *contain* the seven trumpets. It is not a separate judgment itself; indeed, when this seal is opened, all that happens is silence in heaven for a half an hour. So too the seventh trumpet, when scrutinized carefully, is seen to *contain* the seven bowls, because while there are storms and earthquakes after it is sounded, they occur in heaven and not on earth. They create what led Eugene Peterson to entitle his incisive little commentary on the Apocalypse *Reversed Thunder*.[44] This approach preserves the strengths of the other two while remedying their weaknesses.[45] While Draper and Rhodes don't discuss this debate explicitly, it appears their commentary would mesh with this third, telescopic approach, which I also think fits John's visions best.

Ever since Hal Lindsey's *Late, Great Planet Earth*[46] became the best-selling book of "nonfiction" (a somewhat dubious label) in the entire decade of the 1970s, countless individuals around the world have imagined that literal, prolonged, and excruciating human warfare will bring world history to its climax just before Jesus comes back. Of course, Lindsey hardly invented this notion; he merely popularized it on an unprecedented scale, which the sixteen novels in the Left Behind series of the 1990s and 2000s elaborated further.[47] Revelation 9:1–12 has always featured prominently in these kinds of interpretations; since the invention of modern flying machines many people have imagined them to be armed helicopters.[48] D. Kelly Ogden and Andrew C. Skinner observe that "some have wondered if John could be describing fighter aircraft, tanks, flame throwers, missiles, and so forth."[49] Meanwhile, the purely historical or preterist perspective notes the Parthian hordes that threatened Rome in the first century with their long-haired riders swinging maces behind them as they rode on armored horses.[50] Draper and Rhodes, though, rightly highlight the demonic origin of these creatures and speak of "hell-inspired pandemonium"[51] and elaborate:

> The images expose the overall horror of the beasts and their powerfully destructive force. To limit them to helicopters or tanks weakens the message and the warning. Their description serves to emphasize the demonic nature that drives them and the broad power to torment they possess. Besides, there is nothing human associated with them.[52]

Chapter 9:20–21 explains why God permits such horrors; even at this late hour he is giving humanity every chance to repent. That so many people do not is astonishing. In Draper and Rhodes's words, "That they can come through the brutalization of the first and second woes with not a shred of turning from their ways reveals an unimaginable depth of hardheadedness, a hardheadedness built on demonic deception."[53] I fully agree and wonder if this doesn't temper the otherwise highly optimistic Latter-day Saint spirit about how few people are so intransigent that they will remain in hell for all eternity. Consider also the evidence of 20:7–10. That unbelievers could live through a millennium of unparalleled goodness directly attributable to the reign of Christ and the goodness of his people and then rebel the moment that Satan is released to deceive the nations (20:7–9) reinforces my conviction. With C. S. Lewis, I affirm that the "doors of hell" may be "locked on the inside,"[54] but let us never underestimate how many may for eternity prefer to be the master of their own destinies, however sordid, rather than bow the knee to any other person or power. It is tragic, but it rings true to history's experience with the human condition.

The vision of the two witnesses in Revelation 11 is regularly described as the hardest chapter of the apocalypse to interpret.[55] But Draper and Rhodes echo many premillennial interpreters when they see the events occurring in Jerusalem ("the great city . . . where also their Lord was crucified"—verse 8) rather than Rome, and when they understand the survivors of Jerusalem's earthquake being terrified and giving glory to the God of heaven in verse 13 as referring to actual repentance and the conversion of many in Israel or among Jewish people more generally.[56] Draper and Rhodes likewise echo most commentators of all theological stripes in seeing the dragon and two beasts of chapters 12 and 13 as a parody of the Father, Son, and Holy Spirit.[57] Against the somewhat more popular understanding of the mysterious number 666 as gematria (Hebrew numerology) for the name NRWN

QSR (Nero Caesar), they agree with the second-most-common scholarly explanation of the number (as do I) that explains it as the triple imperfection of the Satanic trinity trying to mimic the true Godhead (which would yield 777—the number of completion or perfection in Jewish thought) but always falling just short.[58]

With Richard Bauckham's influential study of the theology of Revelation,[59] Draper and Rhodes take the harvest of the earth and the winepress of God's wrath to refer to the harvest of believers and the judgment of unbelievers, respectively. Again, I tend to concur, even if the majority of scholars take both as parallel metaphors for judgment. We have already mentioned briefly the seven bowl judgments and the nature of the great whore of Babylon, which account for most of chapters 15–17. That brings us to Revelation 18, in which the materialistic nature of the whore is highlighted. In other words, not only is the great, evil end-times empire politically powerful and religiously blasphemous, persecuting the true devotees of Jesus, it is also economically wealthy.[60] Draper and Rhodes provide an important corrective to the typical non-Mormon interpretation that sees this empire fulfilled in forces largely outside the professing church of Jesus Christ, such as totalitarian regimes, the most unethical of the multinational corporations and, at times, even the unbridled militarism of the American empire.[61] False Christianity can also readily, if even unwittingly, side with the beast, empowered by the false prophet and serving the dragon. On the other hand, Draper and Rhodes do not adequately acknowledge the allusions to Rome that regularly permeate every part of the Apocalypse, making the most dangerous threat to the Church at the end of the first century *not* the false teachers and apostates from within but persecution and hostility from without.[62]

With Revelation 19, the stage is set for Christ's return and the marriage feast of the Lamb, where he is "wedded" to all of his followers of all time. At this juncture, Draper and Rhodes helpfully clarify a number of the comments they have made and a plethora of quotations of Church leaders they have utilized regarding the role of good works in a person's salvation. Quoting Joseph Fielding McConkie and Robert L. Millet, they explain:

> In the strictest sense, no one can work out his own salvation. No person can create himself, resurrect himself, ransom himself from

sin, or cleanse his own heart from the taints of the world. These are the actions of a God, of an infinite being. We can seek and ask and petition and supplicate. We can apply his blood, take his name, accept his enabling power, and acquire his nature, but we cannot save ourselves. The Saints of God seek above all things for the sanctifying powers of the Spirit in their lives. Through this process they have their beings changed, and by means of that Spirit they are motivated to righteous works, the works of God. In that sense, Christ has begun to live in them (see Gal. 2:20). Thus Paul implored: "Wherefore, my beloved, as ye have always obeyed, not as in my presence only, but now much more in my absence, work out your own salvation with fear and trembling." And now note the Apostle's words: "For it is God which worketh in you both to will and to do of his good pleasure" (Phil. 2:12–13).[63]

This quotation could just as easily have been placed in the context of the great white throne judgment of Revelation 20.

Had the seven seals not been defined as seven millennia, there would have been no need for Draper and Rhodes (or any other Latter-day Saint) to defend the rather strained idea of the Millennium beginning before the return of Christ so that it could include the tribulation that the seventh seal introduces.[64] There is no reason to see the events at the beginning of Revelation 20 occurring at any earlier point than after the return of Christ with which chapter 19 ends.[65] Indeed, this may be one of the most unfortunate places where the medieval church inserted a chapter break in the entire Bible. Revelation 19:20–21 narrates the capture and demise of two-thirds of the unholy trinity—the beast and the false prophet. One's curiosity is naturally piqued as to what will happen to the third member, the dragon—Satan himself. And the first four verses of chapter 20 answer that question at once. He is bound and thrown into the abyss, which is locked for a thousand years. All these punishments happen at the same time, so that the Millennium begins after Jesus has returned to earth, vanquished his enemies, and confined Satan to prevent him from doing his dirty work on earth as he had previously done, in particular during the tribulation depicted by the seven trumpets and seven bowls immediately preceding Christ's *parousia*.[66]

Draper and Rhodes, following the BYU New Testament rendition, do, nevertheless, recognize what the NIV and several other modern translations do not—that it is not just martyrs who are raised to life during the Millennium but all of God's people.[67] The *kai* before the *hoitines* in the middle of verse 4 could be appositional, renaming the same group of individuals. But it is far more likely to be merely continuative, broadening the group from those who were beheaded for their faith to everyone who never received the mark of the beast or worshipped its image.[68] Draper and Rhodes, again following the BYU New Testament rendition, similarly recognize that the aorist tenses at the end of verse 4 are most likely ingressive—the believers began to live and reign with Christ or, to quote the rendition, "they were brought to life and ruled with Christ a thousand years."[69] This is no flashback to Christ's first coming as in classic amillennialism, making the Millennium coterminous with all of church history. Neither is it the final glorious period of the Christianizing of the planet *prior* to Jesus' Second Coming, as in postmillennialism. It is a discrete period between Christ's return and the new heavens and new earth, to which chapters 21–22 turn.

Fortunately, there is less disagreement among commentators of all theological stripes about the final two chapters of Revelation than there is over many other portions of the book. The eternal state will be more glorious than any of us dare ever imagine. And it will be earthier than much of the history of Christianity has envisioned, because the earth as well as the heavens are re-created. Especially because of verse 24, which teaches that the kings of the earth will bring their splendor into the new earth, Draper and Rhodes recognize that "the old earth is not so much annihilated as reconstituted to become a new celestial orb."[70] What our authors might have added is that here is another mandate to care for our earth, as well as our material universe more generally, because at least some of it will be redeemed.[71]

Almost all branches of Christianity have read between the lines of John's prophecy about the new heavens and new earth because Revelation 21–22 leaves so many unanswered questions. Draper and Rhodes, often following previous Latter-day Saint teaching, are no exception, as they go well beyond the biblical text in talking about eternal service and becoming gods. But no umbrage can be taken to their summarizing statement: John "has placed all history in its cosmic setting and shown its movement to the end of time. But even grander than the historical review stands his powerful and pure testimony of his King and his God, whose power, judgment, and love he has shown none can escape."[72] They do overly narrow the application of John's warnings at the end of the book, based on 22:19, reasoning that a warning that one's share of the tree of life will be taken away from a person who adds or subtracts from the book could only apply to those who once had such a share. But John could just as easily mean the share that a person *could* have had. Especially since he has just mentioned all the wicked who remain outside the new heavens and the new earth—"dogs, and sorcerers, and whoremongers, and murderers, and idolaters" (22:15)—it is unlikely that he is thinking only of those within the church who have tampered with his prophecy.[73]

Our authors close the commentary proper by rightly observing that the warning at the end of Revelation refers only to the words of that book itself and not to the whole Bible. Thus it cannot be used to challenge the Mormon conviction that "plain and precious truths" have been removed from Bible that Joseph Smith restored.[74] But it is disingenuous to cite Bart Ehrman's two books on textual criticism for support,[75] because all Ehrman discusses are the textual variants in ancient copies of biblical books that actually exist. He offers not a shred of evidence that the specific kinds of corruption postulated by Smith ever happened.[76] Fortunately, the commentary proper is not the end of Draper and Rhodes's book. A brief epilogue summarizes and applies John's Apocalypse and ends with an extended passage that well merits recitation:

> In sum, the central message of Revelation is that God, the Almighty, is governing this world. Admittedly, Satan, his followers, those mortals he is able to corrupt, and those who corrupt themselves have and are making a hell of it when they can. But God ever limits their time and effectiveness within the bounds of agency. In the end, he and his Saints will win this battle with a decisive victory. Therefore, it behooves all of us to repent and help him move the work forward.
>
> The point is that none can stop the Lord (see D&C 3:1–3). As his righteous children see this, they react in a magnificent hymn of praise to his power, majesty, and mercy. In the words of the heavenly

choir: "Great and marvelous are thy works, Lord God Almighty; just and true are thy ways, thou King of saints. Who shall not fear thee, O Lord, and glorify thy name? For thou only art holy: for all nations shall come and worship thee; for thy judgments are made manifest." (Revelation 15:3–4)[77]

Adela Yarbro Collins has offered the pithiest summary of the Apocalypse I have ever heard: "Jesus wins!"[78] But Draper and Rhodes offer the necessary unpacking of this summary in language that both captures John's message accurately and highlight humanity's appropriate response of worship.

What should a reviewer say in conclusion? Tayman's perspectives from inside the Latter-day Saint movement almost exactly match mine from outside. If the purpose of this commentary series "is simply to present a substantial contribution to moving forward Mormons' familiarity with important (and most unheard in Mormon circles) aspects of the history, traditions, arguments, and usage and language of the book of Revelation, then its value is great, and is to be recommended." If, as some both inside and outside the Latter-day Saint world have hoped, one of the purposes is "that this volume might serve as a contribution to the outside world of Biblical Scholarship, to be engaged with and to further widen discussion of the concepts within," then "the devotional and seeming uncritical way certain modern doctrinal interpretations 'trump' and give the appearance of discrediting some available historical and otherwise convincing views, will not be conducive to this volume making any significant impact in outside scholastic circles."

In either case, Tayman concludes:

> As a combination educational and devotional tool for the wider LDS Community, however, I see this project's development as an important contribution, and one that should be applauded by those who wish to see, at the very least, a wider understanding of at least some of the concepts and problems expressed by the wider Biblical community that otherwise may have no other way of being "safely" expressed from within. While the answers and issues may not be addressed or resolved how all might ideally like them to be, the fact that issues *are being expressed and acknowledged from a substantial work by a Church-run institution* is in and of itself, at least for me, a major gain.[79]

With this I heartily concur. And with twenty-six more books of the New Testament to go, the series has every opportunity to improve even on whatever deficiencies may attach to this initial volume.

The key hermeneutical issue to be decided and hopefully to be discussed in these subsequent volumes is the relationship between General Authorities' statements, even canonical ones, and the historical-grammatical meaning of the text of the New Testament. Will commentators continue to employ all of the standard tools of interpretation that are used with any other work of ancient literature and human communication unless an authority says something seemingly at odds with that interpretation? Will the authority normally trump the text's plain meaning in those instances? Do Latter-day Saint commentators have the freedom to state their preference for the plain meaning? If not, why not and what are the implications of such a restriction? If they have the freedom to do so but prefer a modern dictum over the ancient historical-grammatical meaning, what are the implications of such a preference? If they continue to demonstrate salutary historical-grammatical interpretive skills except where such a dictum exists and then try to hold the two forms of interpretation together in ways others find contradictory, how can they defend such a hermeneutic? This is not just asking for more explicit clarification that modern prophets carry more authority than ancient scripture but rather for explanation of how they can *ever* rely on mere historical-grammatical interpretation if the possibility of later, potentially contradictory revelation remains that would carry greater authority. Why not simply say we have no idea what the text means unless we have an authoritative interpretation on which to rely? Or do those interpretations themselves reflect patterns that could be extended to other texts? These and related questions will hopefully be addressed as the series emerges.[80]

Notes

1. He also never wrote commentaries on the one-chapter letters of 2 John and 3 John.
2. James M. Hamilton Jr., "Why Didn't Calvin Preach Revelation?," *For His Renown*, June 11, 2013, http://jimhamilton.info/2013/06/11/why-didnt-calvin-preach-revelation/.

3. In addition to those that appear in the notes below, see especially Craig S. Keener, *Revelation* (Grand Rapids, MI: Zondervan, 2000); Grant R. Osborne, *Revelation* (Grand Rapids, MI: Baker, 2002); Ben Witherington III, *Revelation* (Cambridge: Cambridge University Press, 2003); Ian Boxall, *The Revelation of Saint John* (Peabody: Hendrickson, 2006); Stephen S. Smalley, *The Revelation to John* (Downers Grove: IVP, 2005); Brian K. Blount, *Revelation* (Louisville: Westminster John Knox, 2009); and Gordon D. Fee, *Revelation* (Eugene, OR: Cascade, 2011).
4. Robert L. Millet, *Making Sense of the Book of Revelation* (Salt Lake City: Deseret Book, 2011).
5. Richard D. Draper and Michael D. Rhodes, *The Revelation of John the Apostle* (Provo, UT: BYU Studies, 2013). A PDF file of the prepublication manuscript disclosed at least one important reason for the delay of the traditional book form—all Hebrew words and phrases were originally typeset as if they read from left to right, creating gibberish for anyone who can read or even pronounce snippets of the language. The Hebrew was thus simply removed from the Kindle edition and will hopefully be reinserted, this time correctly, in the forthcoming hard copy.
6. G. K. Beale, *The Book of Revelation* (Grand Rapids, MI: Eerdmans, 1999).
7. David E. Aune, *Revelation*, 3 vols. (Dallas: Word, 1997; Nashville: Nelson, 1998).
8. Robert H. Mounce, *The Book of Revelation*, rev. ed. (Grand Rapids, MI: Eerdmans, 1997).
9. R. H. Charles, *A Critical and Exegetical Commentary on the Revelation of St. John*, 2 vols. (New York: Charles Scribner's Sons, 1920).
10. G. B. Caird, *A Commentary on the Revelation of St. John the Divine* (New York: Harper & Row, 1966).
11. J. Massyngberde Ford, *Revelation* (Garden City, NY: Doubleday, 1975).
12. Draper and Rhodes, *The Revelation of John the Apostle*, 12.
13. Draper and Rhodes, *The Revelation of John the Apostle*, 241.
14. Draper and Rhodes, *The Revelation of John the Apostle*, 415. Indeed, David E. Aune (*Revelation 17–22* [Nashville: Nelson, 1998], 920–22) reproduces a sketch of the late first-century coin depicting the goddess Roma as a warrior, sitting on seven hills with her foot dipped in the Tiber River—all possible background imagery for this reference.
15. Draper and Rhodes, *The Revelation of John the Apostle*, 67.
16. Draper and Rhodes, *The Revelation of John the Apostle*, 67.

17. If Greek writers or speakers wanted the pronoun unambiguously to modify only the second noun, they would place it *before* that noun. In this instance, the word order would need to be *tō theō kai autou patri*.
18. Draper and Rhodes, *The Revelation of John the Apostle*, 68.
19. Daniel B. Wallace, *Greek Grammar Beyond the Basics: An Exegetical Syntax of the New Testament* (Grand Rapids, MI: Zondervan, 1996), 241. For this construction in Revelation 1:6 as an example, see p. 244. For a comprehensive treatment of Granville Sharp the man and his grammatical discoveries, see Daniel B. Wallace, *Granville Sharp's Canon and Its Kin: Semantics and Significance* (New York: Peter Lang, 2009).
20. Draper and Rhodes, *The Revelation of John the Apostle*, 68.
21. This is either the "adjunctive" use of *kai* to mean "even" or "also" or the "epexegetical" use, meaning "that is to say." On these and related uses, see F. Blass and A. Debrunner, *A Greek Grammar of the New Testament and Other Early Christian Literature*, ed. Robert W. Funk (Chicago: University of Chicago Press, 1961), 227–29.
22. I am not in a position to know whether Joseph Smith's "revelation" caused him to "misread" the text or whether his "misreading" led to his "revelation."
23. Draper and Rhodes, *The Revelation of John the Apostle*, 68.
24. For Joseph Smith's pilgrimage from creating little more than a sectarian offshoot of Alexander Campbell's larger Restoration project to ever growing heterodoxy, see esp. George B. Arbaugh, *Revelation in Mormonism: Its Changing Forms* (Chicago: University of Chicago Press, 1932).
25. David Tayman, "First Impressions: BYU New Testament Commentary Series, 'The Revelation of John the Apostle,'" *Worlds without End: A Mormon Studies Roundtable*, July 9, 2013, http://www.withoutend.org/impressions-byu-testament-commentary-series-the-revelation-john-apostle/.
26. Tayman, "First Impressions."
27. Draper and Rhodes are summarizing in their own words material from James E. Talmage, *The Great Apostasy* (Salt Lake City: Deseret Book, 1958), 44–45.
28. Draper and Rhodes, *The Revelation of John the Apostle*, 65.
29. Borrowing and modifying the famous metaphor used by Hugh Nibley, *When the Lights Went Out: Three Studies in Ancient Apostasy* (Salt Lake City: Deseret Book, 1970).
30. Draper and Rhodes, *The Revelation of John the Apostle*, 14–56. Cf. Craig L. Blomberg, *From Pentecost to Patmos: An Introduction to Acts through Revelation* (Nashville: B & H, 2006), 509–60.

31. Draper and Rhodes, *The Revelation of John the Apostle*, 20–21.
32. See further Donald Fairbairn, "Contemporary Millennial/Tribulational Debates: Whose Side Was the Early Church On?" in *A Case for Historic Premillennialism: An Alternative to "Left Behind" Eschatology*, ed. Sung Wook Chung and Craig L. Blomberg (Grand Rapids, MI: Baker, 2009), 105–31.
33. Cf. esp. Grant Underwood, *The Millenarian World of Early Mormonism* (Urbana: University of Illinois Press, 1993).
34. Craig L. Blomberg, "The Posttribulationism of the New Testament: Leaving *Left Behind* Behind," in *A Case for Historic Premillennialism*, 61–87.
35. For a more accurate, and balanced, presentation, see W. H. C. Frend, *The Rise of Christianity* (Philadelphia: Fortress, 1984), 119–60.
36. Presumably the 28th edition wasn't yet available when the first round of galley proofs was created. Now that the appearance of the hard copy has been delayed, this portion of the commentary could be updated. Whether it is or not remains to be seen.
37. Draper and Rhodes, *The Revelation of John the Apostle*, 123–24. Cf. M. J. Rudwick and E. M. B. Green, "The Laodicean Lukewarmness," *Expository Times* 69 (1957–58): 176–78; and Stanley E. Porter, "Why the Laodiceans Received Lukewarm Water (Revelation 3:15–18)," *Tyndale Bulletin* 38 (1987): 143–49.
38. Draper and Rhodes, *The Revelation of John the Apostle*, 132.
39. See, e.g., William M. Branham, *An Exposition of the Seven Church Ages* (Jeffersonville, IN: Voice of God Recordings, 1965).
40. Like a few commentators before him, Smith took the conquest, however, to refer to the advance of the gospel. In a context in which all the other seals are negative judgments, though, it is better to follow the majority who see this as the negative force of militarism and political conquest by force. See, e.g., Allen Kerkeslager, "Apollo, Greco-Roman Prophecy, and the Rider on the White Horse in Rev 6:2," *Journal of Biblical Literature* 112 (1993): 116–21.
41. But to make the chronology work even vaguely and generally, Draper and Rhodes turn one of the millennia into more than 1,800 years (the fifth seal spanning the time from the birth of Christ to the Restoration), which hardly fits 1,000 years, even taken as a round number. Draper and Rhodes, *The Revelation of John the Apostle,* 171. Millet (*Making Sense of the Book of Revelation,* 25–27) is more consistent in taking each seal as a thousand years, but he does not explain how 4000 BC can be the beginning of "temporal existence," nor what we are to infer as the longer time continues after AD 2000 (the end of the sixth seal).

42. "These plagues are only preliminary in nature. They announce the coming eschaton or final events, but are not a part of it. Their severity, as bad as it is, is but a gentle prelude to what is coming when the inhabitants of the earth face the full wrath of God." Millet, *Making Sense of the Book of Revelation*, 180.
43. See especially Osborne (*Revelation*, 21–22), who stresses that even the futurist should acknowledge a measure of truth in each of the other three main positions.
44. Eugene H. Peterson, *Reversed Thunder: The Revelation of John and the Praying Imagination* (San Francisco: Harper & Row, 1988). George E. Ladd, in *A Commentary on the Revelation of John* (Grand Rapids, MI: Eerdmans, 1972), 164, explains that the lightning, thunder, earthquake, and hail "are conventional ways of expressing majesty and power attending the manifestation of the divine presence."
45. For further details, see J. Ramsey Michaels, *Interpreting the Book of Revelation* (Grand Rapids, MI: Baker, 1992), 56–58. For helpful schematics to illustrate all three approaches, see H. Wayne House, *Chronological and Background Charts of the New Testament* (Grand Rapids, MI: Zondervan, 1981), 146.
46. Hal Lindsey, *Late, Great Planet Earth* (Grand Rapids, MI: Zondervan, 1970).
47. Tim LaHaye and Jerry B. Jenkins, *Left Behind* (Wheaton: Tyndale, 1995–2007).
48. Cf. Hal Lindsey, *There's a New World Coming: A Prophetic Odyssey* (Santa Ana, CA: Vision House Publishers, 1973), 138–39.
49. D. Kelly Ogden and Andrew C. Skinner, *New Testament Apostles Testify of Christ: A Guide for Acts through Revelation* (Salt Lake City: Deseret Book, 1998), 331.
50. Caird, *The Revelation of St. John the Divine*, 122.
51. Draper and Rhodes, *The Revelation of John the Apostle*, 220.
52. Draper and Rhodes, *The Revelation of John the Apostle*, 224. Cf. David E. Aune, *Revelation 6–16* (Nashville: Nelson, 1998), 539, citing *b. Shabbat* 88a and *b. Pesahim* 112b in the Babylonian Talmud that speak of huge armies of destroying angels sent to wreak spiritual rather than physical havoc.
53. Draper and Rhodes, *The Revelation of John the Apostle*, 231.
54. C. S. Lewis, *The Problem of Pain* (London: Geoffrey Bles, 1940), 115.
55. Most would agree, however, with Rob Dalrymple in *Revelation and the Two Witnesses: The Implications for Understanding John's Depiction of the People of God and His Hortatory Intent* (Eugene, OR: Wipf & Stock, 2011), 47, that four major themes of the chapter are that the people of God are divinely protected, called as witnesses, persecuted, yet ultimately vindicated.

56. Likewise, on both these points, Ladd, *A Commentary on the Revelation of John*, 159–60. Osborne (*Revelation*, 433) strikes perhaps a good balance with his description of this picture as "an amalgamation of Jerusalem and Rome into one unholy capital city of the Antichrist."
57. While Draper does not use the term "trinity," except with reference to the evil parody, Eric D. Huntsman and Cecilia M. Peek ("Imperial Cult and the Beasts of Revelation," in *The Life and Teachings of the New Testament Apostles: From the Day of Pentecost through the Apocalypse*, ed. Richard Neitzel Holzapfel and Thomas A. Wayment [Salt Lake City: Deseret Book, 2010], 248) rightly insist that "if one considers the beasts of Revelation together with the satanic dragon, the text presents a trinity of beasts surely meant to be a perversion of the godly trinity."
58. Cf. especially G. R. Beasley-Murray, *The Book of Revelation* (Grand Rapids, MI: Eerdmans, 1981), 219–21. So also Peterson, *Reversed Thunder*, 126; Millet, *Making Sense of the Book of Revelation*, 43.
59. For considerable detail, see Richard Bauckham, *Climax of Prophecy: Studies on the Book of Revelation* (Edinburgh: T & T Clark, 1993), 238–337.
60. Cf. esp. J. Nelson Kraybill, *Imperial Cult and Commerce in John's Apocalypse* (Sheffield: Sheffield Academic Press, 1996).
61. See, e.g., many of the essays in David Rhoads, ed., *From Every People and Nation: The Book of Revelation in Intercultural Perspective* (Minneapolis: Fortress, 2005).
62. On which, see especially Wes Howard-Brooks and Anthony Gwyther, *Unveiling Empire: Reading Revelation Then and Now* (Maryknoll: Orbis, 1999).
63. Draper and Rhodes, *The Revelation of John the Apostle*, 457, citing Joseph Fielding McConkie and Robert L. Millett, *Doctrinal Commentary on the Book of Mormon* (Salt Lake City: Deseret Book: 1991), 3:258.
64. Contrast Millet, *Making Sense of the Book of Revelation*, 54.
65. As often argued by amillennialists and postmillennialists, who postulate a flashback, as at the beginning of chapter 12.
66. See especially Keener, *Revelation*, 464–65.
67. The 2011 NIV at least added a footnote expressing the alternative translation. The text itself renders the relevant section of verse 4 as "And I saw the souls of those who had been beheaded because of their testimony about Jesus and because of the word of God. They had not worshiped the beast or its image and had not received its mark on their foreheads or their hands." But the footnote adds that the end of

the first sentence and beginning of the second could be rendered as "God; I also saw those who. . . ." The latter is more literal.
68. "Because John envisions the whole church needing to resist the world system, he can portray the church as a martyr church, though his wording can allow for others who have withstood the beast but were not specifically martyred." Keener, *Revelation*, 467.
69. Draper and Rhodes, *The Revelation of John the Apostle*, 477.
70. Draper and Rhodes, *The Revelation of John the Apostle*, 493.
71. See, e.g., David Mathewson, "The Destiny of the Nations in Revelation 21:1–22:5: A Reconsideration," *Tyndale Bulletin* 53 (2002): 121–42.
72. Draper and Rhodes, *The Revelation of John the Apostle*, 530.
73. Beale, *The Book of Revelation*, 1153. Cf. J. William Fuller, "'I Will Not Erase His Name from the Book of Life' (Revelation 3:5)," *Journal of the Evangelical Theological Society* 26 (1984): 297–306.
74. Draper and Rhodes, *The Revelation of John the Apostle*, 536.
75. Draper and Rhodes, *The Revelation of John the Apostle*, 536n90.
76. Bart D. Ehrman, *The Orthodox Corruption of Scripture* (New York: Oxford University Press, 1993); Bart D. Ehrman, *Misquoting Jesus: The Story Behind Who Changed the Bible and Why* (San Francisco: HarperSanFrancisco, 2005).
77. Draper and Rhodes, *The Revelation of John the Apostle*, 541.
78. During a question-and-answer time in a seminar at the national meetings of the Society of Biblical Literature at least twenty-five years ago. I have no further recollection of the specific setting.
79. All three quotations from Tayman, "First Impressions."
80. One thinks of at least partly analogous debates on the use of the Old Testament in the New. A huge literature has examined the variety of methods the New Testament uses in citing and applying the Old Testament. Is the full range of apostolic exegesis, in turn, reproducible? Interpreters are split down the middle but at least the discussions are out in the open and the implications of the various approaches widely analyzed.

Part III
Christianity

Mormons and Evangelicals in Dialogue
Finding the Right Questions

Richard J. Mouw

Harvard scholar Diana Eck is frequently quoted in interfaith discussions as saying that "if you know only one religion, you know no religion."[1] A rabbi friend of mine used the quotation in several public dialogues we did together, and finally I decided to challenge him in a private conversation. "I don't think you really believe that," I said. And since I knew something of his background I went directly to his family history. "Take your grandmother," I said, "living in the ghetto in Eastern Europe. She spent her life as a strictly observant Jew, attending synagogue faithfully, and praying fervently to God several times a day. Do I have it right?" He nodded. "So now take a Jewish sophomore at UCLA—let's say he's nineteen years old. He too is faithful in his observance but not nearly steeped in the tradition as your grandmother was. Unlike her, though, he has the opportunity to take a course on Hindu philosophy. He receives an A for his work in the course, writing a very fine paper comparing the Eastern idea of reincarnation with the Hebrew view of the afterlife. So now he knows more than one religion, which your grandmother did not. Do you really think he has begun to know Judaism better than she did?"

Before he could respond, I continued. "And my grandmother—she came to these shores with her parents as a child. They went through rough times in urban New Jersey. When she married, she gave birth to six children, one of whom died as a teenager when his appendix burst. The Dutch Reformed Church they attended was her haven. She read the Bible and prayed every day. But the fact is that she could not utter one true sentence about any religion but her own. As her grandson, I can write books on the subject of religious pluralism, but I simply refuse to . . ."

My rabbi friend cut me off. He was laughing. "OK, OK, Richard, I get the point. You're right. I promise I will never quote that line from Diana Eck again!"

I'm glad he agreed. I'm convinced I'm basically right about this. But later I did think about it more, and I got back to him with a slightly revised assessment. Diana Eck is wrong to imply that our grandmothers were deficient in their religious "knowing" when compared to the students who take her courses at Harvard. But someplace in her comment there is a truth that is lurking. Our knowledge of our own religion can certainly be enhanced by studying it in comparison to another religious perspective. When I study Islam or rabbinic Judaism, I'm not sure I increase in my knowledge of the God whom I worship. But I do get clearer about the content of my evangelical theology by viewing it in comparison to other systems of thought.

The same applies to ecumenical dialogue. When Protestants engage in explorations with Catholics about the meaning of the sacraments, or the role of Mary in Christ's redemptive mission or papal authority, representatives of both communities often testify that—while the important theological differences have not gone away—they come away from this kind of in-depth conversation with a much clearer grasp of the teachings of their own tradition.

And the gains are not only in technical theological understanding. An "iron-sharpening-iron" kind of theological dialogue can also be the occasion for spiritual growth. In the give-and-take of serious exchanges with people with whom we disagree on profoundly important subjects, we often discover that the exercise has benefited our souls as well as our minds.

RICHARD J. MOUW

I have just referred to two different kinds of serious dialogue about important matters of faith. One kind is properly called interfaith. There is no question, for example, that when Jews dialogue with Buddhists they do so as representatives of different faith communities. In the most obvious sense of the term, Buddhism, Judaism, Islam, and Christianity are different religions.

The other kind of dialogue is typically referred to as ecumenical, a term related to *oikos*, the Greek word for household or family. This terminology is used most often in Christian circles. Ecumenical dialogue takes place between Catholics and Lutherans, or between Methodists and Baptists. But the differences between, say, Orthodox Jews and representatives of the Reform Jewish movement, or between Sunni and Sufi Muslims, can also be thought of as ecumenical. This kind of conversation occurs within a broad religious family which has spawned different family lines.

The beginning of the twenty-first century saw the emergence of a serious ongoing dialogue between representatives of the Mormon and evangelical communities. This dialogue has taken the form of face-to-face group meetings and shared publishing projects—of which this volume is a case in point. Clarification regarding disagreements and commonalities has occurred. Friendships have been formed. There have even been times of praying and singing together.

An interesting question to ask about this particular dialogue is where it belongs with reference to the two categories I have just briefly outlined. Is it interfaith or ecumenical? There is no question that, around the time that our Mormon-evangelical dialogue got started at the turn of this century, if these questions were to be posed to members of both communities, the shared verdict would have come down on the interfaith side of things. One obvious reason for this is that the term *ecumenical* is not common parlance in either community. It has little place in the language of Mormonism; and for evangelicals the term, while fairly well known, is seen as the thing that more liberal types use in order to bring about organizational unity—not a popular cause among evangelicals.

But the underlying issue in the posing of the question is still an interesting one. Properly understood, are Mormons and evangelicals branches of the same broad Christian *oikos*? In good part, long-standing hostility between the two communities has made it difficult to discuss that question calmly. On the evangelical side, the standard assessment of Mormonism in the second half of the twentieth century was that of the "countercult" movement. Mormons, like the Jehovah's Witnesses and the adherents to Christian Science teachings, have so redefined the traditional Christian terms, according to that assessment, that they are not only non-Christian— they are, in effect, *anti*-Christian. On the Latter-day Saints' side, it was not unusual for Mormons to insist, for very different reasons to be sure, that Mormonism was not a branch of Christianity. It has not been uncommon, for example, for folks from each community to refer to what we have initiated in our dialogue as an interfaith effort.

In each case the "different faiths" assessment has been shaped by a century and a half of hostility. Buddhists and Catholics can describe each other as representing different faiths without meaning thereby to insult each other. But the history of Mormon-evangelical relations was antagonistic from the outset. In his canonized First Vision account, Joseph Smith reported that the Son of God had informed him regarding the traditional Christian communities "that all their Creeds were an abomination in his sight."[2] One of the standard terms employed by Mormons in describing the traditional Christian communities was "apostasy"—the abandonment of a faith that was now being restored in the establishment of Mormonism. Nor were representatives of those communities any less condemning of the views expressed by the Prophet and his followers.[3]

But a history of mutual condemnation does not make the ecumenical question irrelevant. The Protestant Reformers often condemned the Catholics as members of a "false church," and the Catholics consistently responded in kind. Some of that still continues today, but in the larger picture, Catholics and Protestants these days do not perpetuate those stereotypes of each other.

Having raised the question about how to characterize our dialogue, I must confess that I do not have a clear answer to offer to the question of whether my discussions with my Mormon friends are ecumenical or interfaith. A few years before I began my initial involvement in the dialogue, I was much influenced by the verdict offered by Jan Shipps in her 1985 study of Mormonism. Shipps, a Methodist scholar who was the first non-Mormon to serve as president of the Mormon History Association, proposed that Mormonism should be seen as a "new religious movement." The relationship of Mormonism to Christianity, she argued, is much like the relationship of Christianity to Judaism.[4] In each case there are both continuities and discontinuities.

In offering that picture, Shipps was clearly suggesting that Mormonism is a different "faith" than Christianity. Mormonism shares much in common with Christianity, of course, just as Christianity shares much in common with Judaism. But they are, as Shipps made her case, different religions. This seemed to sit well with the Mormon academics who admired Shipps's work. Her placement of Mormonism outside of the broad Christian household certainly provoked no outcry from her Mormon colleagues.

Again, I began my active involvement in dialogue with Mormon scholars in general agreement with Shipps's account. I had found it unacceptable simply to relegate Mormonism to cult status. The cult label basically functions, for evangelicals at least, as an instrument of condemnation. Cults are secretive. They are aggressive proselytizers, employing manipulative methods of persuasion. They use language in deceptive ways.

I found Shipps's category of "new religious movement" a helpful way to view Mormonism. It allowed me to approach Mormons with respect and a genuine desire to learn from them. It gave me a framework for exploring both continuities and discontinuities, without descending into accusations about being "pseudo-Christian."

Right around the time that we began our dialogue, however, Jan Shipps published another book, *Sojourner in the Promised Land: Forty Years Among the Mormons.* As her subtitle makes clear, in this volume Shipps was gathering her thoughts together about her four-decade academic sojourn in Mormon studies. The book contains some essays previously published in various journals, plus some essays making their first appearance in this book. In the final section of the book Shipps moves to a directly autobiographical mode. Of special interest for me is her chapter entitled "Is

Mormonism Christian? Reflections on a Complicated Question"—an essay originally published in *BYU Studies* but extensively reworked for the book. Throughout her career of studying Mormonism, she says, there has been "a clear modulation . . . in the way I have approached what Mormonism is and whether it is Christian."[5]

In reflecting back on her "new religious movement" discussion of 1985, Shipps does not retract her placement of Mormonisn within this category. But in explaining it she touches on a nuance that I had missed in my reading of her earlier book. Yes, she had argued there that Mormonism was discontinuous with Christianity in much the same way that Christianity had seen itself with Judaism. But in her reflections on that thesis in her 2000 book, she notes that "just as the early Christians believed that they had found the only proper way to be Jewish, so the early followers of the Mormon prophet believed they had found the only proper way to be Christian."[6]

The point here that I had not adequately attended to in accepting her "new religious movement" placement of Mormonism was that the analogy that she draws in making that decision is itself a complicating factor. There was a time, for example, when Islam occurred as "a new religious movement," and it emerged in an environment deeply formed by Judaism and Christianity. But its relationship to those other religious movements was not the same as Christianity's to Judaism, or Mormonism's to Christianity. Muslims did not see themselves as having discovered "the only proper way" to be a Jew or a Christian. The continuity–discontinuity pattern in Islam's relationship to those other two faiths was not of the intimate sort that Mormonism bears to Christianity, or Christianity to Judaism.

Again, that is an important nuance to the use of the "new religious movement" category. Some movements are "newer" than others. Hinduism and Judaism are different "faiths" than Christianity, but as a Christian I see Christianity in a very obvious way as the *fulfillment* of Judaism in the way that I do not see Christianity in its relationship to Hinduism. My differences with my Jewish friends have much to do with my conviction that there is something significant within their own faith tradition that they fail to understand properly. And my Mormon friends make similar claims about my understanding of Christianity.

RICHARD J. MOUW

After forty years of studying Mormonism as a Methodist, Shipps concludes that to ask whether Mormons are Christians is to pose—to use the phrase included in the title of her essay—"a complicated question." And it has become even more complicated in recent years, she observes, because of what she sees within the Mormon community as "a contemporary rhetorical shift that seems to be turning Mormon into an adjectival modifier used to signify a particular kind of Christian."[7] In the early years, Mormons—like others who claimed a "restorationist" identity—explicitly distanced themselves from the traditional Christian denominations in order to emphasize the ways they were restoring something that had long been corrupted. But in our present context, the Saints "no longer need an *other* to set themselves apart either rhetorically or categorically."[8] Thus, claiming their place within the broad Christian tradition—to be sure, as a purer form than others who claim Christian identity—has become an acceptable posture.

In coming to her own conclusion about whether Mormons are Christians, Shipps points to the ways in which the question of who is truly Christian has loomed large in many splits that have taken place in Christian history. It has been quite common, she argues, for a group that separated from another group—Constantinople from Rome, Protestants from Catholicism, Methodists from Anglicanism—to raise the question of whether what they had left deserved to keep the label "Christian." Her own assessment on who has a right to claim the label, she confesses, is presently an agnostic one. The final verdict must await, she says, "the fullness of time, [when] a decision will be made in a higher court." Until that day arrives, she says, she will live with the knowledge that she is "one who sees 'through a glass darkly,'" which means that all she can do is to "withhold judgment, counting within the definition of Christian any church, sectarian movement, liberal or conservative coalition, or new religious tradition that gathers persons together in the name of Christ and, in so doing, creates genuine community wherein women and men may—to use Methodist phraseology—take up the cross and follow him."[9]

I agree with Jan Shipps that we humans should not second-guess God about what will be revealed at the Last Judgment. None of that releases us, however, from serious attempts to discern the workings of the Spirit in ways that are available to us in our pre-eschaton present situation: "Dear friends, do not believe every spirit, but test the spirits to see whether they are from God" (1 John 4:1, New International Version, hereafter NIV). In our past relations with Mormons, though, we evangelicals have not always gone about this testing-the-spirits in a manner that honors another important biblical mandate. "Always be prepared to give an answer to everyone who asks you to give the reason for the hope that you have," the Apostle Peter instructs believers. Then he immediately adds: "But do this with gentleness and respect" (1 Peter 3:15–16, NIV). We have often fallen short on the "gentleness and respect" part of it.

Gentle respect for people with whom we disagree is key to productive efforts at dialogue. One reason why we evangelicals have had difficulties in this kind of engagement has to do with the way our approaches to other perspectives—and this has certainly been the case with our approach to Mormonism—had been dominated by soteriological and apologetic concerns. We have seen them as souls whose eternal destinies are imperiled, and we have also wanted to disprove key elements in their worldview.

To be sure, there is much merit in caring about salvation and doctrinal truth. But having them dominate our approaches to others can also lead to dangers. The most basic one is also spiritual in nature: the real possibility that we will bear false witness against our non-Christian neighbors. In evangelization contexts, we rightly want to get people to see the inadequacy of their present religious commitments. But this can lead us to portray those commitments in the worst possible light so that Christian belief and practice can clearly be seen as the better way. It is easy in such contexts to emphasize the negative aspects of the other perspective or even to distort the positive elements of that perspective so that things are portrayed as worse than they really are.

The challenge is to seriously engage other religious perspectives while being very careful not to say anything in our theology of religions that would deny what is at the core of our own deepest convictions. Certainly one criterion for the adequacy of an evangelical theology of religions is whether or not our formulations comport well with our attempts to bring the gospel to those who have not yet accepted Christ. Nonetheless, it is a helpful exercise to attempt, temporarily at least—and especially because of our overemphasis in the other direction in the past—to bracket our overt interests in evangelism and apologetics as we think about some broader topics in this area.

This bracketing allows us to offer assessments that are not easy to make when we are concentrating primarily on who is in and who is out. When the main question is whether we have good reasons to believe that, say, a fully committed Buddhist—someone whose understanding of reality is spelled out in consistently Buddhist terms—can go to heaven, then many of us will have to answer in the negative. In this context it is appropriate for evangelicals to say that Buddhism is a false religion in the sense that a person who wants to enter into a saving a relationship with the one true God will not achieve that goal by following the Buddhist path.

But this is not the same as saying that there is no truth in Buddhism. If we can bracket the question of whether Buddhists *qua* Buddhists can be saved, then we are free to evaluate this or that particular Buddhist teaching or practice in terms of whether it illuminates reality, and we may well find many good and true elements in the Buddhist worldview. Indeed, we might even find things in the Buddhist understanding of spiritual reality that can enrich—even by calling our attention to spiritual matters that we have not thought about clearly—our own Christian understanding of religious truth.

Needless to say, the best way of truly attempting to understand another religious perspective is to engage in genuine dialogue with persons who adhere to that perspective. And in order to do this, we need to be clear about the basic *point* of the enterprise. Relativism runs rampant in contemporary culture, in both the high and the low versions, and it is important that we not encourage the dilettantish samplings of various worldviews.

For me a key element for successful dialogue is entering into the engagement with a genuine learning posture. In approaching another religious perspective it is important to see how specific beliefs function within the larger web of beliefs and convictions in that perspective. Evangelicals have often failed to do this in our approach to Mormonism. We have approached

Mormonism as one of many cults and then assessed specific teachings by using what I have called elsewhere a "doctrinal checklists" test.[10] We ask what each group believes about the sole authority of the Bible: Jehovah's Witnesses get a pass on this point, Christian Science and Mormonism a fail. Then we move to the Trinity, the substitutionary Atonement, the Virgin Birth, and so on.

What such an approach fails to take into account is the deep differences among religious perspectives. Bishop Stephen Neill—himself a veteran of decades of interfaith dialogue in India—criticized this comparative-method approach to the study of religions for the way it treats "all religions as commensurables." We cannot simply lay different religious formulations about the divine side by side, Neill says, while ignoring the fact that in doing so we are, in each case, isolating the specific conception from other ideas with which it is interconnected. To do so is to detach the specific ideas of God "from the living experiences which has given rise to them. In so doing we rob them of their life," thus ignoring "the living fabric of the religion from which the idea has been somewhat violently dissevered."[11]

The proper alternative is to enter into the perspective of the person representing another faith, trying as much as possible to place ourselves "within" the framework of the other belief system, in order to probe the deep questions that are being asked within that framework. To do this is to make genuine communication possible. And this, in turn, means setting aside our much-too-common temptation to win rhetorical victories that cut off any interesting conversations.

Our recent efforts at Mormon-evangelical dialogue have been characterized by this empathetic approach: a mutual desire to learn, a spirit of genuine listening. For me this has meant coming to a much better understanding of specific Mormon teachings that had been troubling me deeply.

One of the most challenging issues in this regard is the "being" of God. It is difficult to think of a Mormon teaching that is more offensive to the theological sensitivities of adherents to traditional Christian theology than the notion that the members of the Godhead are "of one species" with human beings.[12] The mainstream of both the Jewish and Christian traditions are united in insisting upon a vast ontological gap between the Creator and human creatures. God and human beings are of different orders of "being." The God of the Bible is seen as the *totaliter aliter*, the Wholly Other who infinitely transcends his creation. From such a perspective, nothing could be further from the truth than the thesis that God and humankind are "of one species."

On the doctrinal checklist approach to get to the point of recognizing that disagreement is basically to shut down the conversation. What evangelicals, along with others in Judaism and Christianity, take to be an essential—even non-negotiable—doctrine about the nature of God stands in stark opposition to Mormon teaching. What more can be said?

The fact is, there *is* much more to be discussed. We can ask why it is that Mormonism wants God to be so like us that Mormons insist upon a "one species" understanding of God and humans. I have explored this question in writing on a couple of occasions with a focus on the historical context in which Mormonism arose,[13] observing that Ralph Waldo Emerson's transcendentalism and Mary Baker Eddy's Christian Science teachings all showed up in the same period as the emergence of Mormonism. Those three metaphysical perspectives obviously differed from each other in key respects. Indeed, in the case of Mormonism and Christian Science, they were exact opposites, with Joseph Smith arguing that everything is physical, so that even God has a physical body, while Mary Baker Eddy espoused the philosophy that everything is spirit, with the appearance of matter resulting from a sinful delusion.

On a deeper level, however, Smith, Emerson, and Eddy shared a common religious motivation. Each of them wanted to bring the realm of the divine nearer—to reduce the ontological distance between God and human beings. The founders of both transcendentalism and Christian Science, for example, would have no difficulty endorsing the Mormon claim that God and human beings are of "the same species," even though they would diverge in their respective metaphysical accounts.

What these reduce-the-distance theologies also had in common was that they emerged in an environment shaped significantly by the high Calvinism of New England Puritanism. And I have observed that it can be plausibly argued that New England theology, while it rightly, from an orthodox Christian perspective, stressed the legitimate *metaphysical* distance between God and his human creatures, at the same time it often fostered an unhealthy *spiritual* distance between the Calvinist deity and his human subjects. Thus it should not surprise us that movements arose to shrink that spiritual distance, even if we evangelicals must deeply regret that they did so by also shrinking the distance of Being, rather than by drawing on corrective teachings—such as the incarnation and the person of the Holy Spirit—that can be found within orthodox Christian theology.

This historical analysis is supported by the case set forth by Janice Knight in her 1994 *Orthodoxies in Massachusetts*. Knight, an English professor at the University of Chicago, distinguishes between two schools of thought within the orthodox Calvinism of American Puritanism. One view, represented by William Ames, depicts God as a distant sovereign before whom human beings must live in reverence in the presence of transcendent mystery. In this conception, a pattern of spirituality developed where the believer's relationship to God was dominated by metaphors like master/servant and king/subject. To be sure, a warmer piety often showed up in this context but always against the background that everything else had to be understood with reference to God as "an exacting lord" and a "demanding covenanter."[14]

Knight finds a significant alternative within Puritanism to Ames's conception of sovereign power as the primary attribute of God. She details the ways in which some American Puritans looked to Richard Sibbes, Ames's contemporary in Old England, for their theological inspiration. The Sibbesians offered a Calvinist conception of God in whom mercy and not power was primary. Here was a clear alternative to Ames's view of a deity to whom, as Knight puts it, "the only bridge was the contractual covenant, not the personal Christ."[15]

Sibbesian Calvinism never abandoned the deep conviction of divine sovereignty. But it did downplay any notion of an *arbitrary* sovereignty by stressing images of divine intimacy, as in Sibbes's assurance that God "applies himself to us, and hath taken upon himself near relations, that he might be near us in goodness. He is a father, and everywhere to maintain us. He is a husband, and everywhere to help. He is a friend, and everywhere to comfort and counsel. So his love it is a near love. Therefore, he has taken upon him the nearest relations, that we may never want [that is, miss out on] God and the testimonies of his love."[16]

One can find clear hints in Mormon writings that Mormonism was in its own way looking for something like the Sibbesian alternative to that strain of Calvinist orthodoxy that emphasized the spiritual distance between God and humanity. One example: the Mormon philosopher Sterling McMurrin saw Mormon metaphysics as seeking to eliminate traditional Christian theology's insistence on the "strange distance that separates God from the world of human struggle, aspiration, and tragedy."[17]

McMurrin's comment points to an important agenda to be addressed by evangelicals and Mormons in dialogue. What are the questions—the deep spiritual questions—to which the "one species" teaching is an answer? What are Mormons attempting to bring about in their own spiritual quests in their efforts to reduce the metaphysical distance between themselves and the members of the Godhead? And—the corresponding topic to explore— what questions are evangelicals trying to answer in their insistence on God's "Wholly Other-ness"?

In the early 1960s there was considerable attention given by Anglo-American philosophers to St. Anselm's well-known "Ontological Argument" for the existence of God, the basic point of which is to show that once we grant the definition of God as "that Being than which no greater can be conceived," then it is impossible to imagine God as nonexistent.

Much of the debate about this argument focused on technical philosophical topics, especially the question whether existence could be thought of as a "property" that something or someone possesses alongside of other properties, such as shape, size, and the like. And it was not uncommon for some Christian believers who witnessed these discussions to question their value. Why would anyone think that one could establish a "proof" for the existence of the God of the Bible by means of an abstract argument regarding "the Being than which no greater can be conceived"? A natural response from a faith perspective was to quote the well-known line attributed to Blaise Pascal: "Not the God of the philosophers, but the God of Abraham, Isaac, and Jacob!"

One philosopher who joined the philosophical fray was Norman Malcolm, a devout Christian and a longtime professor at Cornell University. In an essay he wrote on the subject, he offered his own case for seeing the ontological argument as having some philosophical merit. After making his technical case, though, he also addressed the question of the spiritual relevance of the argument. This kind of argument, he observed, cannot be evaluated properly "without an understanding of the phenomena of human life that give rise to it." Then he offered this explanation:

> There is the phenomenon of feeling guilt for something that one has done or thought or felt or for a disposition one has. One wants to be free of this guilt. But sometimes the guilt is felt to be so great that one is sure that nothing one can do oneself, nor any forgiveness by another human being, would remove it. One feels a guilt that is beyond all measure, a guilt "a greater than which cannot be conceived." Paradoxically, it would seem, one nevertheless has an intense desire to have this incomparable guilt removed. One requires a forgiveness that is beyond all measure, a forgiveness "a greater than which cannot be conceived." Out of such a storm of the soul, I am suggesting, there arises the conception of a forgiving mercy that is limitless, beyond all measure. This is one important feature of the Jewish and Christian conception of God.[18]

I find Malcolm's observations about the importance of an "understanding of the phenomena of human life that give rise to" the conception of a "being than which no greater can be conceived" to be profoundly provocative. Why is it so important for us to be discussing together the nature—the "being"—of God? Malcolm is pointing us in a similar spiritual direction as Sterling McMurrin did when the Mormon philosopher insisted that undergirding the Mormon doctrine of the nature of the divine is to have access to a God who is not far removed from "the world of human struggle, aspiration, and tragedy."

Evangelicals have not typically attributed these spiritual impulses to Mormons. The title of the viciously anti-Mormon film is telling in this regard: we have portrayed Mormons as "God-makers"—people who, rather than submitting to the power and authority of the God of the Bible choose instead to create a God in their own human image in order to lift themselves into the realm of the divine. The fundamental question driving Mormon theology and spirituality in such a depiction is "How can I become my own god?"

I do not recognize that depiction in the Mormons with whom I have been in dialogue. Here, for example, is what my friend Robert Millet has written about the kind of Christianity that he embraces in a very personal way: to be a follower of Jesus, he says, is to be a person "who acknowledges their fallen state and their need for redemption; one who recognizes that the only source of redemption is through the person and power of Jesus of Nazareth, the Messiah, the Savior; one who receives the proffered gift of atonement by covenant with Christ, seeks for, and obtains a remission of sins and a new heart."[19]

In that very evangelical-sounding testimony, Millet uses a form of the verb *proffer* in referring to what is provided in the atoning work of Christ. As one who pays close attention to the specific language employed by my Mormon friends when they describe the Atonement, I have noticed the frequent use of the same verb—not one whose use I come across much elsewhere these days—in writings of other Mormon scholars. Here, for example, is another Latter-day Saint friend, Spencer Fluhman, on the subject of divine grace: Mormons, he writes, "stand with the rest of Christendom, 'all amazed . . . [and] confused at the grace he so fully proffers us.'"[20]

My puzzlement about the use of the verb was solved when I discovered that my Mormon friends were alluding to one of the two or three most frequently sung hymns at Mormon sacrament services, one that begins with this verse:

> I stand all amazed at the love Jesus offers me,
> Confused at the grace that so fully he proffers me.
> I tremble to know that for me he was crucified,
> That for me, a sinner, he suffered, he bled and died.

The hymn goes on to express wonderment that Jesus would leave heaven's throne to "rescue a soul so rebellious and proud as mine," with this chorus after each of the three verses:

> Oh, it is wonderful that he should care for me
> Enough to die for me!
> Oh, it is wonderful, wonderful to me![21]

What do the spiritual dynamics expressed in that hymn mean for our continuing conversations about the "being" of God? Obviously the serious theological disagreement remains. But it does bring the dialogue down to issues that are heartfelt for both evangelicals and Mormons. We each testify that we "stand amazed" at the gift of salvation "proffered" to us by means of the cross of Calvary. When we ask the question "What would it take to save the likes of us?" we both look to that cross in awe and wonder. Where we disagree theologically is in our very different answers to the question of how best to understand the nature of the God who makes that gift possible. Is he the deity who is "of one species" with us, or is he "the Wholly Other," separated from us in his "being" by an infinite ontological gap?

Norman Malcolm's suggested pattern of going from our spiritual need for a Savior to our theological formulations about the nature of God is a helpful one in this regard. Our shared amazement at the gift of salvation has to do with a deep sense of our own sinfulness—each of us sees ourselves as "a soul so rebellious and proud as mine," as the sacrament hymn puts it. A sinfulness "than which no greater can be conceived" requires a love "than which no greater can be conceived." And such a love can be "proffered" only by a Savior "than which no greater can be conceived."

Again, those shared spiritual concerns point us to important questions to pursue with each other in our continuing dialogues. And the arguments are not easy ones to resolve. But it is important to focus on the right questions. If we can discover that we share a deep sense of our own unworthiness, and that we acknowledge together that only a "proffered" gift of amazing grace can rescue us from our guilty condition, this can mean a more productive—spiritually and theologically—stage in our discussions together.

Focusing on the right questions certainly also means a change in the tone of our efforts at mutual understanding—no small accomplishment, given the history of our angry exchanges in the past! It is a step worth taking: engaging in a dialogue that takes place as we stand together at the cross, "amazed at the love Jesus offers" us, and "confused at the grace that so fully he proffers" us there, at Calvary.

Notes

1. Quoted by Ari L. Goldman, *The Search for God at Harvard* (New York: Random House, 1991), 33.
2. Karen Lynn Davidson, David J. Whittaker, Mark Ashurst-McGee, and Richard L. Jensen, eds., *Histories, Volume 1: Joseph Smith Histories, 1832–1844*, vol. 1 of the Histories series of *The Joseph Smith Papers*, ed. Dean C. Jessee, Ronald K. Esplin, and Richard Lyman Bushman (Salt Lake City: Church Historian's Press, 2012), 214.
3. J. Spencer Fluhman provides abundant examples of early anti-Mormon rhetoric in chapters 1 and 2 of his *A Peculiar People: Anti-Mormonism and the Making of Religion in Nineteenth-Century America* (Chapel Hill: University of North Carolina Press, 2012).
4. Jan Shipps, *Mormonism: The Story of a New Religious Tradition* (Urbana: University of Illinois Press, 1985),148–49.
5. Jan Shipps, *Sojourner in the Promised Land: Forty Years Among the Mormons* (Urbana: University of Illinois Press, 2000), 329.
6. Shipps, *Sojourner*, 337–38.
7. Shipps, *Sojourner*, 345.
8. Shipps, *Sojourner*, 347.
9. Shipps, *Sojourner*, 356.
10. See Richard J. Mouw, *Talking with Mormons: An Invitation to Evangelicals* (Grand Rapids, MI: Eerdmans, 2012), 15–17.
11. Stephen Neill, *Christian Faith and Other Faiths: The Christian Dialogue with Other Religions* (New York: Oxford University Press, 1961), 3.
12. See, for example, "Discourse by Elder O. F. Whitney," *Millennial Star*, January 17, 1895, 34.
13. See Richard J. Mouw, "Joseph Smith's Theological Challenges: From Revelation and Authority to Metaphysics," in *The Worlds of Joseph Smith: A Bicentennial Conference at the Library of Congress*, ed. John W. Welch (Provo, UT: Brigham Young University Press, 2006), especially 218–19.

14. Janice Knight, *Orthodoxies in Massachusetts: Rereading American Puritanism* (Cambridge: Harvard University Press, 1994), 78.
15. Knight, *Orthodoxies*, 77.
16. Richard Sibbes, *The Complete Works of Richard Sibbes* (Edinburgh: J. Nichol, 1862–64), 4:196; quoted by Knight, *Orthodoxies*, 83.
17. Sterling M. McMurrin, *The Philosophical Foundations of Mormon Theology* (Salt Lake City: University of Utah Press, 1959), 14.
18. Norman Malcolm's contribution to a symposium on "Contemporary Views of the Ontological Argument," in *The Ontological Argument: From St. Anselm to Contemporary Philosophers*, ed. Alvin Plantinga (Garden City, NY: Anchor Books, 1965), 158.
19. Robert L. Millet, *The Vision of Mormonism: Pressing the Boundaries of Christianity* (St. Paul: Paragon House, 2007), xx.
20. J. Spencer Fluhman, "Authority, Power, and the 'Government of the Church of Christ,'" in *Joseph Smith: The Prophet and Seer*, ed. Richard Neitzel Holzapfel and Kent P. Jackson (Provo, UT: Religious Studies Center, 2010), 225–26.
21. Charles H. Gabriel, "I Stand All Amazed," *Hymns* (Salt Lake City: The Church of Jesus Christ of Latter-day Saints, 1985), no. 193.

Mormonism and the Heresies

Brian D. Birch

Mormonism and Creedal Christianity

On February 23, 2010, Cardinal Francis George delivered Brigham Young University's forum address. As archbishop of Chicago, George was then serving as president of the United States Conference of Catholic Bishops. In the years prior to this address, his organization had been working with Latter-day Saint leaders on humanitarian projects and social issues of mutual interest. That February day was a high-water mark for Mormon interfaith relations. The Lord's Prayer served as the invocation for the event and was offered by a BYU faculty member and devout Catholic. Appropriate to the event, George's remarks focused on areas of common cause among Catholics and Latter-day Saints and emphasized the need for both traditions to advance religious freedom around the world. "However different our historic journeys and creeds might be," he said, "our communities share a common experience of being a religious minority that was persecuted in different ways in mid-19th-century America."[1]

A stark example of these differences was manifest just nine years prior in June 2001, when the Vatican officially ruled that Latter-day Saint baptisms were not legitimate Christian rites. Since the Second Vatican Council (1962–65), the Catholic Church has recognized baptismal ceremonies from other Christian denominations as valid Catholic sacraments. However, questions arose among American bishops as to whether LDS baptisms met the conditions for inclusion, and they forwarded their query to Rome for a ruling. The response came in the form of a *responsum ad dubium* from the Vatican's Congregation for the Doctrine of the Faith, the body charged with the protection of Catholic orthodoxy. The Congregation's response consisted simply of one word: "Negative." Among the more striking features of this case is that the Vatican has ruled on only six baptismal cases since 1970.

Finally, after two months of waiting, an article appeared in the Vatican's official newspaper explaining the Church's rationale for the ruling. The piece was authored by Luis Ladaria, the secretary to the congregation and a member of the Church's International Theological Commission. After a brief excursion into Mormon cosmology, taken in part from Joseph Smith's King Follett Sermon, Ladaria concludes that "the words Father, Son and Holy Spirit, have for the Mormons a meaning totally different from the Christian meaning. The differences are so great that one cannot even consider that this doctrine is a heresy."[2] The reference to heresy is important because, since the Second Vatican Council, the Catholic Church has not disqualified baptisms performed by those who are said to advocate heretical positions. Thus the ruling was a clear and very public effort to place Mormonism outside the pale of Christian ecumenical communion.[3]

Furthermore, between 1995 and 2001, five major denominations formally rejected Mormonism as part of the Christian community of faith. In addition to the Roman Catholic Church, the United Methodist Church, the Presbyterian Church USA, the Southern Baptist Convention, and the Missouri Synod of the Lutheran Church all offered similar rulings on the status of Mormonism.[4]

In the face of these doctrinal repudiations, the LDS Church has accelerated its efforts in the areas of interfaith outreach and cooperation.[5] Coinciding with these activities, there have been serious attempts to more carefully address theological issues related to the rulings of these major denominations.

Notable among these is the fifteen-year Mormon-evangelical dialogue jointly led by Robert L. Millet and Richard J. Mouw. Among the recurrent themes in these dialogues has been the extent to which Mormonism does indeed diverge from theological positions affirmed by creedal Christianity.[6] Latter-day Saint scholars have repeatedly found themselves responding to questions implying that Mormon ideas are too radical to be characterized as legitimately Christian. Importantly, these questions are not coming from strident anti-Mormon voices but from serious, well-respected, and friendly interlocutors.

This dynamic has led to more productive efforts to carefully explicate Mormon concepts such as grace, Atonement, revelation, and the Trinity. It has also pressed Mormons to more carefully consider questions regarding the sources of doctrinal authority and inconsistencies manifested in the historical record. On the other side, evangelical scholars have been led to reconsider characterizations of Mormonism within their communities. Furthermore, they have been exposed to the range of theological ideas within Mormonism and have recognized the more redemptive dimensions of Mormon thought. Gerald McDermott underscored this point in his book-length dialogue with Robert Millet. Regarding their discussion of grace, he states that "what I am now about to say may cause all of my evangelical friends to desert me, or think I have lost it. But I think we evangelicals have something to learn from our Mormon friends on this subject." He goes on: "Perhaps we can learn from Mormons that we have wrongly separated faith from works, that we have created a false dichotomy between justification and sanctification, and that while we are saved from being justified by the law, nevertheless the law is still 'holy, and just, and good.'"[7]

Earlier in 2004, Richard J. Mouw offered his famous "Tabernacle apology" to Latter-day Saints, saying that evangelicals have often "seriously misrepresented the beliefs and practices of the Mormon community." Regarding the dynamics of the Mormon-evangelical dialogue, though Mouw confesses he hasn't succeeded in convincing Mormons to embrace Calvinist Christianity, he does acknowledge that "they've been willing to hear me out. And sometimes—not always, but sometimes—they even sound as though they're moving in the direction of some of the key convictions that are for me rooted in my Calvinism."[8] In the weeks following the dialogue at Wheaton College in 2009, *Christianity Today* reported that "Mouw is not alone in perceiving that Millet and other 'neo-orthodox' thinkers at BYU have been migrating closer to belief in salvation by grace alone."[9] This is hardly a comfort for skeptics of the dialogue within the Latter-day Saint community. From its very beginnings, the effort has had to continually justify its value and demonstrate that its participants are not advocating a developmental view of doctrine.

Noteworthy, however, is the extent to which these concerns are nothing new and have come from both sides of the Mormon intellectual spectrum. Fifty years ago, Sterling McMurrin voiced similar questions regarding theological convergence with mainstream Christianity—and most especially in its more conservative forms. In his *Theological Foundations of the Mormon Religion* (1965), McMurrin was unapologetic in his defense of Mormon heterodoxies. He was particularly fond of showcasing the more liberal strands in Mormon theology and believed them to possess "the authentic spirit of the Mormon religion."[10] In fact, McMurrin's project was designed to call out for criticism precisely the theological tendencies that Mouw and Millet have welcomed and encouraged. Referring to these tendencies as the "old orthodoxy," McMurrin worries that an emphasis on human depravity and helplessness could push Mormonism too close to the doctrine of original sin. The issue was so important to him that he believed how it was treated "may determine much of the character of Mormon theology in the future."[11]

Referring to these trends in Mormon thought as a kind of "Jansenist movement," McMurrin maintained that "such negativism in the assessment of man, whether scriptural or otherwise, is a betrayal of the spirit and dominant character not only of the Mormon theology but also of the Mormon religion, which draws heavily on doctrinal foundations in supporting its practical affirmation of man and its positive moral ideal."[12]

In this respect, McMurrin was prescient. Few would question that a theological pivot has occurred as it relates to questions of redemptive theology. At this point, the dispute surrounds the implications of this new orientation and the extent to which it is a form of revisionism. Though Millet agrees with McMurrin in identifying similar trends as a "movement," it is one that is "in harmony with the teachings of the Book of Mormon and one that may be long overdue."[13] These include the need to emphasize human helplessness in sin and thus the need for a robust theology of grace.

One can certainly contest McMurrin's characterizations, and there has been no shortage of critical responses.[14] Nevertheless, it is a mistake to discount the direction in which he hoped to point the conversation in clarifying the relationship to mainstream Christianity. Though Latter-day Saints possess no obligation to the creedal tradition, they have not been anxious to connect themselves with explicitly heretical positions. Given the politics of interfaith dialogue, there are good reasons for this reluctance, but there are also important respects in which Mormonism resonates more strongly with heresiarchs like Pelagius or Arius than with Augustine or Luther.

With these considerations in mind, the second part of this essay will seek to clarify Mormonism's relationship with two momentous heresies, namely Pelagianism and Arianism. Both of these heresies dealt with critical areas in Christian self-understanding—grace and the Trinity—and have set the theological agenda for the past seventeen centuries.

Pelagianism: Grace and Freedom

McMurrin famously claimed that Mormonism is "essentially Pelagian in its theology" and demonstrates "a quite remarkable similarity to the Pelagian doctrines."[15] We begin here because Pelagianism is often viewed as the most pernicious of all the heresies in the Christian tradition. It is named after Pelagius, a fourth-century monk from Britain whose ideas were hotly contested in the churches of his day. Most notable among his detractors was Augustine, who succeeded in his effort to anathematize Pelagian teachings and whose ideas gave decisive shape to the direction of Christian thought. Augustine's accounts of sin, providence, and grace were developed and sharpened in response to Pelagius, who rejected original sin and argued that human beings naturally possess the freedom to choose between good and evil.

In his treatise "On the Possibility of Not Sinning," Pelagius offers up a moral argument. If God commands the avoidance of sin, then the *ability* to do so must be present. Only an unjust God would command actions impossible to obey. Pelagius declares "how perverse it is to believe God to be capable of something which not even the nature of mortals would respect!"[16] His arguments intend to show both the inconsistency and ethical deficiencies that follow from accounts of human sinfulness as inevitable by necessity. If this were the case, he argues, human beings would be falsely secure in thinking it impossible for them to avoid sin. Given genuine choice, the human being "would have to exert himself to fulfill what he now knows to be possible" and would work "to achieve his purpose for the most part, even if not entirely."[17]

Pelagius's insistence on robust human freedom led to the accusation that he denied the fundamental role of divine grace in salvation. As a result, his works were condemned by the synod of Carthage in 418 and later at the Council of Ephesus in 431.[18]

A generation after Pelagius, another debate arose surrounding the teachings of John Cassian that came to be labeled "semi-Pelagianism." In the attempt to reconcile the Augustine/Pelagius divide, Cassian argued that human freedom is indeed disabled through original sin and yet not entirely dead. Though human beings may freely *initiate* a turn toward God, he argues, the Christian life cannot be *sustained* without the ongoing cooperative grace of God. Though popular for a season, this more moderate position was eventually condemned by the Synod of Orange in 529.[19]

The debate was revitalized yet again during the Dutch Reformation through the writings of Jacob Arminius. Though schooled in Calvinism, Arminius found aspects of its anthropology thoroughly repugnant. He accepted a version of total depravity, but he also argued that the human will must be free to choose God. This led him to propose a restoration of human freedom to respond to the gift of salvation.

Predictably, this led to charges of Pelagianism and eventuated in the Synod of Dort (1618), which condemned the teachings of Arminius and his followers. Despite this ruling, the influence of Arminian ideas continued to spread and eventually made their way to America through John Wesley and Charles Grandison Finney—a contemporary of Joseph Smith. For traditional Calvinists, these positions remain unacceptable because "we can't even believe until God in his grace and in his mercy first changes the disposition of our souls through his sovereign work of regeneration."[20]

This background leads us to a vital component in Arminian (and later Wesleyan) anthropology, namely the concept of *prevenient grace*. In order to rescue Christian anthropology from the menacing implications of total depravity, Arminius emphasized a form of grace that preceded the confession of faith. This grace is said to restore human freedom that was lost in the Fall such that human beings can choose God. As a conditional form of grace, it "creates both awareness and capacity, but neither is saving unless responded to or exercised by one's grace-endowed freedom."[21] Grace thus occurs at two stages and is said to retain two necessary elements of Christian teaching: total depravity and free response to the gospel. Article VIII of Wesley's Articles of Religion states that after the Fall "we have no power to do good works, pleasant and acceptable to God, without the grace of God by Christ."[22] Though not a biblical term, prevenient grace is understood by its advocates as a "theological category developed to capture a central biblical motif."[23]

In the revivalist fervor of his youth, Joseph Smith was exposed to both Calvinist and Wesleyan perspectives. In a remark that portended things to come, he reported that during this critical period "my mind became somewhat partial to the Methodist sect" (Joseph Smith—History 1:8). Given the development of his revelations and reflections, it is apparent that the austerity of Calvinism was repellent to him and remained so from an early age.

The Book of Mormon expresses some key distinctions in these debates. It is closely aligned with positions advocated by other restorationist movements, particularly that of a universal atonement and its role in the restoration of human agency. Among the most important passages is that expressed through the prophet Lehi: "And the Messiah cometh in the fulness of time, that he may redeem the children of men from the fall. And because that they are redeemed from the fall they have become free forever, knowing good from evil; to act for themselves and not to be acted upon, save it be by the punishment of the law at the great and last day, according to the commandments which God hath given" (2 Nephi 2:26). Historically, Latter-day Saints have emphasized the central role of human agency in the cosmological order. Because agency is metaphysically necessary, grace has been seen as a supplement to, and reward for, freely chosen good works.

It is here that important questions emerge and the contest over Mormon anthropology is waged. In what sense is moral agency a *natural* part of human being? In what sense is this agency a gift? How does the restoration of agency in the Atonement work for Latter-day Saints? McMurrin is explicit in his view. "By the fall man gained the possibility of a moral life through the implementation of his freedom, and by the atonement he gained the possibility of salvation in eternal life through merit."[24] This sounds very much like an expression of well-known passages in the Doctrine and Covenants: "Verily I say, men should be anxiously engaged in a good cause, and do many things of their own free will, and bring to pass much righteousness; for *the power is in them*, wherein they are agents unto themselves. And inasmuch as men do good they shall in nowise lose their reward" (D&C 58:27–28; emphasis added).

However, this passage can be taken in at least two very different ways. First, it could be understood as describing the power being "in them" as a necessary and constitutive feature of the human soul "all the way down;" or it could be read more specifically as describing a condition of grace brought about through the universal application of the Atonement.

Returning to prevenient grace, because it "precedes the free determination of the will," it provides the condition for the possibility of a free response to God's *saving* grace.[25] On this account, freedom is possible only because God acts upon an otherwise depraved and fallen soul. Human beings "are dead in trespasses and sins until the prevenient grace of God awakens and enables them to exercise a good will toward God in repentance and faith."[26] Prevenient grace is not sufficient for salvation, but provides only a "grace-endowed freedom" that allows one to embrace God's sanctifying grace.

Millet, in an effort to find common ground with his evangelical interlocutors, explicitly accepts prevenient grace as an acceptable Latter-day Saint theological category. Though prevenient grace is not found in Mormon discourse, Millet employs it in connection to Latter-day Saint categories and distinctions. "The effects of the Fall tend to entice humankind away from God, from godliness, and from an acceptance of the gospel of Jesus Christ. To counteract this influence, there are unconditional blessings and benefits—graces, *prevenient graces*, that flow from the Almighty."[27] The first of these he identifies as the "Light of Christ," which is given to all human beings as a kind of "inner moral monitor" that leads them to the Christian gospel. The second of these benefits is the ability of human beings to choose between good and evil. On this account, the Atonement is understood to liberate humanity from the effects of the Fall and allow for a genuine kind of freedom, otherwise known as "libertarian free will."[28]

Importantly, however, there is a connotation traditionally associated with the term that is left unspecified in Millet's writings. This is the extent to which prevenient grace is said to affect *individual* human capacities, particularly with regard to agency. More specifically, to what extent can prevenient grace be said to be *regenerative* for Mormons? Regeneration was clearly involved in the theologies of Arminius and Wesley, both of whom accepted the doctrine of total depravity and understood prevenient grace as regenerating a devastated human nature. Those who receive it are said to be taken from a state of total enslavement to sin to a state of freedom wherein one is able to choose the saving grace of Christ.[29] Because Millet rejects the doctrine of total depravity, he cannot accept Arminius's and Wesley's notion of prevenient grace whole cloth, or can he?[30] He does talk about grace as a "divine enabling power": "The Lord agrees to do for us what we could never do for ourselves—to forgive our sins, to lift our burdens, to renew our souls and *recreate our nature*, to raise us from the dead and qualify us for glory hereafter."[31] So the interesting question here is the extent to which Millet's anthropology allows for a nature that stands in need of regeneration and, if there is such a need, how this might affect other areas of the Mormon redemptive narrative.

On this latter point, McMurrin is emphatic. Though he does not reject regenerative grace by name, the implication is clear. He declares that "the release from the bad consequences of the fall is fully achieved by Christ's sacrifice and the *individual soul* is unaffected, therefore, by Adam's transgression."[32] As we have seen, McMurrin is most anxious to distance Mormon theology from views that connect the condition of human fallenness with the need to re-create human nature: "The sacrifice of Christ immediately compensates for the act of Adam, and mankind, who had no part in the act, is free of its negative consequences."[33]

This approach hearkens back to the homilies of Brigham Young, who, in an 1882 Tabernacle address, stated that it has been "fully proved" that human beings "naturally love and admire righteousness, justice, and truth more than they do evil." He goes so far as to explicitly refute a staple of biblical theology: "Paul says in his Epistle to the Corinthians, 'But the natural man receiveth not the things of God,' but I say it is the unnatural 'man that receiveth not the things of God.' . . . The natural man is of God. We are the natural sons and daughters of our natural parents, and spiritually we are the natural Children of the Father of light and natural heirs to his kingdom."[34]

President Young's declarations notwithstanding, one of the most oft-quoted passages in the Book of Mormon comes from King Benjamin's sermon in which he states that "the natural man is an enemy to God, and has been from the fall of Adam" (Mosiah 3:19). The 1985 edition of the Latter-day Saint scriptures cross-references this passage with 1 Corinthians 2:14. This is, of course, yet another example of the challenges involved in trying to connect and synthesize the seemingly disparate strands of Mormon thought; yet the implications are critical as they relate to theological discourse.

Millet understands his project as an attempt to provide an account of grace that is more consistent with the Mormon scriptural canon and which may take account of theological insights obtained through his engagement with evangelical Protestant theology. The implication has been the extension of Mormon thought in the direction of Arminian anthropology and away from the Pelagian sensibilities of McMurrin and others who understand the Mormon project as a radical departure from orthodox conceptions of sin, grace, and human freedom.

Arianism: The Begotten Son

The Vatican's ruling on Latter-day Saint baptisms raises a variety of intriguing questions related to theological boundary maintenance. Notable among these is the extent to which Mormon concepts of God depart from the language and intent of the Trinitarian language of Nicea. The issue that led to the creed involved the relationship between the Father and Son. The Gospel of John opens as follows: "In the beginning was the Word, and the Word was with God, and the Word was God." In subsequent verses, the Word is described as being "made flesh" as "the only begotten of the Father" (John 1:1, 14).

Events that led to Nicea were ignited by a young Alexandrian named Arius, who openly challenged Bishop Alexander on the relationship between the Father and the Son. Arius and his followers interpreted the biblical language of John to mean that the Son, though unique, was a created being and thus subordinate to the Father. They describe him as "the perfect creature of God, but not as one of the creatures; offspring, but not as one of things begotten."[35] Arius also relied heavily on biblical passages describing the Jesus as the "firstborn of every creature" (Colossians 1:15) and "firstborn among many brethren" (Romans 8:29). An important consideration for the Arian theologians was the preservation of the oneness and transcendence of the Father. God had to be separate from the world of change and becoming that was said to be inherent in the created order. To qualify this status would make the Father "composite and divisible and mutable and a body" and thus a reducible to a form of blasphemy.

Led by Alexander and later Athanasius, opponents of Arius argued that the divinity of Jesus Christ would be compromised by making the Son a creature. If the Son were not eternally of the same substance with the Father, they argued, he could not be truly divine; and only a divine being is able to save humanity from death and sin.

After lengthy deliberations, the Council of Nicea determined that the Son, though *begotten*, was not *created*. The creedal confession expresses this distinction as follows: "We believe in one Lord, Jesus Christ, the only Son of God, eternally begotten of the Father, God from God, Light from Light, true God from true God, *begotten, not made*, of one Being with the Father."[36]

The theological position of the creed revolved around the Greek term *homoousios*, which has often been translated as "of the same substance." Contra the Arians, the creed employs this term precisely to express the oneness of God and the coeternal status of the Son with the Father. The Nicene position thus came to be articulated in the doctrine of three persons (*hypostases*) in one divine substance (*ousia*).[37]

Arians preferred the weaker *homoiousios*, which means "of *similar* substance." In 360, a "homoian creed" was formulated under the imperial leadership of Constantine's son Constantius II that served as the official statement of orthodoxy for nearly twenty years before reverting back to the Nicene formula. It reads, "We believe in one God, the Father, Almighty, from whom are all things. And in the only-begotten Son of God, who was begotten from God before all ages and before all beginning."[38]

This intriguing and lesser-known part of this story involves an epic theological struggle in which the authoritative position shifts back and forth between variants of Arian and Nicene positions for nearly sixty years. Bishops and emperors alike contended over the correct formula until 381, when the matter was firmly settled at the First Council of Constantinople.

Mormonism and Arianism

Latter-day Saints are widely understood to embrace a form of Arianism in connection with the spirit birth of the Son. Church leadership made this point explicit in their 1916 authoritative document "The Father and the Son," which explicitly identifies the Son as among the created spirit children of the Father. However, the document goes on to point out that "He is essentially greater than any or all others, by reason (1) of His seniority as the oldest or firstborn; (2) of His unique status in the flesh as the offspring of a mortal mother and of an immortal, or resurrected and glorified, Father; (3) of His selection and foreordination as the one and only Redeemer and Savior of the race; and (4) of His transcendent sinlessness."[39]

Thus Arianism and Mormonism share in the effort to maintain both a form of dependence and a unique status for the Son in relationship to the rest of creation. Beyond this, however, their differences quickly emerge. For Arians, affirming a created Son protects the uniqueness and sovereignty of the Father. This sovereignty was conceptualized within an account of creation ex nihilo of which the Son is a part. Though brought into being "before all ages," the Son was, nonetheless, created from nothing and thus in a relation of complete ontological dependence. This position was chided by the Nicene camp as both offensive and unbiblical.

Latter-day Saint theology begins from a different set of initial conditions as seen through their rejection of creation ex nihilo. In one of Joseph Smith's key revelations, the Lord discloses not only that "I was in the beginning with the Father, and am the Firstborn," but that "ye were also in the beginning with the Father" (D&C 93:21, 23). All human souls are coeternal with the Father in the qualified sense that they share with the Son a form of everlasting existence. This shared ontology comes in the form of a more rudimentary and undeveloped state of existence prior to spirit birth known as "intelligence." A pivotal revelation to Joseph Smith in 1833 pronounces that intelligence "was not created or made, neither indeed can be" (D&C 93:29).

Thus, in a narrow sense, Mormonism can join orthodox Christianity in rejecting the Arian slogan "there was a time when He [the Son] was not." However, Mormonism diverges in the way it understands the eternal nature of the Son. Though it is central to Latter-day Saint belief that Jesus Christ is "the Eternal God," this does not necessarily imply that Jesus Christ has been *God* from the eternities.[40] In fact, if the Son is the firstborn of the spirit children, then his spirit had a beginning in time and thus cannot be eternal. Latter-day Saint writers have navigated these straits by describing the Son as an eternal *being*, though not eternal *as God*.

Robert Millet employs this distinction in *Claiming Christ*—his book-length dialogue with Gerald McDermott: "Jesus Christ is truly from everlasting to everlasting. He is, as stated on the title page of the Book of Mormon, 'The Eternal God.' He existed from eternity past, and he will exist into eternity future." Though he explicitly asserts no inconsistency between spirit birth and eternal divinity, he does go on to say that this relationship may serve as a kind of "blessed mystery" not unlike mainstream Christian responses to the Trinitarian relationship.[41]

McDermott, however, does not allow the issue to pass by without further notice. "It is not clear to me what Professor Millet means when he concludes that Jesus 'is the Eternal God.' . . . If Jesus was the eternal God, wouldn't that mean he was just that from before the beginning of time?"[42] This point relies on a commonly held understanding of "eternal" as "everlasting."[43] McDermott would have done well to clarify this meaning because Millet's rejoinder is suggestive of alternative ways of applying this term to the Son. These include etymological issues over the Greek *aeon* and the Hebrew *olam*, both of which can be translated as a finite epoch rather as everlastingness or even timelessness. Of course, these considerations take the debate in a new direction involving the equivocal use of theological concepts—no small issue in religious studies. However, for the purposes of this treatment, it is most useful to employ Joseph Smith's straightforward description of the term in his 1840 statement: "Eternity means that which is without beginning or end."[44]

Finally, we must say a word or two about the concept of *adoptionism*. As we noted above, the common reading of Arianism involves God creating the Son ex nihilo "before all ages." Adoptionism, by contrast, is the position that the Son *grew into* divinity at some point during his lifetime.[45] Traditional candidates for this divination event include Jesus' baptism, resurrection, or ascension. The Mormon twist involves the event occurring in the premortal realm at some point after his spirit birth but before the creation of the world. The adoptionist dynamic plays a rather critical role in tying together the propositional triad we have been considering: (1) the *eternal nature* of the Son, (2) the *spirit birth* of the Son, and (3) the *premortal godhood* of the Son.[46]

Conclusion

As Latter-day Saints extend their efforts to engage more deeply with the Christian community, the opportunities for respectful dialogue and scholarly exchange appear boundless. Furthermore, Mormonism is a theological free agent. It has the ability to find connections and resonance in new and unexpected places, and this includes positions among the traditional Christian heresies. As Joseph Smith famously said, "We should gather all the good and true principles in the world and treasure them up, or we shall not come out true 'Mormons.'"[47]

Notes

1. Francis Cardinal George, "Catholics and Latter-day Saints: Partners in the Defense of Religious Freedom," Brigham Young University forum address, February 23, 2010, 8, speeches.byu.edu.

2. Fr. Luis Ladaria, S.J., "The Question of the Validity of Baptism Conferred in the Church of Jesus Christ of Latter-day Saints," *L'Osservatore Romano*, August 1, 2001, 4. This publication is the official newspaper of the Holy See.

3. See Alonzo Gaskill, "*Maximus Nothus Decretum*: A Look at the Recent Catholic Declaration Regarding Latter-day Saint Baptisms," *FARMS Review* 13, no. 2 (2001): 175–96.

4. See Presbyterian Church, USA, "Position Paper: Relations with the Church of Jesus Christ of Latter-day Saints and Its People" (Salt Lake City: Presbytery of Utah, January 11, 1995); E. Brian and Jennifer L. Hare-Diggs, "Sacramental Faithfulness: Guidelines for Receiving People from The Church of Jesus Christ of Latter-day Saints," General Board of Discipleship of The United Methodist Church, 2000; "The Church of Jesus Christ of Latter-day Saints (Mormonism): Beliefs and Practices," Commission on Theology and Church Relations, the Lutheran Church Missouri Synod. See also Kent P. Jackson, "Are Mormons Christians? Presbyterians, Mormons, and the Question of Religious Definitions," *Nova Religio* 4, no. 1 (October 2000): 52–65.

5. In addition to Cardinal George, the Mormon Church has recently hosted a handful of evangelical leaders and provided them a public platform at Brigham Young University and the Salt Lake Tabernacle to address areas of common interest. Guests have included Al Mohler, president of Southern Baptist Theological Seminary (Louisville, Kentucky); Richard Land, president of Southern Evangelical Seminary (Charlotte, North Carolina); and Ravi Zacharias, founder of Ravi Zacharias International Ministries.

6. See, for example, Kent Jackson, "Are Christians Christians?," in *No Weapon Shall Prosper: New Light on Sensitive Issues*, ed. Robert L. Millet (Provo, UT: Religious Studies Center), 43–59; Bruce D. Porter and Gerald McDermott, "Is Mormonism Christian?," *First Things*, October 2008, 35–41; Richard Mouw, *Talking with Mormons: An Invitation to Evangelicals* (Grand Rapids, MI: Eerdmans, 2012); Richard Mouw, "The Possibility of Joseph Smith: Some Evangelical Probings," in *Joseph Smith Jr.: Reappraisals after Two Centuries*, ed. Reid L. Neilson and Terryl L. Givens (New York: Oxford University Press, 2009), 189–99; Craig L. Blomberg and Stephen E. Robinson, *How Wide the Divide: A Mormon and an Evangelical in Conversation* (Downer's Grove, IL: InterVarsity Press, 2007); Jan Shipps, *Sojourner in the Promised Land: Forty Years among the Mormons* (Urbana: University of Illinois Press, 200), 335–57; and Terryl L. Givens, *Wrestling the*

Angel: The Foundations of Mormon Thought: God, Cosmos, Humanity (New York: Oxford University Press, 2014).

7. Robert L. Millet and Gerald R. McDermott, *Claiming Christ: A Mormon-Evangelical Debate* (Grand Rapids, MI: Brazos Press, 2007), 177.
8. Richard Mouw, *Talking with Mormons: An Invitation to Evangelicals* (Grand Rapids, MI: Eerdmans, 2012), x, 2.
9. Richard N. Ostling, "Most Improbable Dialogue: Mormon Tabernacle Revival Service Is Latest Sign of Openness to Evangelicals," *Christianity Today*, October 30, 2009.
10. Sterling McMurrin, *The Theological Foundations of the Mormon Religion* (Salt Lake City: University of Utah Press, 1965), 111.
11. McMurrin, *Theological Foundations*, 71.
12. McMurrin, *Theological Foundations*, 67–68.
13. Robert L. Millet, "Joseph Smith and Modern Mormonism: Orthodoxy, Neoorthodoxy, Tension, and Tradition," *BYU Studies* 29, no. 3 (1989): 66. See also O. Kendall White, *Mormon Neo-Orthodoxy: A Crisis Theology* (Salt Lake City: Signature Books, 1987); Joseph M. Spencer, "Taking Grace for Granted: A Roundabout Review of Adam Miller's *Immanent Grace*," *Element: The Journal of the Society for Mormon Philosophy and Theology* 4, no. 2 (Fall 2008): 89–108; Blomberg and Robinson, *How Wide the Divide*; Robert L. Millet, *A Different Jesus? The Christ of the Latter-day Saints* (Grand Rapids, MI: Eerdmans, 2005).
14. See the initial responses to *Theological Foundations* in *Dialogue, a Journal of Mormon Thought* 1, no. 1 (Spring 1966): 107–21.
15. McMurrin, *Theological Foundations*, 82.
16. Pelagius, "Letter to Demetrias," in *The Christianity Reader*, ed. Mary Gerhart and Fabian Udoh (Chicago: University of Chicago Press, 2007), 312.
17. Pelagius, "Letter to Demetrias, 313.
18. After being cleared of heresy in the Synod of Jerusalem (c. 412), Pelagius was later excommunicated by Pope Innocent I in 417. However, the condemnation was lifted and then reinstated by Pope Zosimus a year later.
19. Protestant theologians have frequently portrayed the Eastern Orthodox tradition as embracing a form of semi-Pelagianism, though Orthodox theologians have consistently rejected this characterization.
20. R. C. Sproul, "The Pelagian Captivity of the Church," *Modern Reformation* 10, no. 3 (May/June 2001): 25.

21. H. Ray Dunning, *Grace, Faith, and Holiness* (Kansas City: Beacon Hill, 1988), 339.
22. The term "preventing" is used by Wesley and his contemporaries to communicate "preceding" or "prevenient" grace. On the Catholic side, the Council of Trent's "Decree on Justification" states, "If any one saith, that without the prevenient inspiration of the Holy Ghost, and without his help, man can believe, hope, love, or be penitent as he ought, . . . let him be anathema."
23. Dunning, *Grace*, 388.
24. McMurrin, *Theological Foundations*, 71–72.
25. *Oxford Dictionary of the Christian Church*, ed. F. L. Cross and E. A. Livingstone.
26. Roger E. Olson, *Arminian Theology: Myths and Realities* (Downer's Grove, IL: InterVarsity Press, 2006), 159.
27. Robert L. Millet and Gerald McDermott, *Claiming Christ: A Mormon Evangelical Debate* (Grand Rapids, MI: Brazos Press, 2007), 185; emphasis added.
28. Libertarian free will is the *ability to choose* between two or more actions. This stands in contrast to Augustine's and Calvin's compatibilist account in which freedom is understood as merely *acting in accord with one's nature*.
29. See Roger E. Olsen, *Arminian Theology: Myths and Realities* (Downer's Grove, IL: InterVarsity Press, 2006), 137–50.
30. See Millet, *A Different Jesus?*, 82–88.
31. Millet, *A Different Jesus?*, 97; emphasis added.
32. McMurrin, *Theological Foundations*, 83; emphasis added.
33. McMurrin, *Theological Foundations*, 83. Douglas Davies joins McMurrin in arguing that Mormonism's distinctive connection between the Fall of Adam and the Atonement is such that "human nature itself is not infected by any negative inevitability." See his *An Introduction to Mormonism* (Cambridge University Press, 2003), 189.
34. Brigham Young, in *Journal of Discourses* (London: Latter-day Saints' Book Depot, 1862), 9:305. It must be noted that Brigham Young made a number of statements related to human agency that gesture in different directions. See, e.g., *Journal of Discourses*, 2:134; 8:160; 12:323. Young's considered view is difficult to determine, but his diverse thoughts are expressive of the challenge of reconciling agency in connection to the Fall.
35. David M. Gwynn, *Christianity in the Later Roman Empire: A Sourcebook* (New York: Bloomsbury Academic, 2014), 75.

36. As printed in the Lutheran Book of Worship and the Anglican Book of Common Prayer (emphasis added). The Nicene Creed was later modified by the Council of Constantinople in 381. Technically, the above is the Niceno-Constantinopolitan Creed.

37. More precisely, the Greek term *ousia* is often translated as "essence," while *hypostasis* is often translated as "substance"—hence, three substances in one essence. In the Latin, however, the term *ousia* is translated into the term *substantia*, while *hypostasis* is translated as "person." Hence, three persons in one substance. For more, see Pier Beatrice, "The Word 'Homoousios' from Hellenism to Christianity," *Church History: Studies in Christianity and Culture* 71, no. 2 (June 2002): 243–72; T. E. Pollard, *Johannine Christology and the Early Church* (New York: Cambridge University Press, 2005); Lewis Ayers, *Nicea and Its Legacy: An Approach to Fourth-Century Trinitarian Theology* (Oxford: Oxford University Press, 2004); R. P. C. Hanson, *Searching for the Doctrine of God: The Arian Controversy, 318–81* (Grand Rapids, MI: Baker Academic, 2006); and Jaroslav Pelikan, *The Christian Tradition*, vol. 1: *The Emergence of the Catholic Tradition* (Chicago: The University of Chicago Press, 1971).

38. David M. Gwynn, *Christianity in the Later Roman Empire: A Sourcebook* (New York: Bloomsbury Academic, 2014), 75.

39. "The Father and the Son: A Doctrinal Exposition," *Improvement Era*, August 1916, 934–42.

40. Scriptural and authoritative references to eternality of the Son include the title page to the Book of Mormon, which states that the book is intended to convince "Jew and Gentile that Jesus is the Christ, the Eternal God." Though radical in its implications, the concept of intelligence is scarcely mentioned in Mormon scripture—and even these references leave much to the imagination. As a result, two schools of thought emerged regarding the nature of intelligence. The first approach employs the term in the plural and describes "intelligences" as possessing attributes such as consciousness and will. B. H. Roberts and Truman Madsen were well-known advocates of this position. See, for example, B. H. Roberts, *Seventy's Course in Theology*, vol. 2, part 1, lesson 1; and Truman G. Madsen, *Eternal Man* (Salt Lake City: Deseret Book, 1966), chapters 1 and 2. The second position understands intelligence as undifferentiated such that individual identity had a beginning at spirit birth. Orson Pratt, Joseph Fielding Smith, and Bruce R. McConkie defended various forms of this approach. See, for example, Joseph Fielding Smith, *The Progress of Man: The Church of Jesus Christ of Latter-day Saints*

(Salt Lake City: Genealogical Society of Utah, 1936), chapter 1; and Bruce R. McConkie, *Mormon Doctrine*, 2nd ed. (Salt Lake City: Deseret Book, 1966), 278.
41. Robert L. Millet and Gerald McDermott, *Claiming Christ: A Mormon-Evangelical Debate* (Grand Rapids, MI: Brazos Press, 2007), 46. In his other book-length treatment, *A Different Jesus*—written primarily for an evangelical Christian audience—Millet dispenses with the issue in just a few sentences. See Millet, *A Different Jesus?*, 20. Andrew Skinner, Millet's colleague at Brigham Young University, echoes these same ideas but is more confident in his assertion that there is "no contradiction when one understands the true nature and order of existence as revealed by enlightened prophets." See "The Premortal Godhood of Christ: A Restoration Perspective," in *Jesus Christ: Son of God, Savior*, ed. Paul H. Peterson, Gary L. Hatch, and Laura D. Card (Provo, UT: Religious Studies Center, 2002), 50–78.
42. Millet and McDermott, *Claiming Christ*, 58.
43. See, for example, Nicholas Wolterstorff, "God Everlasting," in *Contemporary Philosophy of Religion*, ed. Steven M. Cahn and David Shatz (New York: Oxford University Press, 1982), 181–203; Nelson Pike, *God and Timelessness* (New York: Schocken Books, 1970); and Eleonore Stump and Norman Kretzmann, "Eternity," *Journal of Philosophy* 78 (1981): 429–58.
44. Andrew F. Ehat and Lyndon W. Cook, eds., *The Words of Joseph Smith* (Salt Lake City: Grandin Books, 1991), 61. Another important construal of "eternal" in Mormon theology is found in Smith's application of the term to mean simply another name for God. Thus, rather than understanding "eternal punishment" as a state of everlasting punishment, it is construed to mean merely another name for the punishment of God. "For, behold, I am endless, and the punishment which is given from my hand is endless punishment, for Endless is my name. Wherefore—eternal punishment is God's punishment. Endless punishment is God's punishment" (D&C 19:10–12).
45. Adoptionism was debated and ultimately rejected in second-century synods of Antioch. Advocates of this position have differed regarding the decisive point at which Jesus was adopted as divine Son. Candidates include the baptism, resurrection, and the ascension.
46. For more on Mormon Trinitarian thought, see Craig L. Blomberg and Stephen E. Robinson, "Christ and the Trinity," in *How Wide the Divide: A Mormon and An Evangelical in Conversation* (Downer's Grove, IL: InterVarsity Press, 1997), 77–110; David L. Paulsen, "Joseph Smith and the Social Trinity: An Analysis and Defense of the Social Model of the Godhead," *Faith and Philosophy* 25,

no. 1 (2008): 47–74; Stephen T. Davis, "The Mormon Trinity and Other Trinities," *Element* 2, no. 1 (Spring 2006): 1–14; Daniel C. Peterson, "Mormonism and the Trinity," *Element* 3, nos. 1–2 (Spring/Fall 2007): 1–43; Blake T. Ostler, *Exploring Mormon Thought: Of God and Gods* (Salt Lake City: Greg Kofford Books, 2008); Paul Owen, "The Doctrine of the Trinity in LDS and 'Catholic' Contexts," *Element* 1, no. 1 (Spring 2007): 59–84.

47. Joseph Smith, *History of the Church of Jesus Christ of Latter-day Saints*, ed. B. H. Roberts, 2nd ed. rev. (Salt Lake City: Deseret Book, 1978), 5:517.

Atoning Grace on Progression's Highway
Explorations into Latter-day Saint Theological Anthropology

Cory B. Willson

What you see and what you hear depends a great deal on where you are standing.

C. S. Lewis[1]

A real meeting with a partner of another faith must mean being so open to him that his way of looking at the world becomes a real possibility for me. One has not really heard the message of one of the great religions that have moved millions of people for centuries if one has not been really moved by it, if one has not felt in one's own soul the power of it.

Lesslie Newbigin[2]

Yes, I think we would have to agree that one of Joseph Smith's most significant efforts was to make the Father of the universe more accessible to His family members within that universe, to retrieve the unreachable, unknowable, timeless, and impassible Deity that had been pushed to the grand beyond by traditional Christians.

Robert L. Millet[3]

ATONING GRACE ON PROGRESSION'S HIGHWAY

Introduction

Religious encounter through an insider's experience of the faith. My introduction to interfaith dialogue was under the most enviable of circumstances. In the fall of 2007, I was invited to collaborate on a book by Rabbi Elliot Dorff comparing Jewish and Christian approaches to social ethics—a yearlong endeavor that brought me into contact with the rich Conservative Jewish tradition through one of its leading rabbinic figures.[4] A few months later I received an invitation to join a dialogue group of Latter-day Saint and evangelical scholars. This experience ushered me into an ongoing exploration of the Latter-day Saint faith alongside one of its most prolific theologians and apologists, Robert L. Millet. The juxtaposition of Judaism and Mormonism and my friendships with Rabbi Dorff and Robert Millet have had profound implications for my faith and scholarship. While I remain a committed evangelical Christian, these men have given me exposure to powerful religious faiths that have moved my soul and challenged the way I see the world.

When it comes to comparative religious studies, it is problematic to try to establish commonalities between religions by reducing them to their lowest common denominator—whether that is a belief in a higher being, shared beliefs, or an adherence to a universal moral code.[5] This approach dilutes distinctives and overlooks lived religion in favor of formal doctrine, thereby neglecting the powerful affective dimensions of religion.[6] Another methodological misstep is to study religious traditions as if they were hermetically sealed from each other. While a religion may assert that its scriptures are of divine origin, the theology developed from this revelation is contextual and a response to the lived experiences of a particular religious community as it interacts with other religions. Our religious traditions not only shape *what we see* but what kinds of *questions we ask*.[7] In light of this, comparative theology yields better results when it avoids employing outside criteria to establish common ground between religions. A better approach begins with appreciating the "incommensurable peculiarity" of each religious tradition with its dynamic relationship among the beliefs, practices, and religious experiences and then proceeds to explore how these address the needs of the community and its members.[8]

One does not proceed very far into this type of study of religion, however, before being struck by how daunting a task it is to understand the historical, theological, and sociological complexity of a tradition's self-understanding in relation to other faiths. What appears as a "contradiction" to outsiders is often embraced as a "paradox" by adherents of that religion.[9] Care must be taken to find inroads into indigenous perspectives of another tradition to see how adherents understand their own faith and their relationship to other religious communities.[10]

My encounter with Robert Millet and his scholarly work has taken place in my quest to understand the Latter-day Saints in connection with historic Christianity. Not only is Bob a devout Saint with a testimony of being touched by the grace of God, he is a first-class scholar with an extensive literary corpus devoted to bringing the Latter-day Saint faith into dialogue with other religious traditions. He has shed light on the power and appeal of the lived experience of the Latter-day Saint community, distinguished between central saving beliefs and what he calls nonessential "shelf" doctrines, and helped me understand how this faith has captured the affections and imaginations of sixteen million people and counting.[11]

What follows is an exploration of Millet's reflections on the Latter-day Saint view of humankind in conversation with Jewish and Protestant traditions. It begins by examining how the Mormon cosmic drama cultivates a distinct theological imagination of what it means to be created in God's image and then proceeds to explore the means by which the distance between God and humanity is bridged.[12] Given the vastness of scholarly writings on this subject, I will limit my analysis to one prominent writer within each faith community: Robert Millet, Rabbi Abraham Cohen, and Reformed theologian G. C. Berkouwer. Given the breadth of thought in each religious community, I will not attempt to give a comprehensive account of each tradition's theology. Instead I will allow each of these writers to give an insider's account of the theological anthropology of their tradition and how it relates to the religious experience of the community.[13] For it is when we study the Latter-day Saint tradition in light of other religions—not only in terms of theological differences and similarities but also in terms of the lived experience—that we can appreciate that Mormonism is about more (though not less) than intellectual questions. It is also about a way of life pursued by a community as it attempts to fulfill humanity's deepest desires.[14]

The Image of God across Religious Traditions

Biblical mysteries and a dialectic approach to theology. In the first chapter of Genesis, we are presented with the mystery of human beings created in the image of God (1:27). The context of this verse is God's speaking and creating a separation of light from darkness and water from land to make room for the forming and filling of the earth. In speaking, God acts. The more God acts, the more creation is free to live and move and have its being. He forms boundaries and sets limits for creation's manifold parts and establishes life-giving rhythms of reciprocity and interdependence. While humans are created from the ground and are part of creation, they are set in a unique relation to other creatures for they alone are said to bear God's image and likeness (see Genesis 1:27; cf. Psalm 8:4–8). Within these established boundaries, there is a close relationship between God and humanity and between humanity and creation.

In spite of the popularity of the concept in the history of theology, references to the image of God within scripture are relatively limited—those few instances being Genesis 1:27; 5:1–2; 9:6; 1 Corinthians 11:7; and James 3:9. It may also come as a surprise to modern readers that apart from these few references, scriptures rarely take the image of God as the basis of appeal for moral reform.[15] Complicating matters further, scripture never defines the meaning of this powerful concept. Debates have ensued among theologians and philosophers over the years as to whether humanity's image bearing is to be understood in functional, substantive, or relational terms. Whereas philosophers have tended to elucidate the meaning of the image of God by rooting it to a specific property of the human person (such as reason, conscience, immortality, freedom), the Old and New Testament writers treat it as a deep mystery and speak in paradoxes that frame our thinking.[16] The Psalmist, for example, reflects on the mystery in this way: "What are human beings that you are mindful of them, mortals that you care for (*attend to*) them?" (Psalm 8:4; see also Psalm 144:3; Job 7:17).[17] Scriptures like this offer a vision of humanity, but when we push for tight technical definitions of "image of God," these texts are robbed of their power to convey mystery.

Historic Jewish and Christian traditions as well as The Church of Jesus Christ of Latter-day Saints see this concept of image of God as being authoritative, and yet each one has taken a different route in developing theological anthropologies that attempt to explain and expand on these biblical dialectics.[18] To understand a tradition on its own terms it is necessary to identify the paradoxes it posits concerning the mystery of the human person.

Living with Tensions: Foundational Dialectics of Latter-day Saints

> The scriptures of the Restoration and latter-day prophets affirm that God our Father has a plan for his children, a program established to maximize our growth and ensure our happiness. And yet that fact alone—that there is some divine plan to life—is not as obvious from the Bible as from latter-day scripture.[19]

The cosmic drama of Latter-day Saints. One cannot read far in the religious writings of Latter-day Saints before coming across references to progression, growth, or development. I find this progression narrative to be one of the most prominent features of Mormon thought, providing structure and direction to many other Church doctrines. This narrative is most easily understood as a cosmic drama that unfolds like a three-act play: act 1, premortal existence; act 2, mortal existence; and act 3, postmortal existence.[20] It is within this drama that Millet's theological anthropology can best be appreciated as we see it functioning within the larger theological imagination of the Latter-day Saint faith. The narrative structure provided in this drama holds together important tensions (or dialectics) within Mormon theological anthropology that will be explored more below. These dialectics include the following:

1. God and humanity are "of the same species," yet there remains an immense gap between finite mortal humans and an omnipotent and omniscient God;

2. Each person is on the road of eternal progression, yet all growth and transformation is brought about solely by the atoning grace of God.

1. Divine Species... Separated by an Immense Gap

> In the day that God created man, in the likeness of God made he him; in the image of his own body, male and female, created he them. (Moses 6:8–9)

Divine species. To be God's image bearer is to be of the same (divine) species as God. One of the most striking (and controversial[21]) features of Latter-day Saint faith is its theological anthropology. When the Mormon Church teaches that human beings are created in the image of God, it means that God and humans are of the same species. The implication of this doctrine for what it means to be human and in relationship with God are far-reaching, especially when viewed alongside of historic Jewish and Protestant views of the human person.

The phrase "image of God" is interpreted literally by Latter-day Saints: we are begotten spirit children of the Father who lived with and worshipped the Father before this life in the spirit existence of the first estate. To say that humans were created in the image of God means that they were made in the image of the Eternal Father's spiritual and *physical* bodies.[22] In his "King Follett" discourse just months before he suffered martyrdom, Joseph Smith spoke these words to comfort mourners at a funeral gathering: "God himself was once as we are now, and is an exalted man, and sits enthroned in yonder heavens! . . . If you were to see him today, you would see him like a man in form—like yourselves in all the person, image, and very form as a man."[23] In this address Joseph revealed a doctrine that goes beyond the traditional teachings of both Jews and Christians, which retain a clear distinction between God and humans. What follows in the King Follett discourse is an emphasis on the relational implications of this metaphysical nearness between God and humanity: "For Adam was created in the very fashion, image and likeness of God, and . . . walked, talked and conversed with Him, as one man talks and communes with another."[24]

With these words, Joseph sought to bring God near to the bereaved by emphasizing the relational proximity of God to humanity and of the relatively "short season" in which mortals are separated bodily from the deceased.[25] This existential need is important to note as it weds theology to lived needs in ways that will resurface in this discussion of the Latter-day Saint faith. Critics of the Church often overlook Latter-day Saints' emphasis on Christlikeness in the process of deification.[26] For Mormons, deification is a specific way of understanding eternal life and insists that we will not only be *with* God for all eternity but also will be *like* him.[27] Again the personal and existential takes central focus over metaphysical explanations: "The whole design of the gospel," said President Gordon B. Hinckley, "is to lead us onward and upward to greater achievement, even, eventually, to godhood. . . . [The Eternal Father] wishes for his children that they might approach him in stature and stand beside him resplendent in godly strength and wisdom."[28] Statements like this make clear that in the religious imagination of Latter-day Saints, the primary value conveyed in the doctrine of deification is relational proximity to God as Father.

Yet an immense gap. To be God's image bearer is also to sense the immense gap that separates humans from God. God is near to us in that he has experienced what we experience, even though he has developed infinitely beyond us. It was Lorenzo Snow who picked up on this line of thought from Joseph and stressed the developmental theme embedded in the words "God himself *was once* as we are now." Snow's poetic thought reads:

> As Abra'm, Isaac, Jacob, too,
> First babes, then men—to gods they grew.
> As man now is, our God once was;
> As now God is, so man may be—
> which doth unfold man's destiny.[29]

This couplet draws on the themes of growth and the unfolding of human destiny discussed earlier in the concept of eternal progression. While the metaphysical specificity of God and humanity does become more explicit in Joseph's later teachings, the concept of progression was well established in prior scriptures and teachings. Modern Latter-day Saint scholars have made it clear that there is indeed a gap between God and humanity—but this is not to be conceived of as an ontological "being" gap but rather an immense "developmental" gap.[30] Millet explains: "I may believe that God and man are not of a different species, but the last thing in the world I want to be accused of is shortening the distance between a frail, weak, and imperfect mortal and an omnipotent, omniscient, and perfected God. . . . God is God, and I am a mere mortal. . . . God is *qadosh* . . . 'holy other,' meaning that he is separate and apart from unholiness and profanity."[31]

In what can be considered a common feature in his style, Millet wisely avoids unnecessary and abstract philosophical speculations by consistently distinguishing between what we know and what we don't know about these doctrinal matters of progression and deification. First, it is a clear teaching of The Church of Jesus Christ of Latter-day Saints that humans can indeed become like God. But as to which attributes of God are communicable and which are not, there has been no clear revelation. Second, throughout the process of eternal progression, at no time will humans ever rival God or compete with him for glory. Third, at no point will any other beings be the focus of our worship besides the Father, Son, and Holy Spirit.[32] Within the Latter-day Saint cosmic drama, the doctrine of deification is held in tension with the emphasis on the immense developmental gap separating humans from the eternal and immortal God.

A Dialogue with Judaism on Bridging the Gap between God and Humanity

The preceding section offered an overview of what Latter-day Saints believe is at the heart of the "more" of Mormonism. For those within the faith, the Mormon doctrine of deification adds a personal dimension to their spiritual life: God is not "aloof, passionless, and set free from his children."[33] He is not the god of the Stoics, a remote unmoved mover or first cause. Instead he is touched by our infirmities and shares in our emotions.[34] It is not only the trajectory of human development that is at stake in the doctrine of deification but the relational proximity of God and his compassion for humanity—an expressed existential concern of Joseph's original funeral address and a significant feature of subsequent Latter-day Saint experience. "We worship a divine Being with whom we can identify," writes Millet. "That is to say, his infinity does not preclude either his immediacy or his intimacy."³⁵ By holding together the dialectic of "same species" and the "holy other," Latter-day Saint theology lifts fallen humans up by bringing God near.³⁶ The Talmudic vision of the human person also wrestles with the issue of how to understand the proximity and distance of God to humans.

The image of God: preciousness and finitude. The central Jewish doctrine of humanity is the image of God. A famous saying gets at the heart of the Jewish imagination concerning the mystery of the human person: "A person should always carry around two pieces of paper in his/her pockets. On one should be written, 'For me the world was created,' and on the other, 'I am but dust and ashes.'"³⁷

This saying reveals the immense value that rabbis placed on each individual while nevertheless situating humanity squarely within the boundaries of creaturely status. The Talmud teaches that there is a tremendous privilege in being a human being set apart from other creatures and uniquely stamped with God's image. But it also guards against blurring the boundaries between a finite human person and the holy Creator God.

Kingship and kinship. Metaphysical speculation was not of widespread interest to the rabbis of the Talmud. In its cosmology, the Talmud emphasizes both God's *kingship over* and yet *kinship with* humanity. Since then, modern rabbinic commentaries have incorporated the categories of "transcendence" and "immanence" to discuss the doctrine of God. The Talmud, most likely to guard against the pantheisms of the day, taught that God is eternal and incorporeal and that his abode is in the seventh heaven, an infinite distance from the earth.³⁸ Since that time, strict adherence to the Jewish monotheistic faith has entailed respecting the unbridgeable gulf between the Creator God and human creatures.

It might surprise us then to learn that the Talmud not only speaks of a "gulf" between humans and God the king, but also of a "kinship." Rabbi Abraham Cohen explains, "Pre-eminent above all other creatures [is humanity], the culminating point in the work of Creation." Humans are differentiated in that all other creatures are formed from the earth, while "man's soul is *from heaven* and [his] body *from earth*."³⁹ As image bearers, humans bear a divine semblance afforded to no other creatures. And yet God has placed humans as image bearers in a relationship of kinship with other creatures. Humans share a kinship with God and a kinship with other creatures.

Bridging the gap. For all the emphasis the Talmud places on the gulf between humanity and God, it is the closeness (immanence) of God that is stressed time and again. In the Talmudic view, these two attributes of God are complementary. "How close is God to his creatures?" the Talmud asks. "He is as close as a mouth is to the ear," is the answer.[40] The eternal God is the one who hears the whispered prayer uttered behind the pillar of a synagogue. The immanence of God is seen in the emphasis the Talmud places on his relational proximity and emotional concern for the well-being of humans. God, says the Talmud, shares in our sorrows and longs to abide with his creatures.[41]

It is within this kingship-kinship dialectic that the divine presence was conceived as being present in creation and among humanity through the *Shechinah* glory and the Holy Spirit.[42] The vision of God in the Talmud is not one-sided, writes Rabbi Cohen: "However reluctant the teachers of Israel were to identify God with His Universe and insisted on His being exalted high above the abode of men, yet they thought of the world as permeated through and through with the omnipresent *Shechinah*."[43] In teaching about the immanent presence of God, his emotional intimacy is portrayed in his longing for communion with his people. The Talmud offers the following story of the eschatological Garden of Eden in a meditation on the verse from Leviticus 26:12, "I [God] will walk among you:"

> To what is this like? To a king who went out to walk with this tenant in his orchard; but the tenant hid himself from him. The king called to him, "why do you hide from me? See, I am just the same as you!" Similarly the Holy One, blessed be He, will walk with the righteous in Gan Eden in the Hereafter; and the righteous, on beholding Him, will retreat in terror before him. But He will call to them, "See, I am the same as you!" Since, however, it is possible to imagine that My fear should no longer be upon you, the text declares, "I will be your God, and ye shall be My people."[44]

Commenting on this passage, Rabbi Cohen argues that we detect the "anxiety of the Rabbis" to maintain the "unbridgeable gulf" between God and humanity, even in the life to come. But this distinct anxiety grows out of the commitment to a very real and yet mysterious communion that will be experienced between God and his people. Whatever this future communion will look like, Cohen writes, for the rabbis this meant that God "will still be God and they will be His 'people,' *i.e., human.*"[45]

Discussion: anthropomorphisms and embodiment. After reading a passage like this from the Talmud, we might be better prepared to entertain this question from Millet: "Is there perhaps something in God that corresponds with embodiment?"[46] Is it really that strange that Latter-day Saints speak of God having a physical body and of our future physical presence with God? To be sure, Saints construe kinship with God literally (physically), whereas the rabbis interpret scriptures that speak of God's embodiment as anthropomorphisms. For the rabbis, these texts are seen as metaphors that reveal God's willingness to accommodate to humans by communicating in terms they can understand. Furthermore, the central ethical doctrine in the Talmud is the imitation of God, and such anthropomorphisms are vivid pictures that show God "Himself obeying the precepts which He desires Israel to observe."[47] As God clothes the naked, visits the sick, comforts mourners, and buries the dead, says the Talmud, so should we.[48] In Talmudic ethics, we bear God's image most fully when we imitate him by following the Torah's commands. This is the significance of biblical anthropomorphisms for the Jewish imagination.

Latter-day Saints, by contrast, see scripture's "anthropomorphisms" not as God's *linguistic translation* to accommodate humans but as windows into *cosmological transformation*, revealing the truth that humans and God are of the same species and family. What Latter-day Saints perceive to be at stake in this debate is not merely issues of *ontology* but the reality of *intimacy* that can be experienced with God.

Matters of ontology and intimacy. In a revealing passage about Trinitarian metaphysical formulations of the Godhead, Millet challenges his readers by asking, "Must one really accept the ontological oneness of the members of the Godhead in order to be close to them, to be at peace with them, to feel their power and presence in his or her life?"[49] Within Mormon thought, intimacy and relational unity between the members of the Godhead does not require ontological oneness. Instead, their unity is seen in being of one mind, spirit, and purpose. On this matter of ontology, our reading of the Talmud leads us to ask, "Must one really accept the shared ontology between humans and God in order to find the deep intimacy that God desires with humanity?"

Within the Jewish religious imagination, the tension between finite humans, who are "dust and ashes," and the infinite God, who is "holy other," makes establishing kinship challenging. The fundamental gulf to be bridged is one of intimacy between two different kinds of beings and pushes the Jewish imagination to conceive of how human kinship with God—the Creator and king of the universe—can be experienced in a meaningful way without dishonoring God or undermining humanity's humanness.[50]

Within the Latter-day Saint religious imagination, the fundamental tension is how to hold together the belief that humans are of divine seed while still maintaining the immense gulf between a holy God. This tension is held together within the Latter-day Saint doctrine of deification. What is required to bridge this "developmental" gulf and achieve intimacy is a belief in a *shared ontology* between God and humanity. With this resolution comes a new challenge within the religious imagination of Latter-day Saints: how do we then maintain a sense of awe, grandeur, and the holy "otherness" of God?

Latter-day Saint interpretation of biblical anthropomorphic language extends into realms beyond the bounds of Jewish and traditional Christian orthodoxy. For all the disagreements between these traditions and the metaphysical interpretations of the Bible, Protestants can identify existentially with the human longings for God and our loved ones that Joseph and subsequent Church leaders have sought to address. Whereas the Mormon faith places the stress on the "mindful" and "magnify" parts of biblical teaching (Psalm 8:4; Job 7:17), the Protestant tradition has focused on those texts that emphasize the "What is man?" biblical theme and interpreted them in light of human sin.

Eternal Progression ... by Grace Alone

> Adam fell that men might be, and men are that they may have joy. (2 Nephi 2:25)

> The Fall had a twofold direction—downward, yet forward. It brought man into the world and set his feet upon progression's highway.[51]

> We believe the Fall was a part of God's divine plan and thus laid the foundation for the Atonement itself. In other words, if there had been no Fall, there would have been no Atonement.[52]

Eternal progression. To be God's image bearer is to be engaged in an unfolding drama of growth and development. One of the most prominent areas the Latter-day Saint cosmic drama is found is in the idea of eternal progression. "The concept embodied in the phrase *eternal progression*," writes Millet, "is that men and women have been engaged in spiritual development and moral expansion from eternity past and will do so into eternity future."[53] In the premortal spirit existence, we all lived as spirit sons and daughters with our Eternal Father. In this first estate, we were able to progress and grow as we worshipped the Father and were obedient to him. The Father's plan for our spiritual and moral expansion entailed our leaving the premortal abode and entering mortal existence to take on the "earthly tabernacle" of a baby. In this second estate, we encounter adversity and overcome the physical passions and desires in our mortal existence, add upon prior growth, and "qualify for eternal life in the celestial kingdom of God."[54] Spiritual growth will continue on in the third estate of postmortal existence as we progress *within* (but, in most formulations, not *between*) the celestial, terrestrial, and telestial kingdoms.[55]

It is hard to overemphasize the influence that this narrative trajectory has on all aspects of Mormon thought and lived experience. This progression narrative offers an answer to the purpose of mortal existence, an approach to suffering as part of God's plan for human growth, and hope for the salvation of those who have died without accepting the gospel of Jesus Christ.[56] Viewing the human person within this story of eternal progression provides a teleological structure to which Saints conform their lives.

By grace alone. To be God's image bearer also means that growth and progression occur by *grace alone*. This strong emphasis on eternal progression is often misunderstood by outsiders, especially evangelicals, who have been conditioned to sniff out "works righteousness" hidden in every theological statement that alludes to human potential.[57] One of the most significant contributions that Millet has made to ecumenical discussions is to demonstrate from Latter-day Saint scriptures the prominent role that grace plays in all stages of eternal progression. Alongside the emphasis on progression there is a counterbalancing emphasis on the atoning blood of Jesus. All growth into Christlikeness is by grace alone.[58] This emphasis on growth through atoning grace goes back to Joseph Smith's *Lectures on Faith*, where he (or perhaps an associate) writes, "all those who keep his commands shall grow up *from grace to grace*, and become heirs of the heavenly kingdom, and joint hers with Jesus Christ; possessing the same mind, being transformed into the same image or likeness."[59]

This emphasis on grace within Mormon scriptures themselves is lost on many of those outside of the faith. In language that evangelicals readily recognize, Millet unpacks how this emphasis on grace should be held in tension with the emphasis on progression and deification. He writes: "To clarify, Mormons do not believe they can work themselves into glory. . . . Mormons do not believe they can gain eternal life through human effort. Mormons do not believe that one becomes more and more Christlike through sheer grit and willpower. Central to any and all spiritual progress is the Atonement of Jesus Christ, and it is only by and through his righteousness that we may be pronounced righteous."[60]

Latter-day Saint understandings of grace and works comports better with Arminian than Reformed theology, but in all of this it is possible to see the emphasis on spiritual progress as being wedded to a reliance upon grace. Holding together tensions is part and parcel of any life of faith, and Mormonism is no exception. By insisting on the need for growth in Christlikeness while still emphasizing human insufficiency for such a task, the Saints are taught to look to the atoning work of Christ rather than their own abilities.[61] This raises questions of how a Latter-day Saint conception of human agency comports with divine action and human sin, which will be explored in conversation with Protestant Christianity.

A Dialogue with Traditional Christianity on Growth, Grace, and Sin

The greatness and misery dialectic in traditional Christianity. In his classic work on the image of God, G. C. Berkouwer draws on Blaise Pascal and argues that maintaining *both the greatness and misery* of the human person is essential for upholding the mystery of humanity. Humanity's greatness and misery are inextricably linked to each other, for it is the greatness of the human person that displays the depths of their misery. Created in God's image, humanity stands as a vice-regent over creation under God's rule. It is from this height that we see the tragedy of humanity's fall. Far from relativizing humanity's sin, emphasizing greatness makes the reality of sin all the greater. The parable of the prodigal son in Luke 15:11–32 is paradigmatic for understanding the relationship between human goodness and sin. The fact that the rebellion was committed by the Father's *son* makes his actions all the more painful than it would be if the rebel were a stranger or an enemy. At the same time, the stress on human sin should not be understood to eradicate all human goodness, for scripture teaches that even after the Fall humans remain God's image bearers (see Genesis 5:1–2; 9:6; James 3:9).[62]

Berkouwer notes the ways in which the Protestant tradition has often struggled to uphold humanity's greatness in its desire to reinforce the need for redemption. In so doing the stress on fallenness has all but eclipsed the view of humanity's created goodness (see Genesis 1:31). What is needed, he argues, is to maintain a healthy reciprocal relationship between our vision of human misery as "the misery of a nobleman, the misery of a dethroned king."[63] The problem of the human situation is not simply finitude—"what are humans that you are mindful of them" (Psalm 8:4) for they are "but dust and ashes" (Genesis 18:27)—but they are also "sinful from [their] mother's womb" (Psalm 51:5).[64] It is human misery that has been heavily stressed by Protestant Christians—and not surprisingly—frequently misunderstood by those outside this tradition.

One of the central dialectics in the religious imagination of Protestants is that of Luther's *simul justus et peccator*, simultaneously righteous and a sinner.[65] In this dialectic, the believer is suspended between bondage to sin and his or her justified status as an adopted child of God. Holding on to Luther's paradox has proven to be challenging for Protestants, as seen in our perennial tendency to overlook humanity's goodness and focus on sinfulness. If we are to uphold the view of the human person we see in scripture, we must not *isolate* humanity's greatness from its misery, nor allow the one to *limit* the other.[66] It is only in the eschaton that this lived paradox will be resolved. Any recovery of a Protestant emphasis on the greatness of humanity will need to configure with human sinfulness and finitude.

Discussion. It is important to draw out some implications of what it means to be human in light of the Latter-day Saint dialectic of growth and grace. First, the emphasis on human progress resonates strongly with the embedded potentials of creation and humanity seen in the opening chapters of Genesis. While it is clear from scripture and experience that some development can take place throughout a person's mortal life, this embedded potential will not be fully actualized until the eschatological kingdom of God is established and believers receive resurrected and glorified bodies (see 1 Corinthians 15:42–53). From a Latter-day Saint perspective, what it means to be human in mortal existence is to have a tenacious belief in human potential even in the face of sin, suffering, and adversity.

Given the strong Latter-day Saint emphasis on progression, it is not surprising to find a need to emphasize the atoning grace of Christ as a counterbalance to human potential. The religious imagination of Latter-day Saints *begins with progression* and then proceeds to configure *how sin and grace fits* into this narrative. In short, the cosmic drama makes it easier to hold onto humanity's greatness than its misery. Protestants, on the other hand, tend to *begin with sin* and then are left wrestling with how humanity's greatness can be understood. The resolution to how atoning grace operates on progression's highway for Latter-day Saints is found in the temple. It is in the temple sacraments and ordinances that the atoning work of Jesus is made efficacious and fallen humans have their agency repaired so that spiritual progress can transpire.[67] A new tension arises with this resolution: how does the narrative of progression foster a *rising sense* of dependence on the atoning grace of Jesus?[68]

For Protestants, the challenge to uphold humanity's created goodness in light of sin and finitude finds a partial resolution in the eschatological concepts of the "already" and the "not yet." Already we have been justified in Christ and adopted as God's children, but not yet has our sanctification and conformity to Christlikenss been made complete. All "progress" in sanctification is contingent upon a dependence on the ongoing work of the Holy Spirit and an increasing awareness of our sin.[69] The dialogue between Latter-day Saints and Protestants stands a better chance of being fruitful for God's kingdom if it takes as its primary goal the fostering of dependence upon the Holy Spirit to effect the atoning work of Jesus in our lives.

Conclusion

From a shared belief that human beings are created in the image of God, the Latter-day Saint, Jewish, and Protestant traditions developed religious imaginations that hold together the mystery of the human person in distinct ways. When we study these traditions on their own terms, we come to see the different sorts of questions they bring to their theological inquiry into sacred texts. The Latter-day Saint view of the human person pushes against the orthodox Judeo-Christian ontology and raises questions over the type of intimacy that can be found with God in this life and the next. Protestants can appreciate the deep human desires for communion with God that Latter-day Saints pursue and the physical means of fulfillment the faith offers men and women to sup with God and Christ. It would behoove Protestants not only to respond to Latter-day Saint doctrines, but more important, to allow themselves to be "really moved by" and feel in their "own soul" the powerful way the Latter-day Saints fulfill the human need for communion with God.[70]

There are important theological issues that remain to be explored among Jews, Protestants, and Latter-day Saints. Among them, two stand out most prominently. First, what are the implications of bearing God's image if it is the image of the Triune God and not simply of the Father that we take as our starting point? Second, what difference does it make when the incarnation of Jesus is conceived of as bridging a developmental rather than an ontological gulf? What does it mean from a Latter-day Saint perspective for Jesus to maintain his two natures throughout eternity? For Protestant Christians, these issues point to a key to the Mormon ontology-intimacy dilemma. With the very real spiritual progress in Christlikeness that takes place in this life and in the new creation, humanity's humanness will not be eradicated in the resurrection even though it will be transformed. Indeed, part of the special affection that Protestants and Catholics have for Jesus is bound up with the belief that the intimacy we will experience with God throughout eternity is made possible by the enduring intercession of our High Priest, Jesus, who with resurrected human body is even now in the presence of God the Father.

There are important issues like these that Protestants and Latter-day Saints need to continue to explore together. It is hoped that all future theological dialogue will follow the embodied example of Robert Millet of being grace-centered, convicted and civil, attentive to the nuances between "central, saving" and "shelf" doctrines, and never pursued outside of the awareness of the human desire for communion with God.

Notes

1. C. S. Lewis, *The Magician's Nephew* (New York: Collier Books, 1974), 125.
2. Lesslie Newbigin, "The Basis, Purpose and Manner of Inter-Faith Dialogue," *Scottish Journal of Theology* 30, no. 3 (June 1977): 253–70, 267–68.
3. Robert L. Millet, "We Shall Be Like Him," an address given at the Religious Education Friday faculty forum at Brigham Young University, September 14, 2007.
4. Rabbi Elliot Dorff, *The Jewish Approach to Repairing the World* (Tikkun Olam): *A Brief Introduction for Christians* (Woodstock, UT: Jewish Lights, 2008).
5. This type of approach to comparative religions which treats different religions as commensurable has been thoughtfully critiqued by several authors, including Hendrik Kraemer, *Religion and the Christian Faith* (London: Lutterworth Press, 1956), 77–78; Stephen Neill, *Christian Faith and Other Faiths* (New York: Oxford University Press, 1962), 3–5; 232–33; George A. Lindbeck, *The Nature of Doctrine: Religion and Theology in a Postliberal Age* (Louisville: Westminster John Knox, 1984), 48–49.
6. James K. A. Smith's book, *Desiring the Kingdom: Worship, Worldview, and Cultural Formation* (Grand Rapids, MI: Baker, 2009), offers a poignant apology for attending to the affective dimensions of religious traditions. On the topic of lived religion, see Talal Asad, *Genealogies of Religion: Discipline and Reasons of Power in Christianity and Islam* (Baltimore: The John Hopkins University Press, 1993); David Hall, ed., *Lived Religion in America: Towards a History of Practice* (Princeton: Princeton University Press, 1997).
7. On the role that tradition plays in shaping the types of questions that we ask, as well as the way in which we pursue the answer, see David Kelsey, *Eccentric Existence* (Louisville: Westminster John Knox Press, 2009), 1–3; C. S. Lewis makes a similar point about the relationship between our particular location with what and how we perceive a given phenomenon or issue in his book *The Magician's Nephew*, 125.
8. Kraemer, *Religion and the Christian Faith*, 78.
9. For more on the ways in which paradoxes are perceived as contradictions by those outside of the faith, see Isaac Rottenberg's review of Michael S. Kogan's *Opening the Covenant: A Jewish Theology of Christianity* (Oxford University Press, 2008), available at http://www.isaacrottenberg.com/uploads/pdf/www.isaacrottenberg.com/a_review.pdf.

10. On "insider" perspectives, see Clifford Geertz, "Thick Description: Toward an Interpretive Theory of Culture," in *The Interpretation of Cultures: Selected Essays* (New York: Basic Books, 1973).
11. Richard J. Mouw quoting from his conversation with Robert Millet in *Calvinism and the Las Vegas Airport: Making Connections in Today's World* (Grand Rapids, MI: Zondervan, 2004), 39.
12. For a helpful distillation of Charles Taylor's work on social imaginaries for inter-religious engagement, see William A. Dyrness, *Senses of the Devotion: Interfaith Aesthetics in Buddhist and Muslim Communities* (Eugene: Cascade Books, 2013), 1–30.
13. Nicholas Wolterstorff employs a similar methodology in the third chapter in his book, *Until Justice and Peace Embrace* (Grand Rapids, MI: Eerdmans, 1987), 43.
14. One of the distinct advantages of interfaith dialogue conducted with attentiveness to insider accounts of lived religion is that we become aware of the pretheoretical assumptions driving our theological inquiry. In dialogue with those who do not share our perspective but also ask different questions, we begin to see that theology is always contextual and a response to the lived experiences of a particular religious community. This study on the theological anthropology of Latter-day Saints through the works of Robert Millet has revealed differences in the religious imaginations of Latter-day Saints, Jews, and Protestants. These differences are in large part due to how each tradition understands the fundamental questions that drive each tradition's theological inquiry into what it means to be a human being as God intended, and this in turn is conditioned by their particular history and sociocultural location.
15. David Clines, "Humanity as the Image of God," *Tyndale Bulletin* 19 (1968): 1; cf. G. C. Berkouwer, *Man: The Image of God* (Grand Rapids, MI: Eerdmans, 1962), 67.
16. On the need to approach the mystery of the image of God from a posture of awe, see Berkouwer, *Man: The Image of God*, 36, 74, 194–95. Cf. Richard Middleton, "The Liberating Image? Interpreting the Imago Dei in Context," *Christian Scholars Review* 24, no. 1 (1994): 1–3.
17. For a helpful discussion of the relationship between the Hebrew words *zakar* and *paquad* in this verse, see John Goldingay, *Psalms Volume 1: Psalms 1–41* (Grand Rapids, MI: Baker, 2006, 158–59). Another such paradox can be seen by comparing Psalm 17:8, "Keep me as the apple of your eye," with Psalm 39:5–6, "Everyone is but a breath . . . [and] goes round like a mere phantom."

18. Millet, *The Mormon Faith: A New Look at Christianity* (Salt Lake City: Shadow Mountain, 1998), 194. See also Rabbi Abraham Cohen, *Everyman's Talmud: The Major Teachings of the Rabbinic Sages* (New York: Shocken Books, 1995), 67; and Berkouwer, *Man: The Image of God*, 67.
19. Robert L. Millet, *Selected Writings of Robert L. Millet* (Salt Lake City: Deseret Book, 2000), 147. For additional reflections on the Latter-day Saint progression narrative, see also Millet, *The Mormon Faith*, 58–59; Charles W. Penrose, *"Mormon" Doctrine, Plain and Simple: or, Leaves from the Tree of Life* (Salt Lake City: Geo. Q. Cannon & Sons, 1897), quoted in *LDS Beliefs: A Doctrinal Reference*, ed. Robert L. Millet, Camille Fronk Olson, Andrew C. Skinner, and Brent L. Top (Salt Lake City: Deseret Book, 2011), 610–11; Truman G. Madsen, *Eternal Man* (Salt Lake City: Desert Book, 2013), 3–7, 18; Stephen Webb, *Mormon Christianity: What Other Christians Can Learn from the Latter-day Saints* (New York: Oxford University Press, 2013).
20. Millet, *The Mormon Faith*, 195.
21. Millet, *The Vision of Mormonism: Pressing the Boundaries of Christianity* (St. Paul: Paragon House, 2007), 271.
22. *LDS Beliefs*, 498–501; cf. Millet, *The Mormon Faith*, 55–56; Millet, *Getting at the Truth: Responding to Difficult Questions about LDS Beliefs* (Salt Lake City: Deseret Book, 2004), 110; The First Presidency of The Church of Jesus Christ of Latter-day Saints, "The Origin of Man," 78, quoted in *LDS Beliefs*, 594–95.
23. Joseph Smith, "The King Follett Discourse [part 1]," *Ensign*, April 1971, 15.
24. Joseph Smith, "The King Follett Discourse," 15.
25. Joseph Smith, "The King Follett Discourse [part 2]," *Ensign*, May 1971, 13.
26. Millet, *The Vision of Mormonism*, 271–74.
27. Millet, *The Vision of Mormonism*, 272.
28. Gordon B. Hinckley, in Conference Report, October 1994, 64, quoted in Millet, *The Vision of Mormonism*, 276.
29. Lorenzo Snow's couplet was originally written in June of 1892 and was later published in the *Improvement Era*, June 1919, 660.
30. Richard J. Mouw, in Robert L. Millet, *A Different Jesus? The Christ of the Latter-day Saints* (Grand Rapids, MI: Eerdmans, 2004), 182.
31. Millet, in Robert L. Millet and Gerald R. McDermott, *Claiming Christ: A Mormon-Evangelical Dialogue* (Grand Rapids, MI: Brazos Press, 2007), 85–86.
32. Millet, *Getting at the Truth*, 115.
33. Millet, *Claiming Christ*, 86.

34. Millet, *The Mormon Faith*, 29–30.
35. Millet, *The Vision of Mormonism*, 272.
36. See Richard J. Mouw, "The Possibility of Joseph Smith: Some Evangelical Probings," in *Joseph Smith Jr.: Reappraisals After Two Centuries*, ed. Terryl Givens and Reid L. Neilson (New York: Oxford University Press, 2009), 195.
37. Quoted in Rabbi Elliot Dorff, *The Way into* Tikkun Olam *(Repairing the World)* (Woodstock, UT: Jewish Lights, 2005), 31.
38. Cohen, *Everyman's Talmud*, 42; 27; 4–6; 40. Rabbi Jonathan Sacks is an example of such thought: "Never before or since . . . has God been conceived in so radically transcendent way. God is not to be identified with anything on earth. . . . This ontological divide is fundamental. God is God; humanity is humanity. There can be no blurring of boundaries." Jonathan Sacks, *Covenant and Conversation: Genesis: The Book of Beginnings* (New Milford: Koren Publishers, 2009), 53.
39. Cohen, *Everyman's Talmud*, 67; emphasis added.
40. Cohen, *Everyman's Talmud*, 41, 40.
41. Cohen, *Everyman's Talmud*, 42–43.
42. Cohen, *Everyman's Talmud*, 42–47.
43. Cohen, *Everyman's Talmud*, 47.
44. Cohen, *Everyman's Talmud*, 386.
45. Cohen, *Everyman's Talmud*, 386; emphasis added.
46. Millet, *Getting at the Truth*, 109.
47. Cohen, *Everyman's Talmud*, 7–8.
48. Cohen, *Everyman's Talmud*, 210; cf. Rabbi David J. Wolpe, *The Healer of Shattered Hearts: A Jewish View of God* (New York: Penguin Books, 1990), 59–61.
49. Millet, *Claiming Christ*, 81.
50. Wolpe discusses the ways in which the strict ethical monotheism of the rabbis of the Talmud was experienced as "personal monotheism." The Talmud's way of holding these tensions together is to conceive of God's immanence in the personal presence of the *Shechinah* glory and the Holy Spirit. Wolpe, *The Healer of Shattered Hearts*, 57.
51. Orson F. Whitney, quoted in Millet, *Selected Writings*, 170.
52. Millet, *The Vision of Mormonism*, 40.
53. *LDS Beliefs*, 191–92.
54. *LDS Beliefs*, 191–92, compare 498; and Millet, *The Mormon Faith*, 59; 194, 60.
55. Millet, *The Mormon Faith*, 66–68; *LDS Beliefs*, 609–10.

56. On the purpose of human existence, see Millet, *The Mormon Faith*, 59–60, and Millet, *Getting at the Truth*, 113. To read a heartfelt discussion about suffering and growth, see Millet, *When a Child Wanders* (Salt Lake City: Deseret Book, 1996), 12–13. On hope for those who have died, see *The Mormon Faith*, 59–60, 63–65; Millet, *Getting at the Truth*, 113; Millet, *Claiming Christ*, 71; and *LDS Beliefs*, 596.
57. In her insightful book *Almost Christian*, Kenda Creasy Dean devotes an entire chapter, "Mormon Envy: Sociological Tools for Consequential Faith," to the spiritual lives of Latter-day Saint youth. Yet for all the book's merits, it misleadingly implies that the cultural tools of Latter-day Saints do not comport well with biblical teachings of grace. Kenda Creasy Dean, *Almost Christian: What the Faith of Our Teenagers Is Telling the American Church* (New York: Oxford University Press, 2010), see especially 59–60.
58. Millet, *Selected Writings of Robert L. Millet*, 185. See also his *Grace Works: After All We Can Do* (Salt Lake City: Deseret Book, 2003), and *Getting at the Truth*, 112.
59. *Lectures on Faith*, 5:2 (American Fork: Covenant Communications, 2000), 57–58, emphasis added; cf. Millet, *Getting at the Truth*, 112.
60. Millet, *The Vision of Mormonism*, 277.
61. Millet, *Getting at the Truth*, 107; Millet, *The Vision of Mormonism*, 277; Millet, *Claiming Christ*, 109.
62. Berkouwer, *Man: The Image of God*, 16–17.
63. Berkouwer, *Man: The Image of God*, 17.
64. Berkouwer, *Man: The Image of God*, 196–97.
65. Berkouwer, *Faith and Sanctification* (Grand Rapids, MI: Eerdmans, 1952), 71.
66. Berkouwer, *Man: The Image of God*, 117–8; cf. 129, 144–47.
67. Millet, *Claiming Christ*, 144–46.
68. Berkouwer, *Faith and Sanctification*, 112–13.
69. Berkouwer, *Faith and Sanctification*, 117.
70. Newbigin, "The Basis, Purpose and Manner of Inter-Faith Dialogue," 267–68.

Embers and Bonfires
The Richard L. Evans Professorship and Interfaith Work at BYU

J. B. Haws

The November 2012 presidential election was still over a year away, but the Republican primary race was already heating up when Dallas pastor Robert Jeffress introduced Texas governor Rick Perry to the Values Voter Summit in Washington, DC. And because of what happened during that brief introduction, CNN was waiting for Pastor Jeffress outside the main convention hall. Jeffress had just endorsed Governor Perry as "a genuine follower of Jesus Christ." The subtext of those words was not lost on reporters who well understood the religious overtones of this particular Republican primary race. In everyone's mind, of course, Mitt Romney—a Mormon—was the candidate with the questionable Christian credentials to which Pastor Jeffress had alluded. CNN wanted to press Pastor Jeffress on that point.[1]

In the interview that followed, Jeffress said, "I think Mitt Romney's a good moral man, but I think those of us who are born-again followers of Christ should always prefer a competent Christian to a competent non-Christian like Mitt Romney." Then Pastor Jeffress went one step further. He called The Church of Jesus Christ of Latter-day Saints a cult. Even though one observer noted that "Jeffress stole the Friday news cycle with his comments," Jeffress defended his word choice in that CNN interview. "This isn't news," Jeffress insisted. "This idea that Mormonism is a theological cult is not news either. That has been the historical position of Christianity for a long time."[2]

Few would argue that "historical position" point with Pastor Jeffress. He was right to note that conservative Christians have long viewed Mormonism as heterodox and suspect. Looking back, then, what *did* seem to qualify as "news" was the reaction that the exchange generated over the ensuing weekend—and the number of voices that challenged the appropriateness of the cult label. High on that list was an essay CNN published on its website, two days after the summit, by Richard J. Mouw, president of Fuller Seminary, with this title, "My Take: This Evangelical Says Mormonism Isn't a Cult."

For those who had watched Mormon–evangelical interaction over the past half century (and longer), Mouw's essay did seem to mark a milestone, especially considering Mouw's reasoning: "For the past dozen years, I've been co-chairing, with Professor Robert Millet of Brigham Young University—the respected Mormon school—a behind-closed-doors dialogue between about a dozen evangelicals and an equal number of our Mormon counterparts. . . . I know cults. . . . Religious cults are very much us-versus-them. . . . They don't like to engage in serious, respectful give-and-take dialogue with people with whom they disagree." To Mouw, therefore, the cult classification simply did not fit his experience with Mormonism. "While I am not prepared to reclassify Mormonism as possessing undeniably Christian theology," Mouw wrote, "I do accept many of my Mormon friends as genuine followers of the Jesus whom I worship as the divine Savior."[3]

Significant for the story to be narrated here, the dozen-year dialogue that Mouw referenced flourished under the auspices of an endowed professorship at Brigham Young University—a professorship that is now more than forty years old. Robert Millet assumed that chair only a few months after he and Mouw launched that initial conversation that has had far-reaching influence on Mormonism's place in the American religious landscape. This essay attempts to paint a picture of that professorship, the Richard L. Evans Chair of Religious Understanding, in a pointillist style of sorts—individual dots of color combining to create an image that takes shape when viewed from a distance. In many ways, this "pointillism" characterizes the impact of the Evans Chair on the public's perception of Mormonism. Individual moments and interactions have become parts of a larger whole, and in this case the whole is certainly greater than the sum of its parts.

What seems to be at work here is an "opinion leadership" approach to the shaping of public perception. One way to effect a shift in widespread opinion, of course, is an information blitz, a protracted publicity campaign, for example, to win the hearts and minds of wide swaths of viewers. But such a campaign requires enormous resources to have any kind of national or international reach. On the other hand, forging relationships with opinion leaders can mean that their influence—their social capital—can have a multiplying effect well beyond those initial relationships.[4] In this way and in just over four-plus decades, the holders of the Evans Chair have leveraged the resources of the endowment not only to raise the profile of Mormonism but also to prompt second looks at Latter-day Saint belief and practice—all of which takes aim at the professorship's initial mandate: "promoting understanding among people of differing religious faiths . . . and promot[ing] an enlightening exchange among Latter-day Saints . . . and people of goodwill everywhere."[5]

Truman G. Madsen and the First Two Decades of the Evans Chair

To understand the story of the Richard L. Evans Chair, one must also understand something of the history of the institution where the chair is housed. And for much of that institution's first century, it almost goes without saying that not many academicians thought Mormonism was worthy of notice.

Brigham Young University started as a perennially underfunded academy in 1875. Teacher salaries were sometimes paid in farm produce in those early lean years. Even though it was an LDS Church-owned school, the institution's perpetuity was in doubt until almost the mid-twentieth century as Church authorities weighed the costs and benefits, and as administration attempts to upgrade the faculty met with stops and starts over financial and philosophical concerns.

Outsiders were even less enthusiastic about the prospects of intellectual engagement with Mormonism. In 1917, Yale-educated Walter Prince wrote dismissively that "scholars have not thought it worth while to discuss the notion of [the Book of Mormon's] ancient authorship" because "the odd contents of the volume lamentably or ludicrously fall before every canon of historical criticism."[6] Over the next two decades, Latter-day Saint authorities sought to bolster the historical-critical credentials of its religion faculty by sending several to study at the University of Chicago. What has come to be known in Church circles as the "Chicago Experiment" yielded mixed results—good academic training did not necessarily result in articulate exponents of a uniquely Mormon religious perspective, nor did it seem to promote a two-way exchange of ideas.[7]

While Mormon theology struggled to gain widespread acceptability as a system of thought, the Mormon people themselves made more headway in that direction in the 1930s and 1940s. An aggressive and well-publicized Church welfare plan in response to the Great Depression drew the press to Salt Lake City and a church that only a half century earlier had been castigated for polygamy was now being openly celebrated for provident living and patriotism. While this favorable turn in national media attention was certainly a welcome change for Mormons, there still was the sense that it was the Church's espousal of all-American values—hard work, thrift, neighborliness—rather than the Church's religious *raison d'etre* underpinning those values that won this sometimes-grudging acceptance. Mormon historian Richard Bushman remembered that as a Harvard undergraduate in 1950, his "sophomore tutor in History and Science, the distinguished historian of science I. B. Cohen, casually mentioned during one of our meetings that many people at Harvard thought Mormon theology was garbage."[8] When sociologist Thomas O'Dea published *The Mormons* later in the decade, he recognized that there were those "who emphasize the obsolescence of Mormonism, those who see the end of the movement in a stereotyped lack of creativity and a routine running down, who believe that this Mormon world will end not with a bang but a whimper"—but O'Dea sensed those prognosticators "[were] wrong." Though he may have been challenging much conventional wisdom, he felt that a tidal change was coming. "There is," he wrote, "still too much vitality—the characteristic Mormon vitality—remaining for such a prognosis to be likely."[9]

Visible evidence of that continued vitality was Church growth in the 1950s and 1960s. Church membership more than doubled in those decades. The accompanying building boom gave Mormons a physical presence in hundreds of new locales around the globe. Henry D. Moyle, a senior Church Apostle, summarized the boom this way in 1963: "In the past twelve years, we have built 56% of the meetinghouses we now have in the world, 1,941 in number—more than were built in the preceding 120 years of Church history."[10] Growth at BYU was even more dramatic. In the fifties and sixties, the BYU "student body increased six-fold to more than 25,000, the size of the faculty quadrupled, . . . and the number of permanent buildings jumped more than twenty-fold."[11]

Just as noticeable was growing esteem for the public faces of Mormonism. As recognizable as any such faces were those of the Mormon Tabernacle Choir singers and their announcer, Apostle Richard L. Evans. By the 1960s the choir was already in its fourth decade of continuous nationwide Sunday broadcasts, and Elder Evans provided the inspirational sermon portion of the weekly *Music and the Spoken Word* programs. So broad was the appeal of the choir's music and Evans's nondenominational-sounding homilies that *Time* magazine reported in 1971 that "many of the show's faithful listeners did not realize Evans was a Mormon; they considered themselves followers of 'Richard Evans's church.'"[12]

It was, fittingly, a Richard Evans broadcast that proved to be the point of genesis for the professorship that would eventually bear his name. California industrialist Lowell Berry (not a Latter-day Saint) had become a Richard Evans admirer after tuning in, by chance, to a 1954 "Church of the Air" sermon that Evans was giving entitled "We Are Not Alone in Life." After meeting Evans and developing a friendship with him, Berry called the Mormon Apostle one of "the two greatest Christians he ever met" (the other was Billy Graham).[13] Berry and Evans also shared an enthusiasm for the work of the Rotary Club—Evans was the president of Rotary International in 1966–67. Upon Elder Evans's death in 1971, Lowell Berry proposed to BYU president Dallin H. Oaks that something be done to honor Richard L. Evans. The idea of an endowed professorship emerged. Lowell Berry became an initial underwriter of the chair, and, until his death, he "continued his support over the protest of some of [the] fundamentalist directors" of his foundation.[14]

By November 1972, fifty donors had put forward $600,000 to endow the professorship, and BYU announced that Dr. Truman G. Madsen would be the first occupant of the Richard L. Evans Chair of Christian Understanding.[15] It proved to be a decidedly far-reaching appointment.

Truman Madsen came to the post with contacts and convictions. Before accepting an appointment at BYU in 1960, he had studied at the University of Utah, the University of Southern California, and Harvard; at Harvard he ultimately passed doctoral exams in both philosophy and the history and philosophy of religion. Madsen was no stranger to vigorous religious dialogue—after all, the man had written a Harvard doctoral dissertation that took on Paul Tillich's theology when Tillich was still *at* Harvard—and he was certainly no stranger to the challenge of explaining Mormonism in a variety of settings and contexts. His first decade at BYU was interrupted by a call from Church authorities to serve for three years as president of the Church's New England Mission. In that post, not only did he supervise scores of young volunteer missionaries, he also renewed many of the friendships he had made in Cambridge. Seven years later, when he was appointed to the Evans Chair, he drew on those friendships to take the academic engagement of Mormonism in unprecedented directions.[16]

It is worth noting here that the professorship's potential for impact was not lost on leaders of the LDS Church. By definition, the Church President is also the chairman of Brigham Young University's board of trustees. Harold B. Lee was that president and chairman when the Evans Chair was inaugurated, and he gave Madsen a charge in the form of an analogy. His message to Madsen was that a visit to another institution to deliver a lecture would be the equivalent of Madsen's carrying an "ember" of Mormonism; inviting scholars to visit BYU would be like bringing them to the "blaze."[17] In terms of embers versus bonfires, 1978 stands out in the early history of the Evans Chair.

In March of that year, BYU and Truman Madsen hosted a symposium that one observer called "the watershed event of the decade."[18] A lineup of participants that read like a who's who of American religious scholarship converged on Provo and for two days considered Judeo-Christian parallels in Mormonism. Mormon polymath Hugh Nibley called the group "Number One, top-drawer in their fields"[19]; Madsen simply said, "We aimed high." The modesty in his understatement aside, what should not be missed is the role that Madsen had played in building personal bridges. Krister Stendahl and John Dillenberger had been on the faculty at Harvard when Madsen had been there, and his friendship with them had given Madsen an important starting point to bring in other luminaries like David Noel Freedman, Jacob Milgrom, and Robert Bellah.[20]

As remarkable as that 1978 conference proved to be, though, in hindsight it seems noteworthy more for what it represented than what actually transpired there, without taking anything away from the thoughtfulness of the presented papers. Duke University's W. D. Davies described the conference as "[opening] up the world of Mormon thinking to direct and deliberate confrontation with that of non-Mormon religious scholarship."[21] What the symposium seemed to signal was that Madsen's work was building momentum. This is characteristic of the "pointillist style" referenced above: the discrete, individual interactions that worked together to nudge a variety of thinkers to see things in Mormonism that they never expected to see—to consider, in Madsen's words, "the thrust of Richard L. Evans' life," that "we have more in common than differences."[22]

In advance of the 1978 symposium, for example, Madsen invited Stendahl, the former dean of the Harvard Divinity School and expert on the Gospel of Matthew, to consider the Sermon on the Mount through the lens of the Book of Mormon, since in the Book of Mormon there is an account of the resurrected Jesus delivering a very similar sermon to a first-century New World audience. Stendahl later republished the presentation that he made on this topic at BYU in a Fortress Press collection of his essays entitled *Meanings: The Bible as Document and as Guide*. In introducing the essay, Professor Stendahl gently chastised biblical scholars for being so "cavalier . . . in our attitude toward the biblical 'after-history'" in "authentic writings" of a "revelatory character" like the Book of Mormon.[23] Stendahl compared his studying of Mormonism to "visiting the Christian Church ca. A.D. 150—a fascinating opportunity indeed for a New Testament scholar."[24] John Dillenberger, too, advocated for more academic attention to Mormonism. Dillenberger led the Graduate Theological Union in the 1970s, and he pushed for a Mormon

Studies component in the curriculum there. Truman Madsen filled a three-year "commuter professorship" at the GTU. Dillenberger wrote to Madsen: "Mormonism is such a significant part of the life of the West that a theological university community which ignores it is not doing its task. We have assumed that our communities need an authentic exposure to Mormonism beyond the traditional stereotypes."[25]

This was the case Madsen was trying to make anywhere he could. After just more than a decade into his tenure (1983), Madsen reported that he had been to eighty different universities to offer lectures or meet with scholars. Besides his work at the GTU in Berkeley, he had also filled a visiting professorship at Haifa University in Israel.[26] After another ten years in the position, Madsen had taken "more than five hundred trips to colleges and universities and institutions worldwide," including forty-five directed study tours to Israel and two years as director of BYU's Jerusalem Center for Near Eastern Studies.[27]

Madsen saw his work as establishing relationships with colleagues who would "speak up for the Mormons, at least with understanding"—in academic circles, yes, but also in the public square.[28] One such public-square moment came in 1985. Krister Stendahl was by this time bishop of Stockholm in the Church of Sweden. He led a press conference at a Latter-day Saint meetinghouse in Stockholm to defuse local opposition to an announced Mormon temple there, and he articulated three rules of religious understanding that have since taken on a life of their own: one, when trying to understand another religion, one should ask the adherents of that religion and not its enemies; two, don't compare one's best to their worst; and three, leave room for "holy envy." Stendahl then expressed "holy envy" for the doctrine of baptism for the dead and for the Mormon impulse to extend salvific rites to those who never had that opportunity on earth.[29] Stendahl even wrote an entry on baptism for the dead for Macmillan's *Encyclopedia of Mormonism*, published in 1992.

There is a danger of overreaching when attempting to measure the impact of conversations or impressions or encounters such as these. Still, what should not be discounted are repeated evidences of the Evans Chair's hand in some of the most significant Mormon academic enterprises of the past generation. The *Encyclopedia of Mormonism* project is a prime example of that. In the mid-1980s, more Mormon-related stories—good and bad—hit newsstands across the country than perhaps ever before: the BYU football team won a national championship; Sharlene Wells, the daughter of a General Authority, was Miss America; Mark Hofmann, a Mormon documents dealer-turned-forger murdered two people to hide his tracks; and a rash of violence in several fundamentalist polygamist communities brought new attention to Mormon breakoff groups. Jerry Kaplan, Macmillan's chief executive officer, wanted to know more about the religion, but he was disappointed with the available resources at the New York City public library. He charged his company with changing that. A massive collaboration with Latter-day Saint scholars ensued. Truman Madsen was one of the editors, and he was instrumental in drawing in sixteen non-LDS scholars to contribute to the *Encyclopedia*—a small percentage of the full pool of contributors, but an important indication, and in a groundbreaking publication, of a growing mutual appreciation on the part of both Mormons and outside scholars.[30]

BYU's involvement with the Dead Sea Scrolls translation project is another of those landmark initiatives with an Evans Chair connection. When representatives of Hebrew University approached Madsen, then director of the BYU Jerusalem Center, and asked for his help in rallying Latter-day Saint donors for the Dead Sea Scrolls preservation project, Madsen expressed willingness to help. But he also offered something else: he explained that BYU was pioneering new computer digitization technology that could be used to catalog, display, and search through every scroll fragment. Thus began a partnership that has placed BYU at the forefront of Dead Sea Scrolls scholarship. Harvard's Frank Moore Cross Jr., another friend of Madsen's (and past participant in a BYU-hosted conference), recruited BYU professors to join Dead Sea Scrolls translation teams—and BYU led the way in electronic publishing of the scrolls. In Truman Madsen's estimation, "this put us on the map."[31]

Two Decades of the Evans Chair after Truman Madsen's Retirement

Changes in the Evans professorship after Truman Madsen's retirement in 1994 meant that his tenure would always be unique in the chair's history—but what did not change was that the fingerprints of the chair's occupants would continue to be found on formative, history-making Mormon intellectual enterprises. After Truman Madsen stepped down, the professorship was expanded (now two professors occupy the chair concurrently), and its tenure was limited to two- or three-year terms—all aimed at broadening the chair's reach. And importantly, the professorship was renamed—the Richard L. Evans Chair of *Christian* Understanding became the Richard L. Evans Chair of *Religious* Understanding. The name change reflected the diversity of Truman Madsen's contacts and friendships and interests. In this way—in every way, really—Madsen had set the tone for his successors, of which there have been nearly a dozen to date.

There is more to document in the recent history of this professorship than the constraints of this essay will allow. But two general trends—and the professors who launched those trends—have particular bearing on the question at hand.

First, David L. Paulsen and his engagement with Mormon metaphysics stand out in this regard. Paulsen was one of two Brigham Young University professors who assumed the Evans Chair in 1994. He was a professor of philosophy, and he followed his natural proclivities to make significant inroads in that discipline. Paulsen tapped into his long association with the Society of Christian Philosophers to initiate a two-year "series of mini-seminars on twentieth-century Christian theology—twentieth-century theological movements and theologians."[32] In many cases, the theological "movers" themselves came to BYU to represent their views before faculty and students. The fruit of that long series was a book published by Mercer University Press in 2007 that David Paulsen coedited with Stetson University's Donald Musser: *Mormonism in Dialogue with Contemporary Christian Theologies*. Each of the book's chapters paired a Mormon thinker with a non-LDS thinker to explore a theological theme. Musser's preface was telling. He recounted that on a flight to Utah to meet with David Paulsen, he read a feature in the *Atlanta Journal-Constitution* on "Christianity at 2000." Musser noticed that "there was not a word of reference to The Church of Jesus Christ of Latter-day Saints," even though Mormons "easily outnumber[ed] many of the 'major' groups covered in the article." Musser then admitted that "prior to my intersection with scholars at BYU . . . I would not have noticed [this exclusion]." He even admitted that in the past, he "ducked any duo that [he] thought had a 'Mormon missionary' look." What changed for Musser was that he became "engaged in the conversations contained in this volume"—conversations, importantly, that "pursued neither an apologetic nor a polemical tack," but were "conversations . . . that lead to understanding." Both Paulsen and Musser agreed in the book's introduction that "the similarities surprised both sides. Agreements were far more frequent than many discussants expected at the outset."[33]

Over his career, as David Paulsen wrote about the theological innovations and implications inherent in Mormon cosmology, he detected important changes along the lines of Musser's biographical journey. When Paulsen first published essays on theodicy or divine corporeality, he "[presented] and [defended] Mormon points of view" but "didn't explicitly identify them as such." He had seen the resistance such explicit identification could generate: for example, *Faith and Philosophy*, the journal of the Society of Christian Philosophers, turned down Paulsen's article on "Joseph Smith and the Problem of Evil" because "it dealt explicitly with Joseph Smith." It said something, therefore, when less than twenty years later, this same journal—"the mainline Christian academic journal" in the field—published in 2008 a David Paulsen and Brett McDonald essay entitled "Joseph Smith and the Trinity: An Analysis and a Defense of a Social Model of the Godhead." Paulsen has seen his work in print in journals like the *Harvard Theological Review* and *Analysis*, and in his view, the days of "setting out a Mormon perspective without identifying it as Mormon" are passing; "we don't have to do that anymore," he said in 2007, and for him, that new reality was a "breakthrough."[34]

"Breakthrough" might also well characterize one more Evans Chair holder to be profiled here: Robert Millet. Significantly, this very volume and several of its contributors stand as evidence of the impact of Millet's Evans Chair outreach. Perhaps more than anything else, what set Millet's activities apart was his turn toward evangelical Christianity. Millet assumed the Evans professorship in 2000, just as he was forging a friendship with Utah pastor Greg Johnson, a friendship that had grown initially out of mutual interest and engagement with *How Wide the Divide? A Mormon and an Evangelical in Conversation*. That 1997 book had been coauthored by Stephen Robinson, Millet's BYU religion faculty colleague, and Craig Blomberg of the Denver Seminary, where Greg Johnson had gone to school. Millet and Johnson's early meetings led to an impulse to formalize and expand their conversations. Millet put his Evans Chair resources to good use. Not only did he and Johnson conduct dozens of "An Evangelical and a Latter-day Saint in Conversation" public forums at universities and churches across the United States, but—coming back to the point where this essay began—he also launched the semiannual Mormon-evangelical dialogue group that continued for more than a decade, with Richard Mouw as coleader.

As was the case in that opening CNN vignette, Millet and Mouw's collaborations have led to a number of memorable moments that have challenged preconceptions about Mormon-evangelical interaction.[35] In 2004, when Millet worked with Latter-day Saint authorities to make available the historic Mormon Tabernacle on Temple Square for an evening of preaching with evangelist Ravi Zacharias, Mouw made perhaps the biggest news of the night. In his introductory comments before Zacharias's preaching, Mouw apologized to Latter-day Saints for what he saw as the false witness that evangelicals often bore against Mormons when they caricatured Latter-day Saint faith. Then, when Robert Millet published a 2005 book, *A Different Jesus? The Christ of the Latter-day Saints*, with evangelical powerhouse Eerdmans Publishing, Mouw wrote the foreword and afterword. These statements resonated widely, not just for what they said, but also for what they signaled—something that was not lost on Mormon or evangelical readers.

Realities—and Possibilities

Not everyone was happy, to say the least, with Eerdmans' decision to publish Millet's book or with Mouw's apology at the Tabernacle. Fiery blogs decried Eerdmans' treachery in giving airtime to Latter-day Saint theology through Millet's book or Mouw's shortsightedness in weakening countercult evangelizing.[36] And it is certainly not a one-sided problem. Millet has noted that some Latter-day Saints have questioned his interfaith approach and the approach of several of his BYU colleagues. A few such voices see these professors' presentations of Latter-day Saint doctrine to Protestant groups, especially evangelical Christians, as either "minimalist" or "neo-orthodox" variants of true Mormonism—as "giving away the store."³⁷ The passion generated by these questions about Mormonism's "Christian status" and the appropriateness of religious dialogue brings an important dose of reality to this discussion about the impact of interfaith initiatives.

So, too, does the frankness of Douglas Davies, a scholar at Durham University in the UK who forged close ties with Evans Chair professors beginning with David Paulsen, and whose own work on Mormonism (and his advising of graduate students in that vein) has made important contributions to the field. Davies noted in 2007 that in terms of outside scholars—like him—who at the time were working on Mormon topics in a serious and committed way, "you can count them on the fingers of one hand, by and large."³⁸

Likewise, in the early days of the 2012 presidential campaign's "Mormon moment," Richard Bushman and Terryl Givens had prime vantage points from which to observe America's public perception of Mormonism, not only because they were Mormon historians with a keen eye for cultural clues, but also because they became go-to resources for scores of journalists who wanted to know about the faith. Thinking about the state of things in 2011, Bushman described the middle of the twentieth century as a time when "Americans became convinced that Mormons were good people. . . . That battle," he said, "I think we've won. The second battle, making our theology respectable, we haven't won." Givens similarly observed at the time that "Mormons are perfectly welcomed to dance with the stars, to feed continual streams of great quarterbacks into the NFL, . . . [and] the Mormon Tabernacle Choir continues to sing at the presidential inaugurals, but the theology continues to be marginalized as a system of thought."³⁹

These are important contemporary commentaries about the state of both academic and public engagement with Mormonism, and the realities noted therein call for appropriate restraint. But there are enough signs of a sea change—signs, for example, that Douglas Davies's estimate no longer feels accurate just a few years later,—that for those with an interest in interfaith discussion, optimism does seem to be the order of the day. Discerning evidence of that sea change, though, might be more like noting a rising tide rather than measuring the size of the waves.

On one level, the venues and the voices involved cannot go long unnoticed. Evans Chair–sponsored conferences and lectures have ranged from Harvard to Yale to Notre Dame to Wheaton to Fuller, just to name a few. Sponsored conferences with wide denominational participation over the last decade at BYU have led to important volumes on salvation and authority.[40] A conversation Robert Millet had with Roanoke College's Gerry McDermott sparked what might be the brightest star to date in this constellation of conferences. McDermott and Millet had joined forces in 2003 for a public Mormon-evangelical presentation—and McDermott mentioned in passing that he was participating in a Library of Congress celebration of the tricentennial of Jonathan Edwards's birth. Millet had already been tapped by the LDS Church to represent BYU on a Church committee that was making plans to commemorate the two hundredth anniversary of Joseph Smith's birth, so the Library of Congress idea was serendipitous. The result was the "Worlds of Joseph Smith" conference at the Library of Congress in December 2005, a conference that considered, from various angles, the impact and import of Joseph Smith's life and teachings. Eight of the seventeen presenters were not Latter-day Saints.[41]

There is something to be said, too, of the ripple effect of Evans Chair initiatives. Almost as if in answer to Bushman's or Givens's call for serious attention to Mormon thought, Roman Catholic philosopher Stephen Webb published a bold book with Oxford University Press in 2013, *Mormon Christianity: What Other Christians Can Learn from the Latter-day Saints*. Webb first turned heads in Mormon studies when he published a *First Things* essay entitled "Mormons Are Obsessed with Christ," a personal response to the "Are Mormons Christian?" question that became so charged (again) during Mitt Romney's campaign seasons.[42] The publicity that came to all of Mormondom in connection with those campaigns, of course, seemed to catalyze an academic and interfaith interest in Mormonism that had already been growing, and the sheer volume of media attention meant that the opportunity for exposure to Mormon ideas was greater than ever. Terryl and Fiona Givens felt some hopefulness in that vein in the month after the 2012 elections. "Only by the end of the Romney campaign," they wrote, "did we seem finally to be moving beyond discussion of magic underwear, Missouri Edens, and Kolob. . . . Perhaps Americans can at last begin a conversation about the substance, rather than the esoterica, of Mormon belief."[43]

New forces seem to be in motion that will only contribute to the "substantive" inertia of that interest. The University of Virginia, for example, inaugurated the Richard Lyman Bushman Chair of Mormon Studies in the fall of 2013—another entry to add to Jerry Bradford's 2007 survey, "The Study of Mormonism: A Growing Interest in Academia."[44] And Brigham Young University launched in August 2014 a new Office of Religious Outreach and advisory board, with Robert Millet as its head.

Apart from these visible institutional movements, though, something that Stephen Webb wrote in his book's acknowledgments seems to bring this essay perhaps full circle: "Of all the people I met at BYU, I am most in debt to David Paulsen, a fearless metaphysical pioneer who amiably opened the door for me to the richness of Mormon thought. He is truly a lover of wisdom, my mentor in Mormon studies, and an elder to me in the Christian faith."[45] This direct link between personal interaction and new perspectives on Mormonism speaks to the ideals on which the Richard L. Evans Chair at Brigham Young University was founded. And while *causation* may be difficult to ascertain statistically, public opinion polls do suggest at least a chronological *correlation* between interfaith outreach and growing public familiarity with, and diminishing misconceptions about, Mormonism.[46] From a distance, then, this is a picture that is taking shape—and it is a picture that has room yet to be fully filled out.

NOTES

1. Richard A. Oppel Jr. and Erik Eckholm, "Prominent Pastor Calls Romney's Church a Cult," *New York Times*, October 7, 2011, http://www.nytimes.com/2011/10/08/us/politics/prominent-pastor-calls-romneys-church-a-cult.html. An earlier version of this paper was presented at the annual meetings of the Mormon History Association, and I acknowledge the MHA, with gratitude, for that opportunity.
2. "Perry Supporter Says Romney's Religion 'a Cult,'" *CNN*, October 8, 2011, http://www.cnn.com/2011/10/08/politics/perry-response-mormonism/; Frances Martel, "Anti-Mormon Pastor to Anderson Cooper: Romney May Belong to a 'Cult,' But

He Is Better than Obama," *Mediaite*, October 8, 2011, http://www.mediaite.com /tv/anti-mormon-pastor-to-anderson-cooper-romney-may-belong-to-a-cult -but-he-is-better-than-obama/; Oppel and Eckholm, "Prominent Pastor Calls Romney's Church a Cult."

3. Richard J. Mouw, "My Take: This Evangelical Says Mormonism Isn't a Cult," *CNN*, October 9, 2011, http://religion.blogs.cnn.com/2011/10/09/my-take-this -evangelical-says-mormonism-isnt-a-cult/.

4. I am indebted to Mark Tuttle, a director in the Public Affairs Department of The Church of Jesus Christ of Latter-day Saints, for identifying this philosophical approach in his department's work. See Mark Tuttle, interview by author, August 20, 2008, transcript in possession of the author, 8–9. The approach, which has roots in the "two-step flow" theory of communication, seems to apply here as well. See, for example, Ronald S. Burt, "The Social Capital of Opinion Leaders," *The Annals of the American Academy of Political and Social Science* 566, no. 1 (November 1999): 37–54. See also David E. Campbell, John C. Green, and J. Quin Monson, *Seeking the Promised Land: Mormons and American Politics* (New York: Cambridge University Press, 2014), 184–91, for analysis of survey data that points to the importance of both social contact and factual knowledge in softening "negative attitudes towards Mormons" (187). The implications of their research are significant here, since the work of interfaith outreach fostered by the Evans Chair seems targeted at facilitating both social contact and factual knowledge.

5. Quoted in the pamphlet announcing the chair's establishment, "The Richard L. Evans Chair of Christian Understanding: A Special Heritage in Religion," Dean's Office, Religious Education, Brigham Young University; copy in possession of the author. Stephen David Grover has also written an important history of the Richard L. Evans Chair, drawing on interviews with several past holders of the chair to give insight into their feelings about the purpose and purview of the professorship. See Stephen David Grover, "Building Bridges: The Richard L. Evans Chair of Religious Understanding," *Religious Educator* 9, no. 2 (2008): 45–56; see especially pages 51–53 for perspectives and experiences shared by past Evans professors Fred Woods, Roger Keller, and Darwin Thomas.

6. Walter Prince, quoted in Terryl L. Givens, *By the Hand of Mormon* (Oxford and New York: Oxford University Press, 2002), 144.

7. See Casey P. Griffiths, "The Chicago Experiment: Finding the Voice and Charting the Course of Religious Education in the Church," *BYU Studies* 49, no. 4 (2010): 91–130.

8. Richard Lyman Bushman, *Believing History: Latter-day Saint Essays*, ed. Reid L. Neilson and Jed Woodworth (New York: Columbia University Press, 2004), vii.
9. Thomas F. O'Dea, *The Mormons* (Chicago and London: The University of Chicago Press, 1957), 262.
10. Gregory A. Prince and Wm. Robert Wright, *David O. McKay and the Rise of Modern Mormonism* (Salt Lake City: University of Utah Press, 2005), 208–9.
11. Gary Bergera and Ronald Priddis, *Brigham Young University: A House of Faith* (Salt Lake City: Signature Books, 1985), 26.
12. "Died: Richard L. Evans," *Time*, November 15, 1971, 53.
13. From a two-page, unpublished typescript of personal reminiscences by Truman G. Madsen, "The Richard L. Evans Chair," 1; copy in possession of the author. The background to the establishment of the chair is also explained, with additional details, in the pamphlet announcing the Chair's establishment. See "The Richard L. Evans Chair of Christian Understanding: A Special Heritage in Religion."
14. Madsen, "The Richard L. Evans Chair," 1.
15. From a one-page historical report, "Richard L. Evans Chair of Christian Understanding," file 56-A, Dean's Office, Religious Education, Brigham Young University; copy in possession of the author.
16. This background information is summarized from two helpful biographical essays: Truman G. Madsen, "Truman Madsen, On His Education," and Dillon K. Inouye, "Truman Madsen, Valued Teacher," in *Revelation, Reason, and Faith: Essays in Honor of Truman G. Madsen*, ed. Donald W. Parry, Daniel C. Peterson, and Stephen D. Ricks (Provo, UT: FARMS, 2002).
17. Truman G. Madsen, interview by author, March 22, 2007. See also David Paulsen, interview by author, March 8, 2007; and Robert L. Millet, interview by author, March 16, 2007.
18. From the dust jacket of *Reflections on Mormonism: Judaeo-Christian Parallels*, ed. Truman G. Madsen (Provo, UT: Religious Studies Center, 1978).
19. Inouye, "Truman Madsen, Valued Teacher," xxx.
20. Madsen, interview, March 22, 2007.
21. From the dust jacket of *Reflections on Mormonism*.
22. Madsen, interview, March 22, 2007.
23. Krister Stendahl, "The Sermon on the Mount and Third Nephi in the Book of Mormon," in *Meanings: The Bible as Document and as Guide* (Philadelphia: Fortress Press, 1984), 99.
24. Stendahl, "The Sermon on the Mount," 100.

25. "The Richard L. Evans Chair of Christian Understanding: A Special Heritage in Religion" announcement pamphlet, 8.
26. Madsen, "The Richard L. Evans Chair," 1.
27. Madsen, "Truman Madsen, On His Education," xx.
28. Madsen, interview, March 22, 2007.
29. Madsen, interview, March 22, 2007.
30. Madsen, interview, March 22, 2007. See Mark Hofmann prison interview, quoted in Richard E. Turley Jr., *Victims: The LDS Church and the Mark Hofmann Case* (Urbana: University of Illinois Press, 1992), 317. See also Richard D. Poll, "Review of the *Encyclopedia of Mormonism*," *Journal of Mormon History* 18, no. 2 (Fall 1992): 205–6, for the story of Jerry Kaplan's interest. I am also indebted to John Welch for his retelling of this story.
31. Madsen, interview, March 22, 2007. See also the introduction to Donald Parry and Dana M. Pike, eds., *LDS Perspectives on the Dead Sea Scrolls* (Provo, UT: FARMS, 1997), for a timeline of Latter-Saint involvement with Dead Sea Scrolls scholarship.
32. David L. Paulsen, interview by author, March 8, 2007.
33. David L. Paulsen and Donald W. Musser, *Mormonism in Dialogue with Contemporary Christian Theologies* (Macon, GA: Mercer University Press, 2007), vii, 1.
34. David L. Paulsen, interview, March 8, 2007; see also David L. Paulsen and Brett McDonald, "Joseph Smith and the Trinity: An Analysis and Defense of the Social Model of the Godhead," *Faith and Philosophy* 25, no. 1 (2008): 47–74. All of this seems especially significant given the troubled reaction from some members of the Society of Christian Philosophers when David Paulsen organized regional meetings of the Society at BYU in the early 1990s. The Society later changed its policy about selecting host institutions because of complaints from some members about the BYU events, but other members pushed for the continued inclusion of Mormons as members of the Society. For a concise summary, see "Mormon-Christian Dialogue?," Beliefnet, http://www.beliefnet.com/Faiths/Christianity/Latter-Day-Saints/2001/06/Mormon-Christian-Dialogue.aspx.
35. Also worthy of mention, especially for its bearing on the question of opinion leaders, is Robert Millet and Richard Mouw's participation as panelists at Michael Cromartie's Faith Angle Forum with national journalists in May 2012. See "Evangelicals and Mormons: A Conversation and Dialogue," Ethics and Public Policy Center, May 7, 2012, http://eppc.org/publications/mouw-and-millet/.

36. See, for example, Dr. James White's May 8, 2005, blog entry, "08 May: Paul Owen Finally Lays His Cards on the Table (#1)," at the Alpha and Omega Ministries website, www.aomin.org; also Keith Walker (Evidence Ministries), "A 'Mouwtainous' Mistake: An Open Letter to Richard Mouw and Other Academics Involved in Apologetics to Mormons," *Apologetics Index*, http://www.apologeticsindex.org/cpoint13-1.html.
37. See Millet's comments on various LDS reactions to interfaith dialogue in his "Outreach: Opening the Door or Giving Away the Store?," *Religious Educator* 4, no. 1 (2003), 55–73. An important side story to the impact of the Richard L. Evans work is the impact on Latter-day Saints. For example, a number of chair holders have presented fireside-type meetings for LDS congregations—Church members or full-time missionaries—with the meetings focused on improving religious understanding and tolerance and mutual respect. Significantly, conversations with evangelical Christians led Robert Millet to publish "What Is Our Doctrine?," *Religious Educator* 4, no. 3 (2003): 15–33, an important essay about evaluating sources of authority in Latter-day Saint doctrinal matters. The Church published something similar, officially, in 2007: "Approaching Mormon Doctrine," *Mormon Newsroom*, May 4, 2007, http://www.mormonnewsroom.org/article/approaching-mormon-doctrine. Millet's services as the Evans Chair holder were repeatedly tapped by the Church's Public Affairs Department. See, for example, Robert L. Millet, "Richard L. Evans Professorship: Report of Activities for the Year 2003," 1; copy in author's possession.
38. Douglas Davies, interview by author, March 22, 2007.
39. Richard L. Bushman and Terryl Givens, quoted in J. B. Haws, *The Mormon Image in the American Mind: Fifty Years of Public Perception* (New York and Oxford: Oxford University Press, 2013), 263.
40. See Roger R. Keller and Robert L. Millet, eds., *Salvation in Christ: Comparative Christian Views* (Provo, UT: Religious Studies Center, 2005); Robert L. Millet, ed., *By What Authority? The Vital Question of Religious Authority in Christianity* (Macon, GA: Mercer University Press, 2010).
41. Robert Millet, interview by author, March 16, 2007; Millet, "Richard L. Evans Professorship: Report of Activities for the Year 2003," 7–8. See also the introduction to "The Worlds of Joseph Smith: A Bicentennial Conference at the Library of Congress," *BYU Studies* 44, no. 4 (2005): vii–x.
42. Stephen H. Webb, "Mormonism Obsessed with Christ," *First Things*, February 2012, http://www.firstthings.com/article/2012/02/mormonism-obsessed-with-christ.

43. Terryl and Fiona Givens, "Moving Past the Esoterica," *Patheos*, December 2, 2012, http://www.patheos.com/Mormon/Moving-Past-Esoterica-Terryl-and-Fiona-Givens-12-03-2012.html.
44. M. Gerald Bradford, "The Study of Mormonism: A Growing Interest in Academia," *FARMS Review* 19, no. 1 (2007): 119–74.
45. Stephen Webb, *Mormon Christianity: What Other Christians Can Learn from the Latter-day Saints* (New York: Oxford University Press, 2013).
46. See two examples of this: "Americans Learned Little About the Mormon Faith, But Some Attitudes Have Softened," Pew Forum on Religion and Public Life, December 14, 2012, http://www.pewforum.org/Christian/Mormon/attitudes-toward-mormon-faith.aspx; also "How Americans Feel About Religious Groups," Pew Forum on Religion and Public Life, July 16, 2014, http://www.pewforum.org/2014/07/16/how-americans-feel-about-religious-groups/. It is on this point of the impact of interfaith relationships, too, that the research of David Campbell, John Green, and Quin Monson again becomes so important. In Seeking the Promised Land, they argue that "the role of interfaith relationships in fostering goodwill across religious lines presents Mormons with a problem. . . . The comparison between Jews and Mormons is instructive. There are about as many Mormons as Jews in America, but while Jews are viewed very positively, Mormons rank near the bottom of public perception. It is no coincidence that Jews are the religious group most likely to bridge to people of other faiths, while Mormons are among the least likely to do so" (185); I am indebted to Spencer Fluhman for raising this point. In Campbell, Green, and Monson's words, "More knowledge about Mormonism softens, or even reverses, such negative impressions, as do close personal relationships with Mormons themselves (but not passing acquaintances)" (190).

Sin, Guilt, and Grace
Martin Luther and the Doctrines of the Restoration

Daniel K Judd

In 1973, American psychiatrist Karl Menninger published an intriguing book with the provocative title *Whatever Became of Sin?* One of the reasons Menninger's publication was significant was its timing; the academic community and popular culture were distancing themselves from religion in general and the concepts of sin and guilt in particular. Menninger, founder of the world-renowned Menninger clinic, and well-versed in the biological and sociological origins of mental illness, wrote: "In all of the laments and reproaches made by our [leaders], one misses any mention of 'sin,' a word which used to be a veritable watchword of prophets. . . . Wrong things are being done, we know; tares are being sown in the wheat fields at night. But is no one responsible, no one answerable for these acts? Anxiety and depression we all acknowledge, and even vague guilt feelings; but has no one committed any sins? Where, indeed, did sin go? What became of it?"[1]

Menninger's view met significant opposition. Albert Ellis, a contemporary of Menninger and a well-respected theoretician and psychologist, represented those who spoke out against religious beliefs when he stated, "Religiosity, therefore, is in many respects equivalent to irrational thinking and emotional disturbance. . . . The elegant therapeutic solution to emotional problems is to be quite unreligious. . . . The less religious they are, the more emotionally healthy they will be."[2] Ellis's statement echoes the writings of Sigmund Freud, who considered religion to be "the universal compulsive neurosis of humanity."[3] The writings of Freud and Ellis anticipated many of the current criticisms of religious belief and practice, such as those by Professor Richard Dawkins, who describes religion as a "malignant infection."[4]

With few exceptions, however, research from the early part of the twentieth century to the present has produced very little support for the arguments linking religion and mental illness.[5] The significant majority of studies are supportive of the conclusion that religious belief and practice, and most especially intrinsic religious devotion, facilitates mental health, marital cohesion, and family stability.[6]

While the majority of research relating to mental health is positive with regard to religion's influence, there are important lessons to be learned from the minority of studies that suggest some religious beliefs and practices are detrimental to mental health. There are few influences more destructive in the lives of individuals, families, and nations than religion "gone bad." Conversely, as this paper will suggest, religion in general is an influence for good in the lives of individuals, families, and nations.

The primary intent of this paper is to focus on the core doctrinal principles of sin, guilt, and grace and the blessings made possible through the Atonement of Jesus Christ as they contribute to the temporal and eternal well-being of the human family. Special attention is also given to doctrinal teachings, which if misunderstood and wrongly applied can contribute to individual, familial, and global instability. A major portion of the paper includes examples from the life of the noted Protestant reformer Martin Luther, as illustrations of both the positive and negative influences of genuine and distorted religious belief and practice.

The Doctrine of Sin

G. K. Chesterton, a British writer noted for his insights into Western culture, once wrote a book entitled *What's Wrong with the World*.[7] Legend has it that the title for Chesterton's 1910 publication was inspired by an invitation he and several other British writers were given to write for the *Times*, the well-known London paper, about the problems the world was facing. Apparently, a number of submissions were received, but Chesterton's was the most noteworthy. In answer to the question "What's wrong with the world?" he simply stated, "Dear Sirs, I am. Sincerely yours, G. K. Chesterton."[8]

While not all of the problems in the world have sin as their origin (see John 9:1–3), to ignore the morality of mortality and to relabel all such problems as sickness, mental illness, or even crime is to make a tragic mistake. If we do not understand the relationship among sin, guilt, repentance, and the grace of Jesus Christ, we may never be free of our particular burdens. The consequence of eliminating sin as a source of suffering is to also remove the only remedy that will bring the healing so many seek.

The most common Greek word translated as "sin" in the New Testament is *hamartia*, which more precisely means "missing the mark."[9] While the "mark" we miss when we sin is often interpreted as breaking God's commandments, Elder Neal A. Maxwell taught that the "mark" isn't simply a commandment or principle, but "the mark is Christ."[10] Christ is the mark; the doctrinal principles contained in his gospel are manifestations of his very being. Doctrinal principles, precepts, and laws are vital, but the Savior wasn't just a teacher of the law—he was and is the Law: "Behold, I am the law, and the light. Look unto me, and endure to the end, and ye shall live; for unto him that endureth to the end will I give eternal life" (3 Nephi 15:9).

As we become disciples of Jesus Christ by following his teachings, we acquire his attributes and become as he is. Paul taught the early Saints at Philippi, "I press toward the *mark* for the prize of the high calling of God in Christ Jesus" (Philippians 3:14; emphasis added). Sin distances us from the Savior; following his teachings and example leads us to him.

Beyond the Mark

Paul taught the Saints in Rome, "For all have sinned, and *come short* of the glory of God" (Romans 3:23; emphasis added). The Book of Mormon prophet Jacob taught that we can also transgress the laws of God by going "*beyond* the mark." Jacob taught that "looking beyond the mark" is how the ancient Jews lost the truth they were once blessed to have: "Wherefore, because of their blindness, which blindness came by *looking beyond the mark*, they must needs fall; for God hath taken away his plainness from them, and delivered unto them many things which they cannot understand, because they desired it. And because they desired it God hath done it, that they may stumble" (Jacob 4:14; emphasis added).

The Jews were seeking a savior, but most were not seeking to be saved from sin. The savior they were anticipating would free them from Roman oppression and provide temporal salvation. They missed the mark in failing to accept and follow Jesus Christ as the Messiah.

In our own day, there are those who also go "beyond the mark" as a means of placing themselves above others and the law above the Lawgiver. They, like some of the Pharisees of old, do the right things for the wrong reasons. In Matthew, Christ's critique of the Pharisees relates not to actions but to motivations: "But all their works they do for to be seen of men" (Matthew 23:5). Robert L. Millet writes: "As members of the Church exceed the bounds of propriety and go beyond the established mark, they open themselves to deception and ultimately to destruction. Imbalance leads to instability. If Satan cannot cause us to lie or steal or smoke or be immoral, it just may be that he will cause our strength—our zeal for goodness and righteousness—to become our weakness. He will encourage excess, for surely any virtue, when taken to the extreme, becomes a vice."[11]

Going "beyond the mark" is thus often an expression of legalism or "works righteousness" where individuals attempt to save themselves through obedience to the law. Going "beyond the mark" can be as destructive as falling short of keeping the commandments. This extrinsic form of religious belief and practice, where the focus is on public behavior rather than private worship, is a characteristic common to many in the religious community who experience increased mental and emotional instability.[12] Those who are *extrinsically* religious tend to see religion as a means to achieve the acceptance of the public and other self-focused objectives. *Intrinsically* religious people place the will of God and the good of others before themselves. Intrinsic religious belief and practice is the manner of religion most commonly correlated with increased mental health.[13]

The New Testament's extrinsically motivated Pharisees are examples of those who worshipped the law but rejected the Lawgiver. The Apostle Paul described this same counterfeit righteousness by those in his day who had "a zeal of God, but not according to knowledge" (Romans 10:2). Paul continued his description by teaching that such individuals were "ignorant of God's righteousness, and going about to establish their own righteousness, [and] have not submitted themselves unto the righteousness of God" (Romans 10:3). These scriptural warnings, along with the findings from social science research, give us clear warnings of the dangers of being overzealous in religious belief and practice (see Mosiah 9:3).

Martin Luther

While there are individuals who look and live "beyond the mark" as a means of gratifying their "pride [and] vain ambition" (D&C 121:37), others ignorantly sin in a sincere but misguided attempt to live what they understand to be the gospel of Christ (see Mosiah 3:11). It is a sobering reality that we can sin in ignorance, and though we may not be morally culpable of sin, we nevertheless suffer the consequences of the transgressed law.

One of the most striking examples in Christian history of one who began his ministry focused on the external sacraments of his faith, in what he mistakenly thought was genuine religious devotion, is Martin Luther, one of the fathers of the Reformation. Luther's personal, and later public, battle with the theological counterfeits of legalism, overzealousness, and (arguably) a clinical obsession with scrupulosity, influenced both the Protestant Reformation and the later Restoration through the Prophet Joseph Smith. There is much that people of all faiths can learn from the mistakes of Martin Luther as well as from his significant contributions to both religious belief and practice.

From his own writings we read that Martin Luther began his ministry as a faithful Augustinian monk: "I was a good monk, and kept the rule of my order so strictly that I may say that if ever a monk got to heaven by his monkery, it was I. All my brothers in the monastery who knew me will bear me out. If I had kept on any longer, I should have killed myself with vigils, prayers, reading, and other work."[14]

SIN, GUILT, AND GRACE

The Augustinians were known for their moral and physical discipline. They slept and studied in small and generally unheated rooms. In addition to making vows of chastity, obedience, and poverty, Luther and the other monks of his order engaged in formal worship beginning each day between and 1:00 and 2:00 a.m. These sessions normally lasted forty-five minutes each and were held seven times throughout the day. While the young Luther has been quoted as saying, "The first year in the monastery the devil is very quiet,"[15] things changed dramatically in the years that followed. After an initial year of peace, Luther began to experience feelings of guilt and despair:

> When I was a monk, I made a great effort to live according to the requirements of the monastic rule. I made a practice of confessing and reciting all my sins, but always with prior contrition; I went to confession frequently, and I performed the assigned penances faithfully. Nevertheless, my conscience could never achieve certainty but was always in doubt and said: "You have not done this correctly. You were not contrite enough. You omitted this in your confession." Therefore the longer I tried to heal my uncertain, weak, and troubled conscience with human traditions, the more uncertain, weak, and troubled I continually made it. In this way, by observing human traditions, I transgressed them even more; and by following the righteousness of the monastic order, I was never able to reach it.[16]

For ten years Luther labored with increasing feelings of guilt and doubt. His writings reveal that other monks with whom he served experienced similar feelings: "I saw many who tried with great effort and the best of intentions to do everything possible to appease their conscience. They wore hair shirts; they fasted; they prayed; they tormented and wore out their bodies with various exercises so severely that if they had been made of iron, they would have been crushed. And yet the more they labored, the greater their terrors became."[17]

Searching for Peace

Martin Luther looked to his religion and his religious leaders to help him with his guilt. Specifically, he turned to the sacraments of the Catholic

Church but found that they did not provide the peace he was seeking. Commenting on his participation in the Church's sacraments, Luther recorded the following: "After confession and the celebration of Mass I was never able to find rest in my heart."[18]

Confession became an unfruitful ordeal for both Luther and those to whom he confessed. His biographers note that Luther "confessed frequently, often daily, and for as long as six hours on a single occasion."[19] Johannes von Staupitz, Luther's trusted mentor and the vicar of the Augustinian order in which Luther served, was one of those who received Luther's confessions. Of this relationship, Luther wrote: "I often made confession to Staupitz. . . . He [Staupitz] said, 'I don't understand you.' This was real consolation! Afterward when I went to another confessor I had the same experience. In short, no confessor wanted to have anything to do with me. Then I thought, 'Nobody has this temptation except you,' and I became as dead as a corpse."[20] Father Staupitz endeavored to ease Luther's guilt: "If you expect Christ to forgive you, come in with something to forgive—parricide, blasphemy, adultery—instead of all these little peccadilloes."[21]

If confession did not salve Luther's guilt, neither did fasting from food and drink, which he often did for days at a time. Luther recorded, "I almost fasted myself to death, for again and again I went for three days without taking a drop of water or a morsel of food."[22] While he acknowledged that fasting had a legitimate place in Christian worship, Luther warned that those who practiced fasting beyond its intended purpose (as he had) would "simply ruin their health and drive themselves mad."[23] Luther's increased devotion to prayer, a central part of a monk's daily routine, appears only to have added to his burden. Luther stated, "I chose twenty-one saints and prayed to three every day when I celebrated mass; thus I completed the number every week. I prayed especially to the Blessed Virgin, who with her womanly heart would compassionately appease her Son."[24] Luther reported that instead of bringing the relief he sought, his extra devotion to fasting and prayer "made [his] head split."[25]

Catholic theology at the time included "an individualistic view of sin," but "a corporate view of goodness."[26] Luther had been taught that while everyone must be accountable for every sin they had committed, they were also entitled to the collective goodness of the righteous who had died having acquired more righteousness than they would need to receive salvation in the kingdom of God. This pooled righteousness was available for a price. The transmission of credit from the collective righteousness of the saints to the person in need was referred to as an "indulgence."[27]

One of the means by which this "transfer" of righteousness from one person to another could occur was by making a financial contribution. Other methods included visiting holy sites and viewing sacred relics. During Luther's first visit to Rome he climbed (on his knees) the "Scala Santa" (holy stairway), twenty-eight marble steps Jesus had allegedly ascended when he was brought before Pontius Pilate for judgment. These steps had been transported from Jerusalem to Rome to remind the people of the Savior's unjust trial and crucifixion. Luther biographer Richard Marius notes that those who climbed these steps, offering a prayer on each step, did so with the belief they would be "purged of the necessity of satisfaction for all the sins they had ever committed." Marius recorded that when Luther finished his ascent he questioned the validity of having his sins remitted in this way by asking, "Who can know if it is so?"[28] In the end, Luther concluded that "those who believe that they can be certain of their salvation because they have indulgence letters will be eternally damned, together with their teachers."[29]

Christian psychiatrist Ian Osborn postulates Luther was suffering from obsessive-compulsive disorder.[30] A more precise clinical diagnosis is "scrupulosity," which Latter-day Saint psychiatrist Dawson Hedges and his colleague Chris Miller describe as "a psychological disorder primarily characterized by pathological guilt or obsession associated with moral or religious issues that is often accompanied by compulsive moral or religious observance and is highly distressing and maladaptive."[31]

Obsessive-compulsive disorder, scrupulosity, or any other psychological disorder is not "caused" by religion. Rather, people tend to express their mental confusion through the areas of life that are important to them.[32] "Cultural backgrounds [religious or otherwise] provide the scenery around which emotional problems create the drama."[33] While no mortal can accurately judge the origin of Luther's guilt and despair, it is clear that Luther was desperate to understand and to resolve what he termed "*Anfechtungen,*"³⁴ or what others have described as "the dark night of the soul."³⁵

The Righteousness of God

Martin Luther's experience with the grace of Jesus Christ would eventually bring him peace and ultimately inspire the Reformation. Luther's journey to grace formally began when his vicar, Johannes von Staupitz, invited him to pursue a doctoral degree and lecture on the Bible at Wittenberg University. Luther was stunned with the invitation but accepted the new assignment and began with a serious study of the Bible, beginning with the book of Psalms followed by the books of Romans and Galatians.

What resulted changed the course of history. Luther's so-called "tower experience" was in large part a personal revelation received as he studied and taught the scriptures over a period of years.³⁶ The "tower" was a small room in the tower of the Black Cloister in the Wittenberg monastery. Luther listed and discussed many scriptural texts that were vital to him being "reborn," but the text that was central to his personal transformation came from Romans: "For therein is the righteousness of God revealed from faith to faith: as it is written, The just shall live by faith" (Romans 1:17). In the beginning, Luther struggled to understand the phrase "the righteousness of God." Initially these words angered him to the point that he "hated the righteous God who punishes sinners."³⁷ But a new understanding of "God's righteousness" ultimately changed everything:

> The words "righteous" and "righteousness of God" struck my conscience like lightning. When I heard them I was exceedingly terrified. If God is righteous [I thought], he must punish. But when by God's grace I pondered, in the tower and heated room of this building, over the words, "He who through faith is righteous shall live" [Romans 1:17] and "the righteousness of God" [Romans 3:21], I soon came to the conclusion that if we, as righteous men, ought to live from faith and if the righteousness of God contribute to the salvation of all who believe, then salvation won't be our merit but God's mercy. My spirit was thereby cheered. For it's by the righteousness of God that we're justified and saved through Christ. These words [which

had before terrified me] now became more pleasing to me. The Holy Spirit unveiled the Scriptures for me in this tower.[38]

Eventually, Luther formulated what is now known as the doctrine of "justification by faith." The "righteousness of God" in Romans 1:17 wasn't a description of God's anger towards the sinner, Luther came to believe, but of his mercy and forgiveness available to those who believed in him. Luther taught that the doctrine of justification was the "chief article of Christian doctrine" and that "we must all be justified alone by faith in Jesus Christ, without any contribution from the law or help from our works."[39] Protestant scholar and pastor John F. MacArthur Jr. defines the doctrine of justification as "an act of God whereby He imputes to a believing sinner the full and perfect righteousness of Christ, forgiving the sinner of all unrighteousness, declaring him or her perfectly righteous in God's sight, thus delivering the believer from all condemnation."[40]

What Luther had initially failed to understand, and what he came to see as a failing of Catholicism, was that personal peace and eternal salvation were not rewards for his own good works, but could only come because of "the righteousness of God" that was made possible through the Atonement of Jesus Christ. All the prayers Luther had offered, the fasting he had done, the countless hours of confession he had made, and the indulgences he had received could never earn God's favor and thus bring him blessings of peace and redemption.

Luther's obsessions and compulsions with prayer, fasting, scripture study, and so on do not appear to have been motivated by a pharisaical desire to elicit the praise of his fellow men but by his desire to be accepted by God and be free from guilt and a consuming fear of death and damnation. His religious obsessions with his own problems, however, were a major part of what was preventing his progress. John MacArthur writes, "The root of both psychological and spiritual sickness is preoccupation with self. Ironically, the believer who is consumed with his own problems—even his own spiritual problems—to the exclusion of concern for other believers, suffers from a destructive self-centeredness that not only is the cause of, but is the supreme barrier to the solution of, his own problems."[41]

Luther's new understanding allowed him to accept God's forgiveness and focus on the needs of others. The following is Luther's counsel to a man who was making the same kind of mistakes he had made. Luther's comments provide additional insight into the depth of his new understanding:

> Brother, it is impossible for you to become so righteous in this life that your body is as clear and spotless as the sun. You still have spots and wrinkles (Eph. 5:27), and yet you are holy. But you say: ". . . . But how will I be liberated from sin?" Run to Christ, the Physician, who heals the contrite of heart and saves sinners. Believe in Him. If you believe, you are righteous, because you attribute to God the glory of being almighty, merciful, truthful, etc. You justify and praise God. In short, you attribute divinity and everything to Him. And the sin that still remains in you is not imputed but is forgiven for the sake of Christ, in whom you believe and who is perfectly righteous in a formal sense. His righteousness is yours; your sin is His.[42]

Luther no longer allowed his sins to consume him, for after years of despair he had the conviction that he had been forgiven through his faith in Christ and that the righteousness of God had been imputed to him. This redemptive and enabling power allowed Luther and allows each of us to be forgiven of our sins and do that which we cannot do on our own, and it is the means by which God "consecrates [our] afflictions for [our] gain" (2 Nephi 2:2).

Counterfeit Doctrines

President Joseph F. Smith once taught, "Satan is a skillful imitator, and as genuine gospel truth is given the world in ever-increasing abundance, so he spreads the counterfeit coin of false doctrine . . . 'that were it possible he would deceive the very elect.'"[43] The doctrines of the grace of Christ and the rightful place of good works have been the subjects of the adversary's most effective and destructive deceptions. Because these doctrines are so central to the gospel of Jesus Christ, the adversary has conjured seductive counterfeits that have deceived and will continue to mislead those who hear the gospel message.

Some, citing the tradition of Augustine, Luther, and Calvin, focus on biblical passages such as the Apostle Paul's counsel to the Ephesians: "For by grace are ye saved through faith; and that not of yourselves: it is the gift of God: not of works, lest any man should boast" (Ephesians 2:8–9). Many of these same individuals ignore the next sentence in the text, which reads: "For we are his workmanship, created in Christ Jesus *unto good works*, which God hath before ordained that we should walk in them" (Ephesians 2:10; emphasis added).

Others, following the tradition of churchmen and scholars like the British monk Pelagius, choose not to emphasize grace but to stress the importance of good works and focus on the writings in the Epistle of James: "What doth it profit, my brethren, though a man say he hath faith, and have not works? can faith save him? . . . Even so faith, if it hath not works, is dead, being alone" (James 2:14, 17). Like the young Luther, many of these individuals wrongly believe their good works will save them and fail to understand the importance of "relying *alone* upon the merits of Christ, who was the author and the finisher of their faith" (Moroni 6:4; emphasis added).

Taking the scriptures as a whole, the Savior and his ancient Apostles taught that good works cannot save us, but neither can we be saved without them. Contentious debates about the relationship between grace and good works are rarely instructive or edifying. Those on both sides of the argument generally conclude the debate more firmly entrenched in their own versions of what the Savior and his servants taught concerning the relationship between grace and works. C. S. Lewis described the principle behind this doctrinal dynamic in the following: "He [the devil] always sends errors into the world in pairs of opposites. And he always encourages us to spend a lot of time thinking which is the worse. You see why, of course? He relies on your extra dislike of the one error to draw you gradually into the opposite one. But do not let us be fooled. We have to keep our eyes on the goal and go straight through between both errors."[44]

Taking the doctrine of grace beyond what the Savior and his servants have taught cheapens and changes this most important principle into a distortion that defeats the very purpose of the Atonement of Jesus Christ. Pastor and theologian Dietrich Bonhoeffer taught:

> Cheap grace means the justification of sin without the justification of the sinner. . . . Cheap grace is the preaching of forgiveness without requiring repentance, baptism without church discipline,

> Communion without confession, absolution without personal confession. Cheap grace is grace without discipleship, grace without the cross, grace without Jesus Christ. . . .
>
> [Costly] grace is *costly* because it calls us to follow, and it is *grace* because it calls us to follow *Jesus Christ*. It is costly because it costs a man his life, and it is grace because it gives a man the only true life. It is costly because it condemns sin, and grace because it justifies the sinner. Above all, it is *costly* because it cost God the life of his Son.[45]

Conversely, overstating the place and the importance of good works erroneously elevates humankind to mistakenly believe we can save ourselves. Elder M. Russell Ballard has written:

> No matter how hard we work, no matter how much we obey, no matter how many good things we do in this life, it would not be enough were it not for Jesus Christ and His loving grace. On our own we cannot earn the kingdom of God—no matter what we do. Unfortunately, there are some within the Church who have become so preoccupied with performing good works that they forget that those works—as good as they may be—are hollow unless they are accompanied by a complete dependence on Christ.[46]

Conclusion

A correct understanding of the relationship among sin, the grace of Christ, and good works was integral to the Reformation and vital to the Restoration and is also essential to each of us as we strive to find peace in this world and eternal life in the world to come. Robert Millet wisely concluded, "God and man are at work together in the salvation of the human soul. The real question is not whether we are saved by grace or by works. The real questions are these: In whom do I trust? On whom do I rely?"[47]

The distortion of the importance of good works brings either a sense of self-righteousness to those who experience success from their obedience or despair to those, like the young Martin Luther, who scrupulously keep the commandments without immediate reward. The distortion of the Savior's grace creates at one extreme a false sense of liberty with license to sin, or, less dramatic but just as damning, the false notion that mediocrity is acceptable. These distortions are the adversary's way of tempting us to place a principle above what the Savior and his chosen servants have taught. President Spencer W. Kimball warned, "Whatever thing a man sets his heart and his trust in most is his god; and if his god doesn't also happen to be the true and living God of Israel, that man is laboring in idolatry."[48] A doctrine, true or false, can become an idol just as easily as a material object.

While not all mental and emotional problems have a moral origin, a distorted understanding of grace or good works helps explain the research studies that report elevated scores on various measures of mental instability and family conflict across religions and denominations.[49] Like the young Martin Luther before he came to understand the graciousness of Christ, some individuals work themselves to exhaustion and despair in an attempt to solve personal and familial problems. Other individuals and families fail in their attempts to find peace because they are undisciplined in their discipleship and unwilling to keep the commandments God has given them and claim the blessings that come through obedience.

We learn from the Book of Mormon that humankind is "redeemed, because of the righteousness of [the] Redeemer" (2 Nephi 2:3) and that "no flesh can dwell in the presence of God, save it be through the merits, and mercy, and grace of the Holy Messiah" (2 Nephi 2:8). Nephi described the relationship between grace and works when he recorded that "it is by grace that we are saved, after all we can do" (2 Nephi 25:23). Though much has been written in an attempt to interpret what Nephi meant by the phrase "all we can do," perhaps the best answer is found in the interpretive words of a once-wicked Lamanite leader who had discovered God's forgiveness "through the merits of [God's] son" (Alma 24:10). Anti-Nephi-Lehi said, "And now behold, my brethren, since it has been *all that we could do*, (as we were the most lost of all mankind) *to repent* of all our sins and the many murders which we have committed, and to get God to take them away from our hearts, for it was *all we could do to repent* sufficiently before God that he would take away our stain" (Alma 24:11; emphasis added).

The key is repentance, available only through the Atonement of Christ, which allows us to claim the gift of grace. Perhaps the most significant contribution the Book of Mormon provides in helping us understand the relationship of sin, the grace of Christ, and our own good works is found in the following summary from Moroni's farewell sermon:

> Yea, come unto Christ, and be perfected in him, and deny yourselves of all ungodliness; and if ye shall deny yourselves of all ungodliness, and love God with all your might, mind and strength, then is his grace sufficient for you, that by his grace ye may be perfect in Christ; and if by the grace of God ye are perfect in Christ, ye can in nowise deny the power of God.
>
> And again, if ye by the grace of God are perfect in Christ, and deny not his power, then are ye sanctified in Christ by the grace of God through the shedding of the blood of Christ, which is the covenant of the Father unto the remission of your sins, that ye become holy, without spot. (Moroni 10:32–33)

Notes

1. Karl A. Menninger, *Whatever Became Of Sin?* (New York: Hawthorn Books, 1973), 13.
2. Albert E. Ellis, "Psychotherapy and Atheistic Values: A Response to A. E. Bergin's 'Psychotherapy and Religious Values,'" *Journal of Consulting and Clinical Psychology* 48, no. 5 (1980): 637.
3. Sigmund Freud, *The Future of an Illusion*, trans. W. D. Robson-Scott (New York: Doubleday, 1957), 77–78.
4. Richard Dawkins, *A Devil's Chaplain* (London: Weidenfeld & Nicolson, 2003), 143.
5. Daniel K Judd, "Religious Affiliation and Mental Health," appendix A in *Religion, Mental Health, and the Latter-day Saints*, ed. Daniel K Judd (Provo, UT: Religious Studies Center, 1999), 257.
6. Allen E. Bergin, Kevin S. Masters, and P. Scott Richards, "Religiousness and Mental Health Reconsidered: A Study of an Intrinsically Religious Sample," *Journal of Counseling Psychology* 34, no. 2 (1987): 197–204. See also Daniel

K Judd, "Religiosity, Mental Health, and the Latter-day Saints: A Preliminary Review of Literature (1923–1995)," in *Latter-day Saint Social Life: Social Research on the LDS Church and Its Members*, ed. J. T. Duke (Provo, UT: Religious Studies Center, 1997), 473–97.

7. G. K. Chesterton, *What's Wrong with the World*, 8th ed. (London: Cassell, 1910).
8. G. K. Chesterton, as cited in Phillip Yancey, *Soul Survivor: How My Faith Survived the Church* (New York: Doubleday, 2001), 58.
9. E. P. Sanders, "Sin," in *The Anchor Bible Dictionary*, ed. Daniel Noel Friedman (New York: Doubleday, 1992), 6:41.
10. Neal A. Maxwell, "Jesus of Nazareth, Savior and King," *Ensign*, December 2007, 45.
11. Robert L. Millet, "Pursuing a Sane and Balanced Course," in *Selected Writings of Robert L. Millet* (Salt Lake City: Deseret Book, 2000), 372.
12. Bergin, Masters, and Richards, "Religiousness and Mental Health Reconsidered," 197–204.
13. Bergin, Masters, and Richards, "Religiousness and Mental Health Reconsidered," 197–204.
14. Martin Luther, as cited in Roland C. Bainton, *Here I Stand: A Life of Martin Luther* (1950; repr., Peabody, MA: Hendrickson Publishers, 2012), 26.
15. Martin Luther, as cited in E. H. Erikson, *Young Man Luther: A Study in Psychoanalysis and History* (New York: W. W. Norton, 1993), 130.
16. Jaroslav Pelikan, ed., *Luther's Works* (St. Louis: Concordia Publishing House, 1955), 27:13.
17. Pelikan, *Luther's Works*, 27:13.
18. Pelikan, *Luther's Works*, 5:157.
19. Bainton, *Here I Stand*, 35.
20. Pelikan, *Luther's Works*, 54:94.
21. Bainton, *Here I Stand*, 36.
22. Pelikan, *Luther's Works*, 54:339.
23. Pelikan, *Luther's Works*, 44:74–75.
24. Pelikan, *Luther's Works*, 54:340.
25. Pelikan, *Luther's Works*, 54:85.
26. Bainton, *Here I Stand*, 27.
27. Alister McGrath, *Christianity's Dangerous Idea: The Protestant Revolution—A History from the Sixteenth Century to the Twenty-First* (New York: HarperOne, 2007), 46–47.

28. Richard Marius, *Martin Luther: The Christian between God and Death* (Cambridge: Harvard University Press, 1999), 83.
29. Pelikan, *Luther's Works*, 31:179.
30. Ian Osbourne, *Can Christianity Cure Obsessive-Compulsive Disorder?* (Grand Rapids, MI: Brazos Press, 2008), 62–67.
31. Chris H. Miller and Dawson W. Hedges, "Scrupulosity Disorder: An Overview and Introductory Analysis," *Journal of Anxiety Disorders* 22 (2008): 1042.
32. Both these descriptions, "obsessive-compulsive disorder" and "scrupulosity," are superior to Erik Erikson's diagnosis of an "identity crisis" described in his once popular publication, *Young Man Luther: A Study in Psychoanalysis and History*. Erikson's work was based upon Freudian theory, which has largely been discredited in theory and practice.
33. Joseph W. Ciarrocchi, *The Doubting Disease: Help for Scrupulosity and Religious Compulsions* (Mahwah, NJ: Paulist Press, 1995), 12.
34. Martin Luther, as cited in David P. Scaer, "The Concept of *Anfechtung* in Luther's Thought," *Concordia Theological Quarterly* 47, no. 1 (January 1983): 15–30.
35. Gerald G. May, *The Dark Night of the Soul* (New York: HarperSanFrancisco, 2005).
36. Marius, *Christian between God and Death*, 212–13.
37. Pelikan, *Luther's Works*, 34:336–37.
38. Pelikan, *Luther's Works*, 54:193–94.
39. Pelikan, *Luther's Works*, 35:363.
40. John F. MacArthur Jr., *The Gospel According to Jesus*, rev. ed. (Grand Rapids, MI: Zondervan, 1994), 197.
41. John MacArthur, *The MacArthur New Testament Commentary: Ephesians* (Chicago: Moody Press, 1986), 383.
42. Pelikan, *Luther's Works*, 26:233.
43. Joseph F. Smith, as cited in Daniel H. Ludlow, *Latter-day Prophets Speak* (Salt Lake City: Bookcraft, 1948), 20–21.
44. C. S. Lewis, *Mere Christianity* (New York: Scribner, 1960), 145.
45. Dietrich Bonhoeffer, *The Cost of Discipleship* (New York: Touchstone, 1995), 44–45.
46. M. Russell Ballard, "Building Bridges of Understanding," *Ensign*, June 1998, 65.
47. Robert L. Millet, *After All We Can Do . . . Grace Works* (Salt Lake City: Deseret Book, 2003), 144.
48. Spencer W. Kimball, "The False Gods We Worship," *Ensign*, June 1976, 3.

49. Marleen Williams, "Family Attitudes and Perfectionism As Related to Depression in Latter-day Saint and Protestant Women," in *Religion, Mental Health, and the Latter-day Saints*, 47–66. See also Ronald J. Sider, *The Scandal of the Evangelical Conscience: Why Are Christians Living Just Like the Rest of the World?* (Grand Rapids, MI: Baker Books, 2005), 13–29.

Salvation by Grace, Rewards of Degree by Works
The Soteriology of Doctrine and Covenants 76

Shon D. Hopkin

In a volume dedicated to the work of Latter-day Saint scholar Robert Millet, it seems appropriate to take a closer look at Joseph Smith's understanding of grace, faith, works, and salvation, and, moreover, to do so with sensitivity to Protestant language and concerns. As that interreligious lens is employed, a clearer view of Smith's early soteriology, as found in key scriptural texts, emerges for both Latter-day Saints and those of other faiths, one featuring more similarities between the two traditions than some may expect but also one highlighting important and fundamental differences. I will focus primarily on a close reading of Doctrine and Covenants 76, with a brief overview of Book of Mormon passages, to argue that the soteriology of this text is one in which humankind is saved only by the grace or power of Christ through faith in him but one in which heavenly rewards are a product of works that are themselves made possible through Christ's grace.

Many voices over the preceding two centuries have engaged the topics of grace, faith, and works for Latter-day Saints, and no study can account for the variety of approaches. Much work has already been done by Millet and others to demonstrate that the Latter-day Saint view of salvation is centered on Christ's merits and that salvation is only possible in and through him.[1] This chapter will not attempt to address a full or complete view of Mormon soteriology, nor will it attempt to provide a full discussion of Joseph Smith's soteriology. Rather, this close reading will show that D&C 76 provides a richly Christ-centered foundation for some of the Saints' distinctive beliefs. The primary contributions of this paper include a demonstration that (1) the rhetorical mechanics of D&C 76 are themselves biblical, (2) grace is the foundation in D&C 76 behind the broad distinction between saved and damned, and (3) in its broad strokes, D&C 76 not so much obliterates the classical heaven/hell binary as flips it on its head with its near-Universalism. In no way do I intend to indicate that my interpretation of this text is at all definitive, but I anticipate healthy discussion of the strengths and weaknesses of this reading. I hope to engender continued interfaith discussion and improved understanding surrounding these key issues taught by Joseph Smith.

Grace-based Protestant Soteriology and Protestant Views of Latter-day Saint Soteriology

One of the significant concerns expressed in Protestant discussions of Mormon theology is that Latter-day Saints have a distinctly works-based soteriology. As will be seen, that concern often points most prevalently to the Latter-day Saint concept of "degrees of glory" that first found expression in D&C 76. The problem is not with the focus on Christ; both Latter-day Saints and other Christians see the work of the incarnate Son of God as the center of their faith. According to Helmut Gollwitzer, "In the center of the Christian faith, and consequently the center also of theological reflection, there stand the event of Jesus Christ and the extraordinary statements that the New Testament have made about his universal significance."[2] Joseph Smith's statement, frequently referred to among Latter-day Saints, reads similarly, though written one hundred and fifty years earlier, "The fundamental principles of our religion [are] the testimony of the Apostles and Prophets, concerning Jesus Christ, that He died, was buried, and rose again the third day, and ascended up into heaven; and all other things are only appendages to these, which pertain to our religion."³ Rather, the difference that looms large in many interfaith discussions is the perceived role of grace, faith, and works in salvation for Latter-day Saints. Discussions of the importance of works in Protestant churches are regularly qualified by the reminder that salvation is by grace through faith in the sovereign will of God alone (rather than by works). One review of evangelical theology puts it this way: "For most contemporary evangelicals, 'justification by grace through faith alone' is 'the soul of the Christian gospel.' This is understood to be the heart of the Protestant Reformation. . . . Martin Luther's reading of Paul's letter to the Romans is the foundation of the doctrine of justification by faith alone, but Protestants claim Paul warrants this doctrine, not Luther. . . . The problem is that the law of God must be fulfilled, not merely externally but internally as well. The answer is that only faith in Christ fulfills it."⁴

Those holding to this view are often suspicious of religious language that appears to unduly elevate the importance of Christian works, since that type of language may betray Paul's teachings that "all have sinned, and come short of the glory of God; being justified freely by his grace through the redemption that is in Christ Jesus. . . . Where is boasting then? It is excluded. By what law? of works? Nay: but by the law of faith. Therefore we conclude that a man is justified by faith without the deeds of the law" (Romans 3:23–24, 27–28).⁵ The danger is not only of boasting in one's own righteousness and trusting in one's own deeds but even more of putting man at the center of salvation rather than God. In the same passage, Paul emphasized that he was speaking in order "to declare at this time his [Jesus'] righteousness: that he [Jesus] might be just, and the justifier of him [the Christian] which believeth in Jesus" (Romans 3:26). Anglican theologian N. T. Wright describes the problem in this way: "We are not the centre of the universe. God is not circling around us. We are circling around him. It may look, from our point of view, as though 'me and my salvation' are the be-all and end-all of Christianity. Sadly, many people—many devout Christians!—have preached that way and lived that way. This problem is not peculiar to the churches of the Reformation. It goes back to the high Middle Ages in the western church, and infects Catholic and Protestant, liberal and conservative, high and low church alike."⁶

SALVATION BY GRACE, REWARDS OF DEGREE BY WORKS

Wright's theological concerns are part of the larger dialogue of traditional Protestantism, growing in part out of perceived historical excesses and distortions in the Christian Church beginning in the "high Middle Ages." Viewing Latter-day Saint teachings through that historically developed lens reveals language that appears suspiciously works-centered to many Christians. Statements like the following by former Church President Harold B. Lee seem to some to indicate a soteriology based on works, emphasizing the righteousness of man:

> Any member of the Church who is learning to live perfectly each of the laws that are in the kingdom is learning the way to become perfect. There is no member of this Church who cannot live the law, every law of the gospel perfectly. All of us can learn to talk with God in prayer. All of us can learn to live the Word of Wisdom perfectly. All of us can learn to keep the Sabbath day holy, perfectly. All of you can learn how to keep the law of fasting perfectly. We know how to keep the law of chastity perfectly. Now as we learn to keep one of these laws perfectly we ourselves are on the road to perfection.[7]

In 2013, a former Latter-day Saint expressed her own views that she had been trained by the Church to trust in her own works. Although most Latter-day Saints would likely view her message as a gross mischaracterization of their beliefs, her statements reflect some evangelical concerns with Latter-day Saint theology so closely that they were published in the evangelical magazine *Christianity Today*. In her description, she attacks numerous concepts, including the emphasis on obedience and on ordinances (the Latter-day Saint word for sacraments), as well as the view that salvation may include the ability to become a "god." Each of these beliefs is discussed in D&C 76, as will be seen, although her mention of some unique practices, such as the health code known as the Word of Wisdom or the temple practice known as baptism for the dead, would not be taught by Smith until later. She wrote:

> [As a Latter-day Saint] I looked down on Christians who followed the Bible. They had part of the gospel, but I had the fullness of it. I kept the laws and ordinances of Mormonism. When I took the sacrament of leavened bread and water each week at our Sunday meeting house,

> I was letting the sin janitor sweep away all iniquity. I believed the Mormon Church secured my eternal life. . . . Serving untold hours in church callings, reading Mormon scripture, tithing, attending meetings, keeping a health code, and doing genealogy so we could redeem the dead in the temple—these were a few of our offerings to the Mormon God. . . . Like Heavenly Father and Jesus before him—like Smith himself—Michael [my husband] was working to become a god. This is one reason we attended the temple regularly.[8]

Her statement stands in tension with consistent statements regarding the insufficiency of human works, like the following by Brigham Young, who could hardly be accused of diplomatically softening his views: "The Latter-day Saints believe . . . that Jesus is the Savior of the world; they believe that all who attain to any glory whatever, in any kingdom, will do so because Jesus has purchased it by his atonement."[9] Notwithstanding these and similar teachings and now-decades-old work by leaders and scholars such as Millet, these works-righteousness accusations continue, as seen in the following statement from a theological journal. Notice again the inclusion of concepts first presented in D&C 76 such as entering the celestial kingdom (the concept of "degrees of glory") and becoming gods, along with later teachings and practices like baptisms for the dead.

> At least some of what Millet says has the appearance of actually misleading the reader. For instance, when he discusses that Jesus and Jesus alone "saves," and nothing else, he fails totally in elucidating the point that, in fact, salvation or "immortality" in Mormon thought is provided for all in either the terrestrial or telestial kingdoms except for apostates from the LDS church, the devil and his angels. An evangelical might think that Millet is speaking of salvation as an evangelical does—that a Christian receives the "fullness" of salvation through, by, and because of the work of Christ alone. Not so. It is only through the "ordinances and rituals" of the "fullness" of the gospel provided by latter-day revelation and the "latter-day," i.e., Mormon, restoration that all of salvation is possible. In other words, apart from proxy baptism once dead, only "Temple-worthy" Mormons will enter the celestial kingdom and become gods. They will be the only ones to experience the fullness of salvation. It is omissions like these

that make Millet's book [*A Different Jesus? The Christ of the Latter-day Saints*] so potentially misleading in the supposed rapprochement of evangelical-Mormon relations.[10]

Salvation by the Merits of Christ through Faith Alone

As seen, the Latter-day Saint notion of "degrees of glory" provides an oft-repeated basis for the accusation of works-based salvation. Salvation in the celestial kingdom is (mis)understood by non-Mormon observers (and by some Latter-day Saints, as well) as the only true salvation, a salvation that can only be "earned" by faithfully fulfilling Latter-day Saint ordinances and commandments to the best of one's ability. According to one interpretation, this type of "real" salvation is available to Latter-day Saints through the grace of Christ, but that grace is only available to those who have "earned it" through a rigorous obedience. According to this view, a view that Wilder states she learned during her time as a Latter-day Saint, Mormons are constantly relying on their own efforts rather than on the merits of Christ, full of anxiety and depressed by their inadequacies as they try to earn a prize that will always rest just beyond their reach, and that is only accessible to perfect Mormons who have their lives fully in order. A closer look at Joseph Smith's scriptural teachings regarding salvation in the oft-mentioned "degrees of glory" may help determine whether this viewpoint, held by some outsiders and apparently also held by some within the Latter-day Saint faith, is actually justified and whether it is a true source of distinction.

Before proceeding, it is important to note that Joseph Smith rarely used the technical language of Protestant theology to describe salvation, at least not with the nuance that might be expected from a scholar. He did not know or use the word "soteriology." Although Smith would have understood the ordinary language of Protestantism (see, for example, the concepts of "justification through grace" and "sanctification through grace" in D&C 20:30–31), his training would not have prepared him to frame the discussion in ways that consistently relied on the theological terms of the Reformers. His teachings can nevertheless be viewed and assessed through that lens, particularly if the assessment is attuned to the differences in language and approach that could be attributed to a distinct historical context. In other words, although Mormon teachings can be viewed through a Protestant lens, those teachings should not be expected to sound exactly like they would coming from the mouth of a Protestant Christian.

Although not part of the central thrust of this article, a close reading of D&C 76, Book of Mormon descriptions of salvation provide the earliest point of reference for Joseph Smith's soteriology. Living centuries after Jesus' incarnation, death, resurrection, and subsequent visit to Book of Mormon peoples in the Americas, the last Book of Mormon prophet Moroni provides several statements that appear to fit well within the framework of salvation by faith in the grace of Christ, using language that often mirrors Paul's teachings. "[Those baptized] were numbered among the people of the church of Christ. . . . relying alone upon the merits of Christ, who was the author and finisher of their faith" (Moroni 6:4). He concludes the book with the call to "come unto Christ, and be perfected in him, . . . that by his grace ye may be perfect in Christ; and if by the grace of God ye are perfect in Christ, ye can in nowise deny the power of God" (Moroni 10:32). The phrase elided in the statement above emphasizes the efforts of the Christian to deny ungodliness and to love God completely, which will be discussed below, but the role of Christ as the one in whom perfection can be found corresponds well with Protestant views, as does the emphasis that an ability to acknowledge the power of God springs from his perfecting grace. Nearer the beginning of the Book of Mormon narrative, a similar statement by Nephi appears: "And we talk of Christ, we rejoice in Christ, we preach of Christ, we prophesy of Christ, and we write according to our prophecies, that our children may know to what source they may look for a remission of their sins" (2 Nephi 25:26). A few verses earlier, an oft-quoted teaching of Nephi begins in very grace-based tones but ends—depending on the interpretation—with what is to some a suspicious emphasis on human effort, "For we labor diligently to . . . persuade our children . . . to believe in Christ, and to be reconciled to God; for we know that it is by grace that we are saved, after all we can do" (2 Nephi 25:23).

Notwithstanding its significant emphasis on Christ's role in salvation, the Book of Mormon contains no overt discussion of heaven and hell in terms of "degrees of glory." As important as it is, therefore, in understanding early Latter-day Saint understandings of faith and grace, it is D&C 76 that must be analyzed for Smith's teachings regarding salvation and heavenly degrees of glory. These concepts are based on a heavenly vision given to Smith and Sidney Rigdon on February 16, 1832 (about twenty-two months after the organization of the Church).[11] The entire discussion is framed in the context of Christ's mission and power. D&C 76:22–24 is memorized by Mormon youth as part of their religious training during their high school years:

> And now, after the many testimonies which have been given of him, this is the testimony, last of all, which we give of him: That he lives!
>
> For we saw him, even on the right hand of God; and we heard the voice bearing record that he is the Only Begotten of the Father—
>
> That by him, and through him, and of him, the worlds are and were created, and the inhabitants thereof are begotten sons and daughters unto God.

The rest of D&C 76 describes salvation as starkly divided between the "sons of perdition," for whom there "is no forgiveness in this world or in the world to come" (76:32, 34), and all others, for whom Christ was crucified, "that through him all might be saved whom the Father had put into his power" (D&C 76:42). In order to understand the biblical underpinnings of "degrees of glory" as described in D&C 76, it is crucial to first look closely at a passage that describes the division between the saved and the damned. First, describing the damned:

> Thus saith the Lord concerning all those who know my power, and have been made partakers thereof, and suffered themselves through the power of the devil to be overcome, and to deny the truth and defy my power—
>
> They are they who are the sons of perdition; . . .
>
> For they are vessels of wrath, doomed to suffer the wrath of God, with the devil and his angels in eternity;
>
> Concerning whom I have said there is no forgiveness in this world nor in the world to come—

> Having denied the Holy Spirit after having received it, and having denied the Only Begotten Son of the Father, having crucified him unto themselves and put him to an open shame.
>
> These are they who shall go away into the lake of fire and brimstone, with the devil and his angels—
>
> And the only ones on whom the second death shall have any power;
>
> Yea, verily, the only ones who shall not be redeemed in the due time of the Lord. (D&C 76:31–38)

After pausing to describe inheritors of heavenly glory, as will be discussed, the passage continues to discuss the damned, saying, "They shall go away into everlasting punishment, which is endless punishment, which is eternal punishment, to reign with the devil and his angels in eternity, where their worm dieth not, and the fire is not quenched, which is their torment" (D&C 76:44).

The condition of the sons of perdition appears roughly equivalent with the traditional Christian view of those in hell. The language invokes King James Version phrasing to convey its message, depicting the damned as "vessels of wrath" (Romans 9:22), doomed to suffer "the wrath of God" (John 3:36; Romans 1:18; Revelation 14:10), with "the devil and his angels" (Matthew 25:41) in eternity. These are they who "shall go away into everlasting punishment" (Matthew 25:46) and be "cast into the lake of fire," which "is the second death" (Revelation 20:14), "where their worm dieth not, and the fire is not quenched" (Mark 9:48).

The thrust of the passage, however, bears closest resemblance to the description provided in Hebrews 6:4–6: "For it is impossible for those who were once enlightened, and have tasted of the heavenly gift, and were made partakers of the Holy Ghost, and have tasted the good word of God, and the powers of the world to come, if they shall fall away, to renew them again unto repentance; seeing they crucify to themselves the Son of God afresh, and put him to an open shame."

On the other hand, the condition of those who are not sons of perdition sounds roughly similar to the traditional Christian view of heaven:

> For all the rest shall be brought forth by the resurrection of the dead, through the triumph and the glory of the Lamb, who was slain, who was in the bosom of the Father before the worlds were made.
>
> And this is the gospel, the glad tidings, which the voice out of the heavens bore record unto us—
>
> That he came into the world, even Jesus, to be crucified for the world, and to bear the sins of the world, and to sanctify the world, and to cleanse it from all unrighteousness;
>
> That through him all might be saved whom the Father had put into his power. (D&C 76:39–42)

These passages set the background context for the rest of the discussion in D&C 76 on degrees of glory. The text thus describes the unsaved and the saved before going on to describe various conditions of the saved in more detail. These details also offer a good opportunity to understand Joseph Smith's soteriology and how his view of the difference between heaven and hell (although not using those precise terms) is presented in stark contrast. Smith, rather than being a purveyor of works-only salvation, seems in these passages to have hewn perhaps uncomfortably close to what Protestants then and now might recognize as Christian Universalism.

In the parts of D&C 76 discussed above, there is only one condition set between the unsaved and the saved. The unsaved purposefully and determinedly reject the salvation available to them through Christ, and the saved accept Christ and the salvation he offers them. This view is confirmed by one of the concluding verses of the vision, that may either describe all of the saved or may possibly refer pointedly to those saved in heaven with the lowest (telestial) degree of reward: "These all shall bow the knee, and every tongue shall confess to him who sits upon the throne forever and ever" (D&C 76:110). The message is clear: salvation is available only through Christ's power, and belief in that power or acceptance of Christ is the only separating feature between the two sides. Put in Protestant terms, salvation is by grace through faith in God alone—rather than by works. Some may argue that Mormon teachings regarding salvation clearly require "works," but this view—at least with regards to D&C 76—comes from conflating the view of what is required for salvation in heaven as presented in D&C 76:31–44 with the view of how rewards or degrees of glory within heaven are provided, as described in the remainder of the section and as frequently emphasized by Latter-day Saints. According to D&C 76, salvation in heaven is due solely to God's power through Christ and the individual's choice to accept Christ rather than purposefully deny him.

The role of free will in the Latter-day Saint view of salvation. Although the soteriology presented in D&C 76:31–44 is pointedly centered on Christ, it is not equivalent to a fully Calvinistic soteriology. As Joseph Smith provided prophetic interpretation of the Old and New Testaments in what Latter-day Saints today call the Joseph Smith Translation (JST), he consistently outlined an understanding of salvation that preserved space for mankind's free choice.[12] The importance of the space or ability to choose what God provides for man is known in Mormon scripture as "agency" (D&C 93:31). Joseph Smith did not view God's grace as "irresistible,"[13] because God allowed humankind the ability to accept or resist it. This view is shown in an early passage in the Doctrine and Covenants that employs the familiar Pauline terms of justification and sanctification:

> And we know that justification through the grace of our Lord and Savior Jesus Christ is just and true;
>
> And we know also, that sanctification through the grace of our Lord and Savior Jesus Christ is just and true, to all those who love and serve God with all their mights, minds, and strength.
>
> But there is a possibility that man may fall from grace and depart from the living God;
>
> Therefore let the church take heed and pray always, lest they fall into temptation;
>
> Yea, and even let those who are sanctified take heed also. (D&C 20:30–34)

Joseph Smith taught the principles of justification and sanctification to the early Church, but he made a pointed, purposeful, and consistent move towards the importance of mankind's agency that can be seen in the view of salvation presented in D&C 76:31–44. Although some Latter-day Saints have interpreted 2 Nephi 25:23 differently—conflating the state of salvation or damnation with the rewards available in heavenly degrees of glory—it is more likely through this lens of free will that the

Book of Mormon passage could be read: "It is by grace that we are saved, after all we can do" (2 Nephi 25:23). If this verse is viewed in light of the soteriology of D&C 76, it could be understood as teaching that all must choose Christ in order to receive his saving power. With regards to our salvation, "all we can do" is accept Christ to the best of our ability, with all of our hearts, souls, and minds (see Matthew 22:37). An alternate view, at least as viewed through the lens of Doctrines and Covenants 76, might understand Nephi's words as describing a heavenly salvation that enjoyed the greatest rewards available to the saved, made possible by grace and determined by a life full of good works.

Although the soteriology of Joseph Smith consistently defended the importance of free will, this view did not place man's power at the center of salvation but rather taught clearly that free will, or "agency," was only available through God's power. "In the Garden of Eden, gave I unto man his agency" (Moses 7:32). Robert L. Millet has frequently represented the Mormon view as coinciding with Wesleyan views of prevenient grace,[14] in which fallen mankind is only able to choose (or reject) Christ because God first provided the capacity to do so through his grace and power.[15] According to D&C and the Book of Mormon, Christ is both the "alpha" or the "author" of the faith of mankind and the "omega" or the "finisher" of that faith (see D&C 19:1; Moroni 6:4). In Joseph Smith's soteriology, faith is necessary as a free-will choice, but faith appears to be possible only through God's providing mankind with the ability to exercise it.

Rewards of Degree Based on Works

The remainder of Joseph Smith's heavenly vision describes three degrees of heavenly glory, the "telestial," "terrestrial," and "celestial," in ascending order of glory. One of the final verses of the vision explains why men are assigned to a particular degree of glory: "Every man shall receive according to his own works, his own dominion, in the mansions which are prepared" (D&C 76:111). The rewards are consistently depicted as only available due to the power of Christ, and the glory of degrees still centers on Christ rather than on humankind. Speaking of the highest, or celestial glory, D&C 76:59–61 states:

> Wherefore, all things are theirs, whether life or death, or things present, or things to come, all are theirs and they are Christ's, and Christ is God's.
>
> And they shall overcome all things.
>
> Wherefore, let no man glory in man, but rather let him glory in God, who shall subdue all enemies under his feet.

Good works are viewed, even in this section of D&C 76, as possible only because of the power of God.

The reality pervading the entire section, however, is that the varying degrees of reward (available only through the power of God) are determined by one's works. Inhabitants of the celestial glory are those who "were baptized after the manner of his burial, being buried in the water in his name, and this according to the commandment which he has given" (D&C 76:51). The terrestrial glory is occupied by "they who are honorable men of the earth, who were blinded by the craftiness of men" (D&C 76:75). Those of the telestial glory "are they who are liars, and sorcerers, and adulterers, and whoremongers, and whosoever loves and makes a lie" (D&C 76:103). Whether or not this last group can be said to belong in heaven or not, the point here is that they are assigned to a telestial glory in heaven because of their deeds that led them while on earth to be liars, adulterers, and whoremongers.

According to Hebrews 11:6, "He that cometh to God must believe that he is, and that he is a rewarder of them that diligently seek him." Although the view of degrees of reward determined by works does not coincide with a Calvinistic soteriology, it is a view of salvation that is—in certain respects—compatible with the views of some Protestant thinkers and a view that fits within the spectrum of evangelical thought concerning the "justice of God."[16] Other differences remain to be discussed below that create a sharp divide between Latter-day Saint and Protestant understandings of heaven. The Mormon view is not the same as the Protestant view (nor does it seek to be), but a division of degrees according to works is not necessarily one of those significant divides.

Those rewards have been described by some as "degrees of glory."[17] Evangelical writer Bruce Wilkinson, who received his theological training at Dallas Theological Seminary and Western Conservative Baptist Seminary, has written: "Although your eternal destination is based on your

SALVATION BY GRACE, REWARDS OF DEGREE BY WORKS

belief [in Jesus], how you spend eternity is based on your behavior while on earth." "Your choices on earth have direct consequences on your life in eternity." "There will be degrees of reward in heaven."[18]

Among the most influential of all Christian theologians, Augustine (354–430) taught: "But who can conceive, not to say describe, what degrees of honor and glory shall be awarded to the various degrees of merit? Yet it cannot be doubted that there shall be degrees. And in that blessed city there shall be this great blessing, that no inferior shall envy any superior, as now the archangels are not envied by the angels, because no one will wish to be what he has not received, though bound in strictest concord with him who has received; as in the body the finger does not seek to be the eye, though both members are harmoniously included in the complete structure of the body. And thus, along with this gift, greater or less, each shall receive this further gift of contentment to desire no more than he has."[19] This should not be taken to mean, of course, that Augustine and Joseph Smith understood heaven in the same ways. Rather, this quote shows Augustine's reasoning that some type of heavenly divisions must exist.

Similarly, Jonathan Edwards (1703–1758), often recognized as America's most influential theologian, stated, "There are many mansions in God's house because heaven is intended for various degrees of honor and blessedness. Some are designed to sit in higher places there than others; some are designed to be advanced to higher degrees of honor and glory than others are."[20] John Wesley, the father of Methodism, used similar language: "There is an inconceivable variety in the degrees of reward in the other world. . . . In worldly things men are ambitious to get as high as they can. Christians have a far more noble ambition. The difference between the very highest and the lowest state in the world is nothing to the smallest difference between the degrees of glory."[21]

Doing one's best to obediently live a Christian life, while helped and strengthened by the Spirit through the grace of Christ, can also be understood as sanctification:

> Sanctification of believers in the New Testament is seen primarily as the work of God, of Christ, and especially of the Holy Spirit. . . . Beyond that, sanctification is even understood as a realm of human action. Therefore, *hagiasmos* (the Greek term meaning holiness just

as much as sanctification) can denote a state in which believers find themselves and in which they must remain by living in correspondence to their given holiness, as well as to a state to which they must strive, which they must "pursue," or "complete" in order to attain it. Believers are thus both passive and active in their sanctification.[22]

As can be seen, although not typically seen as synonymous, living the kind of life that will be rewarded in heaven is closely connected to sanctification in some Protestant thought.

A Closer Comparison: Similarities and Differences

Can the rewards of a "telestial" glory truly be described as heaven? In the preceding discussion, I have proposed that the soteriology of D&C 76 fits in broad strokes with a Protestant soteriological view that understands salvation as available only through the grace and power of Christ, with rewards of degree in heaven possible only through the power of Christ but determined by works. The remainder of this chapter will look more closely at some of the potential or actual conflicts with the comparison.

The existence within Smith's soteriological view of a saved group designated for the telestial kingdom (see D&C 76:81–90, 98–112) provides the greatest areas of possible difference with a traditional Protestant view. First, can the rewards of the telestial kingdom appropriately be understood as part of the biblical heaven? The following limitation of reward in that degree of glory might indicate that the answer is no when viewed in the light of a traditional Christian understanding of heaven: "[The telestial] are they who receive not of his fullness in the eternal world, but of the Holy Spirit. . . . And also the telestial receive it of the administering of angels who are appointed to minister for them, or who are appointed to be ministering spirits for them. . . . And they shall be servants of the Most High; but where God and Christ dwell they cannot come, worlds without end" (D&C 76:86, 88, 112).

If inheritors of the telestial glory cannot go where God and Christ dwell, can their salvation truly be said to describe heaven? Protestant Christians are not accustomed to thinking of a variation of rewards in these terms but might be more comfortable with the idea of certain saved beings that are allowed a closer proximity to the throne of God, using imagery provided by Revelation 4:10–11.[23] A closer proximity to the throne of God, of course, indicates that another stands further away and is not allowed into the "presence of God" to the same degree. A reward that does not allow one to stand at the throne of God imposes a similar limitation to a telestial reward that states that where God and Christ "dwell," the saved one can never go, whether this is viewed as a world, a throne, or some other type of location. The telestial glory, existing in the heavenly realm, is in one sense very much still "in the presence" of God; it is the sons of perdition who are described as being cast into the lake of fire and brimstone with the devil and his angels. In fact, whether viewed through a Mormon lens that understands the Holy Ghost as a member of the Godhead, or a Trinitarian lens that views the Holy Ghost as one of three Persons, inhabitants of the telestial glory do dwell in the presence of God—God the Spirit—as they enjoy the presence of the Holy Ghost. Although the wording makes its interpretation inconclusive, the thrust of the quoted passage above may be that the presence of the Holy Ghost is precisely the way in which those of the telestial glory are allowed to enjoy "the fullness" of God's influence. The first phrase states that the telestial receive not of the fullness of the Father but of the Holy Ghost. The following phrase, however, indicates that they receive "it" of ministering angels, possibly referring to God's fullness and modifying the way the first phrase should be read.

The New Testament not only suggests a variety of rewards connected to location but can also be interpreted as suggesting higher degrees of responsibility for some in heaven (as per Luke 19:17, 19) and varying degrees of glory (and power or authority), suggested by the image of a "crown of righteousness" mentioned in 2 Timothy 4:8. D&C 76:79 actually employs the image of the crown to describe a difference in glory, authority, and power between the celestial and terrestrial glories, indicating that those who inherit a terrestrial glory had not been fully valiant in the testimony of Jesus while in mortality, and therefore "they obtain not the crown over the kingdom of our God." The section also describes the differing glories of the celestial, terrestrial, and telestial kingdoms in terms of the light of the sun, moon, and stars (see D&C 76:78, 81), using language that Joseph Smith connected with Paul's discourse on the resurrection of the dead (see 1 Corinthians 15:40–42).

A point of great discomfort for many Protestants when discussing Mormon soteriology, as can be seen in the quotations at the beginning of the paper, is the difference of responsibility, power, and authority known as *theosis* or deification that in this passage is offered as a reward of the celestial glory. Joseph Smith's soteriological connection with *theosis* was first articulated in this section of the D&C (though early Latter-day Saints may not have read the passage as modern Saints do, through the lens of Smith's later teachings): "Wherefore, as it is written, they are gods, even the sons of God—wherefore, all things are theirs, whether life or death, or things present, or things to come, all are theirs and they are Christ's, and Christ is God's" (D&C 76:58–59). The difference in reward described in this passage indicates that Smith's soteriology viewed potentially deified mankind as remaining in the same relationship with Christ and the Father as "sons of God" for all eternity. According to Joseph Smith, although *theosis* was a reward of the highest glory of heaven, with all things being given to the celestially saved, the Christocentric relationship is maintained: "they are Christ's."

While the limited reward of the telestial glory might not sit comfortably with one trained to picture salvation in terms and imagery provided by traditional Christianity, a closer comparison reveals that labeling this teaching as outside the biblical spectrum may not be fully appropriate. Indeed, D&C 76:88 finishes the phrase above by restating that this should be understood as full salvation: "the telestial receive it [God's fullness] of the administering of angels who are appointed to . . . be ministering spirits for them; for they shall be heirs of salvation" (D&C 76:88). According to Smith, he "saw, in the heavenly vision, the glory of the telestial, which surpasses all understanding. And no man knows it except him to whom God has revealed it" (D&C 76:89–90). This echoes Paul's description of future heavenly glory: "But as it is written, Eye hath not seen, nor ear heard, neither have entered into the heart of man, the things which God hath prepared for them that love him. But God hath revealed them unto us by his Spirit: for the Spirit searcheth all things, yea, the deep things of God" (1 Corinthians 2:9–10).

Have those in the telestial kingdom truly accepted Christ? The Latter-day Saint inclusive view of salvation contrasted with Protestant "inclusivism." The second challenge with understanding the telestial glory as reflecting heaven is the description in D&C 76 of the types of individuals who are saved there: "These are they who are liars, and sorcerers, and adulterers, and whoremongers, and whosoever loves and makes a lie. These are they who suffer the wrath of God on earth. These are they who suffer the vengeance of eternal fire. These are they who are cast down to hell and suffer the wrath of Almighty God" (D&C 76:103–6). This passage certainly does not describe anything a traditional Christian would expect to see in heaven. Any view of liars, adulterers, and "those thrust down to hell" as also living in a heavenly, saved condition appears to be a blatant contradiction of terms.

Upon closer reading, however, it becomes clear that the description represents decisions made on earth and prior to the resurrection and judgment. The passage goes on to state, "These are they who are cast down to hell . . . until the fullness of times, when Christ shall have subdued all enemies under his feet, and shall have perfected his work" (D&C 76:106). In other words, the destination of "hell" is not a permanent one but should instead be viewed in light of the Mormon concept of a "spirit prison," where individuals destined for a telestial (or another) glory prepare to dwell there. Elsewhere, Joseph Smith indicated that the *she'ol* of the Hebrew Bible, often translated into English as "hell," referred to the destination of the spirits of the deceased prior to their resurrection.[24] Although, as discussed above, the Doctrine and Covenants describes the future destiny of those who ultimately reject Christ (the sons of perdition) in terms similar to those used by other Christians for "hell," Joseph Smith viewed *she'ol* (called "hell" in D&C 76:106) as distinct from this post-Judgment designation. Further confirmation of the difference between the condition of the figures in mortality and their state when in the telestial glory is found in their description as those who "received not the gospel, neither the testimony of Jesus" (D&C 76:101) in mortality, but in the end "all [of them] shall bow the knee, and every tongue shall confess to him who sits upon the throne forever and ever" (D&C 76:110). The Mormon view of a "spirit world" will be discussed further below.

The view that an individual could not receive the testimony of Jesus while in mortality but still end up in a saved condition might fit on the liberal end of the evangelical belief spectrum as a belief known as "inclusivism." This view holds that Christ's power is essential for salvation but that an epistemological awareness or active faith in Christ is not absolutely necessary to be saved. According to one of the view's proponents,

> The unevangelized are saved or lost on the basis of their commitment, or lack thereof, to the God who saves through the work of Jesus. [Inclusivists] believe that appropriation of salvific grace is mediated through general revelation and God's providential workings in human history. Briefly, inclusivists affirm the particularity and finality of salvation only in Christ but deny that knowledge of his work is necessary for salvation. That is to say, they hold that the work of Jesus is ontologically necessary for salvation (no one would be saved without it) but not epistemologically necessary (one need not be aware of the work in to benefit from it).[25]

This view is not acceptable to Calvinists, most of whom would interpret the ignorant state of those who never learned of Christ as an evidence of their predestination to damnation according to God's foreknowledge and sovereign will. Some other Protestants, however, find this view as rejecting the justice and mercy of God, and the inclusivist view helps them understand how a just and merciful God could deal with those who never knew of Jesus.

Christian apologist C. S. Lewis placed the inclusivist view in the mouth of the lion Aslan, who served in the *Chronicles of Narnia* as a metaphor for Christ. In this passage, Aslan is in conversation with Emesh, a pagan follower of the false god Tash:

> Then I fell at his feet and thought, Surely this is the hour of death, for the Lion (who is worthy of all honour) will know that I have served Tash all my days and not him. . . .
>
> But the Glorious One bent down his golden head and touched my forehead with his tongue and said, Son, thou art welcome.
>
> But I said, Alas Lord, I am no son of thine but the servant of Tash.

SALVATION BY GRACE, REWARDS OF DEGREE BY WORKS

> He answered . . . I take to me the services which thou hast done to him. For I and he are of such different kinds that no service which is vile can be done to me, and none which is not vile can be done to him. Therefore if any man swear by Tash and keep his oath for the oath's sake, it is by me that he has truly sworn, though he know it not, and it is I who reward him. And if any man do a cruelty in my name, then, though he says the name Aslan, it is Tash whom he serves and by Tash his deed is accepted. Dost thou understand, Child?
>
> I said, Lord, though knowest how much I understand. But I said also (for the truth constrained me), Yet I have been seeking Tash all my days.
>
> Beloved, said the Glorious One, unless thy desire had been for me thou wouldst not have sought so long and so truly. For all find what they truly seek.[26]

The Book of Mormon reflects a similar approach as that represented by Lewis, indicating that those who do good are always motivated to do so because they are serving Christ (whether or not they are aware of that reality):

> A bitter fountain cannot bring forth good water; neither can a good fountain bring forth bitter water; wherefore, a man being a servant of the devil cannot follow Christ; and if he follow Christ he cannot be a servant of the devil.
>
> Wherefore, all things which are good cometh of God. . . .
>
> But behold, that which is of God inviteth and enticeth to do good continually; wherefore, everything which inviteth and enticeth to do good, and to love God, and to serve him, is inspired of God.
>
> Wherefore, take heed, my beloved brethren, that ye do not judge that which is evil to be of God, or that which is good and of God to be of the devil. (Moroni 7:11–14)

Mormon goes on to explain in a uniquely Book of Mormon Christocentricity how it is possible that one who has not been taught of Christ could do good with true intent. He states that all humankind is provided with "the Spirit of Christ" (Moroni 7:16), that prompts each individual to do good and draws her or him, consciously or unconsciously, towards

God. This is at least a partial explanation of Smith's soteriological view that even those who did not know of Christ in mortality could accept him by following the Spirit of Christ.

As described in D&C 76, however, Smith's soteriological view was both more liberal and more conservative than inclusivism. On the liberal side, it included even those who had acted in sinful ways during mortality the opportunity to suffer the wrath of God "in hell," be cleansed, accept Christ, and be saved. The ability of the sinner to come unto Christ and be forgiven is not surprising to traditional Christians. The ability to do so after mortality but before resurrection and judgment, while in a spirit world, is more so, although the concept is not completely absent from traditional Christian thought.[27]

On the conservative side, Smith's soteriology divides the saved from the unsaved not simply due to the power of Christ, but based on an actual, purposeful acceptance of Jesus. In D&C 76, it is not sufficient to unknowingly follow Christ. In the end, all will be given a full opportunity to accept or reject Christ. Those who accept him, exercising their faith in him, will be saved with a heavenly degree of glory. The sons of perdition purposefully reject him, turning their backs on Christ and his offer of salvation. This view is strictly Christ-centered both in terms of Christ's power and the necessity of the choice to accept Christ's proffered salvation. The Mormon view of a spirit world, where all who have not had the opportunity in mortality are given a full chance to learn of and accept Christ, is the soteriological teaching of Joseph Smith that allows Latter-day Saints to view God as perfectly just and perfectly merciful, just as inclusivism has fulfilled that function for some Protestants. The concept of the spirit world also helps explain the world view of Latter-day Saints, who are often prepared to appreciate the good in others (even in those who might be characterized as sinners, adulterers, or whoremongers), holding out hope that any good is evidence that the individual will someday be willing to fully accept Christ when some of the impediments of their mortal conditioning and fallen nature may be softened by death and by an interim existence in the spirit world.

Is the Latter-day Saint view of salvation broader than that found in the New Testament? If Joseph Smith's view of salvation is indeed more similar to traditional Christian thought than has at times been understood, viewing it through that lens still reveals significant differences. First, as mentioned above, Joseph Smith's soteriology appears to offer something much closer to a universal salvation than is typically understood in traditional Christian thought, in essence turning the view of the heaven/hell binary on its head. Christians have taken their cues as to the relative scarcity of those who will be saved and the abundance of the damned from Jesus' words in the Sermon on the Mount. "Enter ye in at the strait gate: for wide is the gate, and broad is the way, that leadeth to destruction, and many there be which go in thereat: because strait is the gate, and narrow is the way, which leadeth unto life, and few there be that find it" (Matthew 7:13–14). This description of the "many" destined for "destruction" and the "few" for "life" appears to contrast sharply with the numbers of those saved in the telestial glory of heaven in D&C 76:109: "But behold, and lo, we saw the glory and the inhabitants of the telestial world, that they were as innumerable as the stars in the firmament of heaven, or as the sand upon the seashore." Since Christians have traditionally understood Jesus' words as applying to those in heaven and hell,[28] there can be no doubt that Joseph Smith's view marks a significant point of departure.

Latter-day Saints, however, would interpret Jesus' words differently, and a close analysis of D&C 76 again points toward that difference. Jesus indicated that there would be many who would find "destruction," *apōleian* in the Greek, the same word used for "perdition" elsewhere in the New Testament. *Apōleian* can also refer to destruction or ruin, whether physical or spiritual.[29] Interestingly, Joseph Smith's vision emphasizes that the wrath of God will be poured out upon those who will eventually be saved in the telestial world, devoting numerous verses to make that point:

> These are they who suffer the wrath of God on earth.
> These are they who suffer the vengeance of eternal fire.
> These are they who are cast down to hell and suffer the wrath of Almighty God, until the fullness of times, when Christ shall have subdued all enemies under his feet, and shall have perfected his work. (D&C 76:104–6; see also D&C 76:84–85)

There is no way to know precisely how many inhabitants of the world will become sons of perdition using Joseph Smith's revelatory lens, just as there is no way to know precisely how "many" will be damned using a traditional Christian lens. The similarity of the described quantity in Jesus' words and the account regarding the telestial world, however, is striking.

A statement from a later revelation to Joseph Smith provides another hint regarding a Latter-day Saint interpretation of Jesus' words. Speaking of a celestial salvation in the highest degree of glory, D&C 132:24 states, "This is eternal lives—to know the only wise and true God, and Jesus Christ, whom he hath sent." Put together, these two verses seem to indicate that Latter-day Saints would view the large quantity headed to "destruction" as describing those who will experience God's wrath before being saved with a telestial glory, and that Jesus' statements about "eternal life" would be interpreted (at least in this later revelation) as referring to the rewards available in the celestial degree of salvation, referred to as "eternal lives." Once again, D&C 76 relies on biblical wording and biblical framing but in this case uses that wording in ways that do not match how those verses have been read in Christian thought over the centuries.

Why do Latter-day Saints talk about works so much? If it is correct to say, as proposed in this article, that Joseph Smith's soteriology in D&C 76 provides salvation or damnation based only on an acceptance or complete rejection of Christ's role and power, and that the degrees of glory are offered in consequence of grace-enabled works, each degree of glory representing true salvation, then this understanding highlights another significant shift in focus between Protestant and Latter-day Saint discussions of salvation. Joseph Smith's highly inclusive view of salvation maintains Christ's role at the center and encourages or requires Latter-day Saints to exercise faith in him, but appears to represent a situation in which many or most will attain salvation, while the Protestant view consistently and fervently encourages Christians to rely solely on Christ because their salvation is highly at risk. The Mormon view—relying in part on the soteriology of D&C 76—instead focuses on encouraging a desire for all to obtain the highest degree of glory possible and constantly invites Latter-day Saints to give their all to the best of their ability in that pursuit.

SALVATION BY GRACE, REWARDS OF DEGREE BY WORKS

The Latter-day Saint understanding of degrees of glory continues to emphasize that these rewards are only possible because of Christ, as in Brigham Young's statement above, and that only as the individual exercises faith in Christ will she or he receive the strength to obey in more and more appropriate ways—referred to as sanctification by both Latter-day Saints and Protestants. In other words, even the Mormon view of degrees of glory awarded according to one's works is centered on Christ's power, and Latter-day Saints do not expect to truly "earn" their degree of glory in heaven. Rather as they choose to give themselves completely to Christ, Christ will soften their weaknesses and provide an opportunity for a celestial salvation. However, the distinction does highlight a different focus that would lead Latter-day Saints to do all they can to choose a godly life through the power of the Spirit. This focus on Christ-enabled good works, then, should not be understood as simply a product of the Mormon pioneer heritage, but rather as a function of their unique theology—a unique theology and soteriology that, again, has not been fully described in this reading of D&C 76. Although it is somewhat an oversimplification of all the issues at hand, it could be said that Latter-day Saint discourse tends to focus more on sanctification, whereas Protestant discourse may focus more on justification. Understanding this varying focus would be helpful for both outside observers and Latter-day Saints themselves.

The extensive treatment of degrees of reward in heaven in D&C 76 also means that Latter-day Saints have much more to say about what many of those distinctions will be. It could be said that the Protestant focus provides a broad view of salvation as a whole, while the Mormon focus highlights the great varieties of heavenly situations that will be encountered in the next life in order to encourage themselves and others to seek after the highest rewards available through the grace of Christ. This focus means that most Latter-day Saints would not anticipate a feeling of perfect contentment in a telestial degree of salvation (in distinction to Augustine's statement). Rather, they long for the blessings available only in the celestial glory of salvation.

Viewing the soteriology of D&C 76 through a Protestant lens highlights the fact that this text does not provide a works-based salvation.

Rather it teaches that true salvation is available through the grace of Christ based solely on God's power and our choice to accept the salvation he freely offers to all. Joseph Smith's teachings about the degrees of glory should be understood as heavenly rewards based on works, with Christ still standing at the center. Notwithstanding the similarities that comparing these viewpoints reveals, it also highlights significant differences in biblical interpretation, approach, and focus. The goal of this study is not to explain away those differences, but rather to help the reader understand (1) that Latter-day Saints have more in common with other Christians than both traditional Christians and Latter-day Saint Christians might initially believe, and (2) that viewing Mormon theology through a traditional lens provides a clearer picture of what the differences actually are and why they exist. In the case of this discussion, those points can help Protestants understand why Mormon prophet Harold B. Lee and others would feel comfortable making some of the strongly works-oriented statements quoted above, and why Brigham Young could claim that Latter-day Saints "believe that all who attain to any glory whatever, in any kingdom, will do so because Jesus has purchased it by his Atonement."

As a devoted Latter-day Saint, I find beauty in Protestant understandings of salvation centered on Christ but find great joy in the equally (I believe) Christ-centered soteriology of Joseph Smith. To my mind, that soteriology reveals the compassion, love, wisdom, and justice of God, and provides a nuanced view of God's plan for humankind and of the great variety of human interaction I experience in my life. As a Latter-day Saint, I have been taught to believe that I can merit nothing without Christ and that both my salvation and my subsequent situation in heaven would be impossible without his substitutionary atoning sacrifice. I need Christ every step of the way to lift me from my weaknesses and provide the strength and hope necessary to continue onward. I also believe that God expects me to freely choose to give my whole self in pursuit of a godly life and to completely turn myself over to him to the best of my ability if I desire to gain the "prize of the high calling of God in Christ Jesus" (Philippians 3:14), with all of its attendant blessings.

Notes

1. See, for example, Robert L. Millet, *By Grace Are We Saved* (Salt Lake City: Deseret Book, 1989); Bruce C. Hafen, "Grace," in *Encyclopedia of Mormonism*, ed. Daniel H. Ludlow (New York: Macmillan, 1992), 2:560–62.
2. Helmut Gollwitzer, *An Introduction to Protestant Theology*, trans. David Cairns (Philadelphia: Westminster Press, 1982), 62.
3. B. H. Roberts, *A Comprehensive History of the Church of Jesus Christ of Latter-day Saints*, 7 vols. (Salt Lake City: The Church of Jesus Christ of Latter-day Saints, 1930), 3:30.
4. D. Stephen Long, "Justification and Atonement," in *The Cambridge Companion to Evangelical Theology*, ed. Timothy Larsen and Daniel J. Treier (New York: Cambridge University Press, 2007), 79–80.
5. All biblical quotes are from the King James Version as found in the official scriptures of The Church of Jesus Christ of Latter-day Saints, published in 2013.
6. N. T. Wright, *Justification: God's Plan and Paul's Vision* (Great Britain: Ashford Colour Press, 2009), 7.
7. *Teachings of Harold B. Lee* (Salt Lake City: The Church of Jesus Christ of Latter-day Saints, 2014), 331.
8. Lynn Wilder, "Mormon No More," *Christianity Today*, December 2013, 80.
9. *Teachings of Presidents of the Church: Brigham Young* (Salt Lake City: The Church of Jesus Christ of Latter-day Saints, 1997), 30.
10. R. Philip Roberts, "The SBJT Forum: Speaking the Truth in Love," *Southern Baptist Theological Journal* 9 (2005): 74.
11. See Matthew C. Godfrey, Mark Ashurst-McGee, Grant Underwood, Robert J. Woodford, and William G. Hartley, eds., *Documents, Volume 2: July 1831–January 1833*, vol. 2 of the Documents series of *The Joseph Smith Papers*, ed. Dean C. Jessee, Ronald K. Esplin, Richard Lyman Bushman, and Matthew J. Grow (Salt Lake City: Church Historian's Press, 2013), 179–92.
12. See, for example, JST, Exodus 7:3 and Exodus 9:12 in the Latter-day Saint edition of the Bible.
13. See P. Toon, "Hyper-Calvinism," in *New Dictionary of Theology* (Downer's Grove, IL: InterVarsity Press, 1988), 324.
14. See R. Kearsely, "Grace," in *New Dictionary of Theology*, 280.

15. Robert L. Millet and Gerald McDermott, *Claiming Christ: A Mormon Evangelical Debate* (Grand Rapids, MI: Brazos Press, 2007), 185. See also Brian Birch's discussion of agency, grace, faith, and works in Latter-day Saint thought in "Are Mormons Pelagians? Autonomy, Grace, and Freedom," in *2010 Society for Mormon Philosophy and Theology* (Utah Valley University, March 25, 2010).
16. See H. G. Anderson, et al., eds., *Justification by Faith* (Minneapolis: Lutherans and Catholics in Dialogue VII, 1985); see also P. F. Jensen, "Merit," in *New Theological Dictionary*, 422.
17. My thanks to Robert Millet for directing me to the quotations found in this and the subsequent two paragraphs.
18. Bruce Wilkinson, *A Life God Rewards* (Colorado Springs, CO: WaterBrook Multnomah Publishers, 2002), 23, 25, 98.
19. St. Augustine, *The City of God*, trans. Marcus Dods (New York: Random House, 1978), 865.
20. Edwards, as cited in Wilkinson, *A Life God Rewards*, 119.
21. Wesley, as cited in Wilkinson, *A Life God Rewards*, 120–21.
22. K. Bockmuehl, "Sanctification," in *New Dictionary of Theology*, 613–14.
23. This is certainly not a common interpretation in Christian thought, but the possibility does exist. See, for example, the discussion of Christ's throne in James D. G. Dunn, *The Epistles to the Colossians and to Philemon: a Commentary on the Greek Text*, in *The New International Greek Testament Commentary* (Grand Rapids, MI: Eerdmans, 1996), 204.
24. *The Words of Joseph Smith*, ed. Andrew F. Ehat and Lyndon W. Cook (Provo, UT: Religious Studies Center, 1980), 211–12.
25. John Sanders, *No Other Name: An Investigation into the Destiny of the Unevangelized* (Grand Rapids, MI: Eerdmans, 1992), 215. My thanks to Bryan Ready of Peoria, Illinois, who pointed me to this quotation, and who freely and knowledgably discussed many of the concepts mentioned in this paper from a Reformed perspective.
26. C. S. Lewis, *The Last Battle*, in *The Chronicles of Narnia* (New York: HarperCollins, 1956, 1982), 756–57.
27. For a review of Jewish and Christian thinking on a world of departed spirits that acts as a temporary abode between life and death, see David L. Paulsen et al., "The Harrowing of Hell: Salvation for the Dead in Early Christianity," *Journal of*

Book of Mormon Studies and Other Restoration Scripture 19, no. 1 (2010): 56–77; David L. Paulsen and Brock M. Mason, "Baptism for the Dead in Early Christianity," *Journal of Book of Mormon Studies and Other Restoration Scripture* 19, no. 2 (2010): 22–49.

28. R. T. France, *The Gospel of Matthew* in *New International Commentary on the New Testament* (Grand Rapids, MI: Eerdmans, 2007), 287.
29. Oepke, "ἀπόλλυμι, ἀπώλεια, πολλύων," *Theological Dictionary of the New Testament*, ed. G. Hittel (Grand Rapids, MI: Eerdmans, 1964), 1:396.

What Is Christianity?

Dennis L. Okholm

In the winter semester of 1899–1900 at the University of Berlin, Adolf von Harnack delivered public lectures on the topic "The Essence of Christianity." They were translated for the English-speaking world under the title "What Is Christianity?"[1] In the course of his lectures, Harnack succinctly answered the question, albeit inadequately: "In the combination of these ideas—God the Father, Providence, the position of men as God's children, the infinite value of the human soul—the whole gospel is expressed."[2] And it was Harnack's conviction that this was the gospel as Jesus proclaimed it—a gospel that "has to do with the Father only and not with the Son," because

> no one had ever yet known the Father in the way Jesus knew Him, and to this knowledge of Him he draws other men's attention, and thereby does "the many" an incomparable service. He leads them to God, not only by what he says, but still more by what he is and does, and ultimately by what he suffers.[3]

Such was the concern of this historian of dogma—to get at the kernel of the Christian faith that lies underneath all the incrustations of "Christian"

WHAT IS CHRISTIANITY?

husk that come and go. But Harnack admitted that the kernel can exist among us in no other way, since it is necessary for the gospel to be relevant to contemporary culture:

> The Gospel did not come into the world as a statutory religion, and therefore none of the forms in which it assumed intellectual and social expression—not even the earliest—can be regarded as possessing a classical and permanent character. . . . Not only can it so exist—it must do so, if it is to be the religion of the living and is itself to live. As a Gospel it has only *one* aim—the finding of the living God, the finding of Him by every individual as *his* God, and as the source of strength and joy and peace. How this aim is progressively realized through the centuries—whether with the co-efficients of Hebraism or Hellenism, of the shunning of the world or of civilization, of Gnosticism or of Agnosticism, of ecclesiastical institution or of perfectly free union, or by *whatever other kinds of bark the core may be protected, the sap allowed to rise*—is a matter that is of secondary moment, that is exposed to change, that belongs to the centuries, that comes with them and with them perishes.[4]

Of course, for Harnack the greatest transformation of the new religion occurred in the second century with the beginning of the Hellenization of Christianity—the "work of the Greek spirit on the soil of the Gospel."[5] In that respect, Mormonism and other primitivist movements in the nineteenth century share something in common with Harnack, reacting against the transformation of a living faith into a creed to be believed (though Mormonism would not reject some of the accoutrements that Harnack goes on to list as corrupting transformations of Christianity).

One representative of the Latter-day Saints, Tad R. Callister, resonates with Harnack's approach—albeit with different concerns—arguing in *The Inevitable Apostasy and the Promised Restoration* that with the death of the Apostles a "different church evolved—one without revelation and without priesthood authority," and one in institutional, doctrinal, and moral decay that confused truth and error as it assimilated "the gospel of Christ with the philosophies of me, . . . an appealing composite of New Testament

Christianity, Jewish traditions, Greek philosophy, Graeco-Roman paganism, and the mystery religions.'"[6]

This does not mean that the kernel was entirely lost amidst the chaff. To use a different analogy, protesters and reformers throughout Christian history kept alive the flame that flickered and dimmed.[7] It is not just the likes of Harnack and Callister, who, with their different agendas, argue that somewhere along the way the essence of Christianity was compromised. Anders Nygren made a similar case in *Agape and Eros*, claiming that Christianity was distorted by Augustine's Platonism (for instance) such that he substituted *caritas* for *agape*.[8] Thanks be to God that Martin Luther came to the rescue in and for this Lutheran scholar's account of the matter! Then again, Rudolf Bultmann argued that the kernel of Christianity had to be uncovered even under the casings of scripture.[9] (It is interesting that Harnack, Nygren, and Bultmann were all *Lutheran* theologians.)

Before continuing, we must insist with patristics historian Robert Louis Wilken that the "notion that the development of early Christian thought represented a hellenization of Christianity has outlived its usefulness. The time has come to bid a fond farewell to the ideas of Adolf von Harnack." Wilken argues that it is more accurate to speak of the "Christianization of Hellenism" because Christian thought was generated "from within, from the person of Christ, the Bible, Christian worship, the life of the church. . . . Christian thinking, while working within patterns of thought and conceptions rooted in Greco-Roman culture, transformed them so profoundly that in the end something quite new came into being."[10]

Still, Harnack's question remains: What *is* Christianity? What is the *essence* of Christianity?[11] And, as Craig Blomberg states, it is complicated by the fact that "no formal definition of the term [Christian] ever appears in the Bible."[12] To be clear, we are not asking (in the present context), "Is Mormonism Christian?" nor "Are Mormons Christian?"[13] That line of inquiry cannot be answered until the prior question is answered.

Indeed, it was the question that Joseph Smith asked, surrounded as he was by the answers of a plethora of denominations which he concluded were all wrong and whose creeds were an abomination before God.[14] His question was answered by an appeal for further divine revelation. But there

WHAT IS CHRISTIANITY?

are other ways to go about exploring for an answer—rooting for the kernel, as it were.

One approach is to take seriously the development of doctrine, assuming that the mature tree is a faithful representation of the acorn. That was the project of John Henry Newman, who *did* assume that "a true development retains the *essential idea* of the subject from which it has proceeded" (while "a corruption loses it") and asked, "What then is the true idea of Christianity?"[15] Newman found it in the Church of Rome, to which he converted in 1845 (the year after Joseph Smith was shot in Carthage Jail). For Newman, Christianity is simply defined by the dogma of the Roman Catholic Church as a faithful development of the "original."

But now we have already landed in a morass, since the definition of Christianity, according to Harnack and representatives of the Mormon Church, denies faithful development and insists on a return to the apostolic beginning, while Wilken and Newman would have no problem identifying true Christianity as a contemporary reality that faithfully developed from the apostolic beginning. A host of folks would get in line behind one or the other—even among evangelicals—but they would be lines that seem never to merge, no matter how far down the horizon one looks.

There are some who *try* to get in both lines. A good example would be the evangelical New Testament scholar Scot McKnight.[16] In one essay McKnight rightly cautions us to have epistemic humility, admitting that our "gospel truth" is "only a partial grasp of the ultimate truth." As he puts it, "the Story" is made up of many wiki-stories in the Bible, and we tend to make one of these wiki-stories a "church tradition" among the many other church traditions. But we need this variety because not even Jesus' story can tell the whole Story. Interpretive retellings of the Story never come to a final unrevisable shape. What we do is figure out a plot that *adequately* but *not definitively* holds all the wiki-stories together.

In a second essay that largely holds together with the approach of the first, McKnight makes the case that atonement theories have become the lens through which the Bible is read, so that atonement theories drive the meaning of the gospel. Instead, the gospel that Peter and Paul preached, as recorded in Acts, was not shaped by an atonement theory, even though doctrines such as double imputation, justification, and propitiation are entailments of the gospel. Instead, the gospel sermons in Acts preach how the Old Testament story came to its fulfillment in the story of Jesus—how Israel's story found its conclusive chapter in Jesus' story, without explaining *how* the death of Jesus accomplished anything: "Peter's and Paul's sermons focus on Jesus and run everything through the lens of Israel's story." So the apostolic gospel drove to the conclusion that "the exalted one, Jesus, is the *Messiah of Israel and Lord of all*."[17] What we are to do in response to the apostolic gospel is repent and believe and be baptized to enter into this lordship story.

It is at the end of this essay, however, that one wonders if McKnight has tried to sneak into the other line with Harnack and Mormons, though he would have significant differences with either one's understanding of the apostolic faith. That is, while McKnight is correct to chastise Christians (largely, evangelical types) for reducing the gospel that the apostles preached to a "plan of salvation" seen through the lens of an atonement theory, and while he rightly allows for *development* of doctrines that are entailed in the gospeling of the New Testament—doctrines such as the various atonement theories—he concludes with a statement that doesn't seem to have the tone of epistemic humility nor the status of a wiki-story or a church tradition. Instead, it sounds like the apostolic original to which we need to return, regardless of developments:

> In short, Israel's story longs for a kingdom where God is King and where Israel is God's people in that kingdom. This, I submit to you, is *exactly* who Jesus is—Governor of heaven and earth—and *exactly* what Jesus preached: the kingdom of God. And this is what Paul was preaching in Acts 28. Personal salvation is what happens to people who enter into that story. The gospel is to tell that story aloud and point people to Jesus Christ as the Messiah and Lord.[18]

Given the impasse (if one really can *not* have it both ways or be in *both* lines), it would be helpful to suggest other paradigms.

It seems to me that there are two ways to establish the identity of Christianity. One way would be to draw boundaries consisting of non-negotiables within which a communion that claims to be Christian would need to remain. Think of it as a Christian corral within which groups graze at different locations depending on which part of the pasture fits their particular tastes, all the while remaining within the fenced boundaries.

The problem here is that not everyone will agree on the type or number of fences that surround the faithful. I would think that most self-identifying evangelicals would put up at least four boundaries or nonnegotiables: (1) God is the ultimate source of all that exists, made neither out of preexistent matter nor out of God's being but by the Word of God (Genesis 1:1; Psalm 33:6; Hebrews 11:3); (2) Jesus Christ is fully God and fully human, with implications for insistence on the doctrine of the incarnation (Jesus is fully human: John 1:14 and 1 John 1:1–3) and, for insistence, on the doctrine of the trinity (Jesus is fully divine by nature and eternally so: John 1:1, 5:18, 10:30, 14:9; Acts 20:28; Romans 9:5); (3) it is *only* through the life, death, and resurrection of Jesus Christ that we are saved (Romans 5; 1 Corinthians 15:3, 4; Colossians 1:22–23); and (4) the Bible is *the* (that is, only) unique, reliable, authoritative, inspired witness to Jesus Christ (as illumined by the Holy Spirit; 2 Timothy 3:16–17). My Latter-day Saint friends might want to add another fence (such as the priesthood), reject the first as stated, refine the trinitarian implication of the second, and alter the fourth to include other scriptures. And let's face it: there are some evangelicals who would want to add another fence or two (or more!). So perhaps the paradigm of boundaries may not be as helpful as another model for getting at the essence of Christianity.

What might serve us better is to envision a center from which would radiate tethers that could be extended. (How far the tether stretches would be debated.) This would be something like Harnack's kernel *along with his insistence* that it *must* exist in specific forms of intellectual and social expression. If we could agree on the center, then what radiates from it would allow for various expressions due to chronology, geography, ethnicity, and so on. The tethers might be something like McKnight's church traditions that are *interpretations* of the faith, trying to hold together the wiki-stories that refer to the Story (the center?).

The advantage of this paradigm is that it realizes there is no generic Christianity. There are only particular Christianities. That is, there is Anglican Christianity, Baptist Christianity, Orthodox Christianity, Roman Catholic Christianity, and so on. We could even be more particular: I am a white, male, suburban, Anglican Christian. Yet I have in common the Christian center with a black, female, urban, nondenominational Christian. We are not going to agree on a lot because all Christianity is enculturated, but there will be that essence—that center—which will tie us to the same faith.

Could Mormonism be tethered to this same center? That is similar to the question "Is Mormonism Christian?" *except* that we have not yet answered the prior question "What is Christianity?" or "What *is* the center?" But it seems to me that when we get the answer that I will propose, Mormonism *could* be so tethered *if* it includes the admission that it is just one particular expression of Christianity—specifically an American-bred form of Christianity[19] that does not necessarily include the fulness of Christian truth. Of course, Roman Catholics—and some Baptists!—would have to make the same admission of a degree of impoverishment. And for these iterations of Christianity that is going to be a difficult, if not impossible, admission to make. In the case of Mormonism, it is precisely Smith's discovery of the gold plates that promised revelation of the *fulness* of the everlasting gospel.[20]

This second paradigm does not solve all of our problems, but it might move us closer if we slightly change the metaphor from radiating tethers to a web, and here I have in mind what Quine describes as a "web of belief."[21] In this case a web is spun from the center out. The entire web consists of an internal logic (so this gets associated with a coherentist epistemology), but nesting in its center is, for example, the resurrection of Jesus Christ. It is possible that this conviction could be undone; something *could* count against belief in Jesus' resurrection, but that scenario is not only not expected, it is considered highly improbable, because ejecting that belief would necessitate a paradigm shift (to use the language of Thomas Kuhn) or conversion and the construction of a new web (a new religious orientation). That is, it would be equivalent to a rejection of Christianity.

But, with the center in place, how the web is constructed from the center out tolerates variations such that the resultant web is a *particular* web. And, given that this is a metaphor, various particular webs can have the same center. (Of course, two webs cannot share a common center in *real* life, so we have to keep in mind that this *is* a metaphor.)

WHAT IS CHRISTIANITY?

So what *is* the center? It is Jesus, obviously. But more must be said. It is Jesus as the only completely faithful Israelite who came to address Israel's problem. (In this sense McKnight's summary is spot-on; he especially appeals to Acts 10:23–43.) In other words, the center cannot tolerate the Marcionite heresy that rejects the Old Testament. The biblical story is *one* Story that minimally requires the Hebrew Bible as well as the New Testament.[22] (Even among Orthodox, Roman, and Protestant Christians there are variations in the canon, so "minimal" is not just taking into account Mormons.)

Israel's problem had to do with covenantal obligations and consequences, especially spelled out in Exodus and Deuteronomy. Though her covenantal relationship with Yahweh positioned her to be the conduit of blessing to all nations (Genesis 12, 15, 22), she did not keep her end of the bargain, so she was sent into exile. The faithful Israelite, Jesus, a descendent of Abraham and David, is the Anointed One (the King, the Messiah), who, by his obedience and his death, fulfills the covenant God made with Israel and, by his resurrection victory over death that establishes his lordship (Philippians 2), makes possible the repentant believer's participation in the restored covenant and God's new (renewed) creation. These believers include both Jews and Gentiles (who now participate in Israel's inheritance) as, for instance, Paul lays out in Ephesians 1–3.[23]

The question remains whether adjustments need to be made to the web of evangelical and Mormon expressions of Christianity.

Both N. T. Wright and Scot McKnight—among many others—insist that the evangelical web isn't the best construction radiating out of the center. In fact, McKnight insists that evangelicals[24] have turned the gospel into the "plan of salvation"—turned a story into a doctrine.[25] He is not accusing such folks of denying the center as we have articulated it above, but he *is* insisting that they've moved the center into other locations on the web and placed at the web's center what should have been spun out on the edges—doctrines such as double imputation and justification.

N. T. Wright has a similar complaint and might be paraphrased as accusing evangelicals of putting too much emphasis on "receiving Jesus into my life" rather than *being* received into *Jesus'* life and righteousness. Said differently, Wright's concern is that Paul has been misread: we are not saved by faith *in* Christ, but by the faith *of* Christ—the only faithful Israelite whose status (not moral virtue) God now declares we share as members of God's true family.²⁶ (We should mention that Wright *would* agree with Harnack on one point: Greek philosophy—specifically of the Platonic sort—has distorted Christianity by making salvation an escape from this world rather than a restoration of this world.)²⁷

What about the Mormon web? On the one hand, the web of Mormon beliefs resembles much of what is in the evangelical web. Bob Millet sums it up well:

> In short, the gospel is the good news that Christ came to earth, lived and taught and suffered and died and rose again, all to the end that those who believe and obey might be delivered from death and sin unto eternal life. This good news Latter-day Saints have in common with Christians throughout the world.²⁸

Mormon teaching also insists on a single Story, including a Jesus who was made known from the time of the Old Testament patriarchs.²⁹ Though Mormons hold to a doctrine of dispensationalism³⁰ much like some in Evangelicalism, there is a sense in which they maintain a continuity of the Abrahamic covenant. While Mormonism is a new stage of Israel's history, it participates in the "new and everlasting covenant." Of course, to really be one of the covenant people requires obedience and continued faithfulness to the Mediator of that covenant—Jesus Christ. Furthermore,

> The crowning tie to Israel comes only by the worthy reception of the blessings of the temple, through being endowed and sealed in family units. . . . "The fulfillment, the consummation of these blessings comes as those who have entered the waters of baptism perfect their lives to the point that they may enter the holy temple. Receiving an endowment there seals members of the Church to the Abrahamic covenant."³¹

So there is a degree of correspondence to what we have identified as the center of Christianity. What seems to be missing is the notion that Jesus is Savior precisely because he is the Israelite who fulfilled the covenant (even taking upon himself the punishment required because the covenant has been broken—being sent into exile on the cross, as it were), so that, now, in N. T. Wright's words, we are saved by *his* faith—taken up into his righteousness, not as a moral exchange or fiction, but as a declaration of our status as people who have been immersed into his life and now live by the power of his resurrection.

Millet *does* note that Mormonism teaches Jesus is the "Holy One of Israel" who kept the law of God.[32] With this, it may not take too much of a leap to develop what we have articulated as the center, but in the Latter-day Saint theological literature I have read I have yet to come across an understanding of Jesus that highlights his association with the history of Israel in such a way that salvation is based on Jesus as the *solution to Israel's problem* (as McKnight puts it at one point).[33]

In fact, Mormon theology may share a theological emphasis with evangelicals in that, as Millet discusses Christ's work, double imputation is *the* theory when atonement is discussed so that in *that* sense we are redeemed "because of the righteousness of the Redeemer."

> The means by which the Savior justifies us is wondrous indeed. It entails what might be called "the great exchange." [Martin Luther used this language] . . . The point [in Philippians 3:8–9] is vital: justification comes by faith, by trusting in *Christ's righteousness*, in His merits, mercy, and grace. . . . Paul teaches a profound truth—that as we come unto Christ by the covenant of faith, our Lord's righteousness becomes our righteousness. He justifies us in the sense that he *imputes*—meaning, he reckons to our account—his goodness and takes our sin. This is the great exchange.[34]

It may not take much of a modification of the web's strands to adjust Mormon theology so that the center is recast, but it also may not be possible given its teaching on the unique relationship that Latter-day Saints have with ancient Israel. Hopefully, more can be discussed and developed along the lines that have been suggested.

Given what we have identified as the essence of Christianity, perhaps the right question to ask after answering "What is Christianity?" is not "Are Mormons Christian?" or even "Are evangelicals Christian?" but instead, "To what extent have Mormons or evangelicals constructed the Christian web poorly, misplacing the center—its essence—in the process?" And then we may need to listen to the voices of weavers who will help us reconstruct the web.

Notes

1. See Adolf Harnack, *What Is Christianity?*, trans. Thomas Bailey Saunders (Gloucester, MA: Peter Smith, 1978). This is a reprint of the Harper Torchbook edition that was published in 1957.
2. Harnack, *What Is Christianity?*, 68.
3. Harnack, *What Is Christianity?*, 144.
4. Harnack, *What Is Christianity?*, 191; last emphasis added. Would Harnack have added evangelicalism and Mormonism to the list of "barks" that come and go?
5. See Harnack, *What Is Christianity?*, Lecture XI.
6. Tad R. Callister, *The Inevitable Apostasy and the Promised Restoration* (Salt Lake City: Deseret Book, 2006), 47. Callister is quoting LDS historian Milton V. Backman Jr. He specifically appeals to Harnack's argument on p. 32.
7. This is Boyd K. Packer's metaphor as cited in Robert L. Millet, "Apostasy, Great," in *LDS Beliefs: A Doctrinal Reference*, ed. Robert L. Millet, Camille Fronk Olson, Andrew C. Skinner, and Brent L. Top (Salt Lake City: Deseret Book, 2011), 48–49.
8. See Anders Nygren, *Agape and Eros*, trans. Philip S. Watson (Philadelphia: Westminster, 1953).
9. See Rudolf Bultmann, *Jesus Christ and Mythology* (New York: Charles Scribner's Sons, 1958).
10. Robert Louis Wilken, *The Spirit of Early Christian Thought* (New Haven: Yale University Press, 2003), xvi–xvii.
11. We certainly do not want to answer it with Ludwig Feuerbach who argued that Christian "theology had long since become anthropology," referring to "Man" in a loud voice when it said "God." But he did help to expose the misguided thinking of nineteenth-century liberal theologians (making use of Luther in the process!), as Karl Barth argued in an introductory essay. See Ludwig Feuerbach, *The Essence of Christianity*, trans. George Eliot (New York: Harper & Row, 1957).
12. Craig Blomberg, "Is Mormonism Christian?," in *The New Mormon Challenge: Responding to the Latest Defenses of a Fast-Growing Movement*, ed. Francis J. Beckwith, Carl Mosser, and Paul Owen (Grand Rapids, MI: Zondervan, 2002), 317.

13. This question has been asked by several: Craig Blomberg, "Mormonism," 315–32; Bruce D. Porter and Gerald McDermott, "Is Mormonism Christian?," in *First Things*, October 2008, 35–41; and Stephen E. Robinson, *Are Mormons Christian?* (Salt Lake City: Bookcraft, 1991).
14. Richard Lyman Bushman, *Joseph Smith: Rough Stone Rolling* (New York: Vintage Books, 2005), 40.
15. John Henry Newman, *An Essay on the Development of Christian Doctrine*, ed. J. M. Cameron (Baltimore, MD: Penguin Books, 1974), 241.
16. The following discussion draws from two essays of McKnight's in *Church in the Present Tense*, ed. Kevin Corcoran (Grand Rapids, MI: Brazos, 2011): "Scripture in the Emerging Movement," 105–22, and "Atonement and Gospel," 123–39.
17. McKnight, "Atonement," 134–35.
18. McKnight, "Atonement," 139; emphasis added.
19. See Andrew C. Skinner, "America," in *LDS Beliefs*, 31–35.
20. Bushman, *Smith*, 44.
21. See W. V. Quine and J. S. Ullian, *The Web of Belief*, 2nd ed. (New York: Random House, 1978).
22. N. T. Wright puts it well: "Trying to understand Jesus without understanding what that story [i.e., Israel's] was, how it worked, and what it meant is like trying to understand why someone is hitting a ball with a stick without knowing what baseball, or indeed cricket, is all about." *Simply Christian* (San Francisco: HarperOne, 2010), 71.
23. N. T. Wright summarizes the faith this way: "Christianity is all about the belief that the living God, in fulfillment of his promises and as the climax of the story of Israel, has accomplished all this—the finding, the saving, the giving of new life—in Jesus. He has done it. With Jesus, God's rescue operation has been put into effect once and for all." *Simply Christian*, 92.
24. I assume evangelicals are his primary "target," since he dialogues with those who would identify themselves as evangelicals in the essays to which I have referred.
25. McKnight, "Atonement," 137–38.
26. This is the case Wright makes in *Justification: God's Plan and Paul's Vision* (London: SPCK, 2009). I am not suggesting that McKnight would entirely agree with Wright's interpretation of Paul and it has been debated among evangelicals (for example, see Mark Husbands and Daniel Treier, *Justification: What's at Stake in the Current Debates* (Downers Grove, IL: InterVarsity Press, 2004). But Wright makes some of the same criticisms, such as that justification

has been overemphasized and theologically misread back into the Bible; and Wright and McKnight both place emphasis on the centrality of the covenant and the Story.

27. See N. T. Wright, *Simply Christian*, 114–15; and N. T. Wright, *Surprised by Hope: Rethinking Heaven, the Resurrection, and the Mission of the Church* (San Francisco: HarperOne, 2008).

28. Robert L. Millet, *The Mormon Faith: A New Look at Christianity* (Salt Lake City: Deseret Book, 1998), 49.

29. "If all this [i.e., that Adam & Eve were Christians, Abraham, Moses, Isaiah, Jeremiah, Ezekiel were Christian prophets] seems odd, anachronistic in the sense that there could obviously be no Christianity until the coming to earth of the Christ, Latter-day Saints believe otherwise. They believe and teach that among the plain and precious truths lost from the holy records that became the Bible is the knowledge of Christ's eternal gospel, the message that a gospel or plan of salvation was had from the dawn of time." Millet, *Mormon Faith*, 44. This is something that "traditional" Christians have taught for centuries—let alone Paul in Ephesians 1—in that they have identified Genesis 3:15 as the Protoevangelium—the first announcement of the gospel. In a similar vein, John Calvin insisted that the church existed in its "childhood" as far back as the Patriarchs; see John Calvin, *The Institutes of the Christian Religion*, trans. Ford Lewis Battles, ed. John T. McNeill (Philadelphia: Westminster Press, 1960), II.2.2.

30. See Robert L. Millet, *Mormon Faith*, 44: Latter-day Saints believe in dispensations—periods during which God revealed himself and his plan of salvation—often in response to periods of apostasy. Also, see Millet, *The Vision of Mormonism* (St. Paul: Paragon House, 2007), 34–35; *A Different Jesus? The Christ of Latter Day Saints* (Grand Rapids, MI: Eerdmans, 2005), 88–89. Similarly, see Andrew C. Skinner's article "Israel" in *LDS Beliefs*, 328.

31. Millet, *Mormon Faith*, 122–23. This discussion begins on p. 114 and continues to p. 125: Israel includes more than the Jews; it is increased by the number of people joining the Church and therefore coming into the covenant—Abraham's descendants. Compare Andrew Skinner's comment in his article on Israel in *LDS Beliefs*, 328: "There are natural-born descendants of Israel, and there are those who are adopted into the house of Israel through accepting Jesus Christ and participating in the ordinances of salvation administered by the house of Israel through the true Church." What is troubling about Skinner's comment is that he supports it with Galatians 3:14–29, where Paul is not really speaking about "accepting Jesus

Christ" as much as he is talking about being accepted into Christ. The distinction is important, as we have argued above.

32. Millet, *A Different Jesus?*, 74, 76. Elsewhere Millet likes to identify Jesus as Change Agent, Benefactor, Example, Mediator, and Intercessor. See Millet, *Vision*, 49; and *What Happened to the Cross? Distinctive LDS Teachings* (Salt Lake City: Deseret Book, 2007), 115.

33. McKnight works from sermons in Acts (2, 3, 4, 10, 11, 13, 14, 17), arguing that none of these explains how Jesus' death saves us but only that the story of Jesus is the fulfillment of Israel's story—its conclusive chapter. See "Atonement," 131–33.

34. Millet, *Mormon Faith*, 71–72; see also Millet, *Vision*, 54; Millet, "Atonement," in *LDS Beliefs*, 56–59.

Curriculum Vitae
Professor Emeritus of Ancient Scripture

Robert L. Millet

Personal Data

Date of Birth: December 30, 1947

Place of Birth: Baton Rouge, Louisiana

Married: Shauna Sizemore (1971); six children

Education

PhD, Florida State University (April 1983) in religious studies and psychology

MS, Brigham Young University (April 1973) in psychology and religion

BS, Brigham Young University (May 1971) in psychology

CURRICULUM VITAE

Professional Experience

Professor of Ancient Scripture, Brigham Young University, September 1993–January 2014

Associate Professor of Ancient Scripture, Brigham Young University, September 1987–August 1993

Assistant Professor of Ancient Scripture, Brigham Young University, June 1983–August 1987

Teaching Support Consultant, LDS Church Educational System, Southern States Area, July 1982–June 1983

Instructor in Religion, Florida State University Department of Religion, 1980–81

Director of the Institute of Religion, LDS Church Educational System, Florida State University, August 1977–June 1982

Seminary Instructor, LDS Church Educational System, Salt Lake City, 1975–77

Marriage and Family Therapist, LDS Social Services, Idaho Agency, October 1973–August 1975

Positions or Assignments

Coordinator of Office of Religious Outreach, Brigham Young University, July 2014–

Member of the Advisory Board of BYU Studies, June 2014–

Abraham O. Smoot University Professor, August 2008–2014

Richard L. Evans Professor of Religious Understanding, March 2001–August 2005

Dean of Religious Education, BYU, January 1991–September 2000

Board of Directors, Deseret Book Company, October 1996–March 2009

Member of the Jerusalem Academic Coordinating Committee, January 1991–September 2000

Member of the Advisory Board of *Brigham Young University Studies*, February 1992–May 1994

Chair, Department of Ancient Scripture, BYU, April 1988 to January 1991

Member, University Rank Advancement Council, September 1987–August 1991

Professional Organizations

American Academy of Religion

Society of Biblical Literature

Association of Mormon Counselors and Psychotherapists

Mormon History Association

Phi Kappa Phi

Kappa Omicron Nu

Publications and Writings
Books

1. *Magnifying Priesthood Power* (Bountiful, UT: Horizon Publishers, 1974; rev. ed., 1989).

2. *Studies in Scripture*, vol. 1: *The Doctrine and Covenants* (Sandy, UT: Randall Book Co., 1984). Coedited with Kent P. Jackson.

3. *Studies in Scripture*, vol. 2: *The Pearl of Great Price* (Sandy, UT: Randall Book Co., 1985). Coedited with Kent P. Jackson.

4. *The Joseph Smith Translation: The Restoration of Plain and Precious Things* (Provo, UT: Religious Studies Center, 1985). Coedited with Monte S. Nyman.

5. *Sustaining and Defending the Faith* (Salt Lake City: Bookcraft, 1985). Coauthored with Joseph F. McConkie.

6. *Studies in Scripture*, vol. 3: *The Old Testament. Genesis to 2 Kings* (Sandy, UT: Randall Book, 1986). Coedited with Kent P. Jackson.

7. *The Life Beyond* (Salt Lake City: Bookcraft, 1986). Coauthored with Joseph F. McConkie.

8. *Studies in Scripture*, vol. 5: *The Gospels* (Salt Lake City: Deseret Book 1986). Coedited with Kent P. Jackson.

9. *Studies in Scripture*, vol. 6: *Acts to Revelation* (Salt Lake City: Deseret Book, 1987), Edited.

10. *Doctrinal Commentary on the Book of Mormon*, vol. 1: *First and Second Nephi* (Salt Lake City: Bookcraft, 1987). Coauthored with Joseph F. McConkie.

11. *"To Be Learned Is Good If..."* (Salt Lake City: Bookcraft, 1987). Edited.

12. *Doctrinal Commentary on the Book of Mormon*, vol. 2: *Jacob through Mosiah* (Salt Lake City: Bookcraft, 1988). Coauthored with Joseph F. McConkie.

13. *In His Holy Name* (Salt Lake City: Bookcraft, 1988). Coauthored with Joseph F. McConkie.

14. *The Capstone of Our Religion: Insights into the Doctrine and Covenants* (Salt Lake City: Bookcraft, 1989). Coedited with Larry E. Dahl.

15. *By Grace Are We Saved* (Salt Lake City: Bookcraft, 1989).

16. *Joseph Smith: Selected Sermons and Writings*. Volume in the Sources of American Spirituality Series (Mahweh, New Jersey: Paulist Press, 1989).

17. *The Holy Ghost* (Salt Lake City: Bookcraft, 1989). Coauthored with Joseph F. McConkie.

18. *The Man Adam* (Salt Lake City: Bookcraft, 1990). Coedited with Joseph F. McConkie.

19. *Life in Christ: Discovering the Transforming Power of the Savior* (Salt Lake City: Bookcraft, 1990).

20. *Leben Im Jenseits* (LDS Books, Schubert & Roth OHG, Bad Reichenhall, 1990). Coauthored with Joseph F. McConkie.

21. *An Eye Single to the Glory of God: Reflections on the Cost of Discipleship* (Salt Lake City: Deseret Book, 1991).

22. *Per Mensch Adam* (LDS Books, Schubert & Roth OHG, Bad Reichenhall, 1991). Coedited with Joseph F. McConkie.

23. *Doctrinal Commentary on the Book of Mormon*, vol. 3: *Alma through Helaman* (Salt Lake City: Bookcraft, 1991). Coauthored with Joseph F. McConkie.

24. *El Espiritu Santo* (Buenos Aires: Deseret Sudamerica, 1991). Coauthored with Joseph F. McConkie.

25. *Adan: El Hombre* (Buenos Aires: Deseret Sudamerica, 1991). Coedited with Joseph F. McConkie.

26. *Doctrinal Commentary on the Book of Mormon*, vol. 4: *Third Nephi through Moroni* (Salt Lake City: Bookcraft, 1992). Coauthored with Joseph F. McConkie and Brent L. Top.

27. *Steadfast and Immovable: Striving for Spiritual Maturity* (Salt Lake City: Deseret Book, 1992).

28. *Our Destiny: The Call and Election of the House of Israel* (Salt Lake City: Bookcraft, 1993). Coauthored with Joseph F. McConkie.

29. *The Power of the Word: Saving Doctrines from the Book of Mormon* (Salt Lake City: Deseret Book, 1994).

30. *Christ-Centered Living* (Salt Lake City: Bookcraft, 1994).

31. *Within Reach* (Salt Lake City: Deseret Book, 1995).

32. *Plain and Precious Truths Restored: The Doctrinal and Historical Significance of the Joseph Smith Translation* (Salt Lake City: Bookcraft, 1995). Coedited with Robert J. Matthews.

33. *When a Child Wanders* (Salt Lake City: Deseret Book, 1996).

34. *Joseph Smith: The Choice Seer* (Salt Lake City: Bookcraft, 1996). Coauthored with Joseph F. McConkie.

35. *Alive in Christ: The Miracle of Spiritual Rebirth* (Salt Lake City: Deseret Book, 1997).

36. *The Mormon Faith: A New Look at Christianity* (Salt Lake City: Shadow Mountain, 1998.)

37. *Latter-day Christianity: Ten Basic Issues* (Provo, UT: FARMS and Religious Studies Center, 1998). Coedited with Noel B. Reynolds.

38. *Life After Death* (Salt Lake City: Deseret Book, 1999).

39. *C. S. Lewis: The Man and His Message, A Latter-day Saint Perspective* (Salt Lake City: Bookcraft, 1999). Coedited with Andrew C. Skinner.

40. *Parables and Other Teaching Stories* (Salt Lake City: Shadow Mountain, 1999). Text by Robert L. Millet, artwork by James C. Christensen.

41. *Selected Writings of Robert L. Millet* (Salt Lake City: Deseret Book, 2000).

42. *More Holiness Give Me* (Salt Lake City: Deseret Book, 2001).

43. *Lost and Found: Reflections on the Prodigal Son* (Salt Lake City: Deseret Book, 2001).

44. *"I Will Fear No Evil": How the Lord Sustains Us in Perilous Times* (Salt Lake City: Bookcraft, 2002).

45. *Jesus, the Very Thought of Thee: Daily Reflections on the New Testament* (Salt Lake City: Eagle Gate, 2002). Coauthored with Lloyd D. Newell.

46. *Grace Works* (Salt Lake City: Deseret Book, 2003).

47. *"And When Ye Shall Receive These Things": Daily Reflections on the Book of Mormon* (Salt Lake City: Deseret Book, 2003). Coauthored with Lloyd D. Newell.

48. *Getting at the Truth: Responding to Difficult Questions about LDS Beliefs* (Salt Lake City: Deseret Book, 2004).

49. *"Draw Near Unto Me": Daily Reflections on the Doctrine and Covenants* (Salt Lake City: Deseret Book, 2004). Coauthored with Lloyd D. Newell.

50. *A Different Jesus? The Christ of the Latter-day Saints* (Grand Rapids: Eerdmans, 2005).

51. *Salvation in Christ: Comparative Christian Views* (Provo, UT: Religious Studies Center, 2005). Coedited with Roger R. Keller.

52. *Are We There Yet?* (Salt Lake City: Deseret Book, 2005).

53. *A Lamp Unto My Feet: Daily Reflections on the Old Testament* (Salt Lake City: Deseret Book, 2005). Coauthored with Lloyd D. Newell.

54. *Men of Valor: The Powerful Impact of a Righteous Man* (Salt Lake City: Deseret Book, 2007).

55. *The Vision of Mormonism: Pressing the Boundaries of Christianity* (St. Paul, Minnesota: Paragon House, 2007).

56. *Claiming Christ: A Mormon-Evangelical Debate* (Grand Rapids, Michigan: Brazos Press, 2007). Coauthored with Gerald R. McDermott.

57. *What Happened to the Cross? Distinctive LDS Teachings* (Salt Lake City: Deseret Book, 2007).

58. *Bridging the Divide: The Continuing Conversation Between a Mormon and an Evangelical* (Rhinebeck, New York: Monkfish Publishers, 2007). Coauthored with Gregory C. V. Johnson.

59. *Holding Fast: Dealing with Doubt in the Last Days* (Salt Lake City: Deseret Book, 2008).

60. *Men of Influence: The Power of the Priesthood to Lift the World* (Salt Lake City: Deseret Book, 2009).

61. *Talking with God: Divine Conversations That Transform Daily Life* (Salt Lake City: Deseret Book, 2010).

62. *Modern Mormonism: Myths and Realities* (Salt Lake City: Greg Kofford Books, 2010).

63. *By What Authority? The Vital Place of Religious Authority in Christianity* (Macon, GA: Mercer University Press, 2010). Edited.

64. *Making Sense of the Book of Revelation* (Salt Lake City: Deseret Book, 2011).

65. *LDS Beliefs: A Doctrinal Reference* (Salt Lake City: Deseret Book, 2011). Coauthored with Camille Fronk Olson, Andrew C. Skinner, and Brent L. Top.

66. *Lehi's Dream* (Salt Lake City: Deseret Book, 2011). Artwork by James C. Christensen.

67. *No Weapon Shall Prosper: New Light on Sensitive Issues* (Provo, UT: Religious Studies Center; Salt Lake City: Deseret Book, 2011). Edited.

68. *Coming to Know Christ* (Salt Lake City: Deseret Book, 2012).

69. *Living in the Eleventh Hour* (Salt Lake City: Deseret Book, 2014).

70. *Restored and Restoring: The Unfolding Drama of the Restoration* (Salt Lake City: Eborn Books, 2014).

71. *Living in the Millennium* (Salt Lake City: Deseret Book, 2014).

72. *Men of Covenant: Oaths, Covenants, and Transcendent Promises* (Salt Lake City: Deseret Book, 2015).

73. *Talking Doctrine: Mormons and Evangelicals in Conversation* (Downers Grove, IL: IVP Academic, 2015). Coedited with Richard J. Mouw.

74. *Mormonism: A Guide for the Perplexed* (London: Bloomsbury, 2015). Coauthored with Shon D. Hopkin.

75. *Joseph Smith: A Doctrinal Biography* (Salt Lake City: Deseret Book, 2016).

Articles and Book Chapters

1. "How the Bible Came to Be: Formation, Preservation, and Inspiration," *Third Annual Church Educational System Religious Educators' Symposium—Old Testament* (Salt Lake City: The Church of Jesus Christ of Latter-day Saints, 1979), 234–42.

2. "The Birth of the Messiah: A Closer Look at the Infancy Narrative of Matthew," in *Fourth Annual Church Educational System Religious Educators' Symposium—New Testament* (Salt Lake City: The Church of Jesus Christ of Latter-day Saints, 1980), 138–41.

3. "The Gospel and Psychotherapy: A Mormon Counselor's Dilemma," *Journal of the Association of Mormon Counselors and Psychotherapists*. Vol. 7, no. 2 (April 1981): 11–14, 35. Coauthored with Charles H. Madsen Jr.

4. "Joseph Smith's Eternalism: Foundations for a System of Psychotherapy," *Journal of the Association of Mormon Counselors and Psychotherapists*. Vol. 7, no. 4 (October 1981): 16–24. Coauthored with Charles H. Madsen Jr.

5. "The Vision of the Redemption of the Dead," in *Hearken, O Ye People*. Proceedings of the 1984 Sidney B. Sperry Symposium (Sandy, UT: Randall Book, 1984), 251–69.

6. "Walking in Newness of Life: The Epistle of Paul to the Romans," *Eighth Annual Church Educational System Religious Educators' Symposium—New Testament* (Salt Lake City: The Church of Jesus Christ of Latter-day Saints, 1984), 40–43.

7. "Joseph Smith's Translation of the Bible and the Doctrine and Covenants," in *Studies in Scripture*, 1:132–43.

8. "A Revelation on Priesthood," in *Studies in Scripture*, 1:309–25.

9. "Heavenly Manifestations in the Kirtland Temple," in *Studies in Scripture*, 1:417–31. Coauthored with Milton V. Backman Jr.

10. "A New and Everlasting Covenant," in *Studies in Scripture*, 1:512–25.

CURRICULUM VITAE

11. "Salvation Beyond the Grave," in *Studies in Scripture*, 1:549–63.

12. "A Small Book That Spans Eternity," in *Studies in Scripture*, 2:3–9.

13. "Enoch and His City," in *Studies in Scripture*, 2:131–44.

14. "Joseph Smith's Translation of the Bible: A Historical Overview," in *The Joseph Smith Translation*, 23–49.

15. "The JST and the Synoptic Gospels: Literary Style," in *The Joseph Smith Translation*, 147–62.

16. "Looking Beyond the Mark: Insights from the JST into First Century Judaism," in *The Joseph Smith Translation*, 201–14.

17. "Beyond the Veil: Two Latter-day Visions," *Ensign*, October 1985, 9–13.

18. "Joseph Smith's Translation of the Bible and the Synoptic Problem," *John Whitmer Historical Association Journal* 5 (1985): 41–46.

19. "Joseph Smith and the Gospel of Matthew," *Brigham Young University Studies* 25, no. 3 (Summer 1985): 67–84.

20. "As Delivered from the Beginning: The Formation of the Canonical Gospels," *Apocryphal Writings and the Latter-day Saints*, ed. C. Wilfred Griggs (Provo, UT: Religious Studies Center, 1986), 199–213.

21. "Abinadi's Messianic Sermon," *Tenth Annual Church Educational System Religious Educators' Symposium—Book of Mormon* (Salt Lake City: The Church of Jesus Christ of Latter-day Saints, 1986), 97–103.

22. "The Brass Plates: An Inspired and Expanded Version of the Old Testament," in *The Old Testament and the Latter-day Saints*. Proceedings of the 1986 Sidney B. Sperry Symposium (Sandy, UT: Randall Book, 1986), 409–37.

23. "The Testimony of Matthew," in *Studies in Scripture*, 5:38–60.

24. "The Birth and Childhood of the Messiah," in *Studies in Scripture*, 5:140–59.

25. "Treading the Winepress Alone," in *Studies in Scripture*, 5:430–39.

26. "Joseph Smith and the New Testament," *Ensign*, December 1986, 28–34.

27. "The Saga of the New Testament Church," in *Studies in Scripture*, 6:1–11.

28. "The Just Shall Live by Faith," in *Studies in Scripture*, 6:45–56.

29. "Looking Beyond the Mark: Why Many Did Not Accept the Messiah," *Ensign*, July 1987, 60–64.

30. I HAVE A QUESTION, "Was baptism for the dead a non-Christian practice in New Testament times (see 1 Cor. 15:29), or was it a practice of the Church of Jesus Christ, as it is today?" *Ensign*, July 1987, 60–64.

31. "Nephi on the Destiny of Israel," in *Studies in Scripture*, vol. 7: *1 Nephi to Alma 29*, ed. Kent P. Jackson (Salt Lake City: Deseret Book, 1987), 73–85.

32. "Redemption through the Holy Messiah," in *Studies in Scripture*, 7:115–30.

33. "How Should Our Story Be Told?," in *"To Be Learned Is Good If..."*, 1–8.

34. "Joseph Smith, the Book of Mormon, and the Nature of God," in *"To Be Learned Is Good If..."*, 59–76.

35. "Biblical Criticism and the Four Gospels: A Critical Look," in *To Be Learned Is Good If...,"* 187–204.

36. "The Plates of Brass: A Witness of Christ," *Ensign*, January 1988, 26–29.

37. "Joseph Smith's Translation of the Bible: Impact on Mormon Theology," *Religious Studies and Theology* 7, no. 1 (February 1988): 43–53.

38. "The Ministry of the Father and the Son," in *The Book of Mormon: The Keystone Scripture*, ed. Paul R. Cheesman (Provo, UT: Religious Studies Center, 1988), 44–72.

39. "Another Testament of Jesus Christ," in *The Book of Mormon: First Nephi, The Doctrinal Foundation*, ed. Monte S. Nyman and Charles D. Tate Jr. (Provo, UT: Religious Studies Center, 1988), 161–75.

40. "The Path of Repentance," in *Studies in Scripture*, vol. 8: *Alma 30 to Moroni*, ed. Kent P. Jackson (Salt Lake City: Deseret Book, 1988), 48–55.

41. "Justice, Mercy, and the Life Beyond," in *Studies in Scripture*, 8:56–68.

42. "Learning the Spirit of Revelation," in *The Capstone of Our Religion: Insights into the Doctrine and Covenants*, 41–62.

43. "A New and Everlasting Covenant of Marriage," in *The Capstone of Our Religion: Doctrinal Themes from the Doctrine and Covenants*, 163–82.

44. "Latter-day Insights into the Life Beyond," in *The Capstone of Our Religion: Doctrinal Themes from the Doctrine and Covenants*, 197–215.

45. "The Influence of the Brass Plates on the Teachings in Second Nephi," in *The Book of Mormon: Second Nephi, The Doctrinal Structure*, ed. Monte S. Nyman and Charles D. Tate Jr. (Provo, UT: Religious Studies Center, 1989), 207–25.

46. "Quest for the City of God: The Doctrine of Zion in Modern Revelation," in *Doctrines for Exaltation*. Proceedings of the 1989 Sidney B. Sperry Symposium (Salt Lake City: Deseret Book, 1989), 169–85.

47. "Joseph Smith and Modern Mormonism: Orthodoxy, Neo-Orthodoxy, Tension, and Tradition," *Brigham Young University Studies* 29, no. 3 (Summer 1989): 49–68.

48. "Adam in Eden: The Creation," in *The Man Adam*, 11–24.

49. "Adam: A Latter-day Saint Perspective," in *The Man Adam*, 189–93.

50. "The Supreme Power Over All Things: The Doctrine of the Godhead in the Lectures on Faith," in *The Lectures on Faith in Historical Perspective*,

ed. Larry E. Dahl and Charles D. Tate Jr. (Provo, UT: Religious Studies Center, 1990), 221–40.

51. "Sherem the Anti-Christ," *The Book of Mormon: Jacob through Words of Mormon, To Learn with Joy*, ed. Monte S. Nyman and Charles D. Tate Jr. (Provo, UT: Religious Studies Center, 1990), 175–91.

52. "The House of Israel: From Everlasting to Everlasting," in *A Witness of Jesus Christ*. Proceedings of the 1989 Sidney B. Sperry Symposium (Salt Lake City: Deseret Book, 1990), 178–99.

53. "The Gathering of Israel in the Book of Mormon: A Consistent Pattern," in *Rediscovering the Book of Mormon*, ed. John L. Sorenson and Melvin J. Thorne (Salt Lake City: Deseret Book and FARMS, 1991), 186–96.

54. "The Natural Man: An Enemy to God," in *The Book of Mormon: The Book of Mosiah, Salvation Only through Christ*, ed. Monte S. Nyman and Charles D. Tate Jr. (Provo, UT: Religious Studies Center, 1991), 139–59.

55. "Jesus Christ: Overview," in *Encyclopedia of Mormonism*, 5 vols. (New York: Macmillan, 1992), 2:724–26.

56. "Jesus Christ, Fatherhood and Sonship of," in *Encyclopedia of Mormonism*. 2:739–40.

57. "Alma II," in *Encyclopedia of Mormonism*, 1:33–35.

58. "Putting Off the Natural Man, An Enemy to God," *Ensign*, June 1992, 7–9.

59. "The Love of God and All Men: The Doctrine of Charity in the Book of Mormon," in *Doctrines of the Book of Mormon*. Proceedings of the 1991 Sidney B. Sperry Symposium (Salt Lake City: Deseret Book, 1992), 127–44.

60. "The Holy Order of God," in *The Book of Mormon: Alma, The Testimony of the Word*, ed. Monte S. Nyman and Charles D. Tate Jr. (Provo, UT: Religious Studies Center, 1992), 61–88.

CURRICULUM VITAE

61. "BYU As a Covenant Community: Implications for Excellence, Distinctiveness, and Academic Freedom," Religious Education Faculty Lecture, October 29, 1992, 63 pp.

62. "So Glorious a Record," *Ensign*, December 1992, 7–11.

63. "From Translations to Revelations: Joseph Smith's Translation of the Bible and the Doctrine and Covenants," in *Regional Studies in Latter-day Saint History: New York* (Provo, UT: BYU Department of Church History and Doctrine, 1992), 214–34.

64. "The Only Sure Foundation: Building on the Rock of Our Redeemer," *The Book of Mormon: Helaman through 3 Nephi 8, According to Thy Word*, ed. Monte S. Nyman and Charles D. Tate Jr. (Provo, UT: Religious Studies Center, 1992), 15–37.

65. "Knowledge by Faith: A Concept of Higher Education in Zion," *Second Annual Symposium on Laying the Foundations in Education at BYU*, ed. A. LeGrand Richards and Valerie Holladay (Provo, UT: Brigham Young University, March 1992), 33–40.

66. "The Revelations of the Restoration: Window to the Past, Open Door to the Future," in *The Heavens Are Open*. Proceedings of the 1992 Sidney B. Sperry Symposium (Salt Lake City: Deseret Book, 1993), 17–33.

67. "Joseph Smith Among the Prophets," in *Joseph Smith: The Prophet, the Man*, ed. Susan E. Black and Charles D. Tate Jr. (Provo, UT: Religious Studies Center, 1993), 15–31.

68. "This Is My Gospel," in *The Book of Mormon: 3 Nephi 9–30, This Is My Gospel*, ed. Monte S. Nyman and Charles D. Tate Jr. (Provo, UT: Religious Studies Center, 1993), 1–24.

69. "The Book of Mormon, Historicity, and Faith," in *Journal of Book of Mormon Studies* 2, no. 2 (Fall 1993): 1–13.

70. "The Man Adam," *Ensign*, January 1994, 8–15.

71. "Honoring His Holy Name," *Ensign*, March 1994, 6–11.

72. "By What (Whose) Standards Shall We Judge the Text? A Closer Look at Jesus Christ in the Book of Mormon," in *Review of Books on the Book of Mormon* 6, no. 1 (1994): 187–99.

73. "The Revelation of the Doctrine of Zion," in *Regional Studies in Latter-day Saint Church History: Missouri*, ed. Arnold K. Garr and Clark V. Johnson (Provo, UT: Department of Church History and Doctrine, 1994), 233–40.

74. "Life in the Millennium," in *Watch and Be Ready: Preparing for the Second Coming of the Lord* (Salt Lake City: Deseret Book, 1994), 167–91.

75. "Walking in Newness of Life: Doctrinal Themes of the Apostle Paul," in *The Apostle Paul—His Life and His Testimony*. Proceedings of the 1994 Sidney B. Sperry Symposium (Salt Lake City: Deseret Book, 1994), 132–50.

76. "Alive in Christ: The Salvation of Little Children," in *The Book of Mormon: Fourth Nephi through Moroni, From Zion to Destruction*, ed. Monte S. Nyman and Charles D. Tate Jr. (Provo, UT: Religious Studies Center, 1995), 1–17.

77. "Praise to the Man: Loyalty to the Prophet Joseph Smith," in *Regional Studies in Latter-day Saint Church History: Illinois*, ed. H. Dean Garrett (Provo, UT: Department of Church History and Doctrine, 1995), 1–11.

78. "The Joseph Smith Translation, the Pearl of Great Price, and the Book of Mormon," in *Plain and Precious Truths Restored: The Doctrinal and Historical Significance of the Joseph Smith Translation*, ed. Robert L. Millet and Robert J. Matthews (Salt Lake City: Bookcraft, 1995), 134–46.

79. "Hard Questions about the Joseph Smith Translation," in *Plain and Precious Truths Restored*, 147–62.

80. "The Educational System of The Church of Jesus Christ of Latter-day Saints," in *Religious Higher Education in the United States: A Source Book* (New York: Garland Publishing, 1996), 49–68.

81. "The Regeneration of Fallen Man," in *Nurturing Faith through the Book of Mormon*. Proceedings of the 24th Annual Sidney B. Sperry Symposium, ed. Paul H. Peterson (Salt Lake City: Deseret Book, 1995), 119–48.

82. "Knowledge by Faith," in *Expressions of Faith: Testimonies of Latter-day Saint Scholars*, ed. Susan E. Black (Deseret Book, 1996), 91–101.

83. "So Glorious a Record," *Liahona*, February 1996, 14–20.

84. "The Eternal Gospel," *Ensign*, July 1996, 48–56.

85. "The Second Coming of Christ: Questions and Answers," in *The Doctrine and Covenants: A Book of Answers*. Proceedings of the 25th Annual Sidney B. Sperry Symposium, ed. Leon R. Hartshorn, Dennis A. Wright, and Craig J. Ostler (Salt Lake City: Deseret Book, 1996), 205–25.

86. "Remember the Sabbath Day, to Keep It Holy," in *The Ten Commandments for Today*, ed. John G. Scott (Salt Lake City: Bookcraft, 1997), 67–77.

87. "Prophets and Priesthood in the Old Testament," in *Voices of Old Testament Prophets*. Proceedings of the 26th Annual Sidney B. Sperry Symposium (Salt Lake City: Deseret Book, 1997), 192–215.

88. "The Man Adam," *Liahona*, February 1998, 14–23.

89. "The Ancient Covenant Restored: The Prophet Joseph Smith and the Promises Made to the Fathers," *Ensign*, March 1998, 36–45.

90. "Honoring His Holy Name," *Liahona*, April 1998, 18–24.

91. "The Ministry of the Holy Ghost," in *The Testimony of John the Beloved*. Proceedings of the 27th Annual Sidney B. Sperry Symposium (Salt Lake City: Deseret Book, 1998), 167–85.

92. "'After All We Can Do': The Meaning of Grace in Our Lives," in *May Christ Lift Thee Up*. Proceedings of the 1998 Women's Conference (Salt Lake City: Deseret Book, 1999), 53–71.

93. "C. S. Lewis, The Man and His Message," in *C. S. Lewis. The Man and His Message: A Latter-day Saint Perspective*, ed. Andrew C. Skinner and Robert L. Millet (Salt Lake City: Bookcraft, 1999), 1–7.

94. "C. S. Lewis on the Transformation of Human Nature," in *C. S. Lewis: The Man and His Message*, 143–55.

95. "The Doctrine of Faith," in *The Book of Mormon: The Foundation of Our Faith*. Proceedings of the 28th Sidney B. Sperry Symposium (Salt Lake City: Deseret Book, 1999), 13–23.

96. "The Son of Man," in *The Redeemer: Reflections on the Life and Teachings of Jesus the Christ* (Salt Lake City: Deseret Book, 2000), 1–38.

97. "A New Millennium, A New Religious Landscape," in *Genesis and the Millennium: An Essay on Religious Pluralism in the Twenty-first Century*, ed. Derek H. Davis (Waco, TX: J. M. Dawson Institute of Church-State Studies, Baylor University, 2000), 57–64.

98. "Bearing Pure Testimony," *Religious Educator: Perspectives on the Restored Gospel* 1, no. 1 (2000): 25–46.

99–104. Entries in *Encyclopedia of Latter-day Saint History*, ed. Arnold K. Garr, Donald Q. Cannon, and Richard O. Cowan (Salt Lake City: Deseret Book, 2000):
- Dispensation of the Fulness of Times
- Elias
- Jesus Christ
- Pearl of Great Price
- Vision of the Redemption of the Dead
- Zion

105. "Reproving with Sharpness—When?," *Religious Educator: Perspectives on the Restored Gospel* 2, no. 1 (2001): 83–93. Coauthored with Lloyd D. Newell.

106. "The Historical Jesus: A Latter-day Saint Perspective," in *Historicity and the Latter-day Saint Scriptures*, ed. Paul Y. Hoskisson (Provo, UT: Religious Studies Center, 2001), 171–96.

107. "The Soteriological Problem of Evil," *Religious Educator: Perspectives on the Restored Gospel* 2, no. 2 (2001): 73–82.

108. "A Different Jesus? The Christ of the Restoration," in *Jesus Christ: Son of God, Savior*, ed. Paul H. Peterson, Gary L. Hatch, and Laura D. Card (Provo, UT: Religious Studies Center, 2002), 176–206.

109. "Outreach: Opening the Door or Giving Away the Store?," *Religious Educator: Perspectives on the Restored Gospel* 4, no. 1 (2003): 55–73.

110. "The Doctrine of Merit: The Book of Mormon on the Work of Grace," in *The Fulness of the Gospel: Foundational Teachings from the Book of Mormon*. Proceedings of the 32nd Annual Sidney B. Sperry Symposium (Salt Lake City: Deseret Book and Religious Studies Center, 2003), 111–33.

111–133. The following entries appeared in *Book of Mormon Reference Companion*, ed. Dennis L. Largey (Salt Lake City: Deseret Book, 2003).
- Faith
- Salvation Is Free
- Children of Christ
- Rely
- Jesus Christ, Role as Father and Son
- Alive in Christ
- Doctrine
- In the First Place
- Forbidden Fruit
- Fulness of the Gospel
- Book of Mormon, Record of a Fallen People
- Cross Yourself
- Tongue of Angels
- Sanctified in the Flesh

- Hope
- The Gathering of Israel
- Godhead
- Born Again
- Brass Plates
- The Fall of Adam and Eve
- Book of Mormon, Relation to JST
- Natural Man
- Book of Mormon, Sign of the Father's Work

134. "What Is Our Doctrine?," *Religious Educator: Perspectives on the Restored Gospel* 4, no. 3 (2003): 15–33.

135. "An Everlasting Covenant: The Old Testament through the Lenses of the Restoration," *Religious Educator: Perspectives on the Restored Gospel* 5, no. 1 (2004): 56–69.

136. "The Process of Salvation," in *Salvation in Christ: Comparative Christian Views*, ed. Roger R. Keller and Robert L. Millet (Provo, UT: Religious Studies Center, 2005), 141–81.

137. "Standing in Holy Places—As Individuals and Families," in *Helping and Healing Our Families*, ed. Craig H. Hart, Lloyd D. Newell, Elaine Walton, and David C. Dollahite (Provo, UT: BYU School of Family Life and Deseret Book, 2005), 7–11.

138. "When Children Choose a Different Path," in *Helping and Healing our Families*, ed. Craig H. Hart, Lloyd D. Newell, Elaine Walton, and David C. Dollahite (Provo, UT: BYU School of Family Life and Deseret Book, 2005), 223–27.

139. "Joseph Smith's Christology: After 200 Years," *Brigham Young University Studies* 44, no. 4 (2005): 231–50; also in *The Worlds of Joseph Smith: A Bicentennial Conference at the Library of Congress* (Provo, UT: Brigham Young University Press, 2006), 231–50.

140. "Joseph Smith and 'The Only True and Living Church,'" *A Witness for the Restoration: Essays in Honor of Robert J. Matthews*, ed. Kent

P. Jackson and Andrew C. Skinner (Provo, UT: Religious Studies Center, 2007), 201–31.

141. "How We Know: The Delicate Relationship Between Evidence and Faith," in *A Twenty-Something's Guide to Spirituality*, ed. Jacob Werrett and David Read (Salt Lake City: Deseret Book, 2007), 28–46.

142. "The Most Correct Book: Joseph Smith's Appraisal," in *Living the Book of Mormon: Abiding by Its Precepts*. Proceedings of the 36th Annual Sidney B. Sperry Symposium, ed. Gaye Strathearn and Charles Swift (Provo, UT: Religious Studies Center; Salt Lake City: Deseret Book, 2007), 55–71.

143. "The Prophets and the Restoration of Integrity," in *Moral Foundations: Standing Firm in a World of Shifting Values*, ed. Douglas E. Brinley, Perry W. Carter, and James K. Archibald (Provo, UT: Religious Studies Center, 2007), 47–65.

144. "What Do We Really Believe? Identifying Doctrinal Parameters Within Mormonism," in *Discourses in Mormon Theology*, ed. James M. McLaughlan and Loyd Ericson (Salt Lake City: Greg Kofford Books, 2007), 265–81.

145. "Glorying in the Cross of Christ," in *Behold the Lamb of God: An Easter Celebration*, ed. Richard Neitzel Holzapfel, Frank F. Judd Jr., and Thomas A. Wayment (Provo, UT: Religious Studies Center, 2008), 125–38.

146. "Joseph Smith and the Rise of a World Religion," *Global Mormonism in the 21st Century*, ed. Reid L. Neilson (Provo, UT: Religious Studies Center, 2008), 3–29.

147. "The Quest for Virtue," *Church News*, December 27, 2008, 3, 13.

148. "For Heaven's Sake: A Review of N. T. Wright's *Surprised by Hope*," *Religious Educator: Perspectives on the Restored Gospel* 10, no. 3 (2009): 219–35.

149. "The Christlike Life," *LDS Church News*, January 2, 2010, 5, 14.

150. "A Latter-day Saint Perspective on Biblical Inerrancy," *Religious Educator: Perspectives on the Restored Gospel* 11, no. 1 (2010); 77–89.

151. "Doctrines, Covenants, and Sweet Consolation, 1843," in *Joseph Smith, the Prophet and Seer*, ed. Richard Neitzel Holzapfel and Kent P. Jackson (Provo, UT: Religious Studies Center, 2010), 467–93.

152. "The Book of Mormon, Historicity, and Faith," *The Book of Mormon and Other Restoration Scriptures* 18, no. 2 (2009): 70–76.

153. "Starving Our Doubts and Feeding Our Faith," *Religious Educator: Perspectives on the Restored Gospel* 11, no. 2 (2010): 105–19.

154. "By Their Fruits Ye Shall Know Them," *The Sermon on the Mount in Latter-day Scripture*. Proceedings of the 39th Annual Sidney B. Sperry Symposium, ed. Gaye Strathearn, Thomas A. Wayment, and Daniel L. Belnap (Provo, UT: Religious Studies Center; Salt Lake City: Deseret Book, 2010), 215–229.

155. "Trust Begins with Each of Us," *Church News*, January 1, 2011, 5, 13.

156. "What We Worship," in *My Redeemer Lives*, Brigham Young University Easter Conference, ed. Richard Neitzel Holzapfel and Kent P. Jackson (Provo, UT: Religious Studies Center; Salt Lake City: Deseret Book, 2011), 69–90.

157. "The Quest for Truth: Science and Religion in the Best of All Worlds," *Converging Paths to Truth*, ed. Michael D. Rhodes and J. Ward Moody (Provo, UT: Religious Studies Center; Salt Lake City: Deseret Book, 2011), 79–99.

158. "Feeding the Flock of God: The Vital Role of Sensitive and Loving Priesthood Leaders," in *Voice(s) of Hope: Latter-day Saint Perspectives on Same-Gender Attraction—An Anthology of Gospel Teachings and Personal Essays*, comp. Ty Mansfield (Salt Lake City: Deseret Book, 2011), 258–70.

159. "Teach One Another," *Church News*, December 31, 2011, 3, 15.

160. "Reflections on Apostasy and Restoration," in *No Weapon Shall Prosper: New Light on Sensitive Issues*, ed. Robert L. Millet (Provo, UT: Religious Studies Center; Salt Lake City: Deseret Book, 2011), 19–41.

161. "A Latter-day Saint Perspective on Biblical Inerrancy," in *No Weapon Shall Prosper*, 123–40.

162. "Jesus Christ and Salvation," in *No Weapon Shall Prosper*, 329–44.

163. "God and Man," in *No Weapon Shall Prosper*, 345–78.

164. "Joseph Smith Encounters Calvinism," *BYU Studies* 50, no. 4 (2011): 5–32.

165. "Reconciling the Irreconcilable: Joseph Smith and the Enigma of Mormonism," in *Bountiful Harvest: Essays in Honor of S. Kent Brown*, ed. Andrew C. Skinner, D. Morgan Davis, and Carl Griffin (Provo, UT: Neal A. Maxwell Institute, 2011), 223–46.

166. "Latter-day Saint Christianity," *Religious Educator: Perspectives on the Restored Gospel* 13, no. 1 (2012): 55–67.

167. "The Praying Savior: Insights from the Gospel of 3 Nephi," in *Third Nephi: An Incomparable Scripture*, ed. Andrew C. Skinner and Gaye Strathearn (Provo, UT: Neal A. Maxwell Institute; Salt Lake City: Deseret Book, 2012), 131–46.

168. "Lost and Found: Pondering the Parable of the Prodigal Son," *Studies in the Bible and Antiquity* 4 (2012): 95–115.

169–186. The following entries appeared in the *Doctrine and Covenants Reference Companion*, ed. Dennis L. Largey (Salt Lake City: Deseret Book, 2012):
- Apostasy
- Born of Me
- Christ, Merits of
- City of the Living God
- Glory

- Grace
- Innocent
- Innocent Blood
- Law of the Celestial Kingdom
- New Jerusalem
- Only True and Living Church
- Parable Regarding Lord's Visit to Kingdoms
- Salvation for the Dead
- Sanctify
- Spirit World
- Zion
- Zion of Enoch
- Zion, Redemption of

187. "The Mormon-Evangelical Dialogue," in *The Wiley-Blackwell Companion to Inter-Religious Dialogue*, ed. Catherine Cornille (Oxford: Wiley Blackwell, 2013), 468–78.

188. "How Miracles Are Wrought: Reflections on Faith, Prayer, and Priesthood," *Religious Educator: Perspectives on the Restored Gospel* 14, no. 2 (2013): 11–27.

189. "Leadership within the Church of Jesus Christ of Latter-day Saints," in *Religious Leadership: A Reference Handbook*, 2 vols., ed. Sharon Henderson Callahan (Los Angeles: Sage Publications, 2013), 1:209–15. Coauthored with John Hilton III.

190. "Sacramental Living: Reflections on Latter-day Saint Ritual," in *By Our Rites of Worship*, ed. Daniel L. Belnap (Provo, UT: Religious Studies Center; Salt Lake City: Deseret Book, 2013), 401–17.

191. "What Is Our Doctrine?," in *Common Ground, Different Opinions: Latter-day Saints and Contemporary Issues*, ed. Justin F. White and James E. Faulconer (Salt Lake City: Greg Kofford Books, 2013), 13–33.

192. "The Perils of Grace," *BYU Studies Quarterly* 53, no. 2 (2014): 7–19.

193. "Engaging Intellect and Feeding Faith: A Conversation with Robert L. Millet," interview by Lloyd D. Newell, *Religious Educator: Perspectives on the Restored Gospel* 15, no. 2 (2014): 133–45.

194. "Make Your Calling and Election Sure," in *The Ministry of Peter, the Chief Apostle*. Proceedings of the 43rd Annual Sidney B. Sperry Symposium (Salt Lake City: Deseret Book, 2014), 267–82.

195. "Fostering Real Growth," *Church News*, December 28, 2014, 5.

Acknowledgments

This volume resulted in part from the originating vision of M. Gerald Bradford, executive director of the Neal A. Maxwell Institute for Religious Scholarship at Brigham Young University. Jerry first suggested honoring our colleague Robert Millet with a collection of essays and we have been grateful collaborators in the effort.

We acknowledge the excellence of the three institutions co-publishing this collection. Their staffs have been enthusiastic supporters of the project from the outset and have blended their experience and skill to produce a marvelous tribute: Thomas Wayment, Brent Nordgren, Devan Jensen, Joany Pinegar, Rebecca Bird, Alison Brimley, Shanna D'Avila, Madison Swapp, and Leah Welker at BYU's Religious Studies Center, Gerald Bradford and Joe Bonyata at the Maxwell Institute, and Lisa Roper at Deseret Book Company.

Lastly, we acknowledge Shauna Millet. Those of us who know Bob well understand the depth of his dependence on her support and love. Across a long and busy career in Church education and academia, she has been a steadying and enlivening influence on Bob. Those of us who love him are especially grateful to her!

Contributors

Richard E. Bennett, professor and chair of the Department of Church History and Doctrine at Brigham Young University, is the author of *Mormons at the Missouri: Winter Quarters, 1846–1852* (Norman: University of Oklahoma, 1987, repr., 2004) and its sequel volume, *We'll Find the Place: The Mormon Exodus, 1846–1848* (Norman: University of Oklahoma, 1997, repr., 2009).

Brian D. Birch is director of the Religious Studies Program at Utah Valley University, editor of the *Perspectives on Mormon Theology* series (Greg Kofford Books) and founding editor of *Element: The Journal of the Society for Mormon Philosophy and Theology.*

Craig L. Blomberg is Distinguished Professor of New Testament at Denver Seminary, author or editor of twenty-two books, including most recently *Christians in an Age of Wealth: A Biblical Theology of Stewardship* (Grand Rapids, MI: Zondervan, 2013) and *Can We Still Believe the Bible? An Evangelical Engagement with Contemporary Questions* (Ada, MI: Brazos, 2014).

Richard O. Cowan was a full-time faculty member for fifty-three years and is a professor emeritus of Church history and doctrine at Brigham Young University and author of books dealing with Latter-day Saint temples, history, and doctrine.

Larry E. Dahl is a professor emeritus of Church history and doctrine at Brigham Young University, author of many published articles and several books, and most recently senior editor of the nine-hundred-page *Doctrine and Covenants Reference Companion* (Salt Lake City: Deseret Book, 2012).

J. Spencer Fluhman is an associate professor of history at Brigham Young University, author of the award-winning *"A Peculiar People": Anti-Mormonism and the Making of Religion in Nineteenth-Century America* (Chapel Hill: UNC, 2012), and editor of *Mormon Studies Review*.

Camille Fronk Olson is professor of ancient scripture at Brigham Young University, chair of the Department of Ancient Scripture, and author of *Women of the New Testament* (Salt Lake City: Deseret Book, 2014) and *Women of the Old Testament* (Salt Lake City: Deseret Book, 2009).

Megan Hansen has researched the Joseph Smith Papyri with Dr. Kerry Muhlestein for years and is a grade school teacher in Utah Valley.

J. B. Haws is an assistant professor of Church history and doctrine at Brigham Young University and author of the award-winning *Mormon Image in the American Mind: Fifty Years of Public Perception* (New York: Oxford, 2013).

Shon D. Hopkin is an assistant professor of ancient scripture at Brigham Young University, with research and publications focused on the Hebrew Bible, medieval Judaism, the Book of Mormon, and interfaith understanding.

Paul Y. Hoskisson is a retired professor of ancient scripture at Brigham Young University, former editor of the *Journal of the Book of Mormon and Other Restoration Scripture*, former associate dean of Religious Education, author of numerous articles on the LDS standard works, and former corporate member of the board of trustees of the American Schools of Oriental Research.

CONTRIBUTORS

Daniel K Judd is professor of ancient scripture at Brigham Young University (where he was department chair) and author of *The Fortunate Fall: Understanding the Blessings and Burdens of Adversity* (Salt Lake City: Deseret Book, 2011) and numerous essays exploring the relationship between religion and mental health.

Richard J. Mouw is a professor of faith and public life and former president of Fuller Theological Seminary in Pasadena, California. His recent books include *Talking with Mormons: An Invitation to Evangelicals* (Grand Rapids, MI: Wm. B. Eerdmans, 2012) and *Called to the Life of the Mind: Some Advice for Evangelical Scholars* (Grand Rapids, MI: Wm. B. Eerdmans, 2014).

Kerry Muhlestein is a professor of ancient scripture at Brigham Young University, author of many articles on the Book of Abraham, and director of the BYU Egypt Excavation Project.

Lloyd D. Newell is a professor of Church history and doctrine at Brigham Young University and author of more than a dozen books, including the *The Gospel of Second Chances* (Salt Lake City: Deseret Book, 2013).

Dennis L. Okholm is a professor of theology at Azusa Pacific University, affiliate professor at Fuller Theological Seminary, and author of *Monk Habits: Benedictine Spirituality for Everyday People* (Ada, MI: Brazos, 2007) and *Dangerous Passions, Deadly Sins: Learning Psychology from Ancient Monks* (Ada, MI: Brazos, 2014).

Dana M. Pike, professor of ancient scripture and ancient Near Eastern studies at Brigham Young University, was on the international team of editors for the Dead Sea Scrolls, and currently serves as associate dean of Religious Education at BYU.

Andrew C. Skinner is a professor of ancient scripture and Near Eastern studies at Brigham Young University, author or coauthor of twenty books, numerous articles, and editor of six volumes on religious and historical topics.

Stephen O. Smoot graduated cum laude from Brigham Young University with bachelor's degrees in ancient Near Eastern studies and German studies. He is an editorial consultant for *Interpreter: A Journal of Mormon Scripture* and has published with the Interpreter Foundation, the Neal A.

Maxwell Institute for Religious Scholarship, and the Religious Studies Center at BYU.

Brent L. Top is a professor of Church history and doctrine and dean of Religious Education at Brigham Young University.

John W. Welch is the Robert K. Thomas Professor of Law at Brigham Young University, editor in chief of *BYU Studies Quarterly*, and author of books and articles including *The Sermon on the Mount in the Light of the Temple* (Burlington, UT: Ashgate, 2009), *The Legal Cases in the Book of Mormon* (Provo, UT: FARMS, 2007), and "The Good Samaritan: A Type and Shadow of the Plan of Salvation" (1999).

Cory B. Willson is the Jake and Betsy Tuls Professor of Missiology and Missional Ministry at Calvin Theological Seminary. He is a PhD candidate at Fuller Theological Seminary and the Vrije Universiteit Amsterdam, NL. He is a contributing author to Rabbi Elliot Dorff's *The Jewish Approach to Repairing the World (*Tikkun Olam*): A Brief Introduction for Christians* (Woodstock, UT: Jewish Lights, 2008) and cofounding editor of *Evangelical Interfaith Dialogue* (www.fuller.edu/eifd).

Index

Abraham. *See also* Abrahamic covenant;
Book of Abraham, translation of
blessings for descendant of,
65–67
as friend of God, 125
Abrahamic covenant, 66–67, 365
Adam, creation of, 186n48
adoptionism, 20n20, 262, 267n45
agape, 122–24, 128, 131–33W
agency. *See also* freedom
and control over life, 45–49
importance of, 37–38
LDS views on, 255–57, 339–40
meaning of, 49n1
obedience and, 41–44
in parable of willing and unwilling
two sons, 105–6
paradoxes regarding, 39–41, 49

agency (*continued*)
and rejection of Light of Christ,
53–54
allegorical reading of parables, 99–100,
103–4
Alma the Younger, 38
Ames, William, 242
Ammon, 33, 38
anagogical reading of parables, 100,
104–11
Anselm, St., 243
anthropomorphisms, 279
apōleian, 350
apostasy, 234, 358–59
Arianism, 258–62
Aristotle, 122, 123
Arius, 259
Arminius, Jacob, 254–55

INDEX

astronomy, principles of, outlined in Abraham, 144–46
Atonement. *See also* salvation
    agency and, 255–56
    exaltation through, 73–75
    Fall and, 280
    LDS views on, 245–46
    salvation through, 333
Augustine, 253, 342
Augustinian monks, 315–16
authority
    in parable of willing and unwilling two sons, 104–6
    to perform baptism, 166

baptism
    Catholic rejection of Mormon, 249–50
    covenant of, 35
    early LDS teachings on Flood as, 165–70
    and earth as living entity, 173–78
    Flood of Noah viewed as, 164–65, 184n37, 185n43
    later LDS teachings on Flood as, 170–73
belief, web of, 363
Benjamin, King, 32, 181
Benson, Ezra Taft, xvi–xvii
Berry, Lowell, 295–96
Bible, coming to know Christ through, 83–84
birth, spirit, 8–12, 20n20, 260, 261, 262
blasphemy against Holy Ghost, 59
blessing(s)
    for Abraham and his descendants, 65–67

blessing(s) (*continued*)
    of Atonement, 73–75
    of eternal life, 70–73
    friendship as, 121
    of gift of Holy Ghost, 57–58
    requirements for, 75–78
    Resurrection as unconditional, 67–70
    unconditional, 256–57
    worthiness for, 67
body
    and degrees of glory, 69–70
    Resurrection and, 15, 16, 68
    spirit and, 12–14
Book of Abraham, translation of
    chronology of, 139, 142–46
    early efforts, 140–41
    evidence for 1842 translation of Abraham 3–5, 149–53
    extent of, 147–48
    later efforts, 141–42
    theory and evidence regarding, 153–57
Book of Mormon
    historicity of, 87
    Millet and literalistic appreciation of, xvi–xvii
    teachings on salvation in, 335–36
    as testament of Jesus Christ, 85–86
Book of Moses, 22n39, 174–75
bowl judgments, 214–15
"breath of life," 197–98
Brigham Young University, x–xiii, 293–94, 295, 296–97
Buddhism, 239
Bushman, Richard L., 303

BYU New Testament Commentary
    Series, 205–6
    interpretations at odds with later
        Mormon commentary, 208–11
    points of agreement with non-
        Mormon scholarship, 211–22
    sources in, 206–8

Call, Anson, 147
calling and election made sure, 58–61,
    62
Callister, Tad R., 180, 358–59
Calvin, John, 205
Calvinism, 241–43, 255
Cassian, John, 254
Catholicism, rejection of Mormon
    baptism, 249–50
celestial kingdom, 72–73, 334, 340–41,
    351
celestial law, 69, 179
Chandler, Michael, 140
charity, in friendship, 123–25, 128,
    131–33
Chesterton, G. K., 312–13
"Chicago Experiment," 294
children, obedience of, 102–3
Christian history, 84–86
Christianity. *See also* heresies
    and apostasy, 358–59
    center of, 363–67
    creedal, 249–53
    culturalist, 89
    defining, 359–60
    establishing identity of, 361–62
    existence of, before Christ, 369n29
    generic, 362–63

Christianity (*continued*)
    growth, grace, and sin in traditional,
        282–84
    Harnack on, 357–58
    Mormonism rejected as, 250–51
    Mormonism tethered to, 363
    N. T. Wright on, 368n23
    relationship of Mormonism to,
        235–37
    Scot McKnight on, 360–61
Christian Science, 241
Christocentrism, xvi, 345, 348
Chronicles of Narnia (Lewis), 347–48
Church of Jesus Christ of Latter-day
    Saints, The
    and center of Christianity, 365–67
    comparison of Protestant soteriology
        versus, 343–53
    as cult, 235, 291–92
    grace in soteriology of, 334–40
    growth of, 295
    history of, 81–93
    public perception of, 293–95,
        310n46
    soteriology of, 330–34
    tethered to Christianity, 363
Cohen, I. B., 294
Columbus, Christopher, 53
Comforter
    Holy Ghost as, 51–52
    Jesus Christ as, 62–63
commandments, obedience to, 27–28,
    41–44
community, importance of, 88–89
comparative religious studies, 270–71
competition, and friendship, 125–26

INDEX

confession, of Martin Luther, 316–17
consequences
    of obedience, 42
    of sin, 59–60
Council in Heaven, 106–11, 115n40, 146
Council of Nicea, 258–59
"countercult" movement, 234
counterfeit doctrines, 321–24
covenants
    and Holy Ghost's seal of approval, 58
    and implementation of gospel, 74–75
Cowdery, Oliver, 143, 147–48
creation
    of Adam, 186n48
    in Book of Abraham, 146, 150–51
    of humans in God's image, 272–77
    spiritual and temporal, 5
creedal Christianity, 249–53
Cross, Frank Moore, Jr., 299
cult label, 235, 291–92
culturalist Christianity, 89

damned, 336–37, 351
Davies, Douglas, 303
dead, redemption of, 14
Dead Sea Scrolls translation project, 299
death
    in Ecclesiastes 12:7, 195
    overcoming, 73
    second, 71, 337
    as separation of spirit and body, 13–14, 189–90, 199
deception, 91–92

decisions, making difficult, 47–49. *See also* agency
degrees of glory, 68–69, 333–43, 351–53
deification, 275–77, 280, 345
depression, 130
derek hārûaḥ, 196, 203n26
destiny, 45–46
Dillenberger, John, 297–98
discouragement, 77–78
dispensational futurism/premillennialism, 211–12
"doctrinal checklists" test, 240, 241
Doctrine and Covenants 76, 329–30, 335–40, 345–46, 349, 352–53
Dorff, Elliot, 270
dove, sign of, 64n13
Draper, Richard D., 205. *See also* BYU New Testament Commentary Series

earth
    as female, 186n47
    Flood as cleansing of inhabitants' sins, 181–82, 183n13
    as living entity, 171, 173–78
    new, 219
    and plan of salvation, 180–81
    reason for cleansing of, 178–80
    to wax old, 186–87n52
earthquake, 91
Ecclesiastes 12:7, 189–90, 198–99
    analysis of, 193–98
    broader context of, 192–93
    LDS views on, 190–92
Eck, Diana, 231, 232
ecumenical dialogue, 232, 233–34
Eddy, Mary Baker, 241

Eden, 278
egō, 109
Egyptian papyri, 140, 147–48. *See also* Book of Abraham, translation of
Ehrman, Bart, 220
Einstein, Albert, 126
Elias, 67
Ellis, Albert, 311–12
Elohim, 151–52
Emerson, Ralph Waldo, 241
Encyclopedia of Mormonism, 298–99
endowment, 77, 365
"Epistle to the Church," 145–46
"estate," 19n5
eternal life
    blessing of, 70–73
    and celestial glory, 351
    defined, 24
    and friendship of Jesus Christ, 134
    and knowing God and Jesus Christ, 26–27, 36n3
eternal progression, 273–74, 275–77, 280–84
eternal punishment, 267n44
ethical reading of parables, 99, 102–3
Evans, Richard L., 295
exaltation
    requirements for, 76–77
    versus salvation, 71–73
    through Atonement, 73–75

faith
    and Christian history, 84–85
    justification by, 320
    and parable of unprofitable servant, 29–34

Faith and Philosophy, 301
faith-promoting myths, 91–92
Fall
    Atonement and, 257, 280
    in Book of Abraham, 147–48, 160–61n7
    and cleansing of earth, 180
fasting, of Martin Luther, 317
fate, 45–46
"Father and the Son, The" document, 260
"first estate," 19n5
first resurrection, 69–70, 72
First Vision, 25, 86–87
Flood, 163–64
    as baptism, 184n37, 185n43
    as cleansing of sins of earth's inhabitants, 181–82, 183n13
    early LDS teachings on, 165–70
    and earth as living entity, 173–78
    later LDS teachings on, 170–73
    and plan of salvation, 180–81
    Protestant interpretations of, 164–65
    reason for, 178–80
Florida State University, ix
forgiveness
    Luther's search for, 315–21
    through repentance, 324–25
freedom, 253–54, 265n28. *See also* agency
free will. *See* agency
friendship, 117–18
    and environment of Millennium, 135–36
    Joseph Smith's view of, 118–20
    necessity of, 120–22
    as paradigm, 124–30
    philia and *agape*, 122–24

INDEX

friendship (*continued*)
   sacrifice in, 130–35

Garden of Eden, 278
Genesis 2:7, 197–98
Gentiles, 103–4
George, Cardinal Francis, 249
gifts of the Spirit, 56, 57
ginosko, 26, 27
Givens, Terryl L., 20n20, 303
glory, degrees of, 68–69, 333–43, 351–53
God. *See also* revelatory power of God
   Abraham as friend of, 125
   becoming like, 72
   at center of salvation, 331
   as consuming fire, 16–17
   debate on existence of, 243–44
   eternal nature of, 7
   hand of, 186n48
   and human progression, 273–74
   image of, 272–77
   instruments in hands of, 38–39
   intervention of, 46–47
   knowing, 24, 25–29, 36n3
   parable of unprofitable servant and knowing, 29–34
   in parable of willing and unwilling two sons, 105
   power of, 51–52
   presence of, 200n5, 344
   proximity of, 276–80
   reckoning of time of, 160–61n7
   relationship between Jesus Christ and, 258–61
   righteousness of, 319–20
   seeing, 55–56

God (*continued*)
   seeking guidance from, 47–49
   and separate nature of Godhead, 208–9
   spirits as children of, 9–12, 17–18, 20n19
   transformation through knowing, 23
   views on nature of, 240–46
   will of, 44, 106–11
Godhead
   unity of, 279
   views on nature of, 240–46, 258–62
gods, multiplicity of, 146, 151–52
goodness, of humans, 282–83
good Samaritan, 98
gospel
   based on law, 76–77
   covenants and implementation of, 74–75
   Harnack on, 357–58
grace
   counterfeit doctrines regarding, 321–24
   eternal progression through, 280–82, 284
   in evangelical versus LDS view of salvation, 364–65
   Luther's journey to, 319–20
   Mormon versus evangelical teachings on, 251–52
   and Pelagianism, 254
   prevenient, 255, 256–57
   in Protestant versus LDS soteriology, 330–34
   salvation through, 50n14, 320–21, 334–40

Graduate Theological Union (GTU), 297–98
"Grammar and Alphabet of the Egyptian Language" (GAEL), 144
guilt, of Martin Luther, 316–18

hagiasmos, 342–43
Harnack, Adolf von, 357–58
harvest of earth, in book of Revelation, 217
heaven, 337–38, 343–46
Hebrew aspects of Book of Abraham, 150–53
Hedlock, Reuben, 142–43
hell, 337, 346
heresies
    Arianism, 258–62
    creedal Christianity, 249–53
    Pelagianism, 253–58
historic premillennialism, 212
Holy Ghost
    blasphemy against, 59
    gift of, 56–58
    ratifying power of, 75
    as second phase of Light of Christ, 55–58
    as sign of dove, 64n13
    telestial glory and presence of, 344
    terms for, 51–52
Holy Spirit of Promise, 58, 75
homoian creed, 260
homoiousios, 259–60
How Wide the Divide? (Blomberg & Robinson), xiii
How Wide the Divide? (Millet and Johnson), 301–2
humans
    distance between God and, 277–80
    in God's image, 272–73, 274–76
    greatness and misery of, 282–83
    spiritual progression of, 273–77, 280–84
    views on nature of, 284–85
hypage, 105
hypostasis, 266n37

image of God, 272–77, 285
immortality, versus eternal life, 70–71
inclusivism, 347–49
indulgences, 318
instruments in God's hands, 38–39
intelligence(s), 4–9, 187n53, 261, 266n40. *See also* spirit(s)
interfaith dialogue, 233, 250–51, 287n14
interfaith work, xii–xv, 250. *See also* Richard L. Evans Chair of Religious Understanding
Isaac, 66
Islam, 236
Israel/Israelites, 103–4, 364–66, 368n22, 369n31
"I Stand All Amazed," 245–46

Jacob, 66–67, 181
Jeffery, Duane E., 178–79
Jeffress, Robert, 291–92
Jesus Christ. *See also* Atonement; Light of Christ; Spirit of Christ
    authority of, 104–5
    as center of Christianity, 363–67
    as eternal, 261–62, 266n40

INDEX

Jesus Christ (*continued*)
    as example of sacrifice in friendship, 130–35
    friendship of, 133–34
    as Great Exemplar, 34–35
    historicity of, 84–86
    immortality of soul possible through, 17
    as instrument in God's hands, 39
    knowing, 24, 25–27, 36n3, 83–84
    in LDS soteriology, 351–53
    meekness of, 127–28
    mind of, 28
    Nauvoo points to, 82
    obedience of, 43
    parable of unprofitable servant and knowing, 29–34
    in parable of willing and unwilling two sons, 106–11
    perfection through, 335
    relationship between God and, 258–61
    Resurrection of, 67–68
    and sealing up to eternal life, 60
    as second Comforter, 62–63
    seeing, 55–56
    and separate nature of Godhead, 208–9
    sin and distance from, 313
    submission of, to God's will, 44
    telestial glory and acceptance of, 346–49
    transformation through knowing, 23
    veiled meanings of, 112n5
Jews and Judaism
    look beyond mark, 314

Jews and Judaism (*continued*)
    and proximity of God, 277–80
    public perception of, 310n46
Job, 128–29
Job 27:3, 197
Johnson, Benjamin F., 120
Johnson, Greg, xiii–xiv, 301–2
John the Revelator, 211
Joseph Smith Translation, 207, 209–10, 339
joy, fulness of, 70
Judaism. *See* Jews and Judaism
judgment(s)
    in book of Revelation, 214–15
    in friendship, 128–29
just, resurrection of, 69–70, 72
justification by faith, 320, 331

Kaplan, Jerry, 299
Kimball, Heber C., 177
King Benjamin, 32, 181
King Follett discourse, 5–6, 18n1, 274
King James Version, 207, 209
Knight, Janice, 242
Knight, Joseph, Sr., 119
knowledge
    agency and, 43–44
    through temple work, 77
Kolob, 145

Ladaria, Luis, 250
Lamoni, King, 33
Laodicea, 213
law of Moses, 75
law(s), 42, 43, 76–77
Lectures on Faith, 25–26

Lee, Harold B., 296
Lewis, C. S., 347–48
life eternal. *See* eternal life
Light of Christ
    following, 62
    functions of, 51
    Holy Ghost as second phase of, 55–58
    as light to all, 52–55
    more sure word of prophecy as third phase of, 58–61, 62
    terms for, 51–52
    as unconditional blessing, 257
Lindsey, Hal, 215
literal reading of parables, 99, 101–2
loneliness, 130
love
    expressing, through obedience, 27
    friendship and, 121
    of Jesus Christ, 73–74
loyalty, in friendship, 118–19
Ludlow, Victor W., 172
Luther, Martin, 315–21

Madsen, Truman G., 296
Malcolm, Norman, 244
mark, looking beyond, 313–14
marriage, 74. *See also* sealing
martyrs, 219, 227–28n67
Matthews, Robert J., viii–ix
Maxwell, Neal A., xi–xii
McConkie, Bruce R., 20n19, 171, 179
McDermott, Gerald, 251, 304
McKnight, Scot, 360–61, 364
McMurrin, Sterling, 243, 244, 252–53, 257

meekness, 127–28
Menninger, Karl, 311
mental health, religiosity and, 311–12, 318, 324
mercy, in friendship, 128–29
metamelomai, 108, 114n33
Millennium, 135–36, 216, 218–19
Millet, Robert L.
    career, viii–xii
    early years, vii–viii
    interfaith work, xii–xv, 301–2
    works, xv–xvii, xviii n. 11
mind of Christ, 28
misery, of humans, 282–83
modified futurism, 211–12
moral reading of parables, 99, 102–3
more sure word of prophecy, 58–61, 62
Mormon, 29, 124–25
Mormon-evangelical dialogue
    antagonism in, 234
    as ecumenical or interfaith dialogue, 233–35
    learning posture in, 239–43
    on nature of God, 240–46
    respectfulness in, 237–39
Mormon history, 81–93
Mormonism in Dialogue with Contemporary Christian Theologies (Paulsen and Musser), 300–301
Mormon Tabernacle Choir, 295
Moroni, 181
mortality, as part of plan for eternal progression, 281, 284. *See also* "second estate"
Moses, meekness of, 127. *See also* Book of Moses

INDEX

Mosiah, sons of, 38
Mouw, Richard, xiv, 83, 251–52, 292, 302
Musser, Donald, 300–301
"My Father in Heaven" (Snow), 10–11
myths, faith-promoting, 91–92

natural man, 58, 258
Nauvoo, Illinois, 81–82, 88, 90
Nauvoo Temple, 89
Neill, Stephen, 240
nĕšāmâ, 197
new and everlasting covenant, 74–75, 77, 365
new earth, 219
Newman, John Henry, 360
new Mormon history, 82
"new religious movement," 236
Nicean Creed, 258–59, 266n36
Nygren, Anders, 359

obedience
    agency and, 41–44
    blessings of, 75
    of children, 102–3
    knowing God through, 27–29
    obtaining Jesus' friendship through, 133–34
O'Dea, Thomas, 294
Ogden, D. Kelley, 172
old, waxing, 186–87n52
"O My Father," 10–11
Onesimus, 32–33
opposition, agency and, 42
ordinances, salvation through, 332–33
ousia, 266n37

papyri, 140, 147–48
parable(s)
    allegorical reading of, 99–100, 103–4
    anagogical reading of, 100, 104–11
    ethical reading of, 99, 102–3
    of good Samaritan, 98
    literal reading of, 99, 101–2
    moral reading of, 99, 102–3
    reading, 97–100
    of unprofitable servant, 29–34
    of willing and unwilling two sons, 100–111, 113–14n28
Parry, Donald W., 171–72
Paul, 32–33, 331
Paulsen, David L., 300–301, 305
Pearl of Great Price, 21–22n39
Pelagianism, 253–58
Pelagius, 253–54, 264n18
Penrose, Charles W., 7–8
perfection, 72, 332, 335
"person eternalism," 8–9
Peter, 23, 132–33
Pharisees, 314–15
Phelps, W. W., 165–66
Philemon, 32–33
philia, 12224
philōn, 131, 132–33
plan of salvation, 180–82, 281
plural marriage, 90
power of God, 51–52
Pratt, Orson
    teachings on earth as living entity, 176–77, 179
    teachings on Flood as baptism, 167, 168

410

Pratt, Orson (*continued*)
    teachings on immortality of soul, 7, 10, 13
    teachings on resurrection, 16
Pratt, Parley P., 6, 13
predestination, 45–46
premortal existence, 190–91, 198, 199, 261, 281
prevenient grace, 255, 256–57
priesthood
    made available to all worthy males, 91–92
    and sealing up to eternal life, 60–61
prodigal son, 283
progression, 273–77, 280–84
Protestantism
    comparison of LDS soteriology versus, 343–53
    and goodness and misery of humans, 283–85
    grace-based soteriology of, 330–34
    interpretations of Flood, 164–65
    studying LDS soteriology through lens of, 334–35
    understandings in Restoration, 163
    works in soteriology of, 341
prōtotokos, 207–8
Puritanism, 241–42

qōhelet, 192

redemption of dead, 14
regeneration, 257
religiosity
    extrinsic versus intrinsic, 314–15

religiosity (*continued*)
    mental health and, 311–12, 318, 324
Religious Education, x–xiii
religious knowledge, 231–32
religious studies, 270–71
repentance, 324–25
rest of the Lord, 28
Restoration
    historicity of, 86–88
    Protestant understandings in, 163
Resurrection, 14–17, 67–70, 75–76, 86
Revelation (Book), 205, 211. *See also* BYU New Testament Commentary Series
revelatory power of God
    Holy Ghost, 55–58
    Light of Christ, 52–55
    more sure word of prophecy, 58–61, 62
    terms for, 51–52
Rhodes, Michael D., 205. *See also* BYU New Testament Commentary Series
Richard L. Evans Chair of Religious Understanding, 292–93
    endowment of, 295–96
    following Madsen's retirement, 299–302
    impact on Latter-day Saints, 309n37
    Millet appointed to, xiii
    realities and possibilities concerning, 302–5
    Truman G. Madsen and, 296–99
Richards, F. Kent, 171
righteousness
    collective, 318
    of God, 319–20

INDEX

righteousness (*continued*)
    salvation and, 331–32
Roberts, B. H., 8, 18
Roman Empire, slaves in, 30
Romney, Joseph B., 172
Romney, Mitt, 291
rûaḥ, 194–98, 199, 203n28

sacred spaces, 83, 84, 87–90
sacrifice, in friendship, 130–35
salvation. *See also* Atonement
    comparison of Protestant versus LDS views on, 343–53
    counterfeit doctrines regarding, 321–24
    versus exaltation, 71–73
    and interfaith dialogue, 238–39
    Protestant versus LDS views on, 330–34
    through gift of Holy Ghost, 57
    through grace, 251–52, 320–21, 334–40
    and works, 217–18, 340–43
Samaritan, good, 98
sanctification
    through gift of Holy Ghost, 57
    through Jesus Christ, 352
    works and, 342–43
Satan
    blaming, for sin, 45
    counterfeit doctrines of, 321, 322
    knows God and Jesus Christ, 25
    in parable of willing and unwilling two sons, 109–10, 115n37
    tactics of, 40, 43
Scala Santa, 318

science, Religious Education and, xi
scriptures
    coming to know Christ through, 83–84
    Millet and literalistic appreciation of, xvi–xvii
scrupulosity, 318
seal judgments, 214–15
sealing. *See also* marriage
    and blessings promised to ancient patriarchs, 67
    to eternal life, 60–61
    and exaltation, 76, 77
    by Holy Spirit of Promise, 75
Seattle Special Olympics, 126
second death, 71, 337
"second estate," 19n5, 281. *See also* mortality
second resurrection, 70
Seixas, Rabbi, 150, 151–52
selectivity, in Church history, 90–91
service, knowing God through, 27–29, 32, 33–34
seven cities, of Revelation, 213
seven seals, of Revelation, 213–16, 218, 225n41
Seventy's Course in Theology (Roberts), 8
Sharp, Granville, 208–9
she'ol, 346
"Shinehah," 144
Shipps, Jan, 235–37
Sibbesian Calvinism, 242
simul justus et peccator, 283
sin. *See also* forgiveness; grace; repentance
    avoidance of, 253–54

412

sin (*continued*)
  blaming Satan for, 45
  consequences of, 59–60
  doctrine of, 312–13
  and human goodness, 283
  and looking beyond mark, 313–14
  Martin Luther and, 315–18
  Menninger on disappearance of, 311
666 (number), 216–17
Skinner, Andrew C., 172
Skousen, W. Cleon, 172
slaves, 30–33
Smith, Emma, 120
Smith, Hyrum, 61, 119
Smith, Joseph. *See also* Book of Abraham, translation of
  gains knowledge concerning God and Jesus Christ, 25
  key of, for understanding parables, 100
  soteriology of, 334–35, 338, 340, 349–50, 351–53
  teachings of, on immortality of soul, 3–9, 12–13, 17
  view of, of friendship, 118–20, 135–36
Smith, Joseph Fielding, 171
Snow, Eliza R., 10, 28
Snow, Lorenzo, 167, 275
Society of Christian Philosophers, 300, 308n34
Sojourner in the Promised Land (Shipps), 235–37
Solomon, 192
sons of Mosiah, 38
sons of perdition, 336–37, 346, 349, 351

soul. *See also* spirit(s)
  as eternal, 4–6
  Joseph Smith's teachings on immortality of, 3–4, 17
  origin of, 6–9
  redemption of, 15
  as spirit and body, 12–13
Spackman, Ben, 179
spirit birth, 8–12, 20n20, 260, 261, 262
Spirit of Christ, 348–49
Spirit of God, 175, 179
spirit prison, 346
spirit(s). *See also* intelligence(s); soul
  in all matter, 177
  body and, 12–13
  as children of God, 9–12, 17–18, 20n19
  death and, 13–14, 189–90, 199
  in Ecclesiastes 12:7, 190, 194–98
  premortal existence of, 190–92, 261
  Resurrection and, 14–17, 68
  return to presence of God, 200n5
spiritual gifts, 56, 57
spiritual progression, 273–77, 280–84
spirit world, 13–14, 349
Staupitz, Johannes von, 317
Stendahl, Krister, 297, 298
Sudbury Moose Hall, 83
symbolism
  in parables, 97–99
  in scriptures, 186n48

Talmage, James E., 210–11
Talmud, 277–79
Taylor, John, 169
Tayman, David, 210, 221

INDEX

telestial glory, 341, 350
temple
    and collective and individual memory in Mormonism, 89–90
    and exaltation, 77
    and grace and eternal progression, 284
terrestrial glory, 341, 343–49
terrestrial resurrections, 70
theosis, 345. *See also* deification
time, God's reckoning of, 160–61n7
Times and Seasons, 142–43, 149
transcendentalism, 241
trials, friendship shaped by, 119–20
trumpet judgments, 214–15
two-sons typology, 115–16n41
two witnesses, in book of Revelation, 216–17

unintelligent materials, power of, 187n53
unity, of Godhead, 279
unjust, resurrection of, 70
unprofitable servant, parable of, 29–34

von Staupitz, Johannes, 317

warfare, in book of Revelation, 215–16
waxing old, 186–87n52
"way of the spirit," 196
Webb, Stephen, 304
web of belief, 363
Wesleyanism, 255
West, William, 148
Whitney, Orson F., 169–70
Widtsoe, John A., 170–71
Wilken, Robert Louis, 359

will. *See* agency
willing and unwilling two sons, parable of
    allegorical readings of, 103–4
    anagogical reading of, 104–11
    differences in various versions of, 113–14n28
    moral principles in, 102–3
    objective elements in, 101–2
    setting of, 100–101
will of God, 44, 106–11
wisdom literature, 192
witnesses, in book of Revelation, 216–17
works
    counterfeit doctrines regarding, 321–23
    in LDS soteriology, 351–53
    in Protestant versus LDS soteriology, 330–34
    rewards of degree based on, 340–43
    and salvation, 217–18, 255–56
worthiness, for blessings, 67
Wright, N. T., 364–65

YMCA Hall (Sudbury, Ontario), 83
Young, Brigham
    meekness of, 128
    succession to Church presidency, 91
    teachings on earth as living entity, 177
    teachings on Flood as baptism, 169
    teachings on immortality of soul, 7, 11, 13
    teachings on resurrection, 16
    tries to sell Church properties, 90